The Making of Contemporary Kuwait

This book explores the contemporary history, governance, foreign policy, political economy, culture, and society of Kuwait. It highlights the dynamics of the country, putting forward both an overview of each subject covered and new research findings. It begins by providing a historical understanding of state formation and goes on to examine state structure, including the ruling monarchy, state legitimacy, and the creation of the Constitution and the National Assembly. It considers foreign policy, including the tools of diplomacy, the state's regional and international approach, and the factors that have formed and reformed Kuwait's strategic policy in the global arena. It assesses the economy, including rentierism, the labour market both for locals and for migrants, the class system, and the process of Kuwaitization; and it discusses Kuwaiti society and national identity, as well as investigates issues of women, civil society, youth, and the Bidoon minority. Overall, the book provides a full and detailed analysis of contemporary Kuwait and of the factors which are bringing about new developments.

Mahjoob Zweiri is Professor in Contemporary Politics and History of the Middle East with focus on Iran and the Gulf region, and Director of the Gulf Studies Center at Qatar University.

Sinem Cengiz is Researcher in the Gulf Studies Center at Qatar University with focus on Gulf politics and society.

Durham Modern Middle East and Islamic World Series

Series Editor: Anoushiravan Ehteshami, University of Durham

50. Limited Statehood and Informal Governance in the Middle East and Africa
Edited by Ruth Hanau Santini, Abel Polese and Rob Kevlihan

51. Constituting the Political Economy of the Kurds
Social Embeddedness, Hegemony, and Identity
Omer Tekdemir

52. Reimagining Arab Political Identity
Justice, Women's Rights, and the Arab State
Salam Hawa

53. China's Economic and Political Presence in the Middle East and South Asia
Edited by Mehran Haghirian and Luciano Zaccara

54. Power and Paranoia in Syria-Iraq Relations
The Impact of Hafez Assad and Saddam Hussain
Amjed Rasheed

55. Arab-Iranian Relations since the Arab Uprisings
Mahjoob Zweiri

56. Israel-Asia Relations in the Twenty-First Century
The Search for Partners in a Changing World
Yoram Evron and Rotem Kowner

57. The Making of Contemporary Kuwait
Identity, Politics, and its Survival Strategy
Edited by Mahjoob Zweiri and Sinem Cengiz

For a full list of available titles please visit: https://www.routledge.com/Durham-Modern-Middle-East-and-Islamic-World-Series/book-series/SE0526

The Making of Contemporary Kuwait

Identity, Politics, and Its Survival Strategy

Edited by Mahjoob Zweiri and Sinem Cengiz

LONDON AND NEW YORK

First published 2024
by Routledge
4 Park Square, Milton Park, Abingdon, Oxon OX14 4RN

and by Routledge
605 Third Avenue, New York, NY 10158

Routledge is an imprint of the Taylor & Francis Group, an informa business

© 2024 selection and editorial matter, Mahjoob Zweiri and Sinem Cengiz; individual chapters, the contributors

The right of Mahjoob Zweiri and Sinem Cengiz to be identified as the authors of the editorial material, and of the authors for their individual chapters, has been asserted in accordance with sections 77 and 78 of the Copyright, Designs and Patents Act 1988.

All rights reserved. No part of this book may be reprinted or reproduced or utilised in any form or by any electronic, mechanical, or other means, now known or hereafter invented, including photocopying and recording, or in any information storage or retrieval system, without permission in writing from the publishers.

Trademark notice: Product or corporate names may be trademarks or registered trademarks, and are used only for identification and explanation without intent to infringe.

British Library Cataloguing-in-Publication Data
A catalogue record for this book is available from the British Library

Library of Congress Cataloging-in-Publication Data
Names: Zweiri, Mahjoob, editor. | Cengiz, Sinem, editor.
Title: The making of contemporary Kuwait: identity, politics, and its survival strategy/edited by Mahjoob Zweiri, Sinem Cengiz.
Description: Abingdon, Oxon; New York, NY: Routledge, 2024. |
Series: Durham modern Middle East and Islamic world series |
Includes bibliographical references and index.
Identifiers: LCCN 2023056842 (print) | LCCN 2023056843 (ebook) |
ISBN 9781032563817 (hardback) | ISBN 9781032563831 (paperback) |
ISBN 9781003435259 (ebook)
Subjects: LCSH: Kuwait–Civilization. | Kuwait–Social conditions. |
Kuwait–Politics and government. | National characteristics, Kuwaiti.
Classification: LCC DS247.K84 M355 2024 (print) |
LCC DS247.K84 (ebook) |
DDC 953.67–dc23/eng/20240130
LC record available at https://lccn.loc.gov/2023056842
LC ebook record available at https://lccn.loc.gov/2023056843

ISBN: 978-1-032-56381-7 (hbk)
ISBN: 978-1-032-56383-1 (pbk)
ISBN: 978-1-003-43525-9 (ebk)

DOI: 10.4324/9781003435259

Typeset in Times New Roman
by Deanta Global Publishing Services, Chennai, India

Contents

Preface and Acknowledgements	*vii*
About the Editors	*ix*
List of Contributors	*x*
List of Figures	*xiv*
List of Tables	*xv*

1 Contemporary Kuwait through the State and Society: An Introduction   1

MAHJOOB ZWEIRI AND SINEM CENGIZ

2 Kuwait's Political History: From Tribal Sheikhdom to Semi-democratic State   7

ABDULRAHMAN ALEBRAHIM

3 Kuwait: A Political System in Crisis   26

HAMAD H. ALBLOSHI

4 From Grassroots to Public Diplomacy: *Diwaniyya* as an Alternative Sociopolitical Institution   44

CLEMENS CHAY

5 Kuwait's Foreign Aid: Motivations and Allocations   69

MOHAMMAD YAGHI

6 Intra-Gulf Dynamics: Pursuit of Survival within the GCC   88

KRISTIAN COATES ULRICHSEN

7 Kuwait's Relations with the Global Powers: US, Russia, and China   103

GIORGIO CAFIERO

8 Kuwait and the Palestinian Cause: Mutual Search for National Pride   119

MESHARI HAMAD ALRUWAIH

vi *Contents*

9 Role of Urbanization in Changing Social Norms to Laws: Impact on Status of Kuwaiti Women 138
MUYASSAR H. SULEIMAN

10 Political Economy of Kuwait through the Prism of Its Hydrocarbon Sector 157
NIKOLAY A. KOZHANOV

11 Citizenship, Identity, and Human Rights in Kuwait 176
GHANIM ALNAJJAR

12 Kuwait's Publication Law: A Civil Act to Protect Freedom of Expression 191
TAHANI ALTERKAIT

13 Culture, Politics, and Citizenship in Kuwait 206
COURTNEY FREER

Index *223*

Preface and Acknowledgements

This book is part of a six-volume series that delves into the contemporary politics and history of each Gulf Cooperation Council (GCC) country, particularly focusing on the post-1990s era. The first volume in this series, titled *Contemporary Qatar: Examining State and Society*, is followed by this, the second book in the series, which scrutinizes the state and society of contemporary Kuwait. The subsequent volumes will explore the remaining four GCC states. This comprehensive series seeks to provide insights into the modern history of each GCC state, shedding light on key developments in areas such as foreign policy and state–society relations.

The vast political, economic, and social developments occurring in contemporary Kuwait called for an in-depth study on the state, its presence in the global platform, and its relationship with its society. *Making Contemporary Kuwait: Identity, Politics, and Its Survival Strategy* is a book that is carefully constructed to contain 13 chapters that serve a wide audience. Although the book thoroughly delves into the contemporary era of Kuwait, it also establishes a solid understanding of the history of Kuwait, especially, the evolvement of the state in the post-1990–91 invasion by Iraq.

Over the years, several books and articles have been produced on Kuwait; however, it is the first time that a text truly takes an interdisciplinary approach. This book, which should be of broad interest to academics and researchers, intends to familiarize the reader with the wholly new dynamics in the Gulf country analysed by renowned scholars on Kuwait and the region. Each contributor aimed to offer the reader his or her research and personal expertise on the topics. The inclusion of both Kuwaiti and international scholars enables us to have local insights from first hand and enrich the product as a whole. The diversity of the author's topics and backgrounds enhances the book chapters and enriches the book as a whole. Consequently, the book aims to move beyond the existing literature, offering new insights and sound understanding of the current debates in Kuwait.

There are three main categories in the book, which are politics, economics, and culture and society. Each category presents the reader with a solid understanding of the topics at hand, as the chapters complement one another to offer a holistic study of Kuwait. As editors from the Gulf Studies Center, we hope that the book be considered a vital resource in academia and a fundamental reference for academics around the world.

viii *Preface and Acknowledgements*

We would like to acknowledge the great efforts that have been placed by each contributor in the book. We would also like to thank the Routledge publishing team for their hard work and continuous support.

Mahjoob Zweiri and Sinem Cengiz
Doha, Qatar
November 2023

About the Editors

Mahjoob Zweiri is Director of the Gulf Studies Center. He is Professor in Contemporary Politics and History of the Middle East—with a focus on Iran and the Gulf region—at Qatar University. He was Head of the Humanities Department during 2011–2016. Before joining Qatar University in 2010, Professor Zweiri was a senior researcher in Middle East Politics and Iran at the Center for Strategic Studies, University of Jordan. He was also Visiting Professor to School of Government & International Affairs at Durham University. From March 2003 until December 2006, he was Research Fellow and then Director of the Centre for Iranian Studies in the Institute for Middle Eastern and Islamic Studies at Durham University. Professor Zweiri has more than 85 publications in the areas of Iran and Contemporary Middle East History and Politics, Gulf Studies and Social Sciences in the University of the Future and the Artificial Intelligence, Social Sciences. In addition to Arabic, Professor Zweiri is fluent in Farsi and English.

Sinem Cengiz is Researcher at the Gulf Studies Center. She pursues her PhD on Area Studies at Middle East Technical University in Ankara on Gulf politics. Before joining Qatar University in 2022, she was an assistant for press, political, and cultural affairs at the Embassy of the State of Kuwait in Ankara, Turkey. In addition to her academic and diplomatic track, she holds journalism experiences. She worked as a diplomatic correspondent and reported from several countries in the post-Arab uprisings' era. Since 2016, she is a weekly columnist for *Arab News*, Saudi Arabia's largest English language daily. Cengiz is the author of the book titled *Turkish–Saudi Relations: Cooperation and Competition in the Middle East* published in 2020 and a non-resident fellow at the Washington-based Gulf International Forum. She is also a member of the Women in Foreign Policy (DPK) Initiative. Born and raised in Kuwait, Cengiz is fluent in Turkish, English, and Arabic.

Contributors

Hamad H. Albloshi is Associate Professor of Political Science at Kuwait University. He holds a PhD from the Fletcher School, Tufts University. His many publications include *Karamet Watan: An Unsuccessful Nonviolent Movement* co-authored with Michael Herb (2018), and published by the Middle East Journal, *Sectarianism and Arab Spring: The Case of the Kuwaiti Shi'a* (2016), and *The Eternal Revolution: Hardliners and Conservatives in Iran* (2016). He has published short pieces on current events in both Iran and Kuwait. These pieces appeared on *Al-Monitor*, The Arab Gulf States Institute in Washington (AGSIW), the Italian Institute for International Political Studies (ISPI), Middle East Institute—Singapore, and Amwaj.Media.

Abdulrahman Alebrahim is an independent researcher who received a PhD from the Institute of Arab and Islamic Studies at the University of Exeter in 2017. Alebrahim's primary interests include Gulf Studies, predominately culture and identity. His research has focused on the history of the Gulf, particularly Kuwait and Southern Iraq. He has published on these topics in Arabic peer-reviewed journals. He also published an English book chapter entitled "Kuwaiti-Zubayri Intellectual Relations until the Beginning of the Twentieth Century: 'Abd al-'Aziz al-Rushayd as an Example." Alebrahim's also published in 2019 a book entitled "Kuwait's Politics Before Independence: The Role of the Balancing Powers" under "Exeter Critical Gulf Studies." In 2016, Alebrahim was awarded the State of Kuwait Prize for Historical and Archaeological Studies commending one of his academic publications.

Ghanim AlNajjar is Professor of Political Science at Kuwait University. He established the Centre for Strategic and Future Studies at Kuwait University and has been Visiting Scholar at several universities such as Harvard University, Human Rights Program at the Law School. He has lectured on an occasional basis in more than 43 universities, academic institutions, and think tanks across the world. He introduced, through the Kuwaiti parliament, the first annual report on the human rights situation in Kuwait, and chaired the committee that produced the first report. He was an International Commissioner at the International Commission of Jurists based in Geneva. In recognition of his work in the field of human rights, he earned the International Monitor Award by Human Rights Watch in New York in 1991. Between 2001 and 2009 he was the UN Independent Expert on Human Rights in Somalia, appointed by the UN Secretary General at the time, Kofi Anan. He led and participated in several international investigation and fact-finding missions in more than 13 countries. He participated in several international missions in Iraq between 2003 and 2006. He is a member of the Academic Committee of IIAS at Tsingua University of China. He is a member of the board of the Arab Center for Policy Research in Doha, and member of the board of trustees of the Doha Institute for Graduate Studies. He is a member of the board of the Center of Gulf and Arabian Studies at Kuwait University. He has written extensively in the fields of political science and human rights. He contributes in advisory capacity to several regional and international NGOs such as Amnesty International and Human Rights Watch. He is regular columnists in daily newspapers and other media outlets. His forthcoming joint book in Arabic is *The Stateless (Bidoon) in the Gulf.*

Meshari H. Alruwaih is Assistant Professor of International Relations at Qatar University. He holds a PhD from the School of Government and International Affairs, Durham University, UK. His research interests focus on Islam and Contemporary International Relations, International Relations Theory, Emotions and Foreign Policy, and Regional Transformation.

Alruwaih has published number of works including *States Do not Go to Heaven: Towards a Theory of Islamic Agency in International Relations*, in addition to, *The Agency of the Muslim Researcher in Developing a Theory of Islamic Agency in International Relations,* and *Masarat Al-Salikeen fi Alsiyassa Aldawliyya.* He has also presented a number of research papers in academic conferences including the Annual Convention of the International Studies Association.

Tahani Al Terkait is a researcher on politics focusing on Kuwait, the Gulf region, and the Middle East and teaches politics and international relations in The American University of Kuwait. She earned her PhD in Political Science and International Affairs from Durham University, UK. She defended her thesis in 2017 titled, "The Conceptual and Constitutional Underpinnings of Kuwait's System of Government." She is also a member at the London-based Centre of International Studies and Diplomacy (CISD) where she received her Master's degree in International Studies and Diplomacy from School of Oriental and African Studies—University of London. Before pursuing her higher education, Al Terkait worked for Kuwait's public sector for 15 years serving her country as a diplomat, researcher, and consultant in international relations and public diplomacy. Both her academic and professional experiences have shaped her research interests in democracy, political, and constitutional reforms in Kuwait and the Arab World and gender politics.

Clemens Chay holds a PhD from Durham University and is currently a Research Fellow at the National University of Singapore's Middle East Institute (MEI).

xii *Contributors*

His research focuses on the history and politics of the Gulf states, with a particular emphasis on Kuwait, Qatar, and Oman. At MEI, he was the head of the Gulf research cluster for the 2021/22 academic year. Prior to joining MEI, he was the Al-Sabah doctoral fellow at the School of Government and Affairs (SGIA) at Durham University.

Giorgio Cafiero is the CEO and Founder of Gulf State Analytics, a Washington, D.C.-based geopolitical risk consultancy. He is also an Adjunct Fellow at the American Security Project. Cafiero has written for a variety of public policy research institutions and media outlets including Gulf International Forum, Atlantic Council, Carnegie Endowment for International Peace, *The New Arab*, *Al Jazeera English*, and *TRT World*.

Courtney Freer is Visiting Assistant Professor of Middle Eastern Studies at Emory University. Her academic work focusses on the domestic politics of the Arab Gulf states and Islamism. Courtney is the author of *Rentier Islamism: The Influence of the Muslim Brotherhood in Gulf Monarchies* (Oxford University Press, 2018) and co-author with Alanoud Alsharekh of *Tribalism and Political Power in the Gulf: State-Building and Nation al Identity in Kuwait, Qatar, and the UAE* (Bloomsbury, 2021). Courtney previously worked at the London School of Economics and Political Science (LSE) and the Brookings Doha Center in Qatar. She holds a BA in Near Eastern Studies from Princeton University, an MA in Middle Eastern Studies from The George Washington University, and a DPhil in Politics from the University of Oxford.

Nikolay A. Kozhanov is a Research Associate Professor at the Gulf Studies Center of Qatar University. He is also a Non-Resident Scholar at the Program on Economics and Energy at the Middle East Institute. His research interests are focused on the geopolitics of the Gulf hydrocarbons, Russian foreign policy in the Middle East, and Iran's economy and international relations.

Muyassar H. Suleiman is a PhD candidate in the Gulf Studies Program at Qatar University. Her area of specialty is social and culture issues. She holds a Master of Arts in Gulf Studies. Currently, she is working as a lecturer in the International Affairs Department and a Graduate Research Assistant in the Gulf Studies Program at Qatar University. She has eight publications including academic articles and book chapters. Her latest publications include a book chapter in the book titled *Gulf Studies: Examining History, State and Society* with Mohammed Almusfir by Aljazeera Center for Studies in 2022. She also co-authored a chapter with Mohammed Alzarir for the book *The Formation of Identity in Qatar: Historical Study during 1868–1913* published in June 2022.

Kristian Coates Ulrichsen is the Fellow for the Middle East at Rice University's Baker Institute for Public Policy. His research spans the history, political and international political economy, and international relations of the Gulf states and their changing position within the global order. Coates Ulrichsen is the author of five monographs and the editor of three volumes about the Gulf states, including *Insecure Gulf: The End of Certainty and the Transition to the Post-Oil Era* (2011), *The Gulf States in International Political Economy* (2015), and, most recently, *Qatar and the Gulf Crisis* (2020). Prior to joining the Baker Institute in 2013, Coates Ulrichsen co-directed the Kuwait Programme on Development, Governance, and Globalization in the Gulf states at the London School of Economics and Political Science and was also an Associate Fellow with the Middle East North Africa Programme at Chatham House between 2012 and 2021.

Mohammad Yaghi is a research fellow and programme manager at the Regional Program Gulf States at Konrad-Adenauer-Stiftung (KAS), a German foundation. His research combines the various internal and foreign relations issues of the GCC states. In particular, he focuses on the growing role of the GCC in the MENA region, the Gulf States' security, the GCC's foreign aid, and the social transformation within the Gulf States. Before joining KAS, he was an adjunct professor in the department of political studies at Queens University in Canada teaching comparative politics. Yaghi received his doctorate in Political Science from the University of Guelph in Canada.

Figures

3.1	Number of elected ministers in Kuwait since 1963	31
4.1	Al Babtain *Diwaniyya* in Session (photograph by author, 02/10/2017)	45
4.2	The Thunayyan *diwaniyya* in Jahra, an annex to the house resembling a tent (photograph by author, taken on 17/04/2023)	51
4.3	Men sitting on the *datchas* built from the walls of the Shamlan *diwaniyya* (photograph courtesy of Hamed al-Amiri)	53
4.4	Sheikh Mubarak holding a public audience in the bazaar (photograph by Lt-Commander A.N. Gouldsmith, National Maritime Museum, London)	54
4.5	Ambassador Doug Silliman featured in the 100-*diwaniyas* campaign (*Source:* US Embassy Kuwait Instagram Page)	62
10.1	Oil Export Revenues of Kuwait in 2012–2019 (billion USD). (*Source:* Middle East Economic Survey)	160
10.2	Dynamics of Kuwait's Budget Deficit in 2011–2023 (billion USD)	165

Tables

3.1	Parliaments that were dissolved by the Emir since 1999 and reasons behind each dissolution (Majlia al-ʾumma … marāsīm, 2022)	34
3.2	Number of attempts to impeach prime ministers in Kuwait from 2006 to 2022	37
5.1	Distribution of loans and grants from 1961 until September 2022	76
5.2	KFAED fund to Islamic countries	77
5.3	Distribution of funds and grants to Arab countries from 1961 to September 2022	78
5.4	Distribution of Kuwait's humanitarian assistance from 2013 to April 2023	80
10.1	Real GDP Growth of GCC Member Countries 2012–2022 (%)	159

1 Contemporary Kuwait through the State and Society

An Introduction

Mahjoob Zweiri and Sinem Cengiz

Since the emergence of Kuwait as an independent state in 1961, it has been experiencing a challenging regional atmosphere. The history of regional politics offers valuable insights into the foundations of Kuwait's domestic and foreign policies, its historical evolution, and its development trajectories. The 1970s and 1980s witnessed intensified disputes and substantial shifts in the Gulf regional dynamics, directly impacting Kuwait's security.

The year 1979 marked a significant turning point in the perceptions of Gulf security (Alasfoor, 2007, p. 88). This was the year when domestic, regional, and global powers came to the forefront for the Gulf States. The region became a battleground for conflicts involving powerful regional countries, with differing political ideologies and competing interests of the Western and Communist powers. The Iranian Revolution of 1979 led to the overthrow of Shah Mohammed Reza Pahlavi and the establishment of the Islamic Republic of Iran, triggering profound changes in the region's political structures and international relations. This newly formed state reoriented its position and foreign policy, which entirely changed the security system of the Gulf region. Concerns mounted about the spread of Shia Islam in the Gulf region, which worried Kuwait, Bahrain, and Saudi Arabia that had a significant portion of the Shia population.

During the same year, the Soviet invasion of Afghanistan posed a significant threat to the Gulf countries, as they fundamentally disagreed with the political values of the Soviet Union. Additionally, the growing Soviet influence in Iraq, the revolution in Ethiopia, and the regime in South Yemen further fuelled the concerns of the Gulf States regarding their security and stability. In addition to all these, Egypt's unilateral signing of the Camp David Peace Agreement with Israel a year prior had led to its isolation from the Arab region, where it had traditionally played a central role. The weakening of the Arab League and its relocation from Cairo to Tunis following the Egyptian–Israeli agreement marked the disintegration of the previous concept of collective security among Arab nations. This created a security vacuum in the Arab world.

The outbreak of the war between Iraq and Iran in 1980 marked a critical turning point, destabilizing the region and pushing the Arab Gulf States, including Kuwait, to back Iraq by providing financial support. This war between the two powerful regional states not only changed the regional landscape but also posed several external security concerns for the Gulf countries (Heard-Bey, 2006, p. 200). The

DOI: 10.4324/9781003435259-1

Arab Gulf States found themselves facing the consequences of a prolonged war between two regional powers, which was likely to bring major losses not only to the warring parties but also to all the countries in the region. It is accurate to assert that the complexity of the situation in the region increased further following the Iran–Iraq War of 1980–88 and the strategic threat to the Gulf countries was further heightened by the combination of all these developments.

Amid these regional threats, the Gulf States felt the need to recalibrate their regional policies and fill the void created by the Arab League's reluctance to assume a stronger role. This impetus led to the formation of an organization among Gulf nations. The Gulf Cooperation Council (GCC) was established in 1981 to address the challenges arising from the volatile region. Its first Secretary-General was Abdulla Bishara, who had been Kuwaiti ambassador to Brazil and Argentina and a representative of Kuwait at the United Nations. However, by the early 1990s, Kuwait was confronted by another threat: Iraq's Invasion of the country on August 2, 1990. Understanding Kuwait's historical context is essential for grasping its intricate political and socio-economic relationships with the rest of the world. Kuwait, with its solid institutions, had navigated through several critical phases in its history, drawing important lessons from most of these phases.

The invasion of Kuwait by Iraq in 1990 not only altered the regional balances but also had a profound impact on the country's political history and its foreign policy approach. It also ushered in a new era of relations between the state and society, marking the beginning of a contemporary phase in Kuwait's history. Following the invasion, Kuwait emerged as a visible actor in the international sphere, adopting a policy of neutrality in its foreign policy in order to address its core national policy interests. Thanks to its traditional foreign policy line of non-assertiveness and neutrality, Kuwait has, in recent years, played a crucial role as a mediator in regional disputes, particularly during the Gulf crises, by engaging in dialogue with all the actors in the Middle East. Kuwait has typically walked a thin line when it comes to regional issues, often opting for humanitarian and diplomatic efforts to resolve crises in countries such as Yemen, Syria, Iraq, Libya, and Palestine, rather than taking sides in these conflicts.

Kuwait's stance on the Palestinian issue has also been greatly influenced by the Iraqi invasion of the country in 1990–91. Kuwait stands out as an exception to the trend of normalizing relations with Israel. Kuwait's leadership vigorously supported the Palestinian cause for many decades. Several factors related to Kuwait's political institutions, historical ties to Palestine, and its commitment to Arab and Muslim solidarity have played a significant role in shaping Kuwait's approach to the Palestinian cause.

In addition to diplomatic mediation, Kuwait uses foreign aid as the second effective tool in its foreign policy strategy. Kuwait was also the first Gulf State to provide aid to Arab States, establishing its Kuwait Fund for Arab Economic Development in 1961, the year of its independence. Kuwait has also served as a central hub for hosting humanitarian donor conferences, a role that earned late Kuwait's Emir Sheikh Sabah the title of "world humanitarian leader" for the Gulf state's humanitarian policies. Kuwait's role in regional mediation and its

Introduction: Contemporary Kuwait through State and Society 3

relationship with neighbouring and international states have garnered significant attention.

For a relatively small country like Kuwait, characterized by a diverse population in terms of sociopolitical and sectarian backgrounds, regional tensions can easily lead to domestic repercussions. On that account, the presence of Shia, tribal representatives, secular or conservative members in the parliament is highly crucial for preserving Kuwait's sociopolitical stability. Unlike other Gulf countries, Kuwait has adopted a neutral stance towards the Muslim Brotherhood (*Ikhwan*), not viewing the movement as a fundamental threat to its system or government. The Islamic Constitutional Movement (*hadas*) has been an integral part of Kuwaiti's political culture for many years, enjoying rights to engage in political activism. This pluralist political environment in the country exerts a substantial influence on both its domestic and foreign policy decisions.

From the 19th century onwards, Kuwait has gone through a series of historical events that have shaped it into the state that it is today. Among the GCC countries, Kuwait stands out as an exceptional case, being the first Gulf State to establish an elected parliament and adopt a Constitution in 1962. The Kuwaiti Constitution of 1962 lays down fundamental principles governing the state's structure, its various functions, power limitations, and the state–society relationship. Given the origins and prospects of Kuwait's National Assembly, it is the most powerful parliament amongst the Arab monarchies of the Gulf. Kuwait's parliamentary experience holds a central importance within the Gulf monarchies and serves as a notable example of political participation. Kuwait's vocal parliament is an amalgam of several figures, including liberals, tribal representatives, independents, and pro-Muslim Brotherhood members, each with their own distinct demands and motivations. The agenda for opposition members in Kuwait's parliament encompasses a wide range of issues, spanning from amnesty laws to economic problems, from combating corruption to reforming the electoral system, and from addressing women's rights to resolving the status of bidūns.

Kuwait's political system and its parliamentary politics are complex. The contemporary political crisis in Kuwait has multiple causes, stemming from personal and institutional factors, economic challenges, and the diverse alignments of various political factions. The Kuwaiti parliament serves as both a source of political strength and vulnerability. Despite decades of electoral practices, Kuwait's political arena still lacks significant experience, resulting in ongoing tension between the legislative and the executive branches. This situation has prompted emirs to dissolve parliaments and call for elections—which often leads to turmoil and fails to address underlying issues. In Kuwait's sociopolitical culture, diwaniyya, which has become widespread especially since the 1990s, is of great importance. These are weekly gatherings of men in dedicated salons connected to homes where they discuss political and social issues. Diwaniyya assemblies hold a unique place, bridging the gap between the public and private spheres (Diwan, 2018, p. 3).

In transitional societies like Kuwait, where socio-economic changes have occurred rapidly, socio-economic groupings hold critical importance (Ghabra, 1997, p. 358). Kuwait's population is typically categorized into several dichotomies:

Kuwaitis/non-Kuwaitis; original *(bi-l-aseel)*/naturalized *(bi-l-tajannus)* citizens; Muslims/non-Muslims; Sunnis/Shias; Hadhar/Bedouins; men/women; and adults/children (Al-Nakib, 2015, p. 5). These distinct categories come with varying degrees of legal rights and social belonging. These various societal groups play a crucial role in the political process because political organizations and parties in Kuwait have traditionally established their power bases on religious, ethnic, and tribal identification and social position (Ghabra, 1997, p. 359). Another significant divide is the one between Kuwaitis and stateless individuals (bidūns), whose significant number of presences further adds to the complexity. These divisions play a significant role across all levels of Kuwaiti society. When examining the country's class structure, it is imperative to take into account the situation of Kuwaiti women. In Kuwait, being the first country in the Gulf region to incorporate women into both the public and private sectors, women's labour force participation rate is high compared to other GCC countries (Gulf News, 2016); In fact, in certain professions, women outnumber men. Nevertheless, Kuwaiti women, who secured the right to vote and be elected in 2005, still struggle to obtain some of their social and civil rights. According to Longva (2005, p. 114), neither the concepts of democracy nor autocracy alone suffice to describe Kuwait; instead, the country should rather be defined as an "ethnocracy."

Hence, in contemporary times, Kuwait is undergoing developments that are influenced by its past and will continue to shape its future. The relationship and interaction between state and society should never be underestimated, but it should be rather approached through different angles that examine the shift and evolution of a contemporary patriarchal state from a traditional one. Consequently, the book titled *Making Contemporary Kuwait: Identity, Politics, and its Survival Strategy* is a much-needed and well-constructed book that compiles numerous chapters addressing all aspects of the emergence and existence of the State of Kuwait. The State of Kuwait is a unique case study of a small state that has forged its distinct identity amidst regional balance of power, global political developments, and fluctuating economic states.

The book encompasses 13 comprehensive chapters categorized into five main themes: History, governance, foreign policy, political economy, and society. The chapters on history provide a historical understanding of state formation in Kuwait and current historical trends, while the governance-focused chapters delve into the state's structure, including discussions on the ruling monarchy, state, and power legitimacy, the creation of the Constitution, and the National Assembly. The chapters focussing on foreign policy explore the state's regional and international strategies and the aspects that have formed Kuwait's foreign policy in the global arena. The political economy chapter covers topics such as rentierism, the labour market (both local and migrant), the class system within the state, and the process of Kuwaitization. Lastly, the culture and society chapters examine Kuwaiti's society, national identity, and investigate issues of women, civil society, youth, and bidūns.

In Chapter 2, Abdulrahman Alebrahim provides a reexamination of Kuwait's constitutional development, discusses the constitutional history of Kuwait from 1921 to the 1990s and focusses on the main historical landmarks that have shaped

Introduction: Contemporary Kuwait through State and Society 5

the country's politics and institutions. Alebrahim looks at the early history of Kuwait as a tribal sheikhdom governed by a *Shura*-based system, offering insights into how Kuwait's modern-day politics are rooted in its tumultuous constitutional development.

In Chapter 3, Hamad H. Albloshi offers a historical background of the political system in Kuwait. He argues that the nature of the political system of Kuwait, which is neither parliamentary nor presidential, is the main reason behind this constant crisis as it reduces the chances of cooperation between the executive power and the legislative power. Albloshi offers a unique understanding of the reasons behind the crises between the executive power and the legislative power through historical accounts.

In Chapter 4, Clemens Chay traces the evolution of the *diwaniyyas*, sites of gathering primarily for Kuwaiti men where they sit and engage one another in conversation, through the theme of political mobilization, which provided new impetus to the *diwaniyya*'s usefulness. Chay explains how the *diwaniyya* practice has gained traction in public diplomacy through specific events on Kuwait's timeline.

In Chapter 5, Mohammed Yaghi delves into how internal and external factors have affected the characteristics and allocation of Kuwait's foreign aid, which is employed as a tool to achieve its foreign policy objectives. Yaghi encapsulates the intricate relationship between Kuwait's foreign aid and its foreign policy objectives, all underscored by the imperatives of domestic politics and national security.

In Chapter 6, Kristian Coates Ulrichsen analyses the shifts in Kuwait's regional and foreign policies with a specific focus on the period after the Iraqi invasion in 1990 and liberation following the Gulf War in 1991. Ulrichsen offers a comprehensive understanding of the different tools that Kuwaiti decision-makers and practitioners have and the ways in which those tools have themselves evolved over time.

In Chapter 7, Giorgio Cafiero examines Kuwait's relations with the global actors, namely Russia, China, and the US, examining its motivations behind the balanced approach it adopts in its international relations. Understanding Kuwait's alliance with the US and its partnerships with Russia and China requires a historical context, which Cafiero provides through some key events in the history.

In Chapter 8, Meshari Hamad Alruwaih traces the status of the Palestinian cause among the Kuwaiti public through role theory and the literature on self-conscious emotions. Alruwaih argues that the Palestinian cause has for a long time been present in the development of Kuwait's national self-representation, allowing it to enact successfully the regional role of a "progressive Gulf state" that includes support for the Palestinian cause as a major role feature.

In Chapter 9, Muyassar H. Suleiman analyses the effect of gender inequality on the political and economic development of Kuwait, contending that gender equality, legally, economically, and politically, provides the most viable platform for achieving and realizing national development aspirations in Kuwait. In doing so, Suleiman reveals how structural gender discrimination in public policy challenges and hinders the Kuwait National Development Plan 2035.

In Chapter 10, Nikolay A. Kozhanov scrutinizes the political economy of Kuwait through the prism of its hydrocarbon sector, arguing that the issue of reducing dependence on the oil and gas industry in the national economy is key to solving the problem of Kuwait's diversification plans. Kozhanov argues that this process is lengthy and requires the adoption of a set of measures that he explains in his chapter.

In Chapter 11, Ghanim AlNajjar delves into the function of citizenship in Kuwait, and the role it plays in identifying politics and the formation of the country. He focusses on how the Citizenship Law issued in 1959, two years before independence in 1961, became the focal point in identity politics. AlNajjar provides a comprehensive understanding of both identity politics and the political environment of the country.

In Chapter 12, Tahani Al Terkait analyses the role of the civil society in Kuwait and to the extent to which it is influential in amending laws. AlTerkait interrogates the mechanisms of book censorship in Kuwait, shedding light on the processes that writers and publishers encounter before publishing, circulating, or selling books in the country, while highlighting the vital role that the civic society can play in passing laws and making a difference in their own society.

In Chapter 13, Courtney Freer examines the various efforts undertaken to resolving the status of the bidūn, as well as the dominant social and political discourse about the population. Freer interrogates the ways in which Kuwait's citizenship laws have shaped its culture, politics, and society with reference to the cleavages between citizens and bidūn and between hadhar and badu, as well as how such divisions have (or have not) been reflected in dominant discourse on national heritage and identity.

2 Kuwait's Political History

From Tribal Sheikhdom to Semi-democratic State

Abdulrahman Alebrahim

Introduction

Since 2011, the Arab Spring has revealed a fervent desire for political, economic, and social change among the Arab populations. Although this movement has reached the Gulf states, it has not profoundly impacted their political structures as in countries like Egypt, Tunisia, and Libya. Nonetheless, protests in Saudi Arabia, Kuwait, Oman, and Bahrain and the Arab Spring movement prompted some debate among academic circles about the origins of such movements in recent regional history. In Kuwait, for example, the Arab Spring expedited the government's response to opposition members who demanded the replacement of Prime Minister Sheikh Nasser al-Mohammad al-Sabah. In addition, some voices could be heard from the opposition demanding the establishment of a constitutional monarchy, political parties, and an elected government. By examining the political liberties of Kuwaitis throughout the country's history, these factors sparked a tidal surge of debates in traditional and social media. However, demands for radical political change gradually ceased without fundamental institutional or political changes.

In Kuwait's political history, certain events echo the Arab Spring's demands for further political progress and civil liberties. Most specifically, the events of 1938, as will be seen in this chapter, are a significant landmark in Kuwait's political and constitutional history as they fundamentally transformed Kuwait's political landscape. Nonetheless, except for the events of 1938, opposition factions in Kuwait have never had a sincere desire to alter the political system but merely wished to alter the terms of the political rules in accordance with the immediate interests of each group.

This chapter compels a reexamination of Kuwaits' constitutional development. Keeping this in mind, this chapter will discuss the constitutional history of Kuwait from 1921 to the 1990s, focussing on the main historical landmarks that have shaped the country's politics and institutions. In doing so, the chapter will demonstrate that the legitimate claims articulated since 2011 are not new but have deep roots in Kuwait's political history. In particular, it is argued here that the country's constitutional development still suffers from the failure to account for the role played by a range of significant social forces in the Kuwaiti political scene. This chapter will look at the early history of Kuwait as a tribal sheikhdom governed by a shura-based system. After that, it will discuss the transition of

DOI: 10.4324/9781003435259-2

8 *Abdulrahman Alebrahim*

power in Kuwait from shared authority between the Sheikh and merchants to absolute rule under Mubarak al-Sabah's reign. The death of Salem al-Mubarak resulted in the establishment of participatory governance with the 1921 Shura Council and the 1938–39 Councils, both of which had an impact on the constitutional development of Kuwait as a modern state. This chapter ends with an analysis of Kuwait's political history, focussing on the 1962 Constitution until the Iraqi invasion in the 1990s. We conclude the chapter by offering insights into how Kuwait's modern-day politics are rooted in its tumultuous constitutional development.

Kuwait's Early Beginning: A Shura-based Tribal Sheikhdom

Throughout the 18th century, the Bani Khalid tribe controlled the province of Grane, the original name of Kuwait, and the eastern coast of the Arabian Gulf, and the al-Utub clans of the Anaiza tribe relocated from al-Hadar in central Najd to the Arabian Gulf coast in an attempt to establish a new dominion. Several branches of the al-Sabah, al-Zayed, and al-Khalifa families constituted most of the al-Utub clan and immigrated to Kuwait in 1716 with the permission of Sadun bin Mohammed, the Sheikh of Bani Khalid, who ruled the region then. Soon, the al-Sabah family became a powerful clan in this region, gradually gaining control of the region over the Bani Khalid. However, it is important to note that a significant portion of the early history of Kuwait remains unclear as the first Kuwaiti historians, such as al-Rushaid (1926) and al-Qinai (1988), mainly relied on oral traditions, which are not always historically accurate and often biased.

Although there is no indication in the narratives offered by Kuwaiti historians that a leader was elected to manage the migration of the al-Utub group from Najd, it would be exceedingly rare for such a big tribe to migrate without appointing a figure of authority for such a significant migration. Al-Shamlan (1986) mentions that the notables chose Sabah ibn Jabir as the first Sheikh of Kuwait (r. till 1743) since his father was the leader of al-Utub in Najd. Eickelman (2002) also proposes that tribes commonly had a council of adult males chosen from each branch or *fakhth* to administer the affairs of the tribe. In the case of Kuwait, such a council may have been established by the al-Utub clan to address issues that afflicted families from the Aniza tribe, who shared similar concerns. In addition, it is worth noting that the Islamic faith requires Muslims to designate a leader while travelling in groups of three or more. According to a Prophetic tradition (al-Nawawi, 1998), Prophet Muhammad stated, "If you are travelling with more than two people, one of you must be in charge." Hence, this evidence from the Islamic religion may also refute the claim that the al-Utub clan did not elect a leader nor form a council with decision-making authority or political power since Islam tended to permeate many societal aspects of tribes at that time. Furthermore, although it is unknown precisely when Sabah bin Jabir the First was entrusted with the leadership of the people in Kuwait, sources tend to indicate that he ruled until 1743 and was chosen through a traditional tribal process whereby notables decided that he would represent the newly formed sheikhdom. Nonetheless, he was not allowed absolute authority and,

Kuwait's Political History 9

instead, was compelled to seek the counsel of local notables but could not exercise influence over them or compel them to embrace his viewpoint.

Hence, Sabah was the first to be chosen through tribal procedures or the *Shura* system, a pre-Islamic tradition familiar to Arabs and others. Given its pre-Islamic usage, consultation was not always motivated by a religious motive. Rather, it was associated with a social or political drive, given that consultation inherently implies a social framework. Moreover, with regard to internal politics, before Mubarak acceded to power in 1896, Kuwaitis' political choices were mainly based on a system of dialogue between merchants and the Sheikh, who lacked total authority. The Sheikhs thus often lacked the ability to reject or alter the merchants' choices or agreements, as they were basically on par with the merchants in terms of authority. Hence, the Sheikh often retained his post depending on the merchants' satisfaction and lacked full decision-making authority.

It is also crucial to note that the early ruling system in Kuwait, in the pre-Mubarak era (before 1896), did not indicate that the society had survived for generations without a ruler or lacked a means of resolving conflicts. Consequently, it is fair to say that the al-Sabah based their ruling system on a social contract, which was neither imposed nor derived from an inherited dictatorship. This system of governance, in which there was no clear distinction between the Sheikh and the elite, lasted for an extended period.

Power Sharing between the Sheikh and Merchants

During that period, Kuwait's elite and merchants may have had greater power than the Sheikh himself on certain occasions. For instance, according to Al-Rushaid (1926), Sabah the First (r. till 1743) and Abdullah the First (r.1743–1814) lacked the power and authority to reject a merchant's judgment. Thus, the ruler's power was restricted to the degree that merchants contributed funds to assist with treasury administration, with each merchant's power proportional to their financial contribution. In this respect, al-Rushaid (1926) relates how Jabir bin Abdullah, the third ruler of Kuwait, favoured a local merchant, Ali bin Ibrahim, by not imposing charges on his products entering Kuwait despite levying taxes on other merchants' goods. Al-Rushaid continues and explains how the Sheikh favoured bin Ibrahim over another merchant, Abdullatif al-Khamis; as Sheikh Jabir needed coffee for his personal use and *Majlis*, bin Ibrahim gave the Sheikh eight huge sacks of coffee while al-Khamis only sent a little pouch. This anecdote highlights the intricate links between the financial and governing powers at the time within the Kuwaiti elite. In other words, the merchant who paid the Sheikh the most money had the most influence over his judgments.

Nevertheless, instead of relying primarily on the merchants, the al-Sabah ruling family often sought other sources of revenue. For instance, they made their way via Ottoman remittances and gifts given to the Sheikh. In addition, these two sources of wealth for the al-Sabah family contributed to their partial independence from the merchants, although not enough to secure complete power. For instance, Rashid al-Sadun[1] and Sulayman al-Zuhayr[2] offered their date palm farms, Sufiyya

10 *Abdulrahman Alebrahim*

and al-Faw gardens, to Sheikh Jabir bin Abd Allah in exchange for their protection (*dakhala*) during their stay in Kuwait. Even after Jabir's death, the subsequent rulers of Kuwait benefited from the profits generated through the al-Sufiyya farm, which exceeded 6,000 pounds Sterling in 1898 and an estimated Rs.8,000 in 1909. In addition to profits from gifts, Jabir received an annual payment of 150 *karas*[3] of dates from the Ottomans and his grandson Abdullah was given the title *Qaimaqam*[4] and an annual income. Hence, not only did the rentier aspect of the governing system begin before the discovery of oil, but the money from these two date palm farms also played a crucial role in the sheikhs' capacity to acquire independence from the merchants (al-Rushaid, 1926; al-Shamlan, 1986).

Mubarak's Era: A Shift in Kuwait's Politics

Following the death of Sheikh Jabir in 1859, his son Sabah bin Jabir took over in 1866, when Abdullah bin Sabah ruled until 1892. Although significant in terms of external affairs, the reigns of Sabah and Abdullah did not significantly impact Kuwait's internal politics. However, Abdullah's successor, Mohammed al-Sabah, became the Sheikh of Kuwait in 1892 and attempted to restructure the system of governance, particularly with respect to the al-Sabah family's wealth. For instance, Sheikh Mohammed backed his brother Jarrah's efforts to expand the family holdings in Iraq and sought to develop the Faw date palm farms to increase the ruler's autonomy. Mohammed al-Sabah and Jarrah were cognisant that the more their non-tax earnings, the greater their independence (al-Rushaid, 1926; al-Shamlan, 1986). However, while they were trying to increase the family revenues and distance themselves from the merchants' financial power, they deprived their brother Mubarak who was in charge of the affairs of the Badia (desert), which included, for instance, tribal matters, controlling desert caravans, or ensuring the safety of the city from outsiders' attacks. Hence, for Mubarak, this required access to sufficient funds. Mubarak's conflict with his brothers, Mohammed and Jarrah, culminated in his murdering them to seize power in 1896.

After murdering his brothers Mohammed and Jarrah, Mubarak al-Sabah seized authority and soon faced violent resistance from merchants who supported his deceased brothers Mohammed and Jarrah. For example, Yusuf bin Ibrahim, a well-known Kuwaiti merchant and former advisor of Mohammad and Jarrah, launched military attacks in Kuwait from Iraq with the support of the sons of the murdered Sheikhs, several Kuwaiti notables, and common people. To counter this opposition, Mubarak attempted to conceal his crime by compelling certain Kuwaiti elites to sign a letter accusing Yusuf bin Ibrahim of murdering Mubarak's brothers and demanding his arrest. Nevertheless, several members of the elite, including religious scholars, refused to sign it, and this conflict persisted during his first decade in power (alebrahim, 2019).

Prior to Mubarak's era, Kuwait's political system was not properly structured and mainly consisted of an informal council of elders, senior members of the al-Sabah family, prominent merchants, and clerics. This council took decisions on various matters, and every member could advise and influence the Sheikh's decisions. Al-Shamlan (1986) argues that the sheikhs were comparable to tribal sheikhs insofar as the ruler's authority was restricted, and the elite often had more authority than the ruler, as mentioned above. However, during Mubarak's rule (1896–1915), the political system shifted from a consultation, Shura-based system to an autocratic regime in which a single person exercised absolute power.

This shift in the ruling system, especially after 1906, can largely be explained by the loss of power from his outside enemies. Indeed, his chief adversaries, Yusuf bin Ibrahim and Abdulaziz al-Rasheed, died in 1906. This allowed him to raise taxes on Kuwaitis as he did not need as much military support as before when his chief enemies were alive and threatening his rule. These tax increases had a significant impact on the economy and the welfare of the people.

The tax increases harmed every sector of Kuwait's economy. For example, Mubarak increased annual rents for market shops by 25%, resulting in shopkeepers paying Rs.50 instead of Rs.20. In addition, he levied a new tax on newly constructed homes and another on carpenters. During this time, Mubarak purchased two enormous date farms in Iraq, al-Fadaghiyya and al-Zain, and in 1909, it was estimated that Mubarak earned Rs.800,000 from palm date production. Inevitably, this additional income increased the merchants' animosity towards him and freed him from heavily relying on the merchants through taxes or grants.

Resistance to Mubarak's Rule: Merchants and Religious Scholars

Mubarak's method of authoritarian governance and imposition of taxes generated resistance to his rule. The merchants' immigration in 1910 is a case in point in that respect, as it is evident that they opposed all forms of authoritarianism. This initiative by Kuwait's leading pearl merchants compelled Mubarak to alter some of his policies and his leadership style. For instance, Mubarak's army stationed in Jahra at the time was awaiting instructions to strike Sadun Basha[5] in Southern Iraq. However, when he learnt about the pearl merchants' departure, Mubarak cancelled the military campaign. In addition, following the migration of the wealthiest merchant in Kuwait, Hilal al-Mutairi, Mubarak was fully aware that the situation could harm Kuwait's economy and his authority as a leader, particularly because merchants and divers were eager to leave the country and follow the leading merchants (al-Rushaid, 1926).

Moreover, in 1915, Mubarak's authority was further questioned not only by merchants but by religious elites as well. For instance, he attempted to compel the people of Kuwait to provide support to the British during the First World War, and he instructed his son Jabir to deploy ships carrying Kuwaiti troops to support the emir of al-Mohammarah, Sheikh Khazal, who expressed his support for the British government in 1915 when the Ottoman government declared a jihad against the British and entered the war. However, during the First World War, local religious scholars and merchants spearheaded the resistance against Mubarak in the name of jihad. As a result, many religious Muslim men and local tribesmen joined the Ottoman army against the British. For example, Hafiz Wahbah and Mohammed al-Shanqiti, influential religious scholars of that time, played a significant role

12 *Abdulrahman Alebrahim*

in persuading people not to follow Sheikh Mubarak, warning them that doing so would constitute apostasy from Islam. Despite possibly irritating Sheikh Mubarak, several notables met with his son Jabir while he was absent, informing him that they would neither follow Mubarak nor sacrifice their brothers for Khazal, arguing that this conflict had nothing to do with the Kuwaiti people (al-Shamlan, 1986; Khazal, 1967).

Notwithstanding Mubarak's threats, the Kuwaiti people were adamantly opposed to assisting him and the British in their fight against the Ottoman Empire. They failed when top merchants attempted to convince them to accept Mubarak's demands. People generally adhered to Sheikh al-Shanqiti and Sheikh Hafiz Wahbah's beliefs despite unsuccessful attempts by several prominent individuals to support Khazal.

Salim and Jabir's Rule: The End of an Era

On November 29, 1915, Sheikh Mubarak's son Jabir bin Mubarak ascended to power upon his father's death and took several measures to soften the relationship between the ruler and his people, which had been tense during Mubarak's reign. As a result, Mubarak's one-third estate tax was abolished by Jabir; this tax was charged to a property regardless of how often it was sold. Jabir also returned to their rightful owners the properties seized during his father's reign and granted amnesty to the merchants who violated the British embargo against the Ottomans, allowing their caravans to enter Syria and Hejaz. However, Jabir's rule did not last long as he died in 1917, and his brother Salim bin Mubarak assumed authority. Salim decreased customs duties to 4% and eliminated export taxes. This decision was seen as a gesture of friendliness towards the affluent business class who had suffered financial losses during Mubarak's rule (al-Rushaid, 1926; al-Shamlan, 1986).

However, Salim's early decisions to reduce taxes did not affect his will to control Kuwait's decision-making process. His propensity for authoritarian rule became evident during the 1919 *Himdh* battle, in which Kuwait suffered significant loss of life and property. Following the battle, as Sheikh Salim recognized that a conflict was imminent with Faisal al-Duweish, the Sheikh of the Mutair tribe, he ordered the construction of new city walls surrounding Kuwait without consulting anyone. Despite his affluence, Salim compelled the people of Kuwait to pay for the building costs without him contributing (al-Rushaid, 1926; al-Shamlan, 1986).

Moreover, notwithstanding Sheikh Salim's predisposition towards authoritarianism and unilateralism, he was unable to disregard the views of Kuwaiti elites in all situations. For instance, following the battle of *Jahra* in 1920, where the *Ikhwan,*[6] supporters of Ibn Saud, aided by a coalition of tribes, were defeated by Kuwaitis, Sheikh Salim negotiated the terms of the Ikhwan's withdrawal from Kuwait. Several Kuwaiti notables participated in these conversations, but Sheikh Salim remained mute and rejected all negotiation terms, insisting that Ikhwan must return to Najd unconditionally.

The rule of Mubarak and his sons Jabir and Salim culminated in a shift towards authoritarian decision-making. This mode of leadership affected the political sphere

Kuwait's Political History   13

in Kuwait. From 1896 through 1921, the decision-making system evolved from consultation to absolute dictatorship. This was the first change in Kuwait's political leadership. The second change occurred when merchants refused to nominate a new ruler without organizing a Shura Council, as the next section will demonstrate.

Towards Participatory Rule: The 1921 Shura Council

During Salim's rule, the British suggested forming a Shura Council with members selected from various segments of society, headed by the crown prince at that time, Ahmed al-Jabir. However, this plan never came to life until Salim's unexpected death in 1921, whereby Kuwaiti merchants who had opposed Salim resolved to establish a Shura Council to participate in the decision-making process. For instance, Yusuf al-Qinai, a local merchant and principal of the Mubarakiyya School and religious scholar, encouraged several prominent Kuwaitis to consider forming a Shura Council to avoid an autocratic regime under the new ruler, Sheikh Ahmad al-Jabir. Although some of the notables al-Qinai met agreed with him, such as the *Qibla* merchants, others, the *Sharq* merchants in particular, were more cautious and preferred to postpone taking action until Sheikh Ahmad al-Jabir's return from Najd (al-Rushaid, 1926; al-Shamlan, 1986).

Furthermore, on Sheikh Salim's death, the famous local merchant Nasir al-Bader gathered in his *diwan*[7] with several well-known merchants from Sharq and Qibla. All the men present drafted and signed a petition calling for succession reforms and changes to the political regime by establishing a Shura Council. The petition, which would have been inconceivable under Mubarak's or his sons' rule, was published by al-Wuqayyan (2014) and al-Shamlan (1986) and read as follows[8]:

In the name of Allah, we, the undersigned, have agreed and united by the covenant of Allah on the following clauses:

1. Reform the House of al-Sabah to avoid disagreements over the appointment of the ruler.
2. The candidates for this matter [i.e. the position of ruler] are Sheikh Ahmad al-Jabir, Sheikh Hamad al-Mubarak, and Sheikh 'Abd Allah al-Salim.
3. It is acceptable for the al-Sabah family to reach a consensus on one of the candidates; then this is all right, and if they delegate the matter to the people, then we will appoint [the ruler]. If the government desires to choose one of them, we will accept him.
4. The appointed ruler shall be the president of the Shura Council.
5. Several members of the al-Sabah family and the Kuwaiti people shall be elected to run the affairs of the country on the basis of fairness and justice.

Ahmed al-Jabir agreed to the terms of the merchants' petitions and established the first Shura Council in 1921. Sources do not specify the procedure for choosing council members; however, it appears that members were chosen instead of being elected by the people. Moreover, the names of these council members tend to suggest that they had social and economic influence. It is important to note that

14 *Abdulrahman Alebrahim*

nearly no source explicitly mentions this Council in great length, except for Khazal (1967), who is the only historian to have thoroughly explained the Shura Council, although the author does not cite specific sources.

It is important to note that Ahmed al-Jabir, not in Kuwait at the time of Salim's death, felt compelled to meet the merchants' requests to form the Shura Council. According to a British document from 1921, Ahmad al-Jabir lacked the authority to reject the request to establish a new Shura Council. For instance, the British Political Agent in Kuwait informed the Baghdad High Commissioner that the al-Sabah and prominent families had already agreed to form a Shura Council before Ahmad's arrival, adding that "they [the leading families] were determined to have some say in Kuwait's affairs, and they were not going to be driven to wage war against their will as they have in the past" (British High Commissioner in Baghdad, 1921).[9]

Nonetheless, upon its establishment, the Council did not have a significant impact on the decision-making process, mainly due to the frequent internal disputes between members. This was expected, given that they were elderly and lacked the necessary knowledge and skills to deal with diverse opinions. Several members were known for being obstinate and steadfastly holding to their positions and did not make decisions based on what the majority thought since they each believed their viewpoint to be true. Thus, some members seemed to have lost sight of the intended objective of the Council and started making outrageous statements, while others became disinterested and stopped attending future meetings. While it was against the Council's rules, it is known that members sometimes sent their sons to council meetings instead of them (Khazal, 1967).

Despite its simplicity, the creation of the 1921 Council showed that Kuwait's ruling family and elites understood the necessity of consultation and participation, particularly in light of the events of the preceding 20 years. The Shura Council was a successful beginning for Kuwait's representative system and was regarded as the fundamental building stone for the following councils, even though it was short-lived. The Council's principal objective was to weaken the al-Sabah's absolute power but not solely include merchants in decision-making. This Council was established after the merchants had organized themselves, gained the upper hand against the ruler, and marked a shift from absolute power to shared decision-making. It comprised various segments of Kuwait's civil society. However, the Council gradually lost its importance until its collapse only two months after its establishment. As a result, Sheikh Ahmad resumed absolute authority. Nonetheless, this did not eliminate the Kuwaiti merchants' desire to establish representative councils.

The Shura Council was the first Council to aid the ruler in political decision-making in a clear and organized manner. The acceptance of the ruler by the Council was seen as a great progress with regard to the rights of the people; in fact, it is hitherto regarded as an important accomplishment in Kuwait. Indeed, the nomination of the ruler on the condition that he heeded the counsel of council members marked a significant shift in the political landscape and laid the stage for later events. The written contract between the ruler and council members was a major advance in Kuwait's political and administrative organization and was one of the most important outcomes of the Council's founding. A notable benefit of this Council was the development of the first parliament-like body, which was unusual in the political history of the Arabian Gulf and substantially aided the formation of succeeding councils. In addition, this declaration emphasized judicial independence and the establishment of an appeals court.

From the Shura Council to the Legislative Council

With the dissolution of the 1921 Shura Council, the merchants' efforts to influence decision-making in Kuwait continued. For example, a municipal administration was established in 1930 to handle health and social services. In addition, the first Municipal Council was created two years later, with members elected for the first time in Kuwait's history, although voting was restricted to the merchant class. The successive Municipal Councils played a crucial part in forming Kuwait's Constitution as it was a driving force in moving the country's political system from selection to election. Moreover, in 1936, merchants proposed the formation of an Education Council, which was refused by the then-ruler, Ahmed al-Jabir. However, to convince him to accept this move, the merchants suggested a 0.5% increase in customs taxes. Sheikh Ahmad al-Jabir initially resisted, but owing to his cousin Sheikh Abdullah al-Jabir's perseverance, he agreed to form an elected council for education funded by increased customs taxes on all commodities imported by non-British traders (al-Adsani, 1938).

Learning from the experience of the failed Shura Council of 1921, which was riddled with difficulties due to the lack of systematic procedures, the Education Council enacted an internal law, and young merchants implemented the notion of "the majority decision," which states that a decision cannot be reversed until six months have elapsed after it became law. However, despite reaching an agreement on the overall structure of the Education Council, which was a step towards constructive work, it became evident that certain members were unable to accept the majority rule and attempted to impose their own thoughts and beliefs.

The formation of the Municipal and Education Councils was unquestionably a step towards greater people's involvement in the government and the beginning of contemporary political institutions. The municipality engaged in several activities, such as burying the dead, measuring roads, and shop health and safety inspections, which set the foundation for the establishment of future organizations. The efforts of Kuwaiti merchants were important in the formation of these two councils, as shown by their substantial donations and voluntary participation. These men also agreed to the customs increase to contribute to the general administration budget, exhibiting an understanding of the role people play in ensuring the welfare of the nation.

Unquestionably, both the Municipal and Education Councils set the way for future political growth since voters were persuaded that a progressive approach was the best way to encourage more involvement. Despite this, the two councils remained under the influence of an elite who was unpopular with the Sheikh's entourage, whose interests were in contradiction with those of this reform movement. In

16 *Abdulrahman Alebrahim*

1937, pro-reform members of the Education Council were replaced by pro-Sheikh members; the names of voters were falsified, and when the results were published, reformist members resigned from the two councils. Hence, starting with the founding of the Shura Council in 1921 and, subsequently, the Municipal and Education Councils, the reform movement aspired to turn Kuwait into an institutional and constitutional nation.

In an attempt to help the reformist movement, a number of members resigned from the local Council. These members began organizing themselves and working secretly to change the status quo and included several prominent Kuwaiti merchants who contributed to this political movement. These reform attempts culminated in the founding of the National Bloc by Abdullah Hamad al-Saqir, the son of the first president of the Shura Council in 1921, Abdullatif al-Ghanim, of the wealthy al-Ghanim family, and Khalid Sulaiman al-Adsani, who would become the secretary of the first and second Legislative Councils.

The National Bloc focussed on two objectives: (1) Striving for the establishment of an elected council and (2) Granting the Council the power to supervise, monitor, and organize the Emirate's affairs as a legislative rather than a consultative council. The National Bloc was initially a secret movement with meetings limited only to its founding members, al-Adsani, al-Ghanim, and al-Saqir. Membership then expanded to 12, all of whom were merchants. Soon after this, the National Bloc succeeded in convincing Mohammed Thunayan al-Ghanim, one of the Kuwaiti merchants and a senior merchant, to join the Bloc. The group also sought to encourage Sheikh Yusuf al-Qinai to stand with them and compose a letter to Sheikh Ahmad with their reform proposals, but al-Qinai was not convinced of this move (al-Adsani, 1938). The members of the National Bloc drafted a letter requesting the formation of a legislative council and delegated Mohammed Thunayan al-Ghanim, Abdullah Hamad al-Saqir, and Sulaiman al-Adsani to present it to Ahmed al-Jabir. The letter reads as follows:

> Your Highness, the nation swore its allegiance to you on the day you ascended the throne on the understanding that the principles of your rule would rest on the notions of Shura, which Islam decreed and was adopted by the four Righteous Caliphs, but these notions have been quickly forgotten by both sides in Kuwait due to the unique circumstances the country has endured. This has prompted several of your subjects to offer their advice and counsel to redress the situation and spare you and themselves the vagaries of time and the unpredictability of circumstances and safeguard our country and its sovereignty and independence. They seek to remove the roots of discontent through dialogue and have, therefore, decided to propose the establishment of a legislative council to run the country's affairs. We have authorised the bearers of this letter to discuss the matter with you. We beseech Allah to guide us onto the path of all that is good and righteous. 30 Rabi' al-Awwal, 1357 Hijri (31 May 1938).
>
> (al-Adsani, 1938; alebrahim 2019).

This push for reforms led to the establishment of the First Legislative Council in 1938, which can be considered a significant landmark in Kuwait's constitutional history.

Kuwait's First Legislative Councils (1938–39)

The 1938 merchants' petition reminded the ruler of the social contract binding him with the Kuwaiti merchants, who emphasized that the only way to achieve this was via the creation of a council. The petitioners engaged in discussions with the ruler who agreed to hold elections. About 320 people were summoned to vote and gathered at the diwan of al-Saqir. Compared to Kuwait's population of about 65,000 at the time, the number of voters invited to participate in the election was limited. It is believed that around 10,000 were of *Ajam* (non-Arab) origin, and 18,000 were from Arab and non-Arab Shi'a minorities (al-Jassim, 1997). Thus, a substantial proportion of Kuwaitis were denied the right to vote. The National Bloc received the majority of votes and 8 of the 14 available seats. In addition, 4 more seats were won by National Bloc sympathizers while the remaining 2 members were independent. More specifically, 12 of the 14 members were *Qibla* merchants, which was a strong indicator that the *Qibla* merchants controlled Kuwait's political landscape.

In order to handle the nation's affairs, the Council drafted a constitution, previously prepared by the secretary of the Council, Khalid al-Adsani, and accepted by the members and president of the Council before being approved by the Sheikh. This Constitution comprised five articles.

Article I: The nation, represented by the Council members, is the source of all powers.
Article II: The Council initiates laws in the areas of health, justice, the budget, and construction, emergency, knowledge, and public security.
Article III: The Legislative Council is the reference for all treaties and agreements; it is not considered legal without the consent of the Council.
Article IV: The Legislative Council represents the Court of Appeal.
Article V: The President of the Council represents the executive authority.

The ruler considered the Constitution unnecessary and favoured a gradual reform of the political institutions. His reluctance to approve the Constitution was due to the fact that it shifted all of the Sheikh's authority to the Council. Since he was not used to sharing power, it was only natural that he hesitated before signing the Constitution. The Council addressed him with a forceful letter to reaffirm their commitment to working with him and to remind him of the 1921 covenant binding him with the people. The letter was an indirect threat to Ahmed l-Jaber to persuade him "to be the head of the nation" or accept "all possible consequences." The members of the Council positioned themselves as opponents of the Sheikh, threatening that they would not accept a constitution other than the one they had drafted and

18 *Abdulrahman Alebrahim*

were also prepared for conflict. To exert additional pressure on the Sheikh, the Council asked a number of youths to write pro-Council slogans addressed to the Sheikh on the city walls, such as "Be sincere to the nation, and they will be most sincere to you" and "Long live our Council members who live for the rights of the people" (al-Adsani, 1938).

Several changes were initiated by the Council, but they did not endure long as on December 18, 1938, Sheikh Ahmed al-Jaber dissolved the Legislative Council. Soon after the dissolution, on December 27, new elections were held. The number of voters rose to 400, with 20 candidates, and the election was mostly seen as fair. The National Bloc won the first 17 seats, while their opponents from the previous Council won the remaining 3 seats by a razor-thin margin. On December 29, the Council met to review the draft of the new Constitution, and by the start of the New Year, they had finalized the Constitution. An article was added stating that the ruler had no authority to dissolve the Council except in cases of popular unrest, in which case he was required to hold new elections within a week.

Nevertheless, the ruler rejected the 1939 Constitution and requested from the British Political Agent a copy of the Trans-Jordanian Constitution to serve as a model for Kuwait and sent him the Council's draft Constitution for his review and advice. The Political Agent encouraged the ruler to reject the text and substitute the phrase "independence" with "independence under British protection." In addition, the British advised the Sheikh to dissolve the Council and choose new members from among the prominent Kuwaitis should they reject his revisions. Sheikh Ahmad presented the proposed Constitution to the Council members in February 1939, whose first article called for the elimination of the previous Council statute, which was one of its most significant characteristics. The third article stated that the Council's function would not be legislative but consultative. In doing so, with the help of the British, the Sheikh sought to regain his complete powers and diminish the influence of the Council, which had managed to gain full control over political decision-making and terminated his 17-year reign of autocracy.

Consequently, the ruler declared the Council's dissolution on March 7, 1939, after failing to achieve a consensus on the constitutional issue. Obviously, the Sheikh's decision incited the pro-Council Kuwaiti youth to take action. For instance, Mohammed al-Munais, a member of a middle-class family returning from Basra, addressed a public assembly arguing that the al-Sabah dynasty had lost its authority. As a result, the chief of the Public Security Department, Sheikh Ali al-Khalifa al-Sabah, ordered his arrest; he was later assaulted and imprisoned. This authoritarian move from the ruling family spurred Council supporters to congregate in opposition to al-Munais' detention, including Yusuf al-Marzuq who opened fire on the ruler's guards and caused violent skirmishes between the guards and the Council supporters. Prominent youth figure and Council supporter Mohammed al-Qatami was shot and killed in the exchange, while al-Marzuq, a former council member, sustained a foot wound (al-Adsani, 1938). The next day, al-Munais was executed on allegations of treason. Five Council members were also imprisoned, thereby bringing the political situation under control by the ruler and his allies. The Council's offices were shut down on March 10, 1939, and the ruler was determined not to reiterate this democratic experience.

A Shift in Kuwait Politics: Kuwait Intelligentsia as a New Political Force

From the 1940s onwards, the education system in Kuwait underwent a period of substantial growth, and the oil revenues were instrumental in the formation of a new intelligentsia. This intellectual elite was composed primarily of Arab nationalists such as Ahmad al-Khatib, Jassem al-Qatami, and Abdulaziz Hussain and significantly influenced Kuwait's political life. For instance, during the 1958 Council elections, with 500 voters, more than 12 of the 56 seats were won by members of this new intelligentsia. Prominent members of the ruling family refused to accept the results, most notably because of the presence of three prominent members: Ahmed al-Khatib, Jassem al-Qatami, and al-Khaled. This prompted all Council members to resign in support of these three members (al-Khatib, 2007). Hence, the 1958 Council is said to be the only Council in Kuwait's political history to be dissolved prior to its first meeting. This indicates a shift in the 1930s' and 1940s' political life from a bipolar situation dominated by Sheikhs and merchants to a tripartite era with the new intelligentsia involved in the decision-making process.

1962 Constitution: A Landmark in Kuwait's Post-Independence Politics

After independence in 1961, in response to Iraqi President Abdulkarim Qasim's threats, Kuwait witnessed a great popular movement in support of the ruling family and demonstrated in numbers near the Sheikh's palace, chanting "Hey Bo Salim, arm us, and we are ready." This event had a positive impact on Sheikh Abdullah al-Salim; according to al-Khatib (2007), this was the primary reason for the Sheikh's decision to call for public elections in Kuwait. Due to his inclination towards the parliamentary system and following threats from neighbouring Iraq, the Sheikh decided to hold elections for a new Legislative Council for the first time since the 1939 Council dissolution. This indicates a significant shift in Kuwait's political life as AbdulAllah al-Salim had a deeper reading of the situation; he understood the importance of involving certain segments of the population in the decision-making process, thereby ensuring the stability of the al-Sabah family as legitimate rulers.

Following Kuwait's change from a sheikhdom under British protectorate to a modern nation-state as a result of independence in 1961, the ruler decreed a new law regulating the elections of members of a new Constituent Assembly. The law contained 48 articles and introduced essential changes in the electoral system concerning the right to vote. For instance, Article 9 granted the right to vote to every male, *Kuwaiti bit-ta'sis* (Kuwaiti by origin) above the age of 21 years. It is important to stress here that not all Kuwaiti males had the right to vote as citizenship was divided into two main categories: (1) *Kuwaiti bit-ta'sis*, that is, any individual

20 *Abdulrahman Alebrahim*

residing or owning property in Kuwait before 1920, and (2) Kuwaiti *bi-tajnis* (Kuwaiti by naturalization).

As a matter of comparison, the number of voters rose from 500 for the 1958 elections to 11,288 for the 1961 elections. However, according to official British estimates, the number of voters reached 28,500 during the 1961 elections. This difference between the estimated voters may be due to the fact that the British reports were sent before the end of the legal registration period, on August 27, 1961, while the registration ended on October 19, 1961. Nonetheless, despite this disparity, the number of voters grew significantly, and all eligible Kuwaitis had the right to vote, unlike at the beginning during previous elections when only elites from the merchant class and the intelligentsia had this right (alebrahim, 2019).

The Constituent Assembly elections were held in December 1961; out of the 20 available seats, most were won by the intelligentsia, tribe members, and villagers, including 13 members from different social classes, while only seven were from the merchant class, Shi'a and Sunni. The elected Assembly held its first meeting on January 20, 1962, and elected Abdullateef al-Ghanim as Speaker and Ahmad al-Khatib as Deputy Speaker (alebrahim, 2019). The election of al-Khatib constituted a significant change as he was the first non-merchant individual to hold a political position in Kuwait's political history. As explained by al-Khatib (2007) himself in his memoirs, this displeased the al-Sabah family; he narrates how his chair was symbolically removed, thereby preventing him from chairing sessions in the absence of the speaker. This testimony, however, contradicts official British records stating that Jabir al-Ali al-Sabah, the Minister for Electricity in 1962, indicated that al-Khatib's vice-presidency was secured by al-Sabah sheikhs' ballots (Burdett, 1997). Nonetheless, it remains that the election of al-Khatib as the Deputy Speaker is indicative of a change in Kuwait's political landscape, previously dominated by the pre-independence privileged class.

Heated debates took place in the Constituent Assembly, particularly on the issue of political freedom. For example, while discussing Article 34, al-Khatib insisted on the approval of the establishment of political parties, arguing that failure to do so could not guarantee a sound democratic life due to the central role of political parties in organizing the masses and contributing to the development of the country. However, several members and ministers ultimately rejected this proposal (al-Khatib, 2007). Moreover, Article 2 was also the subject of intense debates as it relates to "Islam as the religion of State" and "the Islamic Sharia as one of the main sources of legislation." For instance, Khalifa Talal al-Jiri, from the Ajman tribe, objected to the wording on the grounds that the phrase "one of the main sources" implied that there could be other sources beside Islam and, therefore, demanded that the phrasing be replaced by "the only source of legislation." However, his request was denied, as many members of the Assembly were merchants whose banking systems were based on usury, and this article would have halted all transactions between banks and corporations abroad (Constituent Assembly, 1962).

The Constitution was finally ratified on November 11, 1962, and published in a special edition of the Official Gazette, *Kuwait Today* (Ministry of Media, 1962).

Kuwait's Political History   21

The Constitution included 183 articles organized into five chapters, including (1) The State and The System of Government, (2) Fundamental Constituents of The Kuwaiti Society, (3) Public Rights and Duties, (4) Powers, and (5) General and Transitional Provisions. A significant change brought about by Articles 80–122 of the Constitution is the mention of the elected National Assembly (*Majlis al-Ummah*) with legislative powers, its duties, powers, and prerogatives (Ministry of Media, 2022).

Political Crises and the Iraqi Invasion

Soon after the adoption of the 1962 Constitution, a series of critical events shook the constitutional foundations of Kuwait's political life. The death of Abdullah al-Salim in 1965 led to several attempts by successive governments to forge the National Assembly elections. The first attempt to rig the elections was in 1967, the first election after the death of Abdullah Al-Salim. Twenty-one candidates ran for election, and six winning members issued a statement accusing the government of rigging the elections (al-Najjar, 2000). The interference in the election by the government did not stop there: the Assembly was dissolved in 1976, changes were made to the electoral districts in 1980, the Assembly was again dissolved in 1986, and attempts were made to introduce a less-independent legislative body to replace the Assembly in 1990.

Abdullah al-Salim can be considered as Kuwait's political "safety valve" to democratic life as he partially believed in preserving the country's democratic experience. It cannot be argued, however, that he had strong beliefs in changing the political system from a sort of autocratic regime to a fully democratic system. Still, he sought to create a modern sheikhdom where the Sheikh always had the upper hand on political matters. Furthermore, from the end of the 1960s until the Iraqi invasion in 1990, the government manipulated political life and attempted several times to put an end to the National Assembly's existence using different methods such as rigging the elections, dissolving the Assembly, or revising the Constitution. However, as Crystal (1995) argues, these attempts only strengthened the opposition's will to push the political boundaries towards more civil liberties. These attempts from the government aimed at silencing the opposition. Most specifically, the reform of the electoral district was made to rally a maximum number of pro-government voters and parliament members and diminish the chances of the opposition, mainly in the *hadhar*[10] districts, to gain seats in the Assembly. This is because there were now more tribe-dominated districts than *hadhar* ones. Consequently, following the 1981 elections, the National Assembly was dominated by the newly elected tribal members and pro-government Islamist groups. These attempts from the government culminated in the dissolution of the National Assembly on July 3, 1986, and the suspension of parliamentary life for four years as a result of the Assembly's interference in oil policies and stock market affairs, as well as allegations of corruption against members of the ruling family (Nosova, 2016).

The dissolution was accompanied by the suspension of several constitutional provisions and press repression. As no date for the Assembly's return was specified

22 *Abdulrahman Alebrahim*

by the Sheikh, political forces opposed the Sheikh's decision to dissolve the parliament or suspend some articles of the Constitution and requested holding new elections, as stipulated in the Constitution. Indeed, as per the Constitution, parliamentary life cannot be suspended for more than a month. However, the government refused to cooperate to end this political crisis and attempted to reform the Constitution, which resulted in a four-year political status quo.

As a result of the government's decisions, a new heterogeneous opposition movement emerged, which was composed of different ideological blocs representing various segments of society. The leaders of this opposition attempted to organize their response to the government through several political moves, petitioning and political gatherings. For instance, petitions to the ruler were written requesting him to reinstate the Assembly and resume parliamentary life, but all their endeavours failed. In addition, on December 4, 1989, a gathering was organized at the *diwaniyya* of a prominent opposition leader, Jasim al-Qatami. As the traditional Kuwaiti *diwaniyya* is a social place where men gather and talk about different topics, this gathering was not legally considered a political gathering, thereby not breaking the Law of Gatherings. Around 700 people attended the *diwaniyya*, and it was then decided to resume such gatherings every Monday at the *diwaniyyas* of former MPs. This marked the 1989 constitutional movement known as *Dawawin al-Ithnain*, the Monday *Diwaniyyas* (Nosova, 2018).

This was met with violent reaction from the government; they attempted to suppress the opposition by banning any further gatherings in *diwaniyyas*. In addition to that, Sheikh Jaber decided to form a new Assembly made of selected and elected members. This move by the ruler was an explicit violation of the provisions of the Constitution, which stipulates that all members of the parliament must be elected. This was a clear breach of the Constitution, as any constitutional reform must be agreed upon by the ruler and Assembly. In the absence of any elected Assembly since the 1986 dissolution, the ruler single-handedly took this unconstitutional decision, thereby reinforcing his autocratic rule. This constituted a step backwards from the 1962 Constitution, as Sheikh Jaber would effectively appoint one-third of the Assembly (25 members), while only two-thirds would be elected. This, therefore, granted him extraordinary powers within the legislative institution.

The new *Majlis* did not get a chance to fulfil its designated term as the elections took place on June 10, 1990, and on August 2, the Iraqi troops invaded Kuwait. Political instability in Kuwait and the vehement opposition to the Sheikh, which lasted for four years, was seen by Saddam as indicative of a divide between Kuwaitis and their ruler. According to Nosova (2016), Kuwait's political status quo created an impression that the population would not stand with the ruling family and would surrender to Iraqis voluntarily, which turned out to be a wrong assumption. Indeed, during the Iraqi invasion, the al-Sabah family and nearly all political blocs and social groups convened in Jiddah, Saudi Arabia. In the meeting, the political opposition requested the reinstatement of parliamentary life in Kuwait under the 1962 constitutional terms, which was accepted by Sheikh Jaber. However, after the withdrawal of Iraqi forces from Kuwait in 1991, the political transition was not straightforward. Not only were the contentious issues of the 1980s, which led to the dissolution of the Assembly in 1986 and the movement of Monday *diwaniyyas* in 1989, not resolved by the invasion but they were also exacerbated.

Conclusion

As discussed in this chapter, since its early beginning as a shura-based semi-tribal sheikhdom, Kuwait has grown into a modern nation-state with unique political institutions in the Arabian Peninsula, as all surrounding GCC countries are ruled by regimes where most people do not have real input on political life. Since the 18th century, Kuwait's political life has often revolved around a bipolar system dominated by the al-Sabah family and powerful merchant families, despite other significant segments playing a non-negligible role in the balancing of powers (alebrahim, 2019, 2021). Moreover, Mubarak and his sons after him ended this power-sharing social contract and dominated the decision-making mechanisms by suppressing all forms of political consultations, thereby accumulating all executive powers. Nonetheless, merchants managed to regain their grasp on political power through the establishment of the 1921 Shura Council, which marked the beginning of Kuwait's participatory, legislative life. This movement culminated in the 1938 and 1939 Councils which were the first elected legislative assemblies with political decision-making powers. In addition, as explained earlier, Kuwait's independence gave birth to the 1962 Constitution, which remains in effect to this date. However, Kuwait's post-independence era, particularly during the 1980s, was characterized by political instability as a result of the successive rulers' attempts to take control of the country's institutions until the Iraqi invasion, which had the unexpected effect of reconciling the ruler and the opposition.

Furthermore, several important political events marked the decades following Kuwait's liberation in 1991. For instance, new elections were held in 1992, the first time since the 1985 elections and the subsequent decision of Jaber to end constitutional life and take full control of political decision-making. Other elections were held in 1996, 1999, and 2003. Moreover, in 2003, an important decision was made by Sheikh Jaber, which detached the function of the Crown Prince from the executive power. Indeed, for the first time in Kuwait's political history, the Crown Prince could no longer be the Prime Minister, although the al-Sabah family kept control of the PM position. Furthermore, on May 16, 2005, for the first time in Kuwait's political history, women were granted the right to vote or stand for office (Shultziner & Tétreault, 2012), and in 2009, four women were elected as members of the Assembly.

Despite going through all these transformations and political turmoils, nowadays, as per the 1962 Constitution, the ruler, being the Head of State, remains effectively in control of all three powers: the executive, legislative, and judiciary. In contrast, the events of 1938, particularly Article I of the 1938 Constitution, represented a significant step forward towards political freedoms: "the nation represented by the Council members [was] the source of all powers." Thus, Council

24   Abdulrahman Alebrahim

members, as per the 1938 Constitution, were effectively in control of the three powers, while the 1962 Constitution transferred these powers from the elected Assembly to the Head of State. It is worth noting, however, that despite Kuwait's current political instability, there have been no attempts neither from the ruler nor from the elected assemblies to reform the Constitution towards granting Kuwaitis more political freedoms or equality, even though such reforms can be achieved as stated by Articles 174–175.

Notes

1 Rashid al-Sadun is one of the leaders of the al-Sadun family who ruled southern Iraq. He owned many palm plantations in Al-Faw and elsewhere in southern Iraq and also had significant political influence.
2 Sulayman al-Zuhayr is a well-known member of the al-Zuhayr merchant family, originally from central Arabia. They settled in Southern Iraq and ruled the Sheikhdom of Al Zubayr in the 18th century.
3 The kara is the unit of measurement for a date's weight; one kara is equivalent to around 3,000 kg.
4 The Qaimaqam was a military rank granted by the Ottomans as an expression of gratitude to individuals for military services accompanied by an annual stipend.
5 Sadun Basha was the leader of the al-Sadun family at the end of the 19th century and the beginning of the 20th century; he participated in many battles against Mubarak al-Sabah and Abdulaziz al-Rashid of Hai'l.
6 The Ikhwan is a religious and military group composed of Bedouin tribesmen from central Arabia who supported King Abdulaziz Ibn Saud at the beginning of the 20th century. This group was known for its strong support of the Wahhabi doctrine and its religious intolerance.
7 The Diwan is a place where Kuwaiti men often meet for social events; it is referred to as the *majlis* in other parts of the Arabian Gulf.
8 Author's translation.
9 IOR/R/15/1/513. Telegram from High Commissioner, Baghdad, to Secretary of State for India, 01 March 1921.
10 The hadhar, as opposed to the nomadic Bedouin living in the desert, are sedentary people who live in cities or villages.

References

al-Adsani, K. S. (1938). *Muthakkirat Khalid Al-adsani, sikritire majlis al-umma al-tasri'iya al-awal wa al-thani [Khaled Al-Adsani memoir] self-published manuscript.*
alebrahim, A. (2019). *Kuwait's politics before independence: The role of the balancing powers.* Gerlach Press.
alebrahim, A. (2021). The balancing powers in Kuwait in the 1938 majlis movement: New insights from the minutes of the legislative council. *AlMuntaqa, 4*(2), 8–26. https://www.jstor.org/stable/48651941
al-Jassim, N. (1997). *Altatwer Al Siyasi wa Al Iqtisadi fe Al-Kuwait bayen Alharbeen: 1914–1939 [Political and economic development in Kuwait between the two wars: 1914–1939] self-published,* 2nd ed.
al-Khatib, A. (2007). *Al-Kuwaiyt: Min al-Emarah ila al-Dawlah, Dhkraiat al-'Amal al-Watani [Kuwait from emirate to state: From the national memory].* Al-Markaz al-Thqafi al-Araby.

Kuwait's Political History   25

al-Najjar, G. (2000). *Madkhal li-l-Tatawwur al-Siyasi fi al-Kuwait [An Introduction to the Political Development of Kuwait]*. Dar Qurtas.

al-Nawawi, Y. bin S. (1998). *Riyadh al-Saliheen*, 3rd ed. Muassassat Al Risaala.

al-Qina'i, Y. (1988). *Safahat Min Ttarikh al-Kuwait" [Pages of Kuwait history]*. That al-Salasil.

al-Rushaid, A. (1926). *Tarikh al-Kuwait [A history of Kuwait]*. al-Matba'a al-Asriyya.

al-Shamlan, S. M. (1986). *Min tarikh al-Kuwait [Of Kuwait's history]*. That al-Salasil.

al-Wuqayyan, K. (2014). *Al-Thaqafa fi al-Kuwait: Bidayat, Ittijahat, Riyadat [Culture in Kuwait. Beginnings, directions, pioneers] self-published*, 6th ed.

British High Commissioner in Baghdad. (1921). Telegram from High Commissioner, Baghdad, to Secretary of State for India, the 1st of March. In IOR/R/15/1/513. Indian Office Records.

Burdett, A. L. P. (1997). *Records of Kuwait, 1961–1965*. Archive Editions.

Constituent Assembly (1962). *Minutes of the constituent assembly, session 19. Kuwait National Assembly. retrieved from the Kuwait National Assembly website:*https://www .kna.kw/PdfHelper?FilePath=rpS1JRuUjqyzPmmqQDsTPrQHd-p1rkaO96Dnnaef27og _JZIAcmzHnuIZcESLrqz74IoRpkgX4DfEWUI4C2rXh1ZtY32sTeH4lZlQPerJKns BqcqMZ7bIJk_ylp6hmpkslRnb3d3Dm5SQv0YZQ82VnLQYo3xUvp6RMhcfSkFpS4

Crystal, J. (1995). *Oil and politics in the gulf: Rulers and merchants in Kuwait and Qatar*. Cambridge University Press.

Eickelman, D. F. (2002). *The Middle East and Central Asia an anthropological approach*, 4th ed. Prentice Hall.

Khazal, H. K. (1967). *Tarikh al-Kuwait al-siyassi [Kuwait political history]*. Dar wa-maktabat al-hilal.

Ministry of Media. (1962). Kuwait's constitution. In *Al-Kuwait al-Yaoum [Kuwait today; Kuwait's official gazette]: Vol. Special Edition* (Issue Year 8). Ministry of Media.

Ministry of Media. (2022). *Kuwait's constitution [English version]*. https://media.gov.kw /assets/img/Ommah22_Awareness/PDF/Follow_the_information_unit/new/consitiution %20-%20English.pdf

Nosova, A. (2016). *The merchant elite and parliamentary politics in Kuwait: The dynamics of business political participation in a rentier state* [Doctoral Thesis]. London School of Economics and Political Science.

Nosova, A. (2018). The voice and loyalty of business in Kuwait: Merchant politics in times of contention. *British Journal of Middle Eastern Studies*, *45*(2). https://doi.org/10.1080 /13530194.2016.1230489

Shultziner, D., & Tétreault, M. A. (2012). Representation and democratic progress in Kuwait. *Representation*, *48*(3). https://doi.org/10.1080/00344893.2012.706981

3 Kuwait

A Political System in Crisis

Hamad H. Albloshi

Introduction

On August 2, 2022, then the crown prince and deputy Emir, Miʻshal Alahmad Alsabah dissolved the National Assembly (*Majlis*) and called for a new parliamentary election (Naar, 2022). The decree was expected because the parliament had a difficult relationship with the executive power since the 2020 election. This action was not unusual since former Emirs had previously dissolved the *Majlis* in 1999, 2006, 2008, 2009, 2011, and 2016. Those dissolutions were based on Article 107 of the Constitution; therefore, they were described as constitutional dissolutions. They contrasted with two other dissolutions that were seen as unconstitutional because they were not followed by new elections. This happened on two occasions in 1976 and 1986. Moreover, the Constitutional Court dissolved parliaments in 2012 and 2013.

When the deputy Emir dissolved the 2020 parliament and called for new elections, the overall atmosphere in the country was positive because a portion of society in Kuwait was against its speaker Marzūq Alghānim. This atmosphere was boosted after the election. However, this did not last for a long time because the relationship between the cabinet of the newly appointed Prime Minister, Ahmad Alnawāf, and the National Assembly deteriorated and led to his resignation. In 2000, after the first constitutional dissolution of parliament, Alnajjar published an article arguing that "Kuwaiti democracy is in serious crisis" (Alnajjar, 2000a). Since then, the crisis has continued to deepen. Only one *Majlis*, 2016 *Majlis*, continued its four-year term since 2003. This chapter seeks to understand the nature of this crisis and the reasons behind it. It is worth noticing that the country has experienced some political developments since the beginning of the 21st century. For example, the position of the Crown Prince was separated from the position of the Prime Minister in 2003; Kuwaiti women gained their political rights in 2005; and the number of electoral districts was reduced from 25 to only 5 districts. However, not all these changes have brought political stability to the country.

The chapter argues that the nature of the political system is the main reason behind this constant crisis because it reduces the chances of cooperation between the executive power and the legislative power, it is responsible for the emergence

DOI: 10.4324/9781003435259-3

Kuwait   27

of disputes among members of the ruling family, and it leads to the emergence of different social movements on the ground. The first section of the chapter will briefly consider the historical background of the political system in Kuwait; it will then discuss its nature in order to understand its links to the crisis in the country, the emergence of disputes among members of the ruling family, and the appearance of different social movements.

Historical Background

Since reaching power as the rulers of Kuwait in the second half of the 18th century,[1] the Sabah family governed based on consultation, or what Ghanim Alnajjar calls "joint governing" (Alnajjar, 2000a). The consultation was with the elite in the country, which consisted of members of the ruling family, merchants, and religious figures. There was an attempt in 1921 to improve this practice and institutionalize it by creating a body to help the ruler govern. Therefore, the Shura Council was founded, but it did not last for a long time because of personal disputes among its members (Alnajjar, 2000b).

There was another attempt to institutionalize the "joint governing" practice in 1938 when the first election in the country was held to elect members of a legislative council. In fact, that council wrote the first Constitution of the country (Alkhamīs, 2020). This council, too, was dissolved, this time by the Emir Ahmad Aljābir who saw it as a threat to his power because the council intervened in his responsibilities (Herb, 2014). This was followed by another election for a new legislative council, which was also dissolved by Aljābir because of its members' disapproval of his draft for a new constitution, which would have turned the council into a consultative one. The dissolution of the *Majlis* was followed by repressive actions that resulted in the detention of some politicians. Two supporters of the council were killed, and some others fled Kuwait and took refuge in Iraq.[2]

As a result, the political freedom in the country was declining until 1950 when 'Abdallah Alsālim reached power after the death of his predecessor Ahmad Aljābir. In the 1950s, Kuwait experienced a revival in political activities. In addition, Kuwait had different elections for small councils, such as religious endowments, education, and the municipality. At the same time, Kuwaitis continued advocating for more participation in decision-making and finally reached their goal in 1961 when Kuwait gained its independence from Great Britain. A few months later, Alsālim called for elections to choose a Constitutional Convention that would be responsible for writing the Constitution. One reason behind Alsālim's decision was his desire to institutionalize the political system by having a constitution and a legislative assembly (Alkhaṭīb, 2007).

The Iraqi threat to Kuwait in 1961 may have played a role in his decision (Herb, 2014). When Kuwait became an independent country, the Iraqi government, led by 'Abdulkarīm Qāsim, refused to recognize its new neighbour and claimed that Kuwait was part of their country. Alsālim wanted to change the negative image of Kuwait perpetuated by the Iraqi government (Alnajjar,

2000b). Therefore, a new political system was born in Kuwait in 1962 when the Constitution was issued. This was not an easy move because not all members of the ruling family supported it.

The rejection of the new system by some members of the Sabah family directly influenced the way that the Constitution was written. Discussions in the Constitutional Convention were intense, as it will be discussed later. The rejection continued with further attempts to undermine the Constitution. This happened on several occasions. The first attempt was in 1967 when the authorities rigged the parliamentary elections (Herb, 2014). Nine years later, the authorities suspended the Constitution and unconstitutionally dissolved the parliament. In 1981, however, parliamentary life was resumed until 1986 when the Constitution was suspended once again. Moreover, in 1990, months before the Iraqi invasion, the authorities decided to create a new parliament with fewer responsibilities. All these actions were faced with popular rejection. Political campaigns were organized to challenge the government; the most important campaign was launched in the late 1980s and was known as *Diwānīyyat al- 'Ithnayn* (Tetreault, 2000).

Considering the history, it can be argued that the path towards a representative system was not an easy one. Kuwaitis endured years of struggle to achieve their current political system, and to date, their struggle is not over, because the system remains in crisis.

Kuwait's Political System: Neither Parliamentary nor Presidential

After issuing the Constitution, the political system in the country was transformed and different institutions appeared such as the National Assembly, and the Cabinet, in addition to other bureaucratic institutions with different responsibilities.

As evidenced previously, the political system in Kuwait is a result of a tense relationship between two forces: The opposition and the ruling family.[3] The people were eager to transform political life and create a fair system of checks and balances, but members of the ruling family were not willing to give up their power. For example, in 1959, an event that was organized by mainly Arab nationalists in Kuwait to celebrate the first anniversary of the establishment of the United Arab Republic (UAR) as a result of the unification between Egypt and Syria, different speeches were delivered. However, the most important one was Jāsim Alqitāmī's who described the political system in Kuwait as a tribal and traditional system and demanded the formation of a democratic system (Alkhaṭīb, 2007). The authorities harshly dealt with the organizers by arresting some of them and expelling several non-Kuwaiti participants. It is true that the relatively free political atmosphere was weakened because of the event; but this did not last for a long time because, as it was mentioned earlier, Kuwait gained its independence in 1961 and within months, the Emir 'Abdallah Alsālim called for a new election to choose 20 members for a Constitutional Convention to write a permanent constitution for the country.

Kuwait was divided into 10 electoral districts, with each electing two members. In addition to them, 11 members of the ruling family were appointed in the Convention as ministers. It is worth noticing that three of the elected members became ministers as well. Therefore, the total number of members of the Convention was 31 (Diyyīn, 1999). Then the Convention formed the Constitutional Committee and elected five of its members to join it in order to review the draft of the constitution. Both the committee and the Convention had intense discussions over different articles of the draft. Even though the members of the ruling family did not participate in the voting process that approved the constitution, they participated in the overall discussions in the committee and the Convention.

It is important to note that there was a vague picture in the minds of the members of the Conviction regarding the upcoming political system in Kuwait. For example, two conflicting opinions appeared in the Constitutional Committee regarding this issue. The first one was promoted by Saʿad Alʿabdallah Alsabah, the Minister of Interior Affairs and the Emir's son, who pushed for adapting a presidential system for the country (Diyyīn, 1999). It can be argued that he was in favour of the presidential system to make the Emir the head of the executive power, and as a result, to weaken the ability of the *Majlis* to question him or challenge the government. His view regarding the presidential system was supported by two members in the committee: Yaʿqūb Alḥumaiḍī and Ḥumūd Alzaid. The latter argued that if the head of the state, the Emir, was also the prime minister, the stability of the executive power would be granted (Diyyīn, 1999). In contrast, other members of the Convention believed in a parliamentary system. For example, Ḥumūd Alkhālid asserted that "the parliamentary system is the best for Kuwait" (Diyyīn, 1999).

The disagreement over the nature of the political system planted the disagreement over specific issues such as the role of the ruling family in the new system, the appointment of ministers (Alnajjar, 2000b), and their right to vote in parliament (Diyyīn, 1999). Ahmad Alkhaṭīb, an Arab nationalist member of the Convention and its deputy, totally opposed the idea of appointing ministers from outside parliament and declared his reservations on appointing members of the ruling family to the cabinet. He believed that appointing ministers from outside the *Majlis* was a dangerous step because "the parliament should be elected, therefore, appointing [people from outside it] damages the spirit of democracy" (Al-Majlis al-Taʾsīsī, 1962). He stressed on the importance of having a monarchical constitution with the Emir having a ceremonial role. He wanted the Kuwaiti system to be similar to other democratic countries with parliamentary systems (Al-Majlis al-Taʾsīsī, References.1962). His comments angered members of the Sabah family in the Convention. For example, Jābir Alali interpreted Alkhaṭīb's comments as an attempt to exclude members of the Sabah family from governing. He even asked the following question: Are the members of the ruling family "traitors and conspirators to be excluded from governing?" (Al-Majlis al-Taʾsīsī, 1962).

At the end, the Constitution merged two different political systems, presidential and parliamentary, into one system. Based on the Explanatory Note on the Constitution, the political system in Kuwait is neither a parliamentary system nor a presidential system. It was intentionally designed this way because, as the Note indicates, "presidential systems are in republican [countries]" (Al-Muthakkara al-Tafsīriyya, 1962). Furthermore, the Note asserts the decision was taken to reject a fully parliamentary system because of the negative outcomes of such

30 *Hamad H. Albloshi*

systems (Al-Muthakkara al-Tafsīriyya, 1962). It can be argued that the system was designed this way because of the ruling family's resistance and reservations. Therefore, the parliament in Kuwait consists of 50 members, as stated in Article 80 of the Constitution, which says, "the National Assembly shall be composed of fifty members elected directly by universal suffrage and secret ballot in accordance with the provisions prescribed by the electoral law" (The Constitution of the State of Kuwait, 1962). The article gives another important indication of the shape of the *Majlis*. It says, "Ministers who are not elected members of the National Assembly shall be considered ex-officio members thereof" (The Constitution of the State of Kuwait, 1962).

Moreover, the ministers, according to Article 56 of the Constitution "shall be appointed from amongst the members of the National Assembly and from others" (The Constitution of the State of Kuwait, 1962). Therefore, they do not all have to be members of parliament, except for at least one. What is important to note is that upon their appointment, they become part of the assembly and have the same rights as other elected members except that they do "not participate in the vote of confidence," according to Article 101 of the Constitution after the impeachment of other ministers (The Constitution of the State of Kuwait, 1962). The appointment of unelected politicians to become ministers and, therefore, members of the National Assembly, gives the ruling family leverage over parliament.

So, the National Assembly can have as many as 65 members or as few as 50 members. Thus, it is in the interest of the ruling family to appoint politicians from outside the National Assembly to have more power in comparison to other MPs. For this reason, when members of the Constitutional Convention wanted half of the cabinet to be from elected MPs, this was not accepted by Saʿad Alʿabdallah. Moreover, when MPs demand half of the cabinet's seats, their requests are denied, such as the case in 1992 and in 2012. Figure 3.1 shows the number of elected ministers in each cabinet from January 1963 to October 2022 (Figure 3.1).

It is important to note that members of the Sabah family are prevented from being legislators; they do not participate in parliamentary elections as candidates. This ban was imposed upon them to ensure fair elections and to protect them from being humiliated during electoral campaigns, as the Explanatory Note describes. The Note asserts that appointing members of the Sabah family as ministers is one way to allow them to serve the country (Al-Muthakkara al-Tafsīriyya, 1962).

The Constitution does not assert that the Prime Minister should be a member of the ruling family, and it does not state that he should come from outside parliament. Article 56 of the Constitution deals with the position of the Prime Minister and asserts that the Emir "after traditional consultations, appoints the Prime Minister and relieves him of office" (The Constitution of the State of Kuwait, 1962). Therefore, the Emir is given the right to appoint the Prime Minister regardless of the parliamentary election results.

Since the appointment of the Prime Minister is not based on the parliamentary elections, the appointments of cabinet ministers are not affected by election results either. The parliament does not appoint ministers and has no right to approve their appointment. Members of parliament can oppose the Prime Minister's choices, but

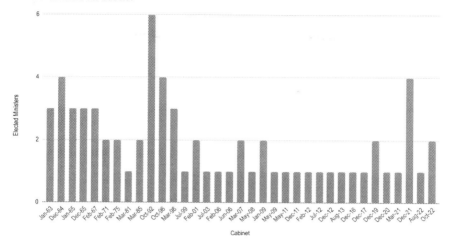

Figure 3.1 Number of elected ministers in Kuwait since 1963[4]

they have no power beyond that. The Constitution does not fully address this issue and does not give the legislators any rights in this regard. They may, however, do two things: First, since members of the cabinet become members of parliament, they need to take an oath. Legislators can prevent this for a certain amount of time by boycotting the sessions, thereby delaying the cabinet from functioning. This occurred in 1964 when some members of the National Assembly refused to attend parliamentary sessions when the new cabinet was scheduled to take the oath (Alkhaṭīb, 2007). Second, legislators can threaten to impeach ministers immediately after the formation of the cabinet. Other than these two steps, members of parliament do not have any legal power to influence the cabinet before its formation.

Endless Crisis

a Politics within the Parliament

When then the crown prince, Miʿshal Alahmad, dissolved the parliament in 2022 and asserted that the government would not interfere in the elections, there was a general understanding that reform is imminent in the country, especially since the former speaker, Marzūq Alghānim, announced his desire not to run in the elections, and the announcement of Ahmad Alsaʿdūn, a former speaker and a politician close to the opposition, to run in the election after ten years of boycotting. The general optimism was boosted when the latter was elected, and Ahmad Alnawāf was appointed as a prime minister instead of Sabah Alkhālid, who was opposed by MPs in the previous parliament. During the first session of the new parliament, Alsaʿdūn was elected as the speaker, and there was hope to transform the political system and make it stable.

However, within a few months, the relationship between the legislative power and the executive power was weakened and the latter resigned as a result of two attempts to impeach two ministers in his cabinet and the government's refusal to back a law to buy citizens' debts (Kuwaiti government resigns after dispute with parliament, 2023). Alnawāf, refused as well to attend parliamentary sessions because he had resigned, and the newly elected *Majlis* was practically suspended for over two months.

The attendance of the cabinet to parliamentary sessions is a disputed matter. Traditionally, the speaker would not begin a session if members of the cabinet were not present, or end it if the last minister decided to leave. This practice has been an interpretation of Article 116 of the Constitution which states " [t]he Cabinet shall be represented at the sitting of the Assembly by the Prime Minister or by some Ministers" (The Constitution of the State of Kuwait, 1962). Alsaʿdūn (Ahmad Alsaʿdūn yudāfiʿ ..., 2023) and Alghānim (Alghānim yarfaʿ al-jalsa ..., References.2022) believe that according to this article, the cabinet must be present. However, there are politicians who believe that this is not the case because of Article 97 of the Constitution, which states "[f]or a meeting of the National Assembly to be valid more than half of the members must be present. Resolutions shall be passed by an absolute majority vote of members present, except in cases where a special majority is required" (The Constitution of the State of Kuwait, 1962). This article does not indicate that the cabinet should be present.

This dispute is constitutional, but it shows that the political system, which was created around the constitution, leads to constant crises, and that the problem is not related to certain politicians. This dispute asserts as well that politicians across the political spectrum might disagree on different issues, but their ability to manoeuvre is limited because of constitutional restrictions. Alsaʿdūn and Alghānim disagree on many issues, but both had to end any parliamentary session when the cabinet was not present. Therefore, the source of the problem in Kuwait is in the nature of its political system.

It is true, as it was mentioned, that the political system in Kuwait is not parliamentary and that parties and political groups do not form the cabinet, but they exist and are part of the overall discussion. The right to form parties is not mentioned in the Constitution, and it does not ban them either. Political groups have been active in the country since the beginning of the 20th century. They have had different demands, which have evolved and modified over the years. At the same time, they represent different social and sectarian segments of society, and different ideological backgrounds.

No political party or group has been able to win a majority in the National Assembly since 1963 because the electoral system encourages individualism. Therefore, in order to counter the weight of the cabinet, legislators have founded different blocs in parliament since 2001. The first bloc was *Kutlat al-ʿAmal al-Shaʿbī*, or the Popular Bloc (Intilāq ḥaraka yiyāsiyya ..., 2014). It was a major step toward organizing the political scene in parliament. The bloc was also significant because it consisted of representatives from all parts of society; it went beyond the sectarian and tribal divisions in the country and was led by Alsaʿdūn. Another bloc, *Kutlat al-ʿAmal al-Waṭanī* (the National Bloc), with a liberal orientation was founded later. The Islamists also decided to have their blocs. In addition, independent legislators also create their own blocs (Assiri, 2012). These blocs can create larger coalitions in parliament and counter the executive power. For example, in the parliamentary election of February 2012, the opposition gained a joint 35 seats and created a larger coalition known as the Majority Bloc, or *Kutlat al-Aghlabiyya*. These blocs can be a source of problem for the cabinet when they try to impose certain issues such as populist legislations, or to use some of its constitutional tools such as impeachment to monitor ministers.

It is true that the cabinet is the most powerful and organized group in the National Assembly because it consists of 16 members, but it must manoeuvre to survive in an individualistic atmosphere in the Assembly. Therefore, the cabinet uses different tools to sustain its power within parliament. For example, the government provides services to its supporters from the legislators and "buys" them as well. This was revealed by a former minister of health, ʿAbdulraḥmān Alʿawaḍī, who declared that he had bribed some MPs by offering them flight tickets, for example. Another good example is when the former Prime Minister, Nāṣir Almuhammad, was accused of bribing the MPs in the 2009 parliament, as it will be explained. Despite this, the authorities find themselves in a position to dissolve parliament, especially when the cabinet finds itself unable to protect a minister from a vote of no confidence or to prevent a legislation it does not support. As it was mentioned, the cabinet has the upper hand in parliament; however, the non-partisan system also allows legislators, who are supportive of the prime minister and his cabinet, to change their alliance when they think that siding with him may harm their chance to be re-elected. Therefore, to overcome this problem, the authorities dissolve the *Majlis*.

As stated earlier, most parliaments since 1999 have been dissolved for a variety of reasons. It is important to note that some reasons given by the authorities were general and vague. Table 3.1 reveals the reasons behind each dissolution since 1999. Most decrees blamed the legislators for the decision (Table 3.1).

Despite this authority to dissolve the Assembly, this action can backfire when it is used. For example, when the political atmosphere is intense, people and members of the opposition are eager to dissolve parliament because they believe the situation on the ground is in their favour. In this case, the opposition gains more seats in the National Assembly, as was seen in the elections of 2006, 2012, and 2022. In these cases, the opposition came back to parliament in a stronger position.

To prevent this from occurring, the authorities are able to manipulate the results by intervening in the elections. They have been intervening in every election to get as many of their supporters to the Assembly and the crown prince's assertion in 2022 that elections would be held without the intervention of the government was a clear indication of previous actions taken by the authorities during parliamentary elections. This act is easier when the country is divided into

34 *Hamad H. Albloshi*

Table 3.1 Parliaments that were dissolved by the Emir since 1999 and reasons behind each dissolution (Majlia al-'umma ... marāsīm, 2022)

Parliament Elected	Year of Dissolutions	Reason
1996	1999	Abuse of constitutional tools by legislators.
2003	2006	Division in parliament, useless discussions that jeopardized its roles and led to flame disputes in society as well as harming the national interests.
2006	2008	To protect national unity.
2008	2009	Disrespecting the Constitution, law, and what had been decided by the Constitutional Court on the constitutional tools to check the executive power's actions.
2009	2011	There is a need to go back to the people to choose their representatives because of threats facing the national interests of the country, and to overcome difficulties.
2013	2016	Instability in the region.
2020	2022	Disputes and lack of cooperation in the National Assembly and behaviours that threaten national unity.

many districts. Therefore, since the first elections, organized after independence in 1961 to choose members of the Conventional Assembly, the ruling family and the opposition have held different views regarding the number of districts. From the beginning, the ruling family wanted to divide the country into many districts. They wanted 20 districts, whilst the leaders of the opposition wanted only one district (Alnajjar, 2000b). In the end, the country was divided into ten districts. In 1981, however, a decree was issued by the former Emir, Jābir Alahmad and the number of districts was increased to 25. This meant more districts with fewer constituencies.

It can be argued that when the number of districts increases, the ability of the authorities to interfere in the elections increases because with a smaller number of constituencies, candidates do not need many votes to win seats in parliament. In some cases, candidates won the elections with only a few hundred votes. For example, in 1981, only 376 people voted for Khālid Aljimai'ān to become a legislator.[5] In small districts with few constituencies, candidates are able to buy votes by bribing people in order to gain their support, or to provide them with advantageous services in the bureaucratic system. Some of these services are illegal. Nevertheless, they are tools in the hands of the authorities which help them increase their number of supporters in parliament. Those who are pro-government are usually given access to the bureaucratic system in order to increase their chances of winning seats.

Kuwait 35

b Disputes within the Ruling Family

Part of the political crisis in Kuwait is related to the competition between members of the ruling family. This is due to the nature of succession in Kuwait, which is horizontal, and not vertical. In other words, the power does not move from father to son, but is based on arrangements within the ruling family. The main condition for a member of the Sabah family to reach power in Kuwait is to be a descendant of Mubārak Alsabah who ruled the country from 1896 to 1915 (The Constitution of the State of Kuwait, 1962). Therefore, each descendant of Mubārak is a legitimate candidate to become the ruler, and this increases competition within the ruling family, which has been evident inside and outside parliament.

The electoral system encourages individualism; therefore, most MPs have been independent legislators since the beginning of parliamentary life in Kuwait. This individualism is exploited by some members of the ruling family to push their agendas. Therefore, some of them form strong relationships with independent MPs. This influences their performance within parliament. Some MPs are pushed to impeach other ministers from the ruling family, or even the Prime Minister. This causes instability in the cabinet and shakes the political system.

Historically, competition existed between two branches of the Sabah family: The Jābir branch and the Sālim branch. In the 1930s, the rivalry was between Ahmad Aljābir and ʿAbdallah Alsālim. This rivalry pushed the latter to support the *Majlis* movement of 1938–1939. The competition was weakened in the 1960s and 1970s because Saʿad Alʿabdallah, from the Alsālim branch, cooperated with Jābir Alahmad, from the Aljābir branch, to weaken Jābir Alali, who belonged to the Alsālim branch.

When Jābir Alahmad died in 2006, the rivalry between the two branches reemerged because Saʿad Alʿabdallah was forced to abdicate. However, the rivalry moved into one branch when the dispute between Ahmad Alfahad and Nāṣir Almuhammad, both from the Jābir branch, became public. In fact, Ahmad Alfahad accused his cousin of conspiring to overthrow the former Emir, Sabah Alahmad, their uncle. Alfahad could influence members within the opposition movement. In the end, he withdrew his accusations and publicly apologized (Sheikh Ahmad Al-Fahad …, 2015).

Recently,, there have been rumours of a new dispute within the ruling family, which was between former Prime Minister, Ahmad Alnawāf, and Ahmad Almiʿshal, son of then the Crown Prince. When a politician, ʿAbdulwahhāb AlʾĪsā, talked about it, Almiʿshal denied it in a statement.

c Political and Social Movements

Since, as mentioned, the political system leads to individualism, political groups and parties do not have the upper hand in the system compared to the authorities. Therefore, they sometimes choose to go to the streets by forming political and social movements which can put pressure on the government to change its actions. In some cases, these movements have been effective.

36 *Hamad H. Albloshi*

These movements have emerged within a social context that is worth mentioning. Kuwaitis belong to different social groups. Religiously, most of them are divided into two groups: Sunnis and Shi'a. They are also divided into two major ethnic groups: Arabs and non-Arabs. Most of the non-Arabs came from Iran over a period of time. Sunnis and Shi'a can be Arabs or Persians. Amongst the Sunni Arabs, there are divisions between those who have an urban background, known as the *ḥaḍar*, and those who have tribal backgrounds, known as Bedouins. The Sabah family has tried to establish balance and harmony between these groups in society. It has also shifted its alliance with these groups from time to time. For example, when the *ḥaḍarīs* were active against the ruling family's policies in the larger part of the 20th century, the latter cooperated with the Shi'a and the Bedouins to counter them. This was obvious in the abovementioned *Majlis* of 1938–39 when the authorities were supported by the Shi'a and the Bedouins to end the *Majlis* movement. The *ḥaḍarīs* faction of society consisted of the business class, as well as the middle class who founded different political groups within the country. They challenged the authorities both inside and outside parliament.

When the Iranian revolution in 1978–79 succeeded in overthrowing the Shah, a portion of the Kuwaiti Shi'a was in favour of it, and their positive relationship with the authorities was damaged. Some of them were adherents of Ayatollah Khomeini, the leader in Tehran, who wanted to expand his revolution to the Gulf monarchical regimes. This relationship worsened when Kuwait supported Iraq in its war against Iran.

In both cases, the Bedouins were close to the government and the ruling family. They have been part of the National Assembly since the 1960s. For most of their history in parliament, they have been in support of the authorities. However, this positive relationship started to change in the 1990s when legislators with tribal and Bedouin backgrounds started to lead the opposition in parliament. Figures such as Musllam Albarrāk, Walīd Aljirī, and Muhammad Alkhalīfa began to oppose the government and challenge it. This group started to gain legitimacy and have more influence among the Bedouin community because of their efforts to monitor the government and focus on fighting corruption. This relationship has worsened in recent years with the emergence of politicians within the country who have attacked the Bedouins and questioned their loyalty, such as Muhammad Aljuwayhil. These individuals were seen as figures supported by the authorities.

This social context is linked to another important issue: The separation between the positions of Crown Prince and the Prime Minister in 2003. This can be described as one of the major changes in the country in two decades. Historically, the Crown Prince was the person who was the head of the executive power. Although there was no ban against his impeachment, he was not cross-examined in parliament because legislators were aware of the consequences and did not want to damage the image of the coming Emir. This taboo was broken after the separation of the two positions. When Sabah Alahmad came to power in 2006, Nawāf Alahmad became the Crown Prince, and their nephew, Nāṣir Almuhammad, was chosen to become the prime minister. The opposition was then freer to counter the prime minister and even to impeach him. During the period between 2006 and 2023, there were 32

Table 3.2 Number of attempts to impeach prime ministers in Kuwait from 2006 to 2022

Prime Minister	Years in Power	Number of Impeachments
Nāṣir Almuhammad	2006–2011	12
Jābir Almubārak	2011–2019	11
Sabah Alkhālid	2019–2022	8
Ahmad Alnawāf	2022– ...	0

attempts to impeach the prime minister. Some requests were publicly discussed, some behind closed doors, and others were not discussed at all either because of the resignation of the cabinet or the dissolution of parliament. Table 3.2 shows the number of attempts to impeach prime ministers in Kuwait since 2006 (Table 3.2).

Nabīha 5 was the event responsible for the usage of the impeachment tool against the prime minister. It was the first major movement in Kuwait since its liberation in 1991. *Nabīha* 5 appeared in 2006 and was dominated by Kuwaiti youths. Until then, the country was divided into 25 districts. The authorities were forced to reduce them to five because of the movement, which believed that reducing the number of districts would reduce corruption by weakening the ability of the government to manipulate the parliamentary elections (Albloshi & Alfahad, 2009). Based on this system, the 50 elected legislators come from five districts in the country, ten from each electoral district. In this system, people had the right to vote for four candidates in their district. However, the new system did not end the government's interference in the election. But it helped political groups to build coalitions during the elections to exchange votes. This proved critical in 2012 when the opposition gained the majority in the *Majlis*.

A few years after *Nabīha* 5 movement, *Irhal Nastaḥiq al-Afḍal* or Leave We Deserve Better, another movement appeared as a result of questions that were raised after allegations of mismanagement of the budget in Almuhammad's office ("Faḥwa taqrīr ..., 2008). In addition, members of the parliament acknowledged that they had received money from him. Ironically, one of his opponents in the opposition movement, Walīd Alṭabṭabāʾī, was amongst those who received money from him for a charity conference, he has claimed (Alṭabṭabāʾī: qaḍiyyat ..., 2009). The problem came to be known as the *checks matter*, or *Qaḍiyyat al-Chaykāt*. Despite the allegations, parliament was not able to hold him accountable. Therefore, after several attempts to impeach Almuhammad, the *Irḥal* campaign was launched.

Almuhammad retained his power after each attempted impeachment because of his appointment by the Emir. Nevertheless, these attempts and the campaigns were important because they highlighted corruption within the country and showed that reforming the system in Kuwait was the route to ending corruption and the misuse of power by the authorities. These events were also linked with evidence of repression against the opposition. The most important event occurred when the Special Forces attacked an event organized by the opposition in the house of one of its members, Jamʿān Alḥirbish, in December 2010. The government had not previously attacked these events; they were considered private gatherings, even though

38 *Hamad H. Albloshi*

some of them were organized for political purposes. Article 38 of the Constitution states that private homes should be respected, "Places of residence shall be inviolable. They may not be entered without the permission of their occupants except in the circumstances and manner specified by law" (The Constitution of the State of Kuwait, 1962). Because the house was not big enough to host all those who attended, people had to sit outside. The authorities interpreted this as an act of disobedience arguing that the law did not allow the attendees to occupy public spaces.

At the same time, disagreements between the cabinet and the opposition within parliament increased, and allegations were made that 15 members of the National Assembly had received bribes from Nāṣir Almuhammad. People were furious when *al-Qabas*, the daily newspaper, published an article claiming some legislators had been bribed by Almuhammad. "Before the new allegations, we were not effective," said Khālid Alfiḍāla, a supporter of the *Irḥal* campaign (Alfiḍāla, 2015). The new scandal revived the movement, demonstrations increased, and the situation escalated and reached its tipping point on November 16, 2011, when protesters stormed the National Assembly with the help of some of its members (Protesters storm …, 2011).

The political upheaval intensified, and one of the largest protests in the history of the country was organized. It is estimated that tens of thousands of Kuwaitis protested and demanded the resignation of the Prime Minister, Almuhammad, and the dissolution of the National Assembly. Before this protest, the Emir contended he would not accept the resignation of Almuhammad. However, shortly thereafter, the latter was out of power and has not returned since. When he resigned, the Emir dissolved parliament and called for new elections, in accordance with the Constitution.

Because of the atmosphere, the opposition gained 35 seats in parliament (Ghabra, 2014), and became the majority, which has rarely occurred in the history of the country. As a result, the opposition formed a bloc known as the Majority Block, or *Kutlat al-Aghlabiyya*. The elections were influenced by the country's continuous political crises and were a direct reaction to the heated political context in Kuwait. Islamists and Bedouins had the advantage in the assembly, and many efforts were made to Islamize the laws. In fact, parliament passed a controversial bill calling for the execution of anyone who insulted God, the Prophet, his wives, and his companions. The Emir, however, vetoed the bill (Al-Kuwait: Rad qānūn …, 2012). The bloc focused on fighting corruption as well.

This was not the end of the story or the end of instability. Parliament was dissolved once again, this time by the Constitutional Court citing irregularities in the dissolution of the 2009 *Majlis*. The situation became further complicated when the Emir issued a decree and changed the electoral system. The decree reduced the citizens' right to vote for four candidates to one during parliamentary elections. This decree weakened the opposition's ability to build coalitions during the elections and prevented them from becoming a majority in the *Majlis*.

The step taken by the Emir led to the emergence of another social movement, *Karāmet Waṭan*, or (the dignity of the nation). The movement proclaimed its rejection of the decree via Twitter, @KarametWatan and its blog. It is not known who administered the Twitter account, but it gathered support and people participated in the rallies that it called for (Albloshi & Herb, 2018). The account was created to force the government to withdraw the decree; however, its purpose changed over time.

The subsequent change was a result of the movement's inability to stop the government from organizing elections based on the new electoral system. The movement also called for the boycott of elections. Politicians, especially the Majority Bloc, supported the movement but the authorities continued to organize the elections, regardless of the opposition's participation. In addition, the Constitutional Court supported the Emir's decision to change the system. In June 2013, a few months after the elections, the Constitutional Court dissolved the new *Majlis* (Westall & Harby, 2013). Elections were reorganized and once more, the opposition boycotted them.

In the meantime, *Karāmet Waṭan* continued its pressures and activities. It organized more rallies, with decreasing numbers of participants. The movement was unsuccessful in forcing the government to withdraw the decree, so instead, it demanded the reformation of the system to turn it into a parliamentary system. Political groups within the opposition demanded the same. For example, *I'tilāf al-Muʿāraḍa* (the Opposition Coalition), an umbrella organization that consisted of different groups, announced in April 2014 a proposal to transform into a parliamentary system (I'tilāf al-muʿāraḍa …, 2014). However, the opposition movement had been weakened, and the rallies stopped. Different views emerged within the movement regarding their relationship to the government, which relied on repression to solve the problem. The government used different tools to weaken the opposition, but the most effective tool was citizenship. In July 2014, the government started to withdraw citizenship from people belonging to the opposition as a means of punishment and prevention (Kuwait Revokes …, 2015).

When parliament was constitutionally dissolved again in 2016, many politicians within the opposition movement decided to participate in the elections. They attempted to gain a majority but failed. Instead, a few of them made it into the *Majlis*. During the campaigns, many of them focused on the issue of citizenship. Since then, they have been attempting to conclude this issue by helping those affected to regain their lost citizenships.

From 2016 to 2022 7 cabinets were formed. Ideally, only two cabinets should have been formed in this period,, but because of the political instability in the country, the number has been high. Moreover, three prime ministers have formed these cabinets.

Conclusion

Kuwait is one of few countries in the region with a parliament that is relatively powerful, compared to its counterparts in the Middle East. However, the Kuwaiti parliament has not been a source of stability, but one of constant crisis and instability. This chapter argues that the nature and design of the political system is the main cause of this continued crisis.

40 Hamad H. Albloshi

Although elections are indeed held for parliament, the political parties do not have the right to form a cabinet. Also, despite the fact that the Constitution does not grant the right to the ruling family, by tradition, the prime minister has always been a member of the Sabah family. This occurred because the Constitution was written as a result of tensions between the ruling family and the opposition, years before independence in 1961. However, the outcomes have benefited the ruling family. They have the right to appoint the prime minister, to choose unelected ministers who have the same rights as other elected legislators, and to become part of parliament. The ruling family can also influence legislators and build coalitions with them against the opposition in the National Assembly. However, the government can lose its leverage over some supporters, and the result is a chaotic scene where legislators shift their allegiances, change their votes, and focus on issues that benefit their own constituencies. When the government finds itself in this position, it uses its right to dissolve parliament and calls for new elections.

When members of parliament cannot force the prime minister to resign, they take to the streets to protest. When members from within the ruling family compete to gain power, they influence legislators, and when the government cannot help a minister, the Emir may dissolve parliament. All these steps are taken because of one major reason: The system is not a partisan system.

The nature of the system will produce more crises. It is not about the people, but the system. If all members of the opposition quit politics, the problems will remain. The intention of those who supported and wrote the Constitution was noble because they wanted to transform Kuwait from a tribal system to an institutionalized one. Some of them were not satisfied with the Constitution in 1962 but supported it nonetheless. For them, the Constitution was a major step forward in the political development of Kuwait. They did not want to delay the emergence of the Constitution because they believed it could and would be changed and improved over time. However, amending the Constitution has been and continues to be a difficult task in Kuwait.

To amend the Constitution, there must be an agreement between members of parliament and the Emir. Article 174 of the Constitution deals with this issue, stating that the Emir or "one-third of the members of the National Assembly have the right" to request an amendment to the Constitution (The Constitution of the State of Kuwait, 1962). The proposed amendments should be supported by a majority in the *Majlis* before they are debated. Then, two-thirds of its members must vote to pass the proposed changes. However, these changes do not come into force before final ratification is given by the Emir. This process makes it hard for any political groups to transform the political system by changing or amending the Constitution.

Therefore, it is difficult for political groups to gain a majority in the National Assembly. They cannot appoint a prime minister, and appointed ministers become part of parliament, while changing the Constitution is extremely difficult because it requires a majority that is hard to reach. The country is trapped in a self-perpetuating cycle of parliamentary crisis, and reformation of its system is the only way to break the cycle. However, the questions remain: Are the people ready to take the necessary steps to reform the system or not? Are the people more democratic than the government? The answer to these questions may not be a positive one, but they do warrant further investigation.

To conclude, Kuwaitis are in a dilemma because of the vicious circle their political system is trapped in. They have not been able to break the cycle despite their history of struggle, their different political groups and parties, their many social movements, and their active civil society. They have attempted, through a variety of channels, to address this crisis but without success or a positive result on the ground. There appears to be no way out of it. This chapter argues that the crisis in Kuwait is a result of its political system, which is neither parliamentary nor presidential. The political system in Kuwait is not functioning effectively because of its vagueness, leading to a constant crisis.

Notes

1 It is worth noticing that unlike other ruling families in the region, the Sabah family did not rely on force to gain power (Aljāssim, 2007, 63).
2 For more information about that, see the memoir of Khālid al-Adsānī, the secretary of the council. An electronic version of the book is available here: http://taqadomi.com/wp -content/uploads/downloads/2011/06/مذكرات-خالد-سليمان-العدساني.pdf.
3 It is important to clarify the meaning of one term that has been used in the political life in the country for a long time: the opposition. Since the beginning of the 20th century, many political groups and parties have appeared in Kuwait. Some of them have been seen as the opposition. However, it is important to note that the opposition in the country is not similar to those in democratic nations. *Al-Muʿāraḍa*, as the opposition is called in Kuwait, has evolved and gone through different phases, and its demands have changed over time. Some political groups have opposed the ruling family when it suspended the Constitution in 1976 and 1986. They have also been critical of the authorities inside the National Assembly. In addition, they have opposed attempts by the government to undermine the power of the *Majlis*, even though it is limited.
4 It is important to note that the chart does not include cabinets that were formed when the *Majlis* was unconstitutionally dissolved in the periods between 1976 to 1981 and from 1986 to 1992. Also, the chart does not include changes in the cabinet. For example, a cabinet might be formed, but one or two of its members would be changed. In other words, the chart includes cabinets that were formed before any other changes. The chart relied on: https://kuwaitpolitics.org/الحكومات/.
5 See: Kuwait Political Database: http://www.kuwaitpolitics.org/DataPage38.htm.

References

Ahmad Alsaʿdūn yudāfiʿ ʿan qarār rafʿ al-jalasāt liʿadam ḥuḍūr al-ḥukūma. (2023, March 5). Alrai Media. Retrieved from https://www.alraimedia.com/article/1630468//محليات مجلس-الأمة/أحمد-السعدون-يدافع-عن-قرار-رفع-الجلسات-لعدم-حضور-الحكومة.
Albloshi, H., & Alfahad, F. (2009). The orange movement of Kuwait: Civic pressure transforms a political system. In M. J. Stephan (Ed.), *Civilian jihad: Nonviolent struggle, democratization, and governance in the middle easted*. New York: Palgrave Macmillan.
Albloshi, H. H., & Herb, M. (2018). Karamet watan: An unsuccessful nonviolent movement. *The Middle East Journal*, *72*(3), 408–430.
Alfiḍāla, K. (2015). H. H. Albloshi, Interviewer.
Alghāim yarfaʿ al-jalsa "al-khāṣa" liʿadam ʿiktiāl al-niṣāb. (2022, January 12). Aljarida. Retrieved from https://www.aljarida.com/articles/1641972768275656800.

42 Hamad H. Albloshi

Alkhaṭīb, A. (2007). *Al-Kuwait min al-imāra Ilā al-dawla: thikrayāt al-ʿamal al-waṭanī wa al-qawmī*. Beirut: al-Markaz al-Thaqāfī al-ʿArabī.

Alkhamīs, M. (2020). *1938 Sharārat al-dīmuqrāṭiyya: ʿarḍ wathāʾiq wa taḥlīl aḥdāth*. Kuwait: Thāt al-Salāsil.

Al-Kuwait: Rad qānūn iʿdām al-musīʾ linnabī wa istiqālat wazīr al-ʿadl wa al-awqāf. (2012, June 15). CNN Arabic. Retrieved from http://archive.arabic.cnn.com/2012/middle_east /6/7/kuwait.shahab/.

Alnajjar, G. (2000b). *Madkhal litaṭawwur al-siyāsī fī al-Kuwait*. Kuwait: Dār Qurṭās.

Alnajjar, G. (2000a). The challenges facing Kuwaiti democracy. *The Middle East Journal*, *54*(2), 242–258.

Alṭabṭabāʾī: qaḍiyyat "al-shayk" sabbabat lī qalaqan. (2009, April 28). Alrai Media. Retrieved from https://www.alraimedia.com/article/112476/قلق-لي-سببت-الشيك-قضية-الطبطبائي/محليات-.

Assiri, A.-R. (2012). *Al-Niẓām al-siyāsī fī al-Kuwait: mabādiʾ wa mumārasāt*. Kuwait.

Diyyīn, A. (1999). *Wilādat dustūr al-Kuwait*. Kuwait: Dār Qurṭās.

Faḥwa taqrīr dīwān al-muḥāsaba bishaʾn maṣrūfāt maktab raʾīs al-wuzarāʾ. (2008, October 23). Alaan. Retrieved from http://www.alaan.cc/pagedetails.asp?nid=21818&cid=30.

Ghabra, S. (2014, May 20). *Kuwait: At the crossroads of change or political stagnation*. Middle East Institute. Retrieved from http://www.mei.edu/content/article/kuwait -crossroads-change-or-political-stagnation.

Hagagy, A. (2023, March 19). *Kuwait court reinstates previous parliament*. Reuters. Retrieved from https://www.reuters.com/world/middle-east/kuwait-court-voids-2022 -legislative-polls-reinstates-disbanded-parliament-2023-03-19/.

Herb, M. (2014). *The wages of oil: Parliaments and economic development in Kuwait and UAE*. Ithaca and London: Cornell University Press.

Inṭilāq ḥaraka yiyāsiyya kuwaitiyya binaqd ḥād linniẓām. (2014, March 16). Noon Post. Retrieved from https://www.noonpost.com/content/2139.

Iʾtilāf al-muʿāraḍa: mashrūʿ al-iṣlāḥ al-siyāsī al-waṭanī (naḥwa iqāmat niẓām dīmuqrāṭī mutakāmil). (2014, 4). Alziadi Q8. Retrieved from http://alziadiq8.com/wp-content/ uploads/2014/04/OpKw.pdf.

Kuwaiti government resigns after dispute with parliament. (2023, January 24). Allazeera. Retrieved from https://www.aljazeera.com/news/2023/1/24/kuwaiti-government-resigns -after-dispute-with-parliament.

Kuwait re-appoints Sheikh Ahmad Nawaf al-Sabah as PM - State news agency. (2023, March 5). Reuters. Retrieved from https://www.reuters.com/world/middle-east/kuwait -re-appoints-sheikh-ahmad-nawaf-al-sabah-pm-state-news-agency-2023-03-05/.

Kuwait revokes citizenship of opposition activists. (2015, February 12). Middle East Eye. Retrieved from http://www.middleeasteye.net/news/kuwait-revokes-citizenship -opposition-activists-254232433.

Majlia al-ʿumma … marāsīm al-ḥal 10 wa ʾasbābuhā. (2022, August 4). Aljarida. Retrieved from https://www.aljarida.com/articles/1659543479280191800.

Naar, I. (2022, August 2). Kuwait's Crown Prince officially dissolves parliament by decree. The National Gulf. Retrieved from https://www.thenationalnews.com/gulf-news/2022 /08/02/kuwaits-crown-prince-officially-dissolves-parliament-by-decree/.

Protesters storm Kuwaiti parliament (2011, November 16). Retrieved from BBC. http:// www.bbc.com/news/world-middle-east-1576802.7.

Sheikh Ahmad Al-Fahad submits public apology to his highness the Amir. (2015, March 26). KUNA. Retrieved from https://www.kuna.net.kw/ArticleDetails.aspx?id=2432212 &Language=en.

Tetreault, M. A. (2000). *Stories of democracy: Politics and society in contemporary Kuwait*. New York: Columbia University Press.

The constitution of the State of Kuwait. (1962). Kuwait: Ministry of Information.

Westall, S., & Harby, M. (2013). Kuwait court orders dissolution of parliament, new elections. Reuters. Retrieved from https://www.reuters.com/article/us-kuwait-court-ruling-idUKBRE95F04320130616.

_____. (1962). *Al-Majlis al-Ta'sīsī*. Kuwait: The National Assembly.

_____. (1962). *Al-Muthakkara al-Tafsīriyya*. Kuwait: The National Assembly.

4 From Grassroots to Public Diplomacy

Diwaniyya as an Alternative Sociopolitical Institution

Clemens Chay

Introduction

While associational life has undeniably altered across the decades, the *diwaniyya* is a persisting element that, at the fundamental level, serves to preserve family cohesiveness and, by extension, the communal spirit. Socialization via this inter-linked space and practice goes beyond (re-)connecting families, to the extent that these spaces are employed for politicking purposes particularly during the electoral campaigning season. The *diwaniyya*'s political role goes as far as supporting the "contending myths"—as coined by the late Mary Ann Tétreault—that stipulates a social contract on two levels: First, of representative government; and second, of a unique distribution of power in the Kuwaiti system. So internalized are these myths within society that there is genuine belief in the historical anecdote about how Kuwait's first ruler, Sabah I, was elected by a group of notable families in a *diwaniyya* tent. While this episode falls into the remit of governance, it is equally evident that the *diwaniyya* tradition would persist as a mark of the past. The descendants of Sabah I, and his successors, who later took on the mantle of Emiri leadership, would also invest time and effort in both hosting a *diwaniyya* session and visiting the *diwawin* of Kuwaiti families. Joint governance, between both ruler and people, is thus exemplified in associational life through *diwaniyya* "hopping."

Hence, the term grassroots diplomacy is particularly noticeable in—and applicable to—the neighbourhoods of old (known as the *fareej*). Through the transmission of cultural capital, denoting the know-how and resources from one generation to another, this practice has not been lost. The emphasis on the family is accompanied by the building of social networks (or the accumulation of social capital), which then shifts the *diwaniyya*'s role into the purview of the public sphere. In an urbanized and contemporary context, accessibility to the *diwaniyya* circuit equates to public outreach, which in turn signifies its usefulness in public diplomacy. Whether for social movements, or interestingly, for foreign diplomats, the *diwaniyya* has the potential to become a vehicle for conveying messages. Shaping optics within the *diwaniyya*, as this chapter will argue, lends itself for use by different segments of the public. This chapter will dissect the sociopolitical relevance of the *diwaniyya* in Kuwaiti society. As a novel outgrowth of governance at the grassroots, the chapter will also touch on how the *diwaniyya* practice has gained traction in public

DOI: 10.4324/9781003435259-4

diplomacy. Finally, the *diwaniyya*'s role in the public sphere will be reassessed with the disruption caused by the Covid-19 pandemic.

The Diwaniyya and Three Standpoints

In a casual conversation with a Qatari friend working in the Foreign Service, he was curious about the steps to obtaining an invitation to a *majlis* in Kuwait, or a *diwaniyya*. A *majlis*, stemming from the root form of the Arabic verb "*jalasa*" (meaning "to sit"), refers to the council or the court—particularly in the Gulf Arab states—where men sit and discuss issues relevant to them (see Figure 4.1). These could range from business dealings to a place where members of the ruling family receive an audience, or where the head of the family holds a gathering. The *diwaniyya* is a similar setup, but applies uniquely to the Kuwaiti context. The difference between the *diwaniyya* and the average Gulf *majlis*? The answer, in brief, is found in my response to my Qatari peer, "You don't need an invitation. You can simply walk in, and you won't be turned away."

How and why this phenomenon came into being deserve a much more elaborate response, which requires a hard look at historical findings. Conceptually, however, the *diwaniyya*, as a protected place of gathering, can be understood from three angles. First, as an idea of gathering manifested historically, and finding relevance in modern society, the *diwaniyya* tradition has been transplanted from councils held in tents into the present-day urbanized context—as an annex to the house or, in lavish cases, as a standalone building fully converted with multiple *diwaniyyas*.[1] It is a prime example of what the American urban sociologist, Lewis Mumford (1937, pp. 86–87) argues, that "social facts are primary, and the physical organization of the city [...] must be subservient to its social needs." Put simply, the *diwaniyya* as

Figure 4.1 Al Babtain *Diwaniyya* in Session (photograph by author, 02/10/2017)

46 *Clemens Chay*

a spatial microcosm of the wider urbanized Kuwaiti landscape, remains a social product of its time—the very same Lefebvrian understanding of urban environments. Ideationally, the relevance of this interlinked space and practice can be broadly attributed to how savvy Kuwaitis have been in navigating social, political, and even business dealings, from the pre- to post-oil eras. These are constructivist qualities—where learners build on existing foundations to learn new ones—where the act of meeting in a *diwaniyya* is "produced, reproduced and altered by the discursive practices of agents [according to their interests]" (Copeland, 2000, p. 190). In each period of Kuwait's development, the *diwaniyya* has found its purpose consistently, as will be discussed in this chapter.

Second, interactions in the *diwaniyya*, at the most fundamental level, persist as a means of sustaining the family unit and, by extension, the Kuwaiti social fabric. Socialization in the *diwaniyya*, as I have argued elsewhere, exemplifies the processes of capital accumulation and transmission (see Chay, 2016). In the Kuwaiti *diwaniyya*, one will find family trees depicting the lineage of specific branches and ancestral portraits. These serve not only as reminders of one's forefathers, but also the type of occupation or business that the family was involved in—which, in many instances, relate to maritime activities in the pre-oil era. According to the French sociologist Pierre Bourdieu (1996, p. 22), these objects, together with the family gatherings held in the *diwaniyya*, constitute "acts of reaffirmation and reinforcement that aim to produce, in a kind of continuous creation, the obliged affections and affective obligations of family feeling [...]."[2] Transmitted hereditarily from one generation to the next, these dispositions and materials on display are what Bourdieu calls cultural capital. Through the recurring family gatherings where senior male members meet the juniors repeatedly, the *diwaniyya* facilitates a continued transmission of cultural capital.

Additionally, by expanding the *diwaniyya*'s accessibility to the public, the space allows for a circulation of social capital. This alternative form of capital is, in Bourdieu's (1986, p. 243) explanation, the "aggregate of the actual or potential resources which are linked to a possession of a durable network of more or less institutionalized relationships of mutual acquaintances and recognition — in other words, to membership in a group." In the Kuwaiti context where the country is governed through "the visible and familiar hierarchy of the state and the less obvious hierarchy of the ruling family" (Herb, 1999, p. 33), the *diwaniyya* network is crucial to sustaining, if not, reproducing inter-family connections. Public access into *diwaniyyas* takes the transmission of social capital to another level: Informal encounters and haphazard meetings in the space accrue unexpected benefits. These are gained by increasing and mobilizing one's network through socialization, and the volume of capital possessed is dependent on the individual with whom the connection is forged at *diwaniyyas*. Personal accounts throughout this chapter, explaining the advantages of *diwaniyya* visits, will illustrate capital transmission.

An understanding of capitals is a befitting segway to the third standpoint on *diwaniyyas*—its role in the public sphere. The political scientist, Mary Ann Tétreault (1993, p. 279), describes how the *diwaniyya*'s ability to "straddle the public–private divide" guarantees its protected status. Holding a session within

From Grassroots to Public Diplomacy 47

the private confines of the house, albeit offering public access, legally exempts the space from giving notice to authorities of a scheduled assembly. As other scholars such as Alnajjar (2000) and Kapiszewsi (2006) have identified, the overlapping of spheres offers room for political mobilization. In a piece for *The Middle East Journal*, Ghanim Alnajjar (2000, p. 257), the Kuwaiti political scientist, wrote:

> There are thousands of diwaniyyas in Kuwait. They are considered social institutions; however, their political role far exceeds the seemingly purely social function for which the institution seems designed. Almost all elections and important political meetings prior to the 1950s were held in diwaniyyas, which put the institution in the forefront of political progress. It has been the place from which election campaigns of the post-independence era have been launched. No candidate can win without meeting with the major diwaniyyas of his constituency.

Campaigning in *diwaniyyas*, including those entailing the tents pitched in the confines of a villa, remains a trend when elections are imminent. The exception is the 2020 election, which, owing to the Covid-19 pandemic, drove electioneering—by both male and female parliamentary candidates—online. The 2022 election, however, marked the comeback of *diwaniyyas*. Embodying civil society but shedding the Western cloak, the *diwaniyya* web work is what Augustus Richard Norton (1993, pp. 213–214) describes as "a precondition for the whole to be the sum of its parts." Norton explains that the rights possessed by the individual in civil society must be reciprocated by his/her duties to the state. Likewise, political participation is a hallmark of the relationship between citizens and rulers in Kuwait—a connection that will be elaborated on later. The *diwaniyya*, then, serves as a mediating platform between state and society, in which members of the ruling Al-Sabah family regularly partake. Not simply holding councils as what is observed in the neighbouring Gulf states, but equally, making their rounds in *diwaniyyas* at the grassroots. This is yet another distinctive feature of Kuwaiti society and politics (Figure 4.1).

Crystallizing a Tradition in Society and Politics

In etymological terms, the term "diwaniyya" has its roots in administration. Alhajeri (2014, p. 268), in his entry for *The Oxford Encyclopedia of Islam and Politics*, wrote that the "diwan" referred to a "registry or a logbook containing army personnel, scribes, and poets." Likewise, the Muslim philosopher Ibn Khaldun (cited in Daghir, 1961), identified the *diwaniyya* as synonymous with the bureau of the clerks under Persian monarchs. Centuries later, the Imperial Divan or Council would constitute the elaborate Ottoman bureaucracy (see, for example, Ágoston & Masters, 2009, p. 486). Fast forward to the present, the diwan retains its administration core in the Gulf Arab states, usually denoting a court or council meant for official gatherings—for instance, the Amiri Diwan, or the ruler's court.

48   *Clemens Chay*

In the Kuwaiti context, unlike the majlis that denoted the venue for men's gatherings elsewhere, the affix "-iyya," when added to "diwan," sheds the official characteristic and adds a layer of informality.

Understanding the Gulf majlis would equally provide areas of contrast to the Kuwaiti *diwaniyya*. Recounting her experience in Bahrain from 1968 to 1972 as the personal assistant to the British Political Resident, Valerie Robinson (2014) wrote:

> The Ruler would receive the Political Resident in his majlis (audience hall), which was often quite a modest affair. Often the hall would be lined with local tribesmen, armed to the teeth, each having a kunja (dagger) in his belt and an ancient rifle over his shoulder. One got quite used to this show of arms, as no tribesmen would care to be seen without those tokens of manhood. The audience with the Ruler would usually be followed by a lunchtime 'fuddle'. In the less sophisticated Gulf states, the food would be served from an enormous dish in the centre of the room, while we all set round on the floor.

Robinson's account of a lavish affair is typical of an official reception in the Gulf. In many instances, the level of reception equally reflects the stature of the host—in the case above, the ruler. This is no exception for the *diwan* or the formal *majlis* in Kuwait. Further, the concept of holding an audience has two implicit connotations: (1) that the relationship between the host and visitor is an asymmetrical one; (2) by extension, the meeting also usually implies that the visitor's presence is aimed at seeking redress, assistance, or quite simply, a symbolic recognition of the other party's higher social status. In such cases, the host chooses the invitees. By contrast, events that transpire in the Kuwaiti *diwaniyya* run deeper into kinship and culture, with more relaxed undertones. Scarce (1985, p. 48), describing the practice in *The Evolving Culture of Kuwait*, writes:

> At home men continue to entertain their friends in either the separate diwaniya apartment or in one of the many sitting rooms; the atmosphere is that of a social club where the members take refreshments, watch television and video programmes, play cards, discuss business and neighbourhood affairs, or sit in companionable silence. Diwaniya sessions usually begin in the early evening after work and may continue late into the night, when a meal will be served [...].

While the *diwaniyya* persists as a "social club" for Kuwaiti men, young and old, this space—usually established by the family—is used for purposes beyond familial gatherings and occasions. During Ramadhan, for instance, while it is customary across the region for members of the ruling family to receive well-wishers in the *diwans* of their palaces, the Kuwaiti case study stands out. Members of the ruling Al-Sabah family would also be seen visiting family *diwaniyyas* across various districts, delivering their congratulatory wishes in person.[3] While these reciprocal

From Grassroots to Public Diplomacy   49

exchanges are far from discount hierarchy, they underscore elements of mutual respect and equality between the Al-Sabah and their constituents—starting from engagement at the grassroots.

Such a relationship, described by Uzi Rabi (2000) as the "First among Equals" system in Kuwait, sets the stage not only for patterns of socialization, but also for political interactions. The first ruler, Sabah I, according to scholarship by Kuwaiti historians, was chosen in a tent meeting among notable families, following an age-old tradition of *Shura*, or consultation, which is codified in constitutional documents (Kha'zal, 1962, p. 42; Al-Qanai, 1957).[4] The tent was a rudimentary form of the *diwaniyya*, where the political ideal of "joint governance"—grounded in tribal custom—was conceived and would later shape the participatory nature of Kuwaiti politics (see, for example, Chay, 2020). As Mary Ann Tétreault's (2000, pp. 41–42) book, *Stories of Democracy*, explained, the authority of the legislative branch in Kuwait's modern-day political system has also been "exercised through nonviolent resistance movements which successfully undermined the legitimacy of the regime in spite of its having halted the parliament's formal role as a legislative body." Some of these movements have employed the *diwaniyya* circuit, as will be detailed in the coming sections. As the Introduction delineated, the overlap across both the public and private spheres, in which the *diwaniyya* operates, equally recognizes the importance of the family as the "corner-stone of society"—which the constitutional wording in Article 9 echoes.[5] In a similar vein, Kuwaiti society is organized, as Kuwaiti academic Hesham al-Awadhi (2013) describes, like a "skeleton" where every "organ" has a role. The *diwaniyya*'s potential to be harnessed in sociopolitical movements is then evident on two levels: (1) its sanctity as a family space but operating in the public sphere; (2) it connects the "organs" of the family structure.

Even in social etiquette at *diwaniyyas*, the practice is representative of the "unique amalgam" of two purportedly contradictory philosophies: "Kuwait for the Kuwaitis" and the ruling Al-Sabah as the head in this "body" or "skeleton" of a family. While this paradox feeds into the "first among equals" notion, it is found in tribal custom reflected in the layout of a tent. When holding council, the leading tribal sheikhs are seated in the innermost length of the tent, similar to where important family members are positioned in the *diwaniyya* today. Distinguished guests are also invited to sit with their hosts, whether in the primordial space or in modern parlance. The audience, however, gathers in the middle for the tent setting, whereas in the *diwaniyya*, they are generally lined across either side of the elders— on benches—in descending order of age with the youngest near the entrance of the room. Kuwaiti males at the *diwaniyya* are expected to be in traditional robes, known as the *dishdasha*, alongside a three-part headdress. Consistent with tribal custom, there is an observance of seniority, and yet, concurrently, there is an implicit equilibrium as the voices are free to correspond with anyone in attendance, providing an element of chance at meeting someone new. These random encounters relate to building the same social capital that helps facilitate social movements.

A simple act of serving coffee, the staple drink obtained strictly from Yemen once upon a time, adopts a similar hierarchical protocol that stemmed from the

50 *Clemens Chay*

tribal custom. In a tent, tribesmen of senior ranks are served coffee, and so are distinguished guests. The level of respect accorded to the guest is shown when the host personally serves the hot beverage. Raswan's (1935, p. 151) account of such hospitality in a tent offers intricate details:

> The coffee made the round. The favoured guests, whom the negro served first (unhappily I belonged to them) were the victims of especial politeness; before the coffee he spat first into the cup and wiped it dry with his shirt-sleeve. Three times I had to endure this rate at the hands of the punctilious coffee-priest, who waited on us with the utmost solemnity on each occasion. Only then might I waggle the cup between my finger-tips in token of thanks and satisfaction and hand it back to him.

The same applies today in the *diwaniyya*, where the *chai* (tea) boy, usually of South Asian descent, would serve the drink to attendees. The process of acculturation carries on wherein fathers take their sons on *diwaniyya* visits, and the young ones are expected to listen more, and speak less. The know-how, the dress code, mannerisms, and the visuals of the family ancestry—these constitute the cultural capital passed down from one generation to the next. As Khaled Bourisly (2009) wrote in his book about his family's history in maritime navigation:

> At one point in the 1940s, my father Homoud Bourisly, and my uncle, Hamad Bourisly, used to take me with them to these evening *dewaniyahs* for a cup of coffee or tea and I would listen to them chatting about freight transport or pearl diving and trading.

What is noteworthy in the conduct of my fieldwork is the (self-)differentiation between the *diwaniyyas* of the *hadhar* (urbanites) and the *bedu* (Bedouins) (see, for example, Al-Haroun and Alajmi, 2018). A recent article in the *Kuwait Times* (2023) goes as far as saying that "each group has different requirements and internal spatial designs" owing to their respective distinct cultural and ethnic personality. From my visits to a myriad of *diwaniyyas*, those situated further away from the city, for instance, in Jahra (some 30 to 40 kilometres from Kuwait City), tend to adhere more strictly to the customs, at least what the hosts deem strictly tribal, particularly in first serving coffee and dates to the guests. Al-Thunayyan (see Figure 4.2) and Al-Enezi are two Jahra-based families that assert such characteristics, although in the *bedu*, once pastoral nomads, are now all but urbanized. Such observations do not dismiss the scholarship on the complexity of the *hadhar-bedu* discourse. Al-Nakib (2014) argued that this binary is an outcome of state-building strategies adopted in the early oil years, linked chiefly to citizenship and housing policies, whereas Longva (2006, p. 184) asserts that "welfare-state systems [akin to Kuwait's] engender processes of ethnicization and the rise of ethnopolitics." Yet, cultural differences, as Longva writes, "should not be overlooked," and so this ascription and self-ascription, also manifested in the *diwaniyya* space, merit further research. Nevertheless, understanding the transmission of capital, which can in

Figure 4.2 The Thunayyan *diwaniyya* in Jahra, an annex to the house resembling a tent (photograph by author, taken on 17/04/2023).

turn lead to questions on identity, is indicative of the relevance that the *diwaniyyas* hold despite the changing Kuwaiti landscape—whether physical, social, or political (Figure 4.2).

Urbanism Then and Now: The *Diwaniyya* in Its Element

Spatial relevance and the *diwaniyya*'s purpose, as a built environment, for the overall physical landscape provide another important analytical angle. Space as a product of the social, a concept by the French sociologist Henri Lefebvre (1991, p. 33), entails an understanding of the "representations of space," which are "tied to the relations of production and to the 'order' which those relations impose." Put simply, societal echelons and the division of labour in urbanism can explain the types of spaces needed in a given landscape. Before the discovery of oil, maritime trade and pearl diving were not the sole revenue-generating activities in Kuwait. The sea, the bazaar, and the desert lay on the same axis, as outlined by the Ali al-Shamlan (2017), the country's former Minister of Higher Education. Historians such as Abu Hakima (1983, p. 97) have gone as far as attributing Kuwait's commercial success to transit trade comprising the transport of goods by caravans—which involved the payment of tributes along the way—and smuggling. Goods offloaded from the port were taken inland, and some of which were sold at the bazaar, while others were taken by caravan into the desert, according to interlocutors.[6] The desert-to-sea connection also means that, unlike most of Gulf historiography revolved around maritime commerce, trade was also conducted across the vast sand dunes.

Pioneering work done by Robert Fletcher (2015) argues that the "desert corridor," as a unit of analysis, unveils histories of communication by land grounded

52   Clemens Chay

in agency, contingency, and power. As an idea emerging from holding council in tents, the *diwaniyya* was also mentioned in early historical records by the British. The first Political Agent to Kuwait, Captain Stuart Knox (1906, pp. 29–30), in his survey of the surroundings, wrote: "He gave us an excellent pillau of fowls in a decent little diwaniya facing the sea at Funtass and was very anxious to know if everything was to my liking." Judging by the location of Funtass (now known as Fintas), placed well into the hinterland and away from the main port, it was almost certain that the *diwaniyya* that Knox referred to was a tent. Sheikh Mubarak al-Sabah, the ruler at that time, was often described in archival records as a wily personality well-versed in desert warfare and, who gave refuge to the great Ibn Saud before he reclaimed the territories to found the third Saudi state.

Arguably the most recurrent aspect of the Gulf, if not, Kuwait historiography is maritime trade. Here the *diwaniyya* slots in nicely into the urbanism of a port town, serving chiefly as a meeting place for stakeholders such as merchants, shipbuilders, sea captains, and pearl divers. *Bas ya Bahar (1972)*, a film directed by Khalid al-Siddiq, roughly translated as *The Cruel Sea*, shows the interdependent relationship of those involved in maritime affairs. In one scene a pearl diver was seeking redress in the *diwaniyya*, having been injured by a shark during a diving trip, and requested his dues from a merchant. Such "unplanned urbanism," as explained by Farah al-Nakib (2016, pp. 36–43) in her seminal book *Kuwait Transformed*, reflects not only functional diversity, but also the built environment relevant for and "intimately linked to the town's port economy." The *diwaniyya*, an idea borne out of tribal custom, found itself transplanted in the courtyard house, as a space for the family and for dispute resolution. In the grand scheme of things, the interconnected mud-houses of the pre-oil port town, known as the *farij*, fostered a sense of communal belonging—and its manifestation was in the *diwaniyya*. The daily life of the pre-oil quarters was also described in Scarce's (1985, p. 48) work, which recounted how men often took their evening meal with their friends in the *diwaniyya*. Life and work, entwined in the *farij*, meant that sea captains would sit on the *datchas* or mud benches built out from the front walls of the *diwaniyyas* (see Figure 4.3). It was where they would watch the ships come and go (Figure 4.3).

The urbanism of that era and the tightly knit community also gave rise to spaces of socialization such as cafés. One famous café that has been preserved from the old *fareej* days is the Bounashi café. Now refurbished, it was the spot where men would wind down after work and a space of information exchange. The coffeehouse is situated in Mubarakiya Souq, the central bazaar, which was, incidentally, also the place where Sheikh Mubarak al-Sabah held a public audience (see Figure 4.4). Enmeshed in this urbanism was the governing structure, which Sheikh Mohammed Sabah al-Salem al-Sabah (2016), the former Minister of Foreign Affairs, explained as a designation of responsibilities. In an interview with the author, he equated the *diwaniyya* to a court at the grassroots:

> It was not something that just happened as a result of modernity, or the ability to have a *diwaniyya*. No, no, it's an indispensable part, it's a pillar of the governing structure. The Emir and his court dispense justice and the application

Figure 4.3 Men sitting on the *datchas* built from the walls of the Shamlan *diwaniyya* (photograph courtesy of Hamed al-Amiri)

of this justice in terms of this law and order. And we have, equally, the other courts of the merchants, organising the economic structure and economic life, and dispensing their economic progress. And you have the third type of courts, the religious, and they have to give their blessings. It is that structure, this is how I understand myself, operating in this domain. For that reason, yes, you would see leaders pay regular visits to *diwaniyyas* as an indispensable part of the ruling apparatus.

The division of tasks that Sheikh Mohammed described reinvokes the previously mentioned skeletal structure of Kuwait society and how the organization of pre-oil life rested on the ruler–merchant equation. In this case, he added a third dimension of religion (Figure 4.4).

The rapid urbanization funded by oil wealth, driven by the 1952 Master Plan, would later drastically change the residential landscape. The revamped housing patterns would in turn have implications for the role of the *diwaniyya*. New neighbourhoods, as described by al-Nakib (2016, p. 71), became "homogenous residential areas, emphasizing detached single-family living on allocated plots," as opposed to the courtyard house setup meant for extended families. With suburbanization, the *diwaniyya* found a new calling—to maintain the social fabric of Kuwait. As extended families were organized into nuclear ones, and the typical residential home became the villa, the *diwaniyya*'s physical form underwent a change as it could now appear as an annex to the house, a standalone building (with multiple *diwaniyyas*), or a room in the entire villa layout with a separate entrance from the main door. While this could generally be attributed to the country's, and by extension, the society's increased affluence, preserving the *diwaniyya*

Figure 4.4 Sheikh Mubarak holding a public audience in the bazaar (photograph by Lt-Commander A.N. Gouldsmith, National Maritime Museum, London)

is akin to preserving the communal spirit of the past, but in remodelled residential quarters. One key difference is that cars are now the primary mode of transport and an integral part of the modern facilities *par excellence*. The *diwaniyya* retains its relevance for the family and the families around Kuwait, simply by giving a space for face-time.

A Vehicle for Sociopolitical Mobilization

The element of face-time, facilitated by the *diwaniyya* where protection is guaranteed, resonates with what the political theorist Hannah Arendt (1958, p. 177) calls a "space of appearance." The space of appearance is a platform created by "action and speech," where the participants find purchase in "discussing and deliberating about matters of public concern." While this could be work-related, as previously mentioned, the *diwaniyya*'s role in the public sphere also means that politicized issues could be expressed in this space. In a subsequent writing, Arendt (1972, p. 151) also contended that power arises when people "act in concert," but legitimacy is derived "from the initial getting together rather than from any action that then may follow." In the same vein, the *diwaniyya* lays the foundation of social connectivity and the congregation on the platform offers a streak of political potential waiting to be harnessed. While there are numerous episodes of political mobilization across Kuwait's timeline, this section will highlight five of them: Two from the pre-oil era to underscore the gravitas of the mercantile elite, one from the period of independence and Arab nationalism, one just before the Iraqi invasion when the parliament was absent, and finally, a more recent example from the 2000s.

From Grassroots to Public Diplomacy 55

Two episodes related to the formation of councils in 1921 and 1938—precursors to the National Assembly—stand out in elucidating the importance of the merchants in pre-oil Kuwait. The notables, gathered in the Al-Saqr *diwaniyya* under the charge of Hamad al-Saqr, banded together to request for the establishment of an advisory council. Their objective was to have a say in the administration of Kuwait (see Crystal, 1990, p. 41). Submitting a petition, which spelt out their demands in black and white, the group articulated their wish to be involved in the appointment of the next ruler (in other words, the successor of Sheikh Salim al-Sabah). This request required the approval of the British, who found the proposed concession excessive, leading to their demise. But al-Rumaihi (1987, pp. 1–2) calls this incident "the beginning of constitutional development in Kuwait." The candidates for succession did eventually come to be chosen in another merchant's *diwaniyya*, but without the presence of any council.

Yet, this experience would set a precedent for the 1938 council. The impetus on the second occasion was driven by maladministration in Sheikh Ahmad al-Jaber's (the next ruler's) charge. According to the India Office Records (1938), Yousif al-Marzuq, a leading merchant offered his *diwaniyya* to elect a 14-member Legislative Assembly, which was aimed at toning authoritarianism down.[7] In what was known as a *Majlis* movement, the council drafted a list of reforms and took societal matters into their own hands. By the end of 1938, this resulted in a scuffle among merchants themselves—those for and others against the *Majlis*. The British said the incident was "not [an] unexpected counter revolution" arising from the refusal of a townsman to "disclose the number of ladies married and unmarried in his house according to a recent law by the *Majlis*" (see Dickson, 1938). As the conflict escalated into a confrontation between the Sabah sheikhs comprising the ruler and the pro-*Majlis* notables, the ruler demanded that the movement surrender the weaponry in its possession, presided over by—interestingly—a certain Sabah sheikh, Abdullah al-Salem. Events that later transpired saw the surrender of the arsenal without bloodshed, only after the ruler had rallied tribesmen to his aid. The council would later be dissolved having gotten on the wrong side of the British when attempting to interfere in external affairs (see Crystal, 1990, pp. 49–55). The council's achievements, however, lie in "electing two prototypical assemblies that wrote Kuwait's first constitution and passed progressive legislation" (Tétreault, 2011, p. 75). The *diwaniyya*'s role, in this stage of Kuwait's development, served as a pre-political space that equally underscored the merchants' central role in decision-making.

With the experiences of the 1921 and 1938 councils, by the 1960s Kuwait entered a new phase of not only independence, but also a climate of Arab nationalism. This period witnessed the drafting of the Constitution and the inauguration of the National Assembly, a stage at which constitutionalism survived, according to Herb (2014, pp. 66–67), owing to the conditions created not only by pre-oil legacies, but also by the agency of Sheikh Abdullah al-Salem. The sheikh, who was the president of the 1938 *Majlis*, succeeded Sheikh Ahmad al-Jaber, and had a "personal commitment to a strong National Assembly." Yet, under the reign of Sheikh Abdullah al-Salem, the room for political freedoms expanded, as observed

56 *Clemens Chay*

by the Kuwait Oil Company President Southwell (1955). Not only was the ban on local press lifted, but also there was a proliferation of clubs such as the Graduates Club and the National Cultural Club, which ran in tandem with "interpersonal networks linking Kuwaiti educators and officials to nationalist activists throughout the region" (see Al-Rashoud, 2019). In this activist climate associated with Arab nationalism, opposition figures emerged in Kuwait such as Ahmad al-Khatib (2007, p. 225) who, in his memoirs, described how *diwaniyyas* were used as a means of campaigning for greater public freedoms. Al-Khatib and Jasim al-Qitami, another leading opposition personality, were closely monitored by the British in fear of causing public unrest. Their activities, described in a report by one British official, were centred on visiting "two to three Diwaniyat" every night with "audiences of 150 to 200," but they "did not wish for violent change" (see Graham, 1967). The activism of the 1960s, in a recent personal conversation with the Director of the Diplomatic Institute, Nasser al-Sabeeh (2023), resonates with the kind of space given to non-governmental organizations (NGOs) in Kuwait today. In "no other Gulf country," according to al-Sabeeh, would NGOs enjoy a similar "amount of room to operate" as they do in Kuwait, particularly "in terms of restrictions" or the lack thereof.

Jasim al-Qitami would feature in another important episode of political mobilization just before the Iraqi invasion. While there are two well-known, unconstitutional dissolutions of the parliament, in 1976 and 1986, it is the latter date when the *diwaniyya* emerged as an alternative space for debate, politicking, and protest. Opposition leaders, at the end of 1989, set to restore the parliament and the Constitution, through what was known as the "Monday *Diwaniyya*" movement, or *Diwaniyya Al-Ithnain*. Starting with al-Qitami's *diwaniyya*, weekly sessions were held to draw in the crowd and rally the people to their cause. This was met by the ire of the authorities, who dispatched the riot police and police dogs to interrupt the proceedings of and disperse the crowd at Mishari al-Anjari's *diwaniyya*—the second session of the movement (see Tétreault, 2000, p. 70; al-Mubaraki, 2008). The use of police dogs, in particular, was considered offensive on the grounds that these were seen as ritually unclean animals in Islam. Then Foreign Minister Sheikh Sabah al-Ahmad would later offer his apology to five opposition leaders in his office, for transgressing what is deemed a private space. Further jostling between the authorities and the movement but the latter would not see the light at the end of the tunnel, as Iraqi forces would later occupy Kuwait in a blatant disregard for national sovereignty. What could be said about the *diwaniyya* in this episode was its role as a counter-space employed as a means of preserving the social contract grounded in "joint governance." This was a reclamation of the access to the public sphere, what Habermas (1974, p. 49) describes as the "guarantee of assembly and association [by citizens] and the freedom to express and publish their opinions— about matters of general interest."

The final episode addressed in this section concerns the 2006 Orange Movement, where activists sought to change the number of electoral constituencies. The tagline of the movement was "*Nabiha Khamsa*" or "We Want Five," which arose from a desire to combat corruption, but later evolved to legally reduce Kuwait's electoral districts from 25 to 5. What is noteworthy in this episode is how information and communication technologies (ICTs) have seeped in—not forgetting the rise of social media. While *Nabiha Khamsa* used blogging to great effect, *diwaniyyas* and other public spaces were used to connect with people physically. Tétreault (2011, pp. 74–83; see also al-Bloshi & Alfahad, 2009) wrote that, by this point, Kuwait's civil society had "cosmopolitan branches reaching well beyond its formal borders," passing the word—through the *diwaniyyas*—to show up in front of the Seif Palace in orange t-shirts and with orange flags. As virtual means of communication run into the mainstream, the physical factor remains a bastion of connectivity. As the section on Covid-19 will reiterate, face-time in *diwaniyyas* continue to remain relevant.

Public Diplomacy in the Diwaniyya: De-Bureaucratizing Formal Conduct

Until this point, it has been established that the *diwaniyya* is an integral part of Kuwait culture. Its malleability in a public sphere with cultural and familial purchase makes it an optimal platform for ascertaining public opinion. This was exactly what a *Wikileaks* cable (2005), crafted by American diplomats, uncovered: Calling the *diwaniyya* a "defining element of Kuwaiti culture," embassy officers were encouraged to tap on its networks to "make and maintain contacts," while "explaining US foreign policy to a diverse audience." Thus far, empirical findings on the *diwaniyya*, as presented in this chapter, presuppose that participants in the *diwaniyya* are predominantly Kuwaiti. Yet, the nesting ground for the *diwaniyya* circuit starts at the grassroots, making the same platform a fertile one for the conduct of public diplomacy by foreign diplomats. "Public diplomacy," a term coined by a retired American foreign service officer Edward Gullion (cited in Pamment, 2014, p. 52), refers to a "form of influence over public opinion which would in turn have an impact upon the conduct of diplomacy." Yet, when a "foreign" agenda is thrown into the mix of a local milieu, often the question is not only whether the skilled foreign practitioner is adaptable to a fresh environment, but also, in this case, whether the message intended for the local Kuwaiti audience is "palatable." Just as the notion of "traditional diplomacy" is challenged by sub-national groups, the literature on public diplomacy is under re-examination to give more *public* emphasis rather than being "a mere ancillary tactic that supports [...] traditional diplomacy efforts" (Snow, 2009, pp. 6–7):

> Traditional diplomacy is government-to-government relations (G2G) and if one were to picture it, it would be a photo op of Secretary of State Condoleezza Rice sitting across the table from the foreign affairs minister in another nation state. Traditional public diplomacy has been about governments talking to global publics (G2P), and includes those efforts to inform, influence and engage those publics in support of national objective and foreign policies. More recently, public diplomacy involves the way in which both government and private individuals and groups influence directly and

58   *Clemens Chay*

indirectly those public attitudes and opinions that bear directly on another government's foreign policy decisions (P2P).

As the diplomatic canon evolves to include how "both government and private individuals and groups influence directly and indirectly" public attitudes, as the above excerpt illuminates, it is equally, if not, more important to question how localised practices shape diplomatic conduct.

Neumann (2005, p. 72) points out that the memory of diplomacy carries with it a "Western history." Indeed, the European diplomatic canon transformed a small international élite in old-style diplomacy into a new, "democratic," and "open" diplomacy (Nicolson, 1961, pp. 39–49). The institutionalization of diplomatic management was compartmentalized into missions, rank, and language, all of which were established at the Congress of Vienna (1814–15); the French language, for instance, acted as the language of diplomacy and intellectual hegemony (Hamilton and Langhorne, 2011, pp. 109–110). The nature of modern diplomacy was thus headed for bureaucratization, as the British example illustrates:

The diplomatist, being a civil servant, is subject to the Foreign Secretary; the Foreign Secretary, being a member of the cabinet, is subject to the majority in parliament; and parliament, being but a representative assembly, is subject to the will of the sovereign people (Nicolson, 1939, p. 82).

Kuwait's induction into the international community, accompanied by its independence in 1961 and an external threat in the form of Iraq, meant that integration into the institutionalized global order was imperative. The Al-Sabah ruling family strategically decided to embark "upon a programme of internal reform and external recognition": First, Kuwait's admission to the Arab League opened the possibility of that organization "assuming responsibility for defending the Shaikhdom"; second, the Kuwait Fund for Arab Economic Development (KFAED) was established as a means of using "wealth as an instrument of foreign policy" in the immediate Arab region; finally, Kuwait's "bargaining position was strengthened" by its admission into the United Nations on May 14, 1963 (see Smith, 1999, pp. 123–129). Kuwait's continued commitment to the bureaucracy of international diplomacy is visibly symbolized by the establishment of the Ministry of Foreign Affairs in 1961, followed by the more recent Saud Al-Nasser Al-Sabah Diplomatic Institute in 2008.

While international recognition for Kuwait meant subscribing to the professional backdrop of diplomacy, or what is known as "Track I diplomacy," diplomacy—as a conduct viewed through the prism of interpersonal communication—need not follow the same path. Berridge (2002, pp. 7–9) writes that diplomatic bureaucracy may not be as influential in "states with shorter diplomatic traditions and highly personalized and arbitrary political leadership." Berridge's statement runs on the back of a Western understanding of "diplomatic tradition" and, equally, an assumption that "personalized" leadership in a monarchical system offers little room for diplomatic exchanges. This chapter has, however, challenged these presuppositions through an understanding of the *diwaniyya* as a platform for diplomacy with *cultural purchase*.

To go further, as the previous sections have shown, the malleability of the *diwaniyya* allows for influence on the public(s) that can extend as far as mobilization. Participant observation during my *diwaniyya* visits allowed me to single out regular visitors consisting of foreign businessmen and diplomats alike. The time and effort invested by personnel from both the British and American embassies stand out from the rest. British officials, by virtue of its historical relationship with Kuwait, exhibit a persisting interest since the Anglo-British agreement was signed at the turn of the 19th century. American prominence, on the other hand, rose in the years after Operation Desert Storm, which saw the US military spearhead coalition efforts to liberate Kuwait from the Iraqi Occupation.[8] As this chapter has illustrated with multiple examples, the British closely examined sociopolitical trends in Kuwait, including those in *diwaniyyas*. Interestingly, by the late 1980s, just before the Iraqi invasion, the former US ambassador to Kuwait, Nathaniel Howell (1989), admitted that "there is no longer any vehicle except the informal *diwaniyya* system by which the [Kuwaiti] families can demand an accounting from the Al-Sabah." By the time, the country was liberated from the Iraqis in 1991, then US ambassador to Kuwait, Edward Gnehm, was instructed by his superior, Edward Drerejian, the former US Assistant Secretary of State, to understand public opinion on the enforcement of a "no-fly" zone over Southern Iraq. The duo would later tell a Kuwaiti cabinet minister, "Let's hit the *diwaniyyas.*"[9]

Testimonies by various diplomats based in Kuwait, now and then, confirm that despite the unofficial nature of *diwaniyya* visits and meetings, the space helped to forge friendships, improve communication, and overcome bureaucratic hurdles on the sidelines. According to the former political and media advisor at the British embassy, Ahmad al-Alowaish (2016), *diwaniyyas* guarantee a "personal connection [...] where people can talk amongst themselves and discuss things as they see, and give their honest opinion in a way that they wouldn't do in an official capacity." Anything but a routine "professionalised" experience, foreign diplomats had to grapple with clashes of expectations and realities, and of orthodoxy and tradition. In an interview with the author, the former British ambassador Matthew Lodge (2016), who served in Kuwait from 2014 to 2017, recounted:

> I have been a career diplomat for about twenty years now, and as I have become more senior myself and engaged in some of the broader aspects— you would call them 'High Level Discussions' in capitals. [...] You would become quite familiar with the way, that, in addition to formal set-piece meetings and engagements, you go and engage with your host country, with senior officials, politicians, parliamentarians, academics in their offices during the working day, and you may come across them occasionally at various, again somewhat set-piece social functions.
>
> Therefore, that was very much, and I should add, my essential part in the building and nurturing of relationships, particularly on a bilateral basis, where we are talking about relationships between two sovereign countries.

60 *Clemens Chay*

> [...] That's a key part of what we do day by day [...] and I think it is fair to say that I arrived in Kuwait two years ago, very much expecting that to be the pattern and rhythm of that sort of engagement—that [bilateral] networking relationship—but actually in reality I found it rather different.

Acutely aware of Britain's historical ties with Kuwait, Lodge admits that his posting to the country constitutes a break from what he was accustomed to—formality and diplomatic hierarchy. His Kuwaiti counterpart in London, also the longest-serving Kuwaiti diplomat to a single country, ambassador Khaled al-Duwaisan (2017), told the author that newly appointed foreign diplomats bound for his country were briefed on the "six channels of informal diplomacy" comprising the *diwaniyya*. Lodge found himself, during his initial days as the head of mission, struggling to understand Kuwaiti society, particularly:

> The impact of social structures and traditions in Kuwaiti society. [...] And of course, people talk to me about the *diwaniyyas*, and they talked about Arab hospitality [...], and the family and tribal linkages within society between the ruling family and other major trading families. The structure of Kuwaiti society in fashion that is actually both broad, but also, and this might sound strange to say, but in some aspects very hierarchical, and in other aspects quite flat.

Crucially, foreign diplomats are required to strategically identify key actors or families outside the top political echelons (i.e. the Al-Sabah), or key parts of the "skeletal" structure that this chapter has explained, including personalities involved in business, education, and energy. Navigating the *diwaniyya* circuit also offers diplomats entry points that bear on the consideration of their country's interests. The British embassy, for instance, stores a list of what they consider strategic *diwaniyyas*, categorized by domain (political, business etc.), and with notes on the day and time of the weekly sessions. Ambassador Lodge explained:

> Because whilst within that relatively privileged strata of society where we are engaging on a daily basis, as an aside, I would notice that the *diwaniyya* culture extends across the whole of Kuwaiti society. But we as foreign diplomats here in Dasman, downtown Kuwait City, even if we are proactive and engaged, I would argue that you only get to see, 10, 15, no more than 20 per cent of the overall activity that goes on. [...] We are sort of existing and operating in a pretty privileged circle, but [...] the combination of family structure, *diwaniyya* culture, small society, local media, both traditional and increasingly social media, all have the effect of pushing much of the business in influencing and shaping opinions outside that Track I business.

In order to gain a holistic purview of Kuwaiti society, Lodge and his team dedicated time outside office hours to travel to *diwaniyyas* on the periphery of the city, for instance, Jahra. Nevertheless, pushing beyond "Track I business," as Lodge

From Grassroots to Public Diplomacy 61

testifies, requires operating on various platforms—formal and informal. Getting underneath the skin of the debate requires a more relaxed atmosphere within the physical confines of the *diwaniyya*. The spontaneous nature of these conversations, as the former economic officer at the US embassy, Charles Fee (2017), told the author, offers a chance to bond with one's opposite number; "to open up because the clock's not ticking and it's not a diversion." Likewise, the former US ambassador to Kuwait, Doug Silliman (2022), who served from 2014 to 2016, admitted to the author in an interview that he always took younger American diplomats to the *diwaniyyas* to "let them have their own conversations" as it was "part of their training as a diplomat." Like the British, the American embassy crafted an Excel spreadsheet with the addresses, contacts, and the weekly sessions of various *diwaniyyas*. For Ambassador Silliman, diplomatic presence in the *diwaniyya* allowed his staff to make sense of Kuwaiti culture:

> Going to *diwaniyyas* also meant giving opportunities to my administrative officers, who usually do visas and passports, and do not really have the opportunity to go out and meet Kuwaitis. For example, [...] if there were women officers who wanted to come along, I made sure to bring them along. They felt that in Kuwait, there seems to be a third gender: male, female, and females who have responsibilities that only male are used to having. The female officers felt that they interact differently in Kuwaiti society compared to being a woman in other societies.

As Silliman described, *diwaniyyas* not only offer an entry point into understanding Kuwaiti culture, but also permit the attendance of female officers who are received in professional capacity. This was a view concurred by Véronique Bertrand-Galli (2018), the former second counsellor at the French embassy in Kuwait, who said that her visits to *diwaniyyas* sharpen her role as the "official representative of her country," an "asexual personality."

Beyond immersion into the culture, the connections forged through the *diwaniyya* circuit facilitate and expedite the organization of official meetings. Appointments organized through the diplomatic establishment undoubtedly instil a sense of formality, but bureaucratic hurdles as the former Indonesian ambassador to Kuwait, Tatang Budie Razak (2017), found out, can be overcome by the social brokerage in *diwaniyyas*. In an interview with the author, he said:

> The Vice Minister's delegation came in the evening and only had half a day here, so of course, formally, we will send a letter to the Ministry of Foreign Affairs, but at the same time, I sent a letter directly to the Minister of Oil here. [...] Because I have a personal relationship, that is very effective. I asked them to please give me a written [answer], [...] and then my personal contact sent a letter to his Sheikh here. So I got the letter [...]. It is very effective. I have a personal relationship [...] because I met them previously [in *diwaniyyas*] so I requested, and they do have some businesses in Indonesia.

62 Clemens Chay

Figure 4.5 Ambassador Doug Silliman featured in the 100-*diwaniyas* campaign (*Source:* US Embassy Kuwait Instagram Page)

The face-time in *diwaniyyas*, emphasized repeatedly throughout this chapter, is vital. As the pioneer of American broadcast journalism, Edward Murrow, famously said, "The real crucial link in international exchange is the last three feet, which is bridged by personal contact, one person talking to another." The "last three feet" as foreign diplomats have increasingly come to learn during their term in Kuwait, are both bridged and facilitated by the *diwaniyya* network.

Although public diplomacy is not always the main agenda for foreign diplomats visiting the *diwaniyya*—as it can be a mere ceremonial appearance to maintain contact, the platform remains viable for those adept at rolling out such campaigns. Ambassador Silliman (2022) shared with the author that the US embassy used the *diwaniyyas* for "public policy messaging," adding that Instagram was also employed as a follow-up to "create a buzz." He was referring to a 100-*diwaniyyas* campaign during Ramadhan 2016 that served as a precursor to the first US–Kuwait Strategic Dialogue (see Figure 4.5). Ultimately, the *diwaniyya* circuit introduces the foreign diplomat into a network of complex relationships that may be taboo to public servants who are required to be as impersonal as possible in the conduct of diplomatic business. To others, such as Alanoud Alsharekh (2017), bypassing formal bureaucratic levels entails "an ethical problem." The sustenance of such a system reflects Kuwait's structural inequalities: Yielding benefits to eligible users while excluding others; its advantages can also turn out to be unevenly distributed as some exploit it more than others. Nevertheless, it remains a point of entry for windows of opportunities to its users, however big or small (Figure 4.5).

The Covid-19 Episode

A final note must be made with reference to the Covid-19 pandemic and its impact on physical interactions. Like the rest of the international community, Kuwaiti authorities imposed restrictions on gatherings to slow down, if not, prevent, the transmission of the virus. Al-Sejari and al-Kandari (2022), in a piece of the *American Journal of Men's Health*, investigated this "complete lockdown on Kuwaiti men's lifestyle behaviour" as the *diwaniyyas* were shut down and their users isolated. Higher rates of depression and other mental disorders were reported because of the inability to socialize, particularly at *diwaniyyas*. To go further, in terms of public space, there was an appetite for other forms of public space, such as the streets in the residential districts. Gomes, al-Ragam, and Alshalfan (2020) observed a 24% increase in neighbourhood mobility as resident left homes to exercise while their children played on the streets. Well-being shifted into focus where spatial policies and urban planning are concerned.

Nevertheless, the thirst for mobility did not stop there—it soon became clear that there was a yearning for face-to-face meetings and socialization. Between 2020 and 2022, two elections took place, one in December 2020 and the other in September 2022. While the 2020 election witnessed a digitization of electoral campaigns, which took candidates to online platforms such as Zoom, the 2022 one marked the return of in-person campaigning as restrictions eased. What is noteworthy were the signs well before the 2022 elections that Kuwaitis longed for interactions in the flesh. In March 2021, amid a political showdown between the executive and legislative branches, then Prime Minister Sheikh Sabah al-Khaled referred a planned opposition-sponsored gathering to the court. The mastermind behind this gathering, Bader al-Dahoum, a controversial figure and MP said the opposition had planned to "organise a large gathering in which thousands would have attended, but [later] agreed to replace it with a press conference" (see Kuwait Times, 2021). Al-Dahoum's membership in the National Assembly would later be nullified. In another instance prior to the September 2022 parliamentary elections, the Ministry of Interior cracked down on members of the public who participated in tribal primaries, which have been outlawed since 1998 (see Kuwait Times, 2022). Although this practice is criminalized by law, the primaries—usually held in *diwaniyyas*—surface from time to time and draw the attention of the authorities. These instances of transgression imply not only an eagerness of a return to normalcy, but also a desire among Kuwaitis for congregation and in-person interactions.

The difference in the lead-up to both the 2020 and 2022 elections, however, was the medium of communication used for circulating electoral explainers. As mentioned earlier, the 2020 election was conducted on the back of largely virtual campaigning. Local political analysts such as Salah al-Jassim and Abdulrazaq al-Shayji took to digital platforms and going on TV shows to provide fresh statistical analysis on the elections. But in the lead-up to the September 2022 elections, Abdullah al-Khonaini (2022), co-founder of the parliamentary watch known as Raqib 50, told the author that local dynamics were shaken up:

> Fast forward to today, surprisingly, it is back to traditional ways. […] Ahmed al-Saadoun (former Speaker of the National Assembly from 1985–99) is going to *diwaniyyas*. When you listen to it, you'll be asking "why would Ahmed al-Saadoun go to *diwaniyyas*?" He is so well-known that people would come to him rather than him going to *diwaniyyas*. But the *diwaniyya* is now on a strong comeback compared to 2020. Not only was there a hunger

64   *Clemens Chay*

for face-to-face interactions, but the political analysts themselves also shifted their base of communications from the TV programmes into the *diwaniyyas*. Al-Khonaini added that a strong speech by the Crown Prince Sheikh Meshaal al-Ahmad, calling for national unity, prompted these analysts to return to the traditional means of circulating information—the *diwaniyyas*.

Conclusion: A Tradition Alive and Well

This chapter has dissected a well-embedded and interlinked Kuwaiti space and practice, the *diwaniyya*, from multiple angles. As the Introduction set out, urbanism, capitals, and the public sphere provide important conceptual vantage points to understand this uniquely Kuwaiti phenomenon, which will complement the chapters in this volume covering history, governance, foreign policy, and society. While it is tempting to attribute the *diwaniyya* platform to civil society, one must, as Norton (1993, pp. 213–214) suggests, shelve the Western "lineage of the concept." Rather, the existence of a civil society, as he writes, "implies a shared sense of identity, by means of, at least, tacit agreement over the rough boundaries of the political unit." A sense of citizenship, with associated rights and responsibilities, make up this concept. Likewise, in the Kuwaiti context, the idea of joint governance, which set the trajectory for a participatory nature of politics, became entrenched in the Kuwaiti psyche. Politicking in the *diwaniyyas* then became a means of fulfilling the responsibilities of the citizenry.

However, Norton (1993, p. 214) also argues that civil society is "more than admixture of various forms of association," and instead stresses on civility—implying "tolerance, the willingness of individuals to accept disparate political views and social attitudes; sometimes to accept the profoundly important idea that there is no right answer." This is a fitting description of the interactions in the *diwaniyya*, which is fundamentally a social space encapsulated in the family. The social dimension facilitates both grassroots diplomacy and public diplomacy. Despite the internal squabbles, the family remains a unit that strives to retain a degree of cohesion. The same applies to the Kuwaiti *diwaniyya* and, while the mushrooming of cafés as many have observed are catered for the younger generation, this new trend is unable to reproduce the family factor. The practice as a traditional male preserve remains imperfect, but access to the *diwaniyya* has widened over the years to include both youth and women—two groups that negotiate the space differently.

Notes

1 The plural form of "*diwaniyya*," orthographically and colloquially, is known as the "*diwawin*" (plr.). However, for consistency, "*diwaniyyas*" will be employed throughout this chapter.
2 *Diwaniyyas* are equally used for family occasions such as weddings and funerals.
3 The day and time of the week indicating the *diwaniyya*'s opening hours to receive guests during Ramadhan are transmitted in a list via local news outlets, for instance, *Al Qabas*.
4 The Constitution's Explanatory Memorandum (EM) specifically describes Kuwait's governance as one that "will not lose its popular character in the parliamentary over-

sight or defy the traditional heritage of *Shura* (consultation)." AlTerkait's (2017) thesis expertly identifies traditional and modern elements in the Kuwaiti Constitution.

5 A reference to the Kuwaiti Constitution may be found at: www.wipo.int/edocs/lexdocs/laws/en/kw/kw004en.pdf.

6 This detail forms part of the author's research notes in a 2017 visit to Kuwait.

7 Crystal (1990: 47–55) provides a very comprehensive account of the 1938 episode that left an indelible imprint on the politics of Kuwait. A detailed account of the reforms sought can be found in IOR:R/15/5/468, File 45/23 I (D 140): Kuwait Reforms, which is also available online at: https://www.qdl.qa/en/archive/81055/vdc_100000000193.0x0001b9. An overview of the majlis movement is also found on: https://www.qdl.qa/en/kuwait%E2%80%99s-majlis-movement-national-and-regional-developments-brought-focus.

8 To understand how the Gulf region underwent a transition from being under British protection to an American one, see Macris (2010). For a more Kuwait-focused study, refer to Joyce (2014).

9 This anecdote was recounted by Ali al-Shamlan (2013), the former Minister of Higher Education, in an interview with the author. The cabinet minister in this example was Al-Shamlan himself.

References

Primary Sources

1.1 Interviews

Al-Alowaish, Ahmad. Interview by author, Kuwait City, September 14, 2016.

Al-Awadhi, Hesham. Interview by author, Salmiya, May 7, 2013.

Al-Duwaisan, Khaled. Interview by author, London, March 6, 2017.

Al-Khonaini, Abdullah. Zoom interview with author, September 6, 2022.

Al-Sabah, Mohammed Sabah al-Salem. Interview by author, Kuwait City, September 29, 2016.

Al-Sebeeh, Nasser. Interview by author, Kuwait City, April 16, 2023.

Al-Shamlan, Ali Abdallah. Interview by author, Surra, April 11, 2017.

Alsharekh, Alanoud. Interview by author, Khaldiyah, April 3, 2017.

Bertrand-Galli, Véronique. Interview by author, Kuwait City, May 16, 2018.

Budie Razak, Tatang. Interview by author, Daiya, April 11, 2017.

Fee, Charles. Interview by author, Salmiya, September 21, 2017.

Lodge, Matthew. Interview by author, Kuwait City, September 25, 2016.

Silliman, Doug. Zoom interview with author, March 14, 2022.

1.2 Archival Documents

1.2.1 The National Archives (TNA), London, UK

FO 960 Indian Office and Foreign Office: Political Agency and Embassy, Kuwait FO 960/2/1013: J. Graham, *Meeting with Jasim Al-Qitami*, 28 November 1967

1.2.2 Rush, A.D.L. (ed.), 1989. Records of Kuwait 1899–1961: Internal Affairs 1, Slough: Archive Editions.

Knox, S., 1906. *Bushire enclosing notes of Political Agent's tour in March 1906 of Southern Kuwait, 28 March,* pp. 29–30.

66 *Clemens Chay*

1.2.3 Rush, A.D.L. ed., 1989. Records of Kuwait 1899–1961: Internal Affairs 3, Slough: Archive Editions.

Southwell, C.A.P., 1955. *Kuwait Oil Company to Mr L A C Fry, Foreign Office, with enclosures, 21 February*, pp. 143–159.

1.2.4 Middle East Centre Archives, St. Anthony's College, Oxford University, UK

GB165-0085: Lt Colonel Harold Dickson collection (HRP Dickson Box 4).
GB165-0594: Valerie Nelson collection.

1.2.5 Qatar Digital Library (QDL)

File 45/23 I (D 140): Kuwait Reforms, 1938. ww.qdl.qa/en/archive/81055/vdc_100000000 193.0x0001b9.

1.2.6 Film

Bas ya Bahar, 1972. Directed by Khalid Al-Siddiq. Kuwait: State of Kuwait.

1.2.7 US Government Cables

Howell, Nathaniel. The Merchant Families Lose Ground to the Al-Sabah. *WikiLeaks*, August 1, 1989. https://wikileaks.org/plusd/cables/89KUWAIT3922_a.html.
US Embassy in Kuwait, 2005. *The Diwaniyya: A Defining Element of Kuwaiti Culture*, July 18. https://wikileaks.org/plusd/cables/05KUWAIT3178_a.html.

1.3 Publications

Bourisly, K.H. (2009). *Shipmasters of Kuwait: 1613 to 1962*. Kuwait (s.n.).
Raswan, C.R. (1935). *The Black Tents of Arabia: My Life Among the Bedouins*. Hutchinson.
Al-Mubaraki, Y. (2008). *Hin Isti'ad al-Sha'b al-Kuwayty Dusturahu: Waqa'i wa Watha'iq Diwawin al-Ithnayn 1990–1986 [Facts and Documentation of the Monday Diwaniyyas 1986–1990]*. Kuwait National Bookshop.

Secondary Sources

Abu-Hakima, A. M. (1983). *The modern history of Kuwait (1750–1965)*. Luzac and Company.
Ágoston, G., & Masters, B. (2009). *Encyclopedia of the Ottoman Empire*. Facts on File Inc.
Al-Abdulhadi, K. (2023). *Diwaniyas: The differences between hadhar and bedu*. https://www.kuwaittimes.com/diwaniyas-the-differences-between-hadhar-and-bedu/
Albloshi, H., & Alfahad, F. (2009). The orange movement of Kuwait: Civic pressure supports a political system. In M. Stepha (Ed.), *Civilian jihad: Nonviolent struggle, democratization, and governance in the Middle East* (pp. 219–232). Springer.
Alhajeri, A. M. (2014). Dīwānīyah. In E. Shahin (Ed.), *The Oxford Encyclopedia of Islam and politics* (pp. 268–269). Oxford University Press.
Al-Haroun, Y. A., & Alajmi, M. (2018). Understandings into socio-cultural spaces between the Hadhar and Badu House in Kuwait. *International Journal of Architectural Research*, *12*(3), 68–89.

From Grassroots to Public Diplomacy   67

Alnajjar, G. (2000). The challenges facing Kuwaiti democracy. *Middle East Journal, 54*(2), 242–258.

Al-Nakib, F. (2014). Revisiting http://example.com?id=journal"searchen housing, and the construction of a dichotomy. *International Journal of Middle East Studies, 46*(01), 5–30.

Al-Nakib, F. (2016). *Kuwait transformed: A history of oil and urban life*. Stanford University Press.

Al-Khatib, A., 2007. Al-Duktur Ahmad al-Khatib yatadhakkir: al-Kuwayt min al-Imara ila al-Dawla [Memoirs of Dr Ahmad al-Khatib: Kuwait from Emirate to State]. G. Alnajjar, ed., Casablanca: al-Markaz al-Thaqafi al-Arabi.

Al-Qanai, Y. ibn 'Isa. (1957). *Safahat min al-Tarikh al-Kuwayt [Pages from the History of Kuwait]*, 5th ed. Dhat al-Salasil.

Al-Rashoud, T. (2019). From Muscat to the Maghreb: Pan-Arab networks, anti-colonial groups, and Kuwait's Arab scholarships (1953–1961). *International Journal of Archaeology and Social Sciences in the Arabian Peninsula, 12*, 1–31.

Al-Rumaihi, A.H., 1987. Political Reform Movements in the History of Kuwait, In: BRISMES 253 (British Society for Middle Eastern Studies), 37th BRISMES Annual Conference. 12-15 July.

Al-Sejari, M. M., & al-Kandari, Y. Y. (2022). A changing in social lifestyle for men during the COVID-19 lockdown and its relationship to mental health: Kuwaiti Diwaniyyah as an example. *American Journal of Men's Health, 16*(2), 1–9.

AlTerkait, T. (2017). *The constitutional and conceptual underpinnings of Kuwait's system of government* [PhD Thesis]. Durham University.

Arendt, H. (1958). *The human condition*. Chicago University Press.

Arendt, H. (1972). *Crises of the republic*. Harcourt Brace Jovanovich.

Berridge, G. R. (2002). *Diplomacy: Theory and practice*, 2nd ed. Palgrave.

Bourdieu, P. (1986). The forms of capital. In J. G. Richardson (Ed.), *Handbook of theory and research for the sociology of education* (pp. 241–258). Greenwood Press.

Bourdieu, P. (1996). On the family as a realized category. *Theory, Culture and Society, 13*(3), 19–26.

Chay, C. (2016). The Dīwāniyya tradition in modern Kuwait: An interlinked space and practice. *Journal of Arabian Studies, 6*(1), 1–28.

Chay, C. (2020). Parliamentary politics in Kuwait. In M. Kamrava (Ed.), *The Routledge handbook of Persian Gulf politics* (pp. 327–345). Routledge.

Copeland, D. C. (2000). The constructivist challenge to structural realism: A review essay. *International Security, 25*(2), 187–212.

Crystal, J. (1990). *Oil and politics in the gulf: Rulers and merchants in Kuwait and Qatar*. Cambridge University Press.

Cull, N. (2006). *"Public diplomacy" before Gullion: The evolution of a phrase*. http://uscpublicdiplomacy.org/blog/060418_public_diplomacy_before_gullion_the_evolution_of_a_phrase

Fletcher, R. S. (2015). *British imperialism and "the tribal question": Desert administration and nomadic societies in the Middle East, 1919–1936*. Oxford University Press.

Gomes, A., Al-Ragam, A., & Alshalfan, S. (2020). *Reflections on COVID-19 and public space use in Kuwait: The potential of a new 'normal'*. https://blogs.lse.ac.uk/mec/2020/05/06/reflections-on-covid-19-and-public-space-use-in-kuwait-the-potential-of-a-new-normal/

Habermas, J. (1974). The public sphere: An encyclopedia article. *New German Critique, 3*, 43–55.

Hamilton, K., & Langhorne, R. (2011). *The practice of diplomacy: Its evolution, theory and administration*, 2nd ed. Routledge.

Harold Nicolson, *Diplomacy* (London, 1939), subsequently revised in 1950 and again in 1963, and reprinted by the Institute for the Study of Diplomacy, Washington DC, in 1988.

Herb, M. (1999). *All in the family: Absolutism, revolution, and democracy in the Middle Eastern monarchies*. State University of New York Press.

68 Clemens Chay

Herb, M. (2014). *The wages of oil: Parliaments and economic development in Kuwait and the UAE.* Cornell University Press.

Joyce, M. (2014). *Kuwait, 1945–1996: An Anglo-American perspective.* Taylor & Francis.

Kapiszewski, A. (2006). Elections and parliamentary activity in the GCC states: Broadening political participation in the gulf monarchies. In A. Khlaf & G. Luciani (Eds.), *Constitutional reform and political participation in the gulf* (pp. 88–131). Gulf Research Center.

Kha'zal, S. H. K. (1962). *Tarikh al-Kuwayt al-siyasi [the political history of Kuwait] vol. 1.* Dar al-Hilal.

Knox, S., 1906. *Bushire enclosing notes of Political Agent's tour in March 1906 of Southern Kuwait, 28 March,* pp. 29–30.

Kuwait Times. (2021). *Monster jams amid chaotic start to curfew.* https://www.kuwaittimes .com/monster-traffic-jams-amid-chaotic-start-to-curfew/

Kuwait Times. (2022). *Many Arrested for Taking Part in Banned Tribal Primary Elections.* https://www.kuwaittimes.com/many-arrested-for-taking-part-in-banned-tribal-primary -elections/

Kuwaiti Constitution. (1962, November). www.wipo.int/edocs/lexdocs/laws/en/kw/ kw004en.pdf

Lefebvre, H. (1991). *The production of space,* D. Nicholson-Smith (trans.). Basil Blackwell Ltd.

Longva, A. N. (2006). Nationalism in pre-modern guise: The discourse on hadhar and Badu in Kuwait. *International Journal of Middle East Studies, 38*(2), 171–187.

Macris, J. (2010). *The politics and security of the gulf: Anglo-American hegemony and the shaping of a region.* Routledge.

Mumford, L. (1937). Architectural reader. In L. Richard & F. Stout (Eds.), *The City reader* (pp. 85–89). Routledge.

Neumann, I. B. (2005). To be a diplomat. *International Studies Perspectives, 6*(1), 72–93.

Nicolson, H. (1961). Diplomacy then and now. *Foreign Affairs, 11*(1), 39–49.

Norton, A. R. (1993). The future of civil society in the Middle East. *Middle East Journal, 47*(2), 205–216.

Otte, T. G. (2001). Nicolson. In G. R. Berridge, M. Keens-Soper & T. G. Otte (Eds.), *Diplomatic theory from Machiavelli to Kissinger* (pp. 151–180). Palgrave Macmillan.

Pamment, J., 2014. Articulating influence: Toward a research agenda for interpreting the evaluation of soft power, public diplomacy and nation brands. Public Relations Review, 40(1), pp. 50–59.

Rabi, U. (2000). The Kuwaiti royal family in the postliberation period: Reinstitutionalizing the "first among equals" system in Kuwait. In J. Kostiner (Ed.), *Middle East monarchies: The challenge of modernity* (pp. 151–166). Lynne Rienner Publications.

Raswan, C.R., 1935. The Black Tents of Arabia: My Life Among the Bedouins, London: Hutchinson.

Scarce, J. M. (1985). *The evolving culture of Kuwait.* Stationery Office Books.

Smith, S. C. (1999). *Kuwait, 1950–1965: Britain, the Al-Sabah, and oil.* Oxford University Press.

Snow, N. (2009). Rethinking public diplomacy. In N. Snow & P. M. Taylor (Eds.), *The Routledge handbook of public diplomacy* (pp. 3–11). Routledge.

Tétreault, M. A. (1993). Civil society in Kuwait: Protected spaces and women's rights. *Middle East Journal, 47*(2), 275–291.

Tétreault, M. A. (2000). *Stories of democracy.* Columbia University Press.

Tétreault, M. A. (2011). Bottom-up democratization in Kuwait. In M. A. Tétreault, G. Okruhlik & A. Kapiszewski (Eds.), *Political change in the Arab Gulf states: Stuck in transition* (pp. 73–98). Lynne Rienner Publications.

5   Kuwait's Foreign Aid
Motivations and Allocations

Mohammad Yaghi

Introduction

Since gaining independence in 1961, Kuwait has been preoccupied with survival, recognizing early on the significance of foreign aid as a tool for shaping Arab and international support. Determining the precise amount of foreign aid disbursed by Kuwait since its independence poses challenges due to the multitude of agencies involved and certain undocumented transactions. However, by drawing upon data from the Kuwait Fund for Arab Economic Development (KFAED) and the Financial Track Service of the United Nations Office for the Coordination of Humanitarian Affairs (UNOCHA), it can be reasonably affirmed that Kuwait has committed a substantial sum of funds to further its foreign policy objectives. For instance, the KFAED reports that Kuwait has extended loans totalling $21.9 billion from 1961 to 2022, while UNOCHA's records show that Kuwait has allocated $2.7 billion in humanitarian assistance between 2003 and 2022.

This chapter delves into an exploration of the motivations behind and allocation patterns of Kuwait's foreign aid. It posits that Kuwait's domestic politics and security considerations have significantly influenced its foreign aid policies since the country's inception. The chapter commences by providing a theoretical foundation for understanding the interplay between foreign aid and foreign policy objectives, asserting that these two facets are inseparable. Furthermore, it contends that small affluent states lacking military capabilities can wield their financial resources to deter threats by cultivating influential and crucial alliances. Subsequently, the chapter outlines the determinants that have guided Kuwait's foreign aid decisions, maintaining that domestic politics and survival strategies have been instrumental in shaping the nation's foreign aid policies since its independence. It then offers a concise overview of the diverse agencies employed by Kuwait to channel its foreign aid.

Following this, the chapter employs data from sources such as KFAED, the United Nations Relief and Works Agency (UNRWA), and the Financial Track Service of UNOCHA to analyse and elucidate discernible patterns in Kuwait's foreign aid. The section prior to the conclusion is dedicated to examining Kuwait's foreign aid during critical junctures. It argues that Kuwait has judiciously utilized its financial assets to safeguard against perceived threats emanating from Iraq and Iran, as well as to forestall the spread of the 2011 Arab uprisings into the Gulf

DOI: 10.4324/9781003435259-5

70 *Mohammad Yaghi*

region. In conclusion, the chapter offers a summary of its findings, encapsulating the intricate relationship between Kuwait's foreign aid and its foreign policy objectives, all underscored by the imperatives of domestic politics and national security.

The Intersection of Foreign Aid and Foreign Policy

Foreign aid encompasses the transfer of money, goods, or technical assistance from affluent and technologically advanced nations to support the development and humanitarian needs of developing states. These aids can manifest in various forms, such as grants, credits, loans, or technical cooperation (Goldstein & Pevehouse, 2002, pp. 295–296). It is crucial to recognize that foreign aid is inextricably linked to foreign policy objectives. Given that a country's foreign policy aims to influence other nations' actions, it relies on two primary approaches: Coercion through force and attraction through incentives. The use of force is not only costly, both politically and economically, but also necessitates military superiority over adversaries. In contrast, enticement through foreign aid serves as a tool employed by policymakers to achieve their overarching goal of pacifying, strengthening, protecting, or reshaping specific countries without resorting to violence (Taffet, 2012, p. 2). It's noteworthy that even small, affluent countries lacking military capabilities can wield foreign aid effectively.

As a foreign policy instrument, economic cooperation in the form of state-to-state aid has long been employed by prosperous, technologically advanced nations to project their influence and further their political and economic interests (Bindra, 2018). Foreign aid, comprising material goods or services controlled by donors, has been common practice since the onset of the Cold War following WWII (Hattori, 2001). Various scholars have investigated the impact of foreign aid on recipient countries from the perspectives of their respective international relations paradigms. For realists, foreign aid functions as a foreign policy tool designed to influence the political behaviour of recipient nations (Hook, 1995; McKinlay & Mughan, 1984). Liberals, on the other hand, argue that foreign aid promotes the socioeconomic and political development of recipient countries (Lumsdaine, 1993; Riddell, 1996). Conversely, some contend that foreign aid can impede the development trajectory of recipient nations (Wood, 1986).

While foreign aid as a foreign policy tool has existed over time, its institutionalization began with the creation of the Bretton Woods institutions—the World Bank and the International Monetary Fund—following WWII. Further institutionalization occurred when the Organisation for Economic Co-operation and Development (OECD) established the Development Assistance Committee (DAC) in 1960, charging it with the mandate to "assist countries and areas in the process of economic development" (OECD, 2006, p. 7). The rise of the US and the former Soviet Union as post-WWII victors, along with their competition for allies, global influence, and ideological supremacy at a time when European states were grappling with physical and economic devastation, solidified foreign aid as a reliable tool for enticing nations to align with one of the two superpowers. Notably, the Marshall Plan in 1947, involving an expenditure exceeding $17 billion to assist Western

European nations in their development, exemplified such an instrument employed to attract these countries to align with the US (Taffet, 2012, p. 3).

Even small, wealthy states lacking military might can employ their financial resources to deter threats and secure alliances. Kuwait stands as an early exemplar of this strategy. Despite being a developing nation, upon gaining independence in 1961, Kuwait possessed significant financial resources. The discovery of oil in 1938 allowed Kuwait to generate £90 million in the early 1950s (Marlowe, 1962). This revenue surged to $300 million in the mid-1950s (and further increased to $800 million by the late 1960s), at a time when Kuwait's population numbered less than 200,000, making it the world's highest per capita income nation for several years. In 1960, Kuwait held 15 per cent of the world's proven oil reserves and was exporting 80 million tons of oil annually, with Kuwait receiving half of the profits (Nath, 1972, p. 342). Approximately 40–50 per cent of its oil income was channelled into savings during the 1959–1968 decade, with half being utilized for domestic development and the remainder sent abroad, contributing to government reserves, commercial bank deposits, and private investors' holdings. As a city-state with limited opportunities for domestic investment, Kuwait's capital exports reached $300 million in 1967–1968 (Ibid., p. 343). In fact, Kuwait's investments in Britain in the early 1960s reached £100 million annually (Bishku, 1991, p. 81).

Kuwait's abundant financial resources enabled it, from the outset of independence, to utilize foreign aid as a means to further its interests. However, the allocation of this aid was closely intertwined with its domestic politics and survival strategies, as explored in the following section.

Determinants of Kuwait's Foreign Aid Policy

Kuwait's foreign policy is rooted in three fundamental imperatives, as articulated by Abdul-Reda Assiri (1990, pp. xiv–xv): The promotion of Arabic ideology and Islamic values, the imperative of political and security survival, and the aspiration to "invest and share the nation's wealth with less fortunate Arab and Muslim countries." Consequently, Kuwait has endeavoured to position itself "toward the center of ideological cleavages within the Arab World" and has employed "dinar diplomacy" to uphold this stance. Additional insights from political analysts, such as Theodore Karasik and Tristan Ober (May 21, 2019), contend that Kuwait "strives to maintain relative neutrality on most regional affairs" while prioritizing a foreign policy rooted in multilateralism, diplomacy, and collaboration with its closest Arab/Islamic allies and Western partners. Istiqlal Alazimi (2022) posits that Kuwait's foreign policy is geared towards preserving the cohesion of its population and ensuring security by cultivating friendships, addressing challenges, and maintaining a neutral stance.

Nevertheless, despite the emphasis on Kuwait's foreign policy neutrality by certain scholars, Kuwait's historical record reveals a maverick foreign policy that oscillates between a balance of power and neutrality, contingent upon the imperatives of its survival as a vulnerable state (Ahrari, 1993). Building upon the perspectives of these scholars, it can be argued that domestic politics and security

72 Mohammad Yaghi

considerations have been pivotal factors shaping Kuwait's foreign policies since its independence, including its approach to foreign aid.

Domestic Factors

While the revenue generated from oil, commencing in 1938, liberated the Kuwaiti ruling family from their historical reliance on merchant families, who had hitherto derived their income from the pearl industry (Crystal, 1990), Kuwait's political trajectory within the Arab Gulf region unfolds as a distinctive narrative. The origins of Kuwait's political system can be traced back to the late 18th century when merchant families elected Sheikh Abdullah al-Sabah as the emir, entrusting him with safeguarding the city's interests. In this context, the emir consolidated his authority within a framework of consultation (Shura) and consent.

This political system underwent significant development in the early 20th century with the introduction of the first constitutional document. This document asserted the community's right to address succession crises within the Sabah family and established the concept of electing a Shura Council. Although the first elections did not occur until 1938, a new Constitution was drafted the same year, proclaiming that "the people [of Kuwait] are the source of all authorities," and that the "National Assembly alone possesses the right to legislate." Kuwait's present political framework is rooted in the 1962 Constitution, which vests sovereignty in the Kuwaiti people, enabling them to elect their representatives to the parliament (Majlis) through regular and free elections. The Constitution additionally endows the parliament with significant authority, granting it the prerogative to approve the heir to the throne, nominated by the Emir, as a prerequisite for ascending to the position of Emir. It bestows the parliament with the right to interrogate all ministers, including the prime minister, and to remove them from office through parliamentary votes. Furthermore, all legislative acts necessitate approval from both the parliament and the Emir (Salem, 2007, pp. 1–4). Finally, the Constitution confers greater influence upon parliament members in managing the state's expenditures. Notably, the ruling family in Kuwait receives a set of annual allowances totalling KD50 million (Nath, 1972), distinct from ownership of the oil revenue.

Given the substantial powers vested in the parliament, domestic politics in Kuwait plays a pivotal role in determining the allocation of foreign aid. As we shall explore below, the advocacy of pan-Arab and Islamic values during specific time periods predominantly reflects the orientations of domestic forces that influence Kuwaiti public opinion and the composition of the parliament.

Survival

In addition to domestic politics, the survival of Kuwait as a sovereign state played a pivotal role in determining the allocation of its foreign aid. Situated amidst three influential regional powers—Iran, Iraq, and Saudi Arabia—each with whom Kuwait either had border disputes or ideological concerns, safeguarding its survival emerged as a paramount concern for the country's leadership. Notably, Kuwait's

Kuwait's Foreign Aid 73

relations with Iraq have consistently been a source of considerable unease, as Iraq has never genuinely recognized Kuwait's sovereignty. Several events reflecting Iraq's stance towards Kuwait have significantly shaped the trajectory of Kuwaiti–Iraqi relations, influencing the national attitudes, sentiments, and trust between the two parties and, by extension, Kuwait's foreign aid policies (Assiri, 1990, p. 10).

In brief, since Iraq's independence in 1932, successive Iraqi rulers have laid claim to Kuwait, asserting that it was historically part of Iraq, administered by the governor of Basra during the Ottoman era (Bishku, 1991). Despite the 1922 conference at Uqair in Eastern Arabia, convened by Britain and attended by representatives from Najd, Iraq, and Kuwait to delineate their territorial boundaries, it was Sir Percy Cox, the British High Commissioner in Baghdad, who ultimately demarcated the borders, allotting Iraq a mere 25-mile coastline along the Arabian Gulf. This decision engendered enduring grievances in Iraq that were never reconciled (Bishku, 1991, p. 79).

In 1932, King Ghazi of Iraq initiated a public campaign advocating for the annexation of Kuwait, which persisted until his demise in 1939 (Elliot, 1996). Furthermore, a week following Kuwait's declaration of independence on June 19, 1961, Iraq's President Abdelkarim Qasim asserted his nation's claim over Kuwait during a press conference, proclaiming that "Kuwait is an integral part of Iraq" and announcing his intention to issue a presidential decree designating the Emir of Kuwait as "the Prefect of the Kuwait district of the Basra Liwa" (Assiri, 1990, p. 19). In 1969, Iraq's troops crossed into nearby Kuwaiti territory, occupying an area of approximately one square mile as a precautionary measure to safeguard the Um Qasr port, following the deterioration of relations with Iran. They withdrew only after eight years (Bishku, 1991, p. 87). Ultimately, Iraq realized its threat to Kuwait and invaded in 1990. From 1961 until the occupation in 1990, Kuwait's foreign aid policies were profoundly influenced by the imperative to shield itself from the looming Iraqi threat. Subsequent to Kuwait's liberation in 1991, the nation leveraged its financial resources to reward Arab countries that supported it and to penalize those that aligned with Iraq.

Sources of Kuwait's Foreign Aid

The challenge of survival has compelled Kuwait, since gaining independence, to engage in what the Kuwaiti scholar Abdel-Reda Assiri aptly termed "dinar diplomacy." This involves using its considerable financial resources to advance its foreign policy objectives. However, owing to the multitude of channels through which Kuwait disburses funds to recipients, determining the precise amount of financial aid and the number of recipients can be a daunting task. A study conducted by Sarah Alzaid in 2012 on Kuwait's foreign aid identified 16 foreign aid-providing agencies, including the Ministry of Finance, the Kuwait Fund for Arab Economic Development (KFAED), Zakat House, Kuwait Finance House, Kuwait Real Estate Investment Consortium, Social Reform Society, International Islamic Charitable Organization, Alnajat Charity Association, Kuwait Society for Relief, Direct Aid

74   *Mohammad Yaghi*

(formerly known as African Muslims Committee), Society for the Revival of Islamic Heritage, and Sheikh Abdullah Nouri Charity.

Moreover, Kuwait joined the OCED–DAC in 2018 (OCED, Kuwait, n.d.), rendering the data available on the DAC website insufficient for tracking the country's foreign aid activities. Nevertheless, relying on figures from KFAED and UNOCHA (as elaborated below), it is safe to assert that Kuwait has contributed a substantial amount of funds to further its foreign policy objectives. For instance, data from KFAED indicates that Kuwait has extended loans totalling $21.9 billion from 1961 to 2022, while the UNOCHA website indicates that Kuwait has provided $2.7 billion in humanitarian assistance between 2003 and 2022.

Furthermore, Kuwait's Official Development Assistance to Gross National Income (ODA/GNI) ratio reached 0.87 per cent in 2016, surpassing the United Nations' target of 0.7 per cent (OECD Library, 2018: 419). In fact, OCED–DAC reports spanning from 2013 to 2020 reveal that Kuwait's average ODA/GNI ratio during this period was 0.35 per cent, exceeding the 0.31 per cent average of OCED countries. However, these figures do not accurately reflect the actual magnitude of Kuwait's foreign aid, as a substantial portion of it went unreported.

The subsequent sections of this chapter will utilize data from KFAED, UNOCHA, international media sources, and scholarly writings to discern patterns in Kuwait's foreign aid policies and elucidate how Kuwait leveraged its financial resources during critical junctures, such as Iraq's invasion of Kuwait in 1990 and the Arab Protests of 2011.

Patterns in Kuwait Foreign Aid

Data from KFAED and UNOCHA unequivocally demonstrate Kuwait's strategic utilization of its financial assets to cultivate regional and international alliances, with a primary focus on garnering political backing for its own survival. Kuwait has also judiciously directed its funds towards underpinning the resolutions of Arab Leaders' Summits, facilitating the reconstruction of Arab nations affected by conflicts with Israel, and providing support to the Palestinian cause. Furthermore, Kuwait has been actively engaged in positioning itself as a humanitarian leader, a move designed to bolster its standing in international politics. While the data underscores that a substantial portion of Kuwait's foreign aid has been channeled to Arab and Islamic states, it is noteworthy that numerous other developing nations across the globe have also benefited from Kuwait's largesse.

Gaining Regional and International Allies

As previously elucidated, Kuwait faced a critical survival challenge immediately following its independence in 1961, as Iraq laid claim to Kuwait's territories and amassed troops for a potential occupation. Despite having the option to invoke a friendship treaty with Britain for protection, Kuwait preferred to address the issue within the framework of the Arab League (Assiri, 1990, p. 22). Egypt's Nasser regime played a pivotal role in securing recognition and Kuwait's admission into the Arab League, offering protection against Iraq. However, Nasser imposed two conditions: The withdrawal of British troops from Kuwait and Kuwait's commitment to sharing its wealth with other Arab nations (Assiri, 1990, p. 23). It was within this context that Kuwait recognized the strategic value of "dinar diplomacy" as a tool in its foreign policy arsenal. As a "price for Arab protection," Kuwait established the Kuwait Fund for Arab Economic Development (KAFED) in 1961, initially endowed with $140 million (Assiri, 1990, p. 26). While initially focused on Arab countries, KAFED expanded its mandate to encompass all developing countries, aiming to cultivate allies on a global scale.

During the 1960s, the influence of the pan-Arab movement held sway both in Kuwait and across the Arab region. In Kuwait, adherents of Arab nationalism dominated the parliament (Zahlan, 2016, p. 40), while Nasser's pan-Arab regime enjoyed widespread support from the populations of various Arab countries (Zahlan, 2016, p. 37). In this context, KAFED's mission was primarily geared towards supporting Arab nations in their pursuit of social and economic development. However, Kuwait altered KAFED's mandate in 1974, extending it to non-Arab countries, partly due to the waning influence of Nasser's regime following its defeat in the 1967 war with Israel, which eroded the pan-Arab movement's strength in both Kuwait and the broader Arab region. Additionally, this shift was influenced by the rise of Islamist movements within Kuwait and accusations by Western countries that the surge in oil prices after the 1973 Arab–Israeli War hindered the economic development of developing nations. Consequently, Kuwait amended the legislation governing KAFED's operations, both in terms of funding size and geographical scope. Funding increased from $680 million in the 1960s to $3,400 million in 1974, with coverage expanded to include all other developing nations. By 1981, KAFED's capital had further increased to $6,800 million, reflecting both heightened demand for project financing and Kuwait's accumulation of wealth from the soaring oil prices during the 1970s (KFAED, September 30, 2022, p. 2).

KAFED offers loans, technical assistance, and grants, and manages urgent grants provided by the Kuwaiti government to finance projects such as housing, schools, hospitals, and other essential infrastructure in emergency situations, including natural disasters. Initially, KAFED focused on financing projects in agriculture, transportation, communication, energy, industry, water, and sewage. However, post-2001, it expanded its portfolio to include projects related to health and education to align with the Millennium Development Goals (MDGs) (KFAED, September 30, 2022, p. 2).

As of 2022, KAFED had disbursed loans amounting to "$21.9 billion, benefiting 105 countries, including 16 Arab countries; 41 African countries; 19 countries in East, South Asia, and the Pacific; 17 countries in Central Asia and Europe; and 12 countries in Latin America and the Caribbean region." Additionally, KAFED provided $1,187 million in technical assistance and grants (KFAED, September 30, 2022, p. 3). Concerning government grants, KAFED managed $6,891 million, benefiting "16 Arab countries, 20 African countries, two Central Asian and European Countries, four South East Asian and Pacific countries, and one country in Latin America and the Caribbean region, and two institutions" (KFAED, September 30, 2022, p. 4).

76 Mohammad Yaghi

Table 5.1 Distribution of loans and grants from 1961 until September 2022

Countries	Loans in US$ (Million)	Grants in US$ (Million)
Arab countries	12,359	6,717
Central, Asia, and Europe Countries	1,265	17
Central, South, and East African Countries	1,482	19
West African Countries	2,462	99
East, South Asia, and the Pacific Countries	3,568	32
Latin America and the Caribbean Countries	744	8
Institutions	112	
Total	**21,992**	**6,891**

Source: KFAED publications. Loans, Grants and Technical Assistance for Arab Countries, 30 September 2022. https://bit.ly/4490idn

While the KAFED data (refer to Table 5.1) illustrates that all grants and over half of the loans were directed towards Arab countries, the remaining funds reached recipients spanning five continents, underscoring Kuwait's endeavour to cultivate friends and allies on a global scale. This strategic approach yielded significant dividends in 1990 when Iraq invaded Kuwait, as 19 out of the 39 states that deployed troops to liberate Kuwait were recipients of Kuwait's foreign aid (CNN Editorial Research, July 24, 2022) (Table 5.1).

The data also underscore Kuwait's distinct focus on providing assistance to Islamic states, driven in part by its own national identity as an Islamic state and in part by the growing influence of Islamists in Kuwait's political landscape since the 1970s. As displayed in Table 5.2, Kuwait directed a substantial amount of aid to Muslim countries, with $3,779 million in loans, $57 million in technical assistance and grants, and $117 million in government grants allocated between 1974 and 2019. It is worth noting that these figures do not encompass aid extended to Muslim states in Europe and the former Soviet Union (Table 5.2).

Support for Arab countries

Scholars have asserted that Gulf aid serves various purposes, including supporting shared foreign policies arising from Arab leaders' summits, rewarding allies in military conflicts, forging strategic alliances, and stabilizing Arab countries with similar political orientations as Gulf States' regimes (Young, 2017; Villanger, 2007; Momani & Enis, 2012; Cochrane, 2021; Kibria et al., 2021). The KFAED data substantiate this argument.

As depicted in Table 5.3, Egypt, Syria, Lebanon, and Jordan have been the primary recipients of funds disbursed by the KFAED. These countries collectively received $8,504 million out of the $20,536 million allocated by the KFAED in loans, technical assistance, and government grants between 1961 and 2022, constituting

Table 5.2 KFAED fund to Islamic countries

Countries	Loans in US$ Million	Tech. Assistance and Grants in US$ Million	Government Grants in US$ Million
Afghanistan	29	31	10
Bangladesh	657	1	10
Indonesia	201		
Malaysia	53		
Maldives	147	5	2
Pakistan	441		
Papua New Guinea	10		
Mozambique	87	2	6
Uganda	87	1	7
Benin	146	1	5
Burkina Faso	226	1	12
Cameroon	107		
Chad	112	1	7
Gambia	152	3	3
Guinea	216	3	4
Guinea-Bissau	42		7
Mali	204	1	23
Niger	127	4	5
Senegal	487	2	10
Sierra Leone	130		3
Togo	118	1	3
Total	**3779**	**57**	**117**

Source: Gathered by the author from KFAED publications. https://bit.ly/3oU8vSs

nearly 41 per cent of the total funds. This is partly attributed to these states being designated as "frontier states" in the confrontation with Israel during the September 1967 Arab Summit in Khartoum, following the 1967 war. This designation aligns with Article 4 of the Khartoum Summit's resolutions, which emphasized that the Arab Gulf States would actively support the efforts of those Arab states affected by aggression and resource loss, assisting them in overcoming the consequences of such aggression. Furthermore, Article 5 of the summit approved Kuwait's proposal to establish an Arab Economic and Social Development Fund based on the recommendations of the Baghdad conference of Arab Ministers of Finance, Economy, and Oil (Arab Summit, September 1, 1967).

The commitment to adhere to the decisions of Arab summits is also evident in Kuwait's decision to suspend its financial support to Egypt after Egypt's signing of the Camp David peace treaty with Israel in 1978. Records from the KFAED show that between 1978 and 1988, KFAED refrained from providing any financial assistance to Egypt, in alignment with the Arab Summit's resolutions in Baghdad. These resolutions included freezing Egypt's membership in the Arab League, relocating the Arab League's headquarters from Egypt to Tunisia, and refraining

78 *Mohammad Yaghi*

from providing economic or financial assistance from Arab funds, banks, and other financial institutions associated with the Arab League and joint Arab cooperation (Lavy, 1984).

Furthermore, it is evident that Kuwait has allocated a substantial portion of its funds to Arab regimes sharing similar political orientations. These regimes include monarchies situated in the Gulf region, such as Oman and Bahrain, as well as those espousing similar policies, such as Morocco and Jordan. As indicated in Table 5.3, these four countries collectively received $9,573 million, with a significant portion disbursed in 2012 following the 2011 Arab protests. Specifically, Bahrain, Jordan, Morocco, and Oman received grants amounting to $1,500, $1,250, $1,250, and $2,000 million, respectively, categorized under "support and implementation of development projects" in KFAED's publications.

Lastly, Table 5.3 highlights Kuwait's support for the reconstruction efforts in southern Lebanon following its liberation from Israeli occupation in 2000 and in the aftermath of the 2006 conflict between Israel and Hezbollah. Kuwait provided Lebanon with grants of $20 million and $311 million, respectively. Similar assistance was extended to Palestine, where Kuwait contributed $315 million and $200 million for the reconstruction of Gaza following the conflicts in 2008/9 and 2014 between the Palestinians and Israel.

Table 5.3 Distribution of funds and grants to Arab countries from 1961 to September 2022

Countries	Loans in US $ (Million)	Tech. Assistance and Grants in US $ (Million)	Government Grants in US $ (Million)	Total
Algeria	70	0	10	80
Bahrain	769	123	1500	2.392
Union of the Comoros	21	2	10	33
Djibouti	305	2	60	367
Egypt	3,533	13	15	3561
Iraq	96	0	302	398
Jordan	767	11	1,250	2,028
Lebanon	917	12	419	1,384
Mauritania	398	4	13	415
Morocco	1,288	4	1250	2,542
Oman	611	0	2,000	2,611
Palestine	0	230	315	545
Somalia	91	2	28	121
Sudan	1,017	1	57	1,075
Syria	1,065	380	86	1,531
Tunisia	904	1	0	905
Yemen	507	10	67	584
Total	**12,359**	**795**	**7,382**	**20,536**

Source: KFAED publications. Loans, Grants and Technical Assistance for Arab Countries, 30 September 2022. https://bit.ly/4490idn. The author gathered and sorted the data from the KFAED's publication.

Support for the Palestinians

The records from the KFAED do not encompass Kuwait's aid to the Palestinians beyond its assistance for Gaza's reconstruction, as mentioned earlier. However, historically, Kuwait was one of the most significant contributors to the Palestinians from 1961 until 1990 when Iraq occupied Kuwait. Following the occupation, Kuwait suspended its financial support to the Palestinians due to the Palestinian Liberation Organization's (PLO) stance regarding Iraq's invasion of Kuwait. At that time, the PLO neither condemned the Iraqi invasion nor supported the US-led military campaign to liberate Kuwait. Instead, the PLO sought an "Arab solution" to the crisis, as opposed to an international one (Al Jazeera, n.d).

Subsequently, records of the Palestinian Authority indicate that Kuwait halted its assistance to the Palestinians between 1990 and 2001. However, aid resumed in 2002 and continued thereafter. In addition to grants for Gaza's reconstruction, Kuwait provided the Palestinian Authority with $758 million between 2002 and 2022. Out of these funds, $483 million were allocated to support the PA budget (Palestine Economy, n.d).

Furthermore, records from the United Nations Relief and Works Agency for Palestinian Refugees in the Near East (UNRWA) spanning from 2006 to 2022 show that Kuwait extended support amounting to $211 million. This funding was provided by various Kuwaiti entities, including the Kuwait government, KFAED, Kuwait Red Crescent, Kuwait Zakat House, and Kuwait Patient Helping Fund (UNRWA, n.d). It is reasonable to assume that Kuwait contributed more funds to UNRWA, but the organization's website only displays contributions received since 2006.

Prior to 1990, Kuwait's government, according to Abdel-Reda Assiri (1990, p. 40), allocated $892 million to the PLO between 1961 and 1989. Additionally, Kuwait deducted 5 per cent from the salaries of Palestinians working in Kuwait starting in 1965 and channelled these deductions to the PLO. By 1989, the cumulative deducted amount was estimated to be $122.5 million.

This substantial support for the Palestinians prior to Iraq's invasion of Kuwait in 1990 not only underscores the Kuwaiti populace's consensus on backing the Palestinian cause but also reflects the influence Palestinians held in Kuwait. Following their expulsion or displacement during the 1948 Arab–Israeli War, Kuwait served as a major refuge for Palestinians. By 1989, nearly 400,000 Palestinians were residing in Kuwait, comprising almost 20 per cent of the total population of 2 million, with 700,000 being Kuwaiti nationals (Lesch, 1991).

Humanitarian Actor

Kuwait has also aimed to position itself as a regional hub for humanitarian aid and reconstruction, particularly after UN Secretary-General Ban Ki-moon designated the Emir of Kuwait as a "Humanitarian Leader" and Kuwait as an "international humanitarian center" in 2014 (Leichtman, 2017, p. 2). As depicted in Table 5.4, Kuwait's contributions to humanitarian causes were limited up until 2013,

80 Mohammad Yaghi

Table 5.4 Distribution of Kuwait's humanitarian assistance from 2013 to April 2023

Year	Amount in US$ Million	First 5 Beneficiaries	Notes
2003	27.7	Iraq and Afghanistan	99.3% Iraq
2004	11	Sudan and others	84.6% Sudan (emergency shelter)
2005	13.3	Not specified, Pakistan	26.5% Pakistan
2006	34.4	Lebanon, Iran, Palestine, not specified	87.8% Lebanon
2007	13.7	Bangladesh, Lebanon	73.1% Bangladesh
2008	95.6	Palestine, not specified, Myanmar, Albania, Iraq	83.5% Palestine (mostly through world bank)
2009	40.3	Palestine, not specified, Lebanon	84.8% Palestine (mostly through UNRWA)
2010	10.6	Pakistan, Haiti, Yemen, not specified	87.4% Pakistan (mostly through Pakistan government)
2011	13.6	Somalia, not specified	87.7% Somalia (mostly through Kuwait Red Crescent)
2012	11.5	Lebanon, not specified, Syria, Philippine, Jordan	45.4% Lebanon (mostly through Kuwait Red Crescent)
2013	323.6	Lebanon, Jordan, Syria, not specified, Turkey	26.7% Lebanon (mostly through UN High Commissioner for Refugees)
2014	351	Not specified, Syria, Jordan, Lebanon, Iraq	31% not specified (mostly through UN High Commissioner for Refugees)
2015	463.5	Not specified, Syria, Jordan, Lebanon, Iraq	28.2% not specified (mostly through UN High Commissioner for Refugees)
2016	308	Lebanon, not specified, Iraq, Yemen, Jordan	18.1% Lebanon (mostly through Lebanon government)
2017	162	Iraq, Turkey, Syria, Lebanon, Jordan	16.9% Iraq (mostly through Turkey government)
2018	446.5	Yemen, not specified, Syria, Iraq, Lebanon	70% Yemen (mostly through UN Children's Fund)
2019	178.2	Yemen, Syria, Iraq, Lebanon, not specified	66.8% Yemen (mostly through World Food Program)
2020	142.2	Not specified, Global, Lebanon, Iraq, Palestine	34.1% not specified (World Health Organization)
2021	1.6	South Sudan, Uganda, Sudan, Honduras, Mozambique	32.1% South Sudan (mostly through World Food Program)
2022	13.6	Afghanistan, Syria, Somalia, Palestine, Ukraine	43.1% Afghanistan (mostly through UN Children's Fund)
2023	100.5	Syria, Turkey, Afghanistan, not specified	48.6% Syria (mostly through UN Children's Fund)
Total	**2762.4**		

Source: UNOCHA Financial Tracking Service. https://bit.ly/3LiiZCG

totalling only $271.7 million between 2003 and 2012. However, starting in 2013, Kuwait significantly increased its humanitarian assistance, providing $2,490.7 million between 2013 and April 2023. A substantial portion of these funds was directed towards assisting Syrian refugees in Lebanon, Jordan, Turkey, and within Syria. Kuwait is recognized as "the largest non-Western donor and the fourth largest donor to [UN humanitarian efforts in Syria]" (Dickinson, December 16, 2013, p. 7). For instance, at the January 2013 UN donor conference on Syria, which Kuwait hosted, Kuwait pledged over $300 million in government grants, and independent Kuwaiti charities raised $183 million for humanitarian aid (The New Humanitarian, February 1, 2013). Between 2013 and 2016, Kuwait hosted three international donor conferences to support the Syrian people and co-chaired two donor conferences in London (2016) and Brussels (2017), contributing over $1.6 billion, which was distributed through regional and international agencies (KUNA, November 28, 2017).

In 2018 and 2019, Kuwait redirected its humanitarian assistance efforts towards Yemen, providing $431.5 million to international organizations involved in relief efforts out of the $624.7 million it contributed during those two years. These figures underscore Kuwait's commitment to supporting Saudi Arabia's policies in Yemen. In both Syria and Yemen, these funds were channelled to beneficiaries through international organizations such as the World Food Program, the UN High Commissioner for Refugees, and the UN Children's Fund (FTS, UNOCHA, n.d.).

As a regional hub for reconstruction, Kuwait played a significant role in February 2018 when it hosted and co-chaired a conference with the European Union aimed at rebuilding Iraq. The Islamic State (also known as Da'esh), a terrorist group that had captured nearly one-third of Iraq in 2014 and 2015, was defeated in December 2017. However, the conflict had exacted a heavy toll, resulting in thousands of casualties, millions of displaced individuals, and the destruction of almost 150,000 homes (GIF, February 14, 2018). Reconstruction was deemed vital to stabilize Iraq by creating job opportunities, addressing displacement issues, and mitigating the long-standing political and sectarian violence that had plagued the country for decades.

Despite still receiving reparation payments from Iraq for its 1990 invasion at the time, Kuwait made a substantial commitment by pledging $1 billion in loans and committing an additional $1 billion as investments, surpassing the contributions of any other Gulf State. The closest contributor in terms of financial assistance to Iraq was Saudi Arabia, which pledged $1 billion through the Saudi Fund for Development and an additional $500 million in export credit (GIF, February 14, 2018).

Kuwait's Foreign Aid at Critical Junctures

During critical junctures involving Iraq, such as the first Gulf War (1980–1988) and the second Gulf War in 1991, as well as during the period of the 2011 Arab uprisings, Kuwait strategically utilized foreign aid to safeguard its survival. During

82 Mohammad Yaghi

these pivotal moments, Kuwait leveraged its financial assets to reward countries that played a role in ensuring its survival while withholding financial assistance from states perceived as undermining its interests. In the following two subsections, I will provide a detailed account of Kuwait's foreign aid to Iraq and its foreign aid policy during the 2011 Arab uprisings.

Foreign Aid to Iraq

The initial instance of Iraq receiving foreign aid from Kuwait dates back to 1963 when a coup d'état toppled the regime of Abd al-Karim Qasim in Iraq. Under the leadership of Abdulsalam Aref, the new regime officially recognized Kuwait's independence and committed to respecting the borders established in a letter sent by King Ghazi of Iraq to Kuwaiti leaders in 1932. In return for this recognition, Kuwait extended an $80 million interest-free loan to Iraq, repayable over 25 years (Assiri, 1990, p. 25). However, Kuwait refrained from providing Iraq with further financial assistance when it became apparent during border negotiations that Iraq's recognition of Kuwait should not be interpreted as an acknowledgement of Kuwait's territorial status quo. Iraq sought to expand its Gulf borders or gain control over the Kuwaiti islands of Warba and Bubiyan for security and trade-related reasons (Bishku, 1991, p. 87).

Kuwait's security concerns were exacerbated when the Islamic revolution in Iran, which began in 1979, aimed to export its revolutionary ideals to neighbouring countries (Cordesman, 2018). Fearing that Kuwait's Shia population, constituting 20–25 per cent of the Kuwaiti populace, might serve as a fifth column for Iran, the Kuwaiti government initiated a restructuring of its internal police force. This restructuring involved coercing the early retirement of 26 high-ranking police officers and gradually removing or demoting Shiites from sensitive security and military positions (Assiri, 1990, p. 68).

Amid the dual threats posed by Iraq and Iran, Kuwait aligned itself with Iraq when the war between the two nations erupted in 1980. Over the course of the war, from 1980 to 1988, Kuwait provided Iraq with "$13.2 billion in non-collectible 'financial-political subsidies.'" Of this sum, "$6 billion was in direct cash forms," with an additional $7.2 billion being indirectly provided through the sale of oil "from [Kuwait–Iraq] neutral zone on behalf of Iraq" (Assiri, 1990, pp. 70–71). Collectively, the financial aid Iraq received from the Gulf States during the war reached $40 billion (Hinrichsen, 2019, p. 10). Consequently, when Iraq subsequently turned against Kuwait after the war concluded in 1988, demanding debt relief, additional loans, and a reduction in oil production to ensure high oil prices while simultaneously threatening military action if its demands were not met (Jones, 2012, p. 155), Kuwait was deeply offended. After all, Kuwait had not only supported Iraq during the war but also contributed to its conclusion by internationalizing the conflict through its policy of reflagging its oil tankers (Ramazani, 1988). Iraq eventually occupied Kuwait in August 1990.

Following the liberation of Kuwait in 1991, there was a dramatic shift in its foreign aid policy. Arab nations that had contributed to Kuwait's liberation were

Kuwait's Foreign Aid   83

financially rewarded, while those that had aligned with Iraq faced financial penalties. Egypt, for example, which had sent 45,000 troops to join US forces in liberating Kuwait, received direct aid, new loans, and debt forgiveness. As Abdennour Benantar (2007, p. 61) noted, the six Gulf States collectively planned an annual emergency aid fund of $1 to 2 billion for Egypt and forgave Egypt $13 billion of its debt. Similarly, Syria received $2 billion in cash from the Gulf States for deploying troops in support of Kuwait's liberation (Shad et al.,, 1995, p. 86). Conversely, Kuwait imposed punitive measures on Jordan, the PLO, Yemen, and Sudan for their support of Saddam Hussein's regime. According to KFAED data (as of September 30, 2022), funds to Jordan, Yemen, Sudan, and the Palestinians were only reinstated in 2004, 2009, 2002, and 2000, respectively. Jordan and the Palestinians were particularly impacted, with "thousands of [them] coerced into leaving or expelled outright amid hostility from Kuwaitis who suspected them of disloyalty" (Reuters Staff, April 15, 2013).

Kuwait and the 2011 Arab Protests

In contrast to numerous Arab countries like Tunisia, Egypt, Libya, Syria, Yemen, and Bahrain, Kuwait experienced relatively mild protests in 2011 and 2012 (Shultziner & Tétreault, 2012). However, Kuwait's ruling elites perceived the 2011 Arab protests as a potential threat to their survival and consequently adjusted their foreign aid policies. This is evident in Kuwait's financial support to the monarchies of Bahrain, Oman, Jordan, and Morocco, which received grants totalling $2 billion, $1.25 billion, and $1.25 billion, respectively, in late 2012, as indicated in Table 5.2. Additionally, Kuwait supported the military coup that occurred in Egypt in July 2013. While KFAED's records show a $54 million contribution to the elected government in June 2012, it appears that this funding was part of phase 2 of a project initiated in 2008, specifically the expansion of natural gas distribution networks in Cairo and Giza (KFAED, 2022, p. 19). However, following the July 2013 military coup, KFAED (2022, pp. 19–20) significantly increased its support to Egypt, providing $288 million from October 2013 to December 2014. It's important to note that KFAED is just one of the agencies in Kuwait used by the government to channel bilateral financial assistance. According to Chatham House and the Carnegie Endowment, Kuwait provided the Egyptian government, after the military coup, with $4 billion in the form of a deposit to Egypt's central bank to bolster its monetary reserves, with payments made in September 2013 and April 2015 (Butter, April 20, 2020, p. 8; also see Dunne, June 9, 2020).

Contrary to this trend is Kuwait's support for the opposition to the Syrian regime. In part, Kuwait supported the removal of Assad's regime by tacitly allowing non-state institutions and private citizens to provide financial support to the opposition, including extremist factions. Reports have indicated that private individuals, including influential figures such as businessmen and Members of Parliament, as well as charitable organizations like Mercy International (linked to the Muslim Brotherhood's Social Reform Society) and the Revival of the

84 *Mohammad Yaghi*

Islamic Heritage Society (a Salafi group), collected hundreds of millions of US dollars for the opposition, with some of these funds reaching extremist groups like Al-Nusra and the Islamic State (Hubbard, November 12, 2013; Dickinson, October 2, 2014).

The allowance of financial support to the Syrian opposition seems to defy the aforementioned trend of Kuwait financially supporting many Arab regimes following the 2011 Arab uprisings. This can be attributed to several factors. First, Kuwait's foreign policy is grounded in principles of multilateralism and diplomacy, emphasizing close cooperation with its key Arab and Western partners (Karasik & Ober, May 21, 2019). When the GCC States, the Arab League, and Western Allies collectively took action against the Syrian regime and supported the opposition, Kuwait's leaders found themselves compelled to align with this consensus. Second, Kuwait's foreign aid policies towards Syria reflected its domestic political landscape, particularly the divide within Kuwait's Parliament between the government and the opposition. At that time, the majority within the opposition consisted mainly of members affiliated with the Muslim Brotherhood and Salafists. These groups had been opposed to the Syrian regime from the onset of the protests in Syria and actively engaged in funding the opposition, including fundraising efforts through local charity telethons on specific Kuwaiti television networks (Dickinson, October 2, 2014; Karasik & Ober, May 21, 2019). Finally, Kuwait has been eager to position itself as a regional hub for humanitarian aid and reconstruction (Leichtman, 2017). Numerous international organizations have accused Assad's regime of deliberately targeting innocent civilians and causing numerous humanitarian crises. Therefore, Kuwait's actions align with its aspiration to maintain an image as a champion of humanitarian causes.

Conclusion

This chapter underscores Kuwait's early recognition of the significance of foreign aid in achieving its foreign policy objectives, particularly in its ongoing struggle for survival since gaining independence, especially in its confrontations with Iraq. Kuwait has strategically leveraged foreign and humanitarian aid to accumulate political capital, a strategy underscored by the establishment of the Kuwait Arab Fund for Economic Development (KAFED) in the same year as its independence. Initially, KAFED provided loans and grants exclusively to Arab countries, but over time, it expanded its mandate and budget to encompass all developing nations.

Kuwait's "dinar diplomacy" has played a pivotal role in the nation's survival. During the 1960s, this policy facilitated Kuwait's admission to the Arab League, thereby thwarting Iraq's annexation ambitions. Although unable to prevent the Iraqi occupation of Kuwait in 1990, it played a crucial role in forging the international coalition forces that liberated the country in 1991. Regionally, Kuwait used its foreign aid to secure political support in alignment with decisions made during Arab summits. It also championed the Palestinian cause and contributed to the reconstruction of southern Lebanon and Gaza following conflicts with Israel,

Kuwait's Foreign Aid   85

which garnered respect from the Arab public. On an international stage, since 2013, Kuwait has positioned itself as a global humanitarian and reconstruction hub, providing $2.5 billion in humanitarian assistance to Syrian refugees, the Yemeni population, and other nations facing humanitarian or natural disasters.

Kuwait's foreign fund is inherently linked to its domestic politics. Support for Arab and Islamic nations is not solely rooted in the state's identity but also influenced by the political forces that hold sway in Kuwait's Parliament. When the pan-Arab movement held prominence in parliament, foreign aid predominantly targeted Arab countries. Conversely, when Islamist groups gained substantial influence in Kuwait's domestic politics, Kuwait broadened its foreign aid to encompass Islamic nations. This partially explains Kuwait's support for opposition forces in Syria.

At critical junctures, Kuwait's foreign aid has been directed towards safeguarding its own survival. When Kuwait perceived the potential spillover of the Iranian Islamic revolution in the late 1970s, it aligned itself with Iraq in its war against Iran, providing substantial financial support amounting to $13 billion. Similarly, Kuwait expended billions of US dollars to prevent the 2011 Arab uprisings from spreading to monarchies in the Gulf and other Arab regions. Moreover, Kuwait supported the July 2013 military coup in Egypt, which resulted in the overthrow of a democratically elected government.

Lastly, Kuwait has employed its foreign aid as a diplomatic tool, using it both as a reward for supporters and as a means to punish defectors. Countries that backed Kuwait's liberation in 1991, such as Egypt and Syria, received financial support and debt forgiveness. Conversely, nations that sided with Saddam Hussein's regime, including Jordan, Yemen, Sudan, and the Palestine Liberation Organization (PLO), faced years of exclusion from Kuwait's financial assistance.

References

Ahrari, M. E. (1993). Rational foreign policy Behaviour of a weak state: The case of Kuwait. *Australian Journal of International Affairs*, *47*(1), 131–148.

Alazami, I. (2022). Kuwaiti foreign policy objectives, and its characteristics, and instruments. *World Research of Political Science Journal*, *5*(1), 111–124.

Aljazeera. (n.d.). *Arafat's costly Gulf War choice*. Aljazeera. https://bit.ly/427xq33

Alzaid, S. (2012). *The influence of financial Kuwaiti Aids on its Arab relations* [Master's Degree Dissertation]. https://bit.ly/3VjgXqj

Arab Summit. (1967, September 1). *Khartoum resolutions*. Yale Law School. https://bit.ly/3ABR77E

Assiri, A. R. (1990). *Kuwait's foreign policy: City-state in world politics*. Westview Press.

Benantar, A. (2007). Egypt and the war on Iraq: Implications for domestic politics. *Journal of Third World Studies*, *24*(1), 227–246.

Bindra, S. S. (2018). Foreign aid and foreign policy. *World Affairs: The Journal of International Issues*, *22*(3), 126–141.

Bishku, M. B. (1991). Iraq's claim to Kuwait: A historical overview. *American-Arab Affairs*, *37*, 77.

Butter, D. (2020). *Egypt and the Gulf. Allies and rivals* [Research paper], 20. Chatham House. https://bit.ly/3ABRsHs

86 *Mohammad Yaghi*

CNN Editorial Research. (2022, July 24). *Gulf War fast facts*. CNN Website. https://bit.ly/3ALi8Fv

Cochrane, L. (2021). The United Arab Emirates as a global donor: What a decade of foreign aid data transparency reveals. *Development Studies Research, 8*(1), 49–62.

Cordesman, A. H. (2018). *Kuwait: Recovery and security after the Gulf War*. Routledge.

Crystal, J. (1990). *Oil and politics in the Gulf: Rulers and merchants in Kuwait and Qatar (No. 24)*. Cambridge University Press.

Dickinson, E. (2013, December 16). *Playing with fire: Why private gulf financing for Syria's extremist rebels risks igniting sectarian conflict at home*. Brookings. https://bit.ly/40QfJE8

Dickinson, E. (2014, October 2). *Kuwait: The crisis in Syria comes home*. European Council on Foreign Relations. https://bit.ly/44ggiKA

Dunn, M. (2020, June 9). *Egypt: Looking elsewhere to meet bottomless needs*. Carnegie Endowment for International Peace. https://bit.ly/3VgD1lo

Elliot, M. (1996). The death of King Ghazi: Iraqi politics, Britain and Kuwait in 1939. *Contemporary British History, 10*(3), 63–81.

FTS, UNOCHA. (n.d.). *Kuwait, Government of 2023, donor data*. https://bit.ly/3LiiZCG. OCHA Financial Tracking Service.

GIF. (2018, February 14). *Allies promise Iraq $30 billion, falling short of Baghdad's appeal*. Gulf International Forum. https://bit.ly/3LFrVmZ

Goldstein, J., & Pevehouse, J. C. (2002). *International relations: Brief edition*. Longman.

Hattori, T. (2001). Reconceptualizing foreign aid. *Review of International Political Economy, 8*(4), 633–660.

Hinrichsen, S. (2019). *Tracing Iraqi sovereign debt through defaults and restructuring*. Economic History Department, London School of Economics And Political Science.

Hook, S. W. (1995). National interest and foreign aid. Lynne Rienner Publishers.

Hubbard, B. (2013, November 12). Private donors' funds add wild card to war in Syria. *New York Times*. https://bit.ly/3NrT9yH

Jones, T. C. (2012). America, oil, and war in the Middle East. *Journal of American History, 99*(1), 208–218.

KFAED. (2022, September 30). *Loans, grants, and technical assistance for Arab countries*. KFAED Website. https://bit.ly/4490idn

Kibria, A., Oladi, R., & Bosworth, R. (2021). The political economy of aid allocation: The case of Arab donors. *The World Economy, 44*(8), 2460–2495.

KUNA. (2017, 28 November). *Kuwait: Permanent solution to Syria crisis only through political Means*. Kuwait News Agency. https://bit.ly/3LkRMz1

Karasik, T., & Ober, T. (2019, May 21). *Kuwait's apprehension about normalizing relations with Syria*. Atlantic Council. https://bit.ly/3Lj1mCD

Lavy, V. (1984). The economic embargo of Egypt by Arab states: Myth and reality. *Middle East Journal, 38*(3), 419–432.

Leichtman, M. A. (2017). *Kuwaiti humanitarianism: The history and expansion of Kuwait's foreign assistance policies*. Stimson Center.

Lesch, A. M. (1991). Palestinians in Kuwait. *Journal of Palestine Studies, 20*(4), 42–54.

Lumsdaine, D. H. (1993). *Moral vision in international politics: The foreign aid regime, 1949–1989*. Princeton University Press.

Marlowe, J. (1962). *The Persian Gulf in the twentieth century*. Cresset Press.

McKinlay, R. D., & Mughan, A. (1984). *Aid and arms to the third world: An analysis of the distribution and impact of US official transfers*. Pinter.

Momani, B., & Ennis, C. A. (2012). Between caution and controversy: Lessons from the Gulf Arab states as (re-) emerging donors. *Cambridge Review of International Affairs, 25*(4), 605–627.

Nath, V. (1972). Review of economic development and regional cooperation: Kuwait, by R. El Mallakh. *Economic Development and Cultural Change, 20*(2), 342–349.

OCED, Kuwait. (n.d). *Kuwait becomes participant in the OECD Development Assistance Committee (DAC)*. OCED Website. https://bit.ly/426jerd

OECD Library. (2018). *Development co-operation report 2018: Joining forces to leave no one behind*. OCED Library. https://bit.ly/3AFRaiM

OECD. (2006). DAC in dates. The History of OECD's Development Assistance Committee. https://bit.ly/3HryQgZ

Palestine Economy. (n.d.). *Donors*. Palestine Economy Website. https://bit.ly/41OHdeR

Ramazani, R. K. (1988). The Iran-Iraq War and the Persian Gulf crisis. *Current History*, 87(526), 61–88.

Reuters Staff. (2013, April 15). *Palestinian leader makes first Kuwait visit for over 20 years*. Reuters. https://bit.ly/3Vg2k7o

Riddell, R. C. (1996). The moral case for post—Cold War development aid. *International Journal*, 51(2), 191–210.

Salem, P. (2007, July 16). *Kuwait: Politics in a participatory emirate*. Carnegie Papers, Carnegie Middle East. Center. https://bit.ly/44rq9NR

Shad, T. I., Shad, T. L., Boucher, S., & Reddish, J. G. (1995). Syrian foreign policy in the post-Soviet era. *Arab Studies Quarterly*, 17(1/2), 77–94.

Shultziner, D., & Tétreault, M. A. (2012). Representation and democratic progress in Kuwait. *Representation*, 48(3), 281–293.

Taffet, J. (2012). *Foreign aid as foreign policy: The alliance for progress in Latin America*. Routledge.

The New Humanitarian. (2013, February 1). *Breakdown of Syria aid pledges in Kuwait*. The New Humanitarian Website. https://bit.ly/3VILWSW

UNRWA. (n.d.). *Donors charts*. UNRWA website. https://www.unrwa.org/how-you-can-help/government-partners/funding-trends/donor-charts

Villanger, E. (2007, December). Arab foreign aid: Disbursement patterns, aid policies and motives. *Forum for Development Studies*, 34(2), 223–256.

Wood, R. E. (1986). *From Marshall Plan to debt crisis: Foreign aid and development choices in the world economy, 355*. University of California Press.

Young, K. E. (2017). A new politics of GCC economic statecraft: The case of UAE aid and financial intervention in Egypt. *Journal of Arabian Studies*, 7(1), 113–136.

Zahlan, R. S. (2016). *The making of the modern Gulf states*. Routledge.

6 Intra-Gulf Dynamics

Pursuit of Survival within the GCC

Kristian Coates Ulrichsen

Introduction

Established in 1981 with significant input from Kuwait's long-standing foreign minister, and future Emir, Sheikh Sabah al-Ahmad al-Sabah, the Gulf Cooperation Council (GCC) remained a priority for Kuwait for the remainder of Sheikh Sabah's long life. The effort with which Sheikh Sabah led Kuwaiti attempts to mediate in the "Gulf crises" first in 2013–14 and again in and after 2017 illustrate Kuwaiti policymakers' commitment to the GCC as an institution and as a reality. This, in turn, reflects the value that Kuwait places in the GCC as an entity that can leverage power when it acts collectively, but only if there is a workable balance of relationships within the institution itself. Again, these are issues that relate directly to Kuwait's positioning as a small state in the regional and international system, for whom balancing relationships is an important tool in the pursuit of survival. This chapter examines how Kuwaiti foreign policy has sought to identify and pursue a pragmatic approach to regional affairs within the framework of the GCC.

There are four sections to this chapter. It begins with a historical outline of how generations of leaders in Kuwait have sought to navigate a careful path that recognized the linkages between internal and external (in) security, and the emirate's vulnerability to regional fissures it could not necessarily influence. The second section explores Kuwait's role in creating the GCC in 1981 and in steering the institution through its formative years, which, for Kuwait, included the existential period of the Iraqi invasion in August 1990 and the subsequent seven-month-long occupation. This leads into the third section, which analyses how Kuwait has engaged within the GCC to maximize the value in engaging collectively while working to minimize, or at least contain, the disruptive impact of intra-GCC sources of friction. The chapter ends with a section that looks ahead to the future both of the GCC after the resolution of the 2017–20 Gulf crisis and of Kuwait's role within it following the death in 2020 of Emir Sabah.

Kuwait as a Balancing Actor

As a small country sandwiched between three much larger and conventionally more powerful neighbours, with records of territorial expansionism and irredentist design, Kuwait historically has had to pursue strategies of survival based on

DOI: 10.4324/9781003435259-6

Intra-Gulf Dynamics 89

balancing competing interests and leveraging key relationships. Social and political dynamics within Kuwait additionally have underscored the vulnerability of the emirate (and, since 1961, the state) to regional fissures and the interaction between domestic politics and external events. Writing in 1991, a period when Kuwait's regional situation became a matter of global concern, Mary Ann Tetreault observed that security and autonomy were two objectives of Kuwaiti rulers throughout the twentieth century, and that "Their choice of security strategies has been shaped by the desire to maximize their independence from domestic social groups as well as from external allies" (Tetreault, 1991, p. 566).

A robust literature examines the role of small states in world politics and explores not just the vulnerabilities of constraints which face small states but also the range of strategic choices and policy outcomes available to them. This literature moved debates on small states beyond early scholarship in international relations, especially among realist thinkers, which often reduced the agency of small states to little more than a choice between "bandwagonning" and "balancing" (Cooper & Momani, 2011, p. 115). For Kuwait, and the other small emirates on the eastern coastline of the Arabian Peninsula, a basic imbalance in size and conventional forms of "power" was an inescapable reality as a regional system took shape in the 20th century which featured three much larger states—Iran, Iraq, and Saudi Arabia, alongside five states of varying degrees of smallness (Kuwait, Bahrain, Qatar, the United Arab Emirates, and Oman), with Yemen situated uneasily on the periphery (Miller, 2016, p. 8). Within this system, there were opportunities for rulers of the smaller emirates to maneuver among the larger powers to gain a degree of freedom of action as well as a guarantor of security. This has been a feature of Kuwaiti regional diplomacy for more than a century since the leadership of Sheikh Mohammed "al Kabir" (the Great) who played regional and international interests off to his advantage in the 1890s and 1900s (Anscombe, 1997, p. 172).

Uniquely among the Gulf States, Kuwait is surrounded by all three larger regional states. To its north lies Iraq, to its west and south is Saudi Arabia, while Kuwait and Iran share a maritime boundary, which has yet to be fully demarcated and has held back development of an offshore gas field in the Gulf (Mills, 2022). All three have, at different times in the twentieth century, posed a physical and territorial threat to Kuwait. The (British-adjudicated) Conference of 'Uqair in 1922, which settled post-First World War territorial boundaries between the Sultanate of Najd (which became the Kingdom of Saudi Arabia in 1932) and the newly formed (British-controlled) mandate of Iraq, allocated two-thirds of Kuwait's geographical territory to Najd (Al-Nakib, 2012, p. 34). The ruler of Najd, Abdulaziz bin Abdulrahman Al Saud (known also as Ibn Saud), subsequently imposed a somewhat porous and never absolute blockade of desert trade with Kuwait that lasted nevertheless for most of the period between 1921 and 1935 (Toth, 2005, p. 148). Ties between Kuwait and Saudi Arabia did improve once the relationship was one of independent nation states, after 1961, and when it was supported within the framework of the GCC, after 1981.

If relations with Saudi Arabia were a periodic source of tension for successive rulers of Kuwait, those with Iraq were a near-constant source of danger for much

90 *Kristian Coates Ulrichsen*

of the 20th century, spanning multiple (and very different) eras in Iraq's political landscape, from the monarchy to the military and to Saddam Hussein. Agreements with the Ottoman authorities in 1899 and 1914 had detached Kuwait from the *vilayet* of Basra and established an administratively distinct emirate under the control of the al-Sabah family, which had emerged as the rulers of Kuwait in the eighteenth century (Abu-Hakima, 1983, p. 1). In 1938, Iraqi media promoted the amalgamation of Kuwait with Iraq in the name of pan-Arabism while the following year King Ghazi told Kuwaitis "Our history supports the annexation of Kuwait to Iraq. We live and die under the Hashemite flag" (Al-Marashi, 2009, p. 452). Later, in the 1950s, the government in Baghdad pressured the authorities in Kuwait to cede the island of Warbah, strategically located at the mouth of the Shatt al-Arab, to give Iraq direct sea and port access to the Gulf (al-Sabah, 2015, p. 107).

The toppling of the monarchy in the July 1958 revolution and its replacement, first, by a military regime and later by the Ba'ath party, did not substantively change the threat posed by Iraq to Kuwait. In June 1961, just six days after Kuwait became an independent sovereign state, Iraq's Prime Minister, 'Abd al-Karim Qasim, moved troops towards the southern border. Britain hurriedly mobilized 7,000 troops who landed in Kuwait to forestall a feared Iraqi invasion, and remained there until an Arab League force replaced them in October 1961 (Smith, 2001, p. 160). The Iraq–Kuwait border was also the site of repeated incidents, in 1954, 1967, 1972, 1973, 1974, and 1976–77, a pattern of activity which led many international observers of the Gulf to fail to appreciate the significance of Saddam Hussein's buildup of troops prior to the full-scale invasion of Kuwait in August 1990, due to a feeling that, in the words of the British Ambassador to Saudi Arabia at the time, "at the most the Iraqis might go for a limited objective (…) such as the Rumaila oilfield or a repetition of previous border incursions" (Munro, 1996, p. 39). The Iraqi threat remained even after their forces were expelled from Kuwait in the Gulf War, with the deployment of Republican Guard units towards the border in October 1994 prompting the Bill Clinton administration to send US forces back to Kuwait (and to Saudi Arabia) in large numbers (Cordeseman, 1997, p. 127).

Kuwait's "smallness" and regional positioning led to several distinct characteristics of foreign policymaking that became associated with the six decades in public life of Sheikh Sabah al-Ahmad al-Sabah, Foreign Minister between 1963 and 2003, Prime Minister from 2003 to 2006, and Emir from 2006 until 2020. Support for Arab causes was one hallmark which reflected its strong ideological foothold in Kuwait in the 1940s and 1950s and was evident in the financial and other assistance Kuwait gave to less-developed emirates elsewhere in the Gulf in the 1960s (Al-Rashoud, 2021, pp. 12–13). So too was the use of aid and development policy as tools of foreign policy through the creation of institutions such as the Kuwait Fund for Arab Economic Development (KFAED) and the Arab Fund for Economic and Social Development (AFESD, also headquartered in Kuwait City) to spread "Arab wealth" regionally (Khalaf, 1992, p. 68). In 1990, however, and to the shock and considerable dismay of many in Kuwait, several of the largest recipients of Kuwait aid since 1961—Jordan, Sudan, Yemen, and the Palestinian

Liberation Organization (PLO)—either supported Iraq or chose to remain neutral in the aftermath of the invasion of Kuwait (Halliday, 2005, p. 65).

Involvement in regional diplomacy and mediation was another characteristic of Kuwaiti foreign policy. Although most closely connected with Sheikh Sabah, during his long tenure as Foreign Minister and then again as Emir, most notably in the two intra-GCC crises in the 2010s, one of the first examples of Kuwaiti mediation occurred decades earlier, in 1938, during a period of tension between Qatar and Bahrain over the disputed Hawar Islands (Wiegand, 2012, p. 82). During his 40 years as foreign minister, Sheikh Sabah crafted an extensive record in mediation that began in the 1960s and culminated in his shuttle diplomacy in June 2017 that prevented the Qatar blockade from escalating into military action (Kabalan, 2018, p. 26). Examples of issues that Sheikh Sabah mediated included disputes between Abu Dhabi and Dubai during the negotiations to create the United Arab Emirates (1968–71), an impasse between Iran and Bahrain in 1968, friction between North and South Yemen (1972 and 1978), tension between Saudi Arabia and Libya in 1982, a boundary dispute between Oman and Yemen in 1984, and a breakdown in relations between Saudi Arabia and Qatar in 2003 (Coates Ulrichsen, 2021, pp. 120–121).

Creation of the GCC

Proposals for the formation of a regional organization in the Arabian Peninsula (and potentially also spanning the Gulf) had been raised periodically in the decade which separated the British withdrawal from the region in 1971 and the eventual creation of the GCC in 1981. Like Bahrain, Qatar, and the Trucial States, which became the United Arab Emirates (UAE), Kuwait had been a British-protected state, but Kuwait's independence had come in 1961, a decade before the other emirates followed suit. Just as the massing of Iraqi troops on Kuwait's border illustrated the threat to a newly independent small state from a far larger regional neighbour, so, too, did Bahrain and the UAE face challenges, from Iran and Saudi Arabia. A spurious yet long-standing Iranian territorial claim to Bahrain was resolved by a United Nations fact-finding mission in 1970 after two years of negotiation between British and Iranian officials (Alvandi, 2010, p. 158). The mission concluded that the overwhelming majority of Bahraini citizens supported independence and Iran renounced its claim to Bahrain which it has nevertheless periodically revived (Gordon, 1971, p. 563).

For its part, the UAE faced immediate challenges both from Iran and from Saudi Arabia. Iranian forces seized and occupied three islands in the Strait of Hormuz belonging to the emirates of Sharjah and Ras al-Khaimah one day before the withdrawal of British protection from the Trucial States (and two days before the official formation of the UAE) in 1971 (Louis, 2003, p. 102). Iran subsequently militarized the islands and deployed units of the Iranian Revolutionary Guards Corps to them in 1992 (Caldwell, 1996, pp. 53–54). Saudi Arabia withheld diplomatic recognition of the UAE until a boundary agreement was reached in 1974 that allocated to Riyadh territory along the eastern coastline of the Arabian Peninsula

92   *Kristian Coates Ulrichsen*

which later was found to be rich in oil and which caused years of ill-feeling in Abu Dhabi (Al-Mazrouei, 2016, p. 184). Other, more ideological, threats to regional security came from groups such as the Popular Front for the Liberation of Oman and the Arabian Gulf (PFLOAG) and from Iraq's Ba'ath Party and Muammar Qaddafi's regime in Libya which provided material support for them in the 1970s (Kechichian, 1999, p. 239).

Questions over the composition of any regional institution, and specifically whether Iran and Iraq (but never Yemen) should be included, held back several separate initiatives in the 1970s. Discussions for an eight-member organization (incorporating Iran and Iraq) took place in Jeddah in 1975 and Muscat in 1976 but failed to overcome differences in perspective and priority (Jones & Ridout, 2015, p. 185). By 1980, the impact of the Iranian revolution and the outbreak of the Iran–Iraq War meant that Iran and Iraq were excluded from the Gulf States' vision of regional arrangements at a time of great external uncertainty. In practice, what emerged was a bloc of relatively like-minded hereditary states that came together at considerable speed in a matter of months in 1981 as the GCC was born from "the exigencies of realpolitik, to shield the member states, as well as their societies from unconventional threats" (Assiri, 1990, p. 76).

That Kuwait played a leading role in the deliberations in the run-up to the creation of the GCC, and, subsequently, in the steering of the new organization, reflected the balance of interests that guided officials and policymaking. Proximity to the war-zone in the northern Gulf and the overspill of geopolitical and sectarian tensions meant that Kuwait was directly affected by the twin shocks of the revolution in Iran and the war with Iraq, as were states such as Saudi Arabia and Bahrain (Plotkin Boghardt, 2006, p. 10). A series of preliminary informal conversations among rulers and their circles produced three different approaches to regional coordination from Kuwait, Oman, and Saudi Arabia that emphasized, respectively, economic integration, military cooperation, and collective security. It was the Kuwaiti focus on economic over security issues, borne in part out of the country's careful balancing in regional and international affairs, which eventually won the day (Heard-Bey, 2006, p. 201). Moreover, it was Sheikh Sabah al-Ahmad who prepared a working paper to regional governments proposing the establishment of the GCC, and who met subsequently with his five foreign minister counterparts in Riyadh and Muscat to discuss the plan. It was in Muscat in March 1981 that the proposal to create the GCC was formally accepted, and a senior Kuwaiti diplomat, Abdulla Bishara, was appointed its Secretary-General (Al-Ebraheem, 2016, pp. 69–70).

From the start, the fact that the GCC was formed at speed and largely as a reaction to regional developments meant that a series of uneasy compromises lay at the heart of what was ultimately a loose organizational structure. Looking back at the end of the twentieth century on its creation, Emirati political scientist Abdulkhaleq Abdulla suggested that the GCC was "a panic response to a situation of profound uncertainty" between 1979 and 1981' and added that "its nature and what it stands for was hardly clear at the outset" and was little clearer by the time he was writing, in 1999, by which time, he argued, the GCC had evolved "into all things for all people" (Abdulla, 1999, pp. 153–154). The new body lacked an integrative supranational decision-making apparatus, akin to the European Commission, and the six-member governments retained responsibility for almost all aspects of political and economic policy and resisted any encroachment on matters of sovereignty (Baaboud, 2005, p. 148). As Christian Koch observed in 2012, it was the flexibility within the GCC that enabled the organization to survive even as consensus on key aspects of foreign (and domestic) policy remained elusive (Koch, 2012).

The GCC has shown its durability even if it did not live up to the rosy future predicted by Emir Isa bin Salman Al Khalifa of Bahrain, who hailed the GCC as a river that would "irrigate the path of the future where it meets with the streams of good and aspires to the coasts of glory" (Miller, 2016, p. 9). Member governments have struggled to reach consensus on "big-ticket" items such as major foreign policy issues, especially as they relate to relationships with neighbouring states such as Iran, Iraq, and Yemen. Agreement on security and defense policy has similarly been contentious and difficult to achieve, due in part to the different levels of threat perception and prioritization among the six-member states. Yet, the GCC has survived for more than forty years, a period which included the invasion and occupation of Kuwait by Iraq in 1990–91 as well as a decade of internal division and rifts which followed the Arab uprisings in 2011. In the next section of this chapter, the analysis turns to how Kuwaiti officials navigated a pathway that balanced, not always easily, national interests with collective objectives within the framework of the GCC.

Pursuit of Interests within the GCC

Before any examination of how generations of Kuwaiti policymakers have engaged in the GCC, it is necessary to outline baseline considerations that have guided the projection of Kuwaiti interests since 1981. These have largely remained constant in spite of significant changes in the broader regional context as well as in the dynamics among GCC members as well. The most important interest is that Kuwait has sought to avoid entanglement in regional power blocs, whether inside or outside the GCC, in a manner consistent with the balancing of regional and international relationships. Throughout Kuwait's membership of the GCC, Sheikh Sabah, as Foreign Minister or later as Emir, used his diplomatic experience to try to resolve points of tension and/or mediate when serious issues arose. This became more difficult in the 2010s when regional geopolitics grew more polarized and "camps" emerged within the GCC which set Qatar against the trio of Saudi Arabia, Bahrain, and the UAE. Kuwait's stance was rooted in a pragmatic acknowledgement of the limitations of the power of small states and an awareness of the benefits that could accrue from collective action on issues of mutual interest (Coates Ulrichsen, 2021, p. 127).

A separate consideration is that Kuwait's hybrid political system, which incorporates an assertive parliament of elected members alongside a cabinet appointed by and in the name of the Emir, does mean that Kuwaiti officials have less domestic freedom of action than many of their regional peers. Although the ability of parliamentarians to introduce legislation and act in a manner that is genuinely

94   *Kristian Coates Ulrichsen*

autonomous from state interests is limited, MPs can, and do, exert an influence on executive decision-making. The threat of hostile parliamentary questioning (known in Kuwait as interpellation), followed by a potential vote of no confidence in a Cabinet minister, has functioned as a constraint on policymaking in the past (Herb, 2009, p. 136). So, too, has the ability of MPs to block measures they do not support or which they believe are not in the "national" interest, however they may define it. An example of the practical impact of this cautionary approach came as MPs from across the political spectrum opposed the approval of a GCC-wide internal security pact in 1982 and again in 1994 on constitutional grounds (Kechichian, 2014).

Kuwait is also distinct among GCC states for having suffered the most cathartic, existential crisis any nation can face that of military invasion and foreign occupation. Oman is the only other Arab Gulf state that has experienced significant conflict in its modern history in the form of the Dhofar War in its southwestern governorate between 1962 and 1975, before the GCC was created and a remote era for many (Takriti, 2016, p. 6). For Kuwait, the Iraqi assault on August 2, 1990, and the policy responses to the invasion demonstrated that, for all the emphasis on GCC "solidarity," it was a partnership with an extra-regional security guarantor, the United States, which proved vital to the survival of Kuwait as a state. While Saudi Arabia and the other GCC states contributed to and participated in the coalition which liberated Kuwait in the Gulf War in 1991, it was U.S. military assistance which provided the bulk of the multinational force, and it was to the U.S. that Kuwait (and other GCC states) turned to sign defence cooperation agreements after the war ended (Cordesman, 1997, p. 128).

Policymakers in Kuwait therefore remain cognizant that the maintenance of security and stability remains reliant on a careful equilibrium that balances regional and international considerations. As early as 1983, Bishara, the Kuwaiti Secretary-General of the GCC, acknowledged that, militarily, "Our ambitions are enormous, but our capabilities are not" and the events of 1990 illustrated that little had changed, when Kuwaiti officials first contacted the US rather than Saudi counterparts for assistance (Miller, 2016, p. 69). On the one occasion in 1986, during the Iran–Iraq War when Kuwait requested that the GCC deploy a contingent of Peninsula Shield Forces to Bubiyan Island to protect the northern border from the fighting on the nearby al-Faw Peninsula, the GCC denied the request. The reason given was that there was concern among some GCC states, especially in Oman and the UAE, that stationing the troops across from Iranian-controlled Iraqi territory, risked provoking Iranian backlash and was a confrontation too far (Assiri, 1990, pp. 101-2). Surprised and stung by the decision, Kuwaiti leaders had no option but to request international support from the US, the UK, France, Italy, and the Soviet Union for maritime security and the protection of Kuwaiti merchant shipping in Gulf waters (Jones and Stone, 1997, p. 6).

The advantage Kuwait has developed over the four-decade-long history of the GCC is that its ability to resist being drawn into geopolitical disputes, both within and beyond the bloc, has earned its credibility as a mediator with the intent and the capacity to generate diplomatic outcomes. For Kuwait to be accepted by other parties as an interlocutor, it had to be seen to be a (relatively) impartial actor engaging to secure regional balance rather than to swing the outcome for one side or another. To an extent, this credibility was bound up with the personality of Emir Sabah and his 60-year involvement in foreign affairs that cast him both as a regional elder statesman and as a senior diplomat (Altiok, 2003, pp. 608–609). An example of how the Kuwaiti leadership could exercise such a role came in January and February 2017 when Emir Sabah reached out to Iranian President Hasan Rouhani to seek to find a way to de-escalate intra-regional tensions, and then met with Oman's Sultan Qaboos to coordinate a diplomatic approach.

Emir Sabah's approach to Iran and subsequent coordination with Sultan Qaboos ultimately failed to bring about a diplomatic rapprochement between Iran and GCC states, notably Saudi Arabia, Bahrain, and the UAE, but it did reveal several of the characteristics of Kuwait's regional engagement (Coates Ulrichsen, 2017). The Emir perceived that tension in the region after the January 2016 storming of Saudi diplomatic facilities in Iran, itself following the execution of the Saudi Shi'a cleric Nimr al-Nimr, was a threat to regional stability with a sectarian dimension that could cause blowback across the Gulf but also within Kuwait. In June 2015, Kuwait had suffered a terrorist attack, carried out by a Saudi suicide bomber in the name of the so-called Islamic State, against a Shi'a mosque, a choice of target designed to enflame sectarian tension. That this did not happen was largely due to Emir Sabah's response as he brushed aside security concerns to hurry to the mosque to offer condolences, condemned the attack against "my children," and attended joint Sunni–Shi'a prayers alongside thousands (Gulf States Newsletter, 2015, p. 18).

In 2017, the fact that it was Emir Sabah who organized the production and delivery of a letter to the Iranian leadership on behalf of the GCC illustrated how Kuwaiti authorities sought to utilize their workable relations with multiple (often antagonistic) parties to good effect. In 2014, the Emir had paid the first state visit to Iran by a Kuwaiti leader since the 1979 revolution that toppled the Shah and brought to power the Ayatollah-led Islamic Republic. The fact that Kuwait was not seen to be involved in geopolitical or sectarian conflicts in the Gulf meant it was acceptable to Iran as a diplomatic partner, but, crucially, as a fellow GCC state, Kuwait was acceptable also to Saudi Arabia and the UAE in a way Qatar, for example, would not have been, given Riyadh and Abu Dhabi's own animosity towards Doha in the 2010s. That left Kuwait and Oman, and Emir Sabah travelled to Muscat to confer with Sultan Qaboos after President Rouhani had paid visits to both their capitals in February 2017 (Asharq al-Awsat, 2017). Emir Sabah drew upon the relationships he had built over decades with leaders on both sides of the Gulf to act as a representative of the GCC and as a regional statesman perceived by all sides to be above the fray. Diplomatic activity took place on both a personal level and on an institutional basis, consistent with the regional context of top-down leadership in which decision-making remained highly personalized at times.

Within the framework of the GCC and its institutions, Kuwait participates on two distinct levels, as do the other five member states. One level is political, the participation of the head of state or government at the annual leaders' summit which rotated around the six capital cities until 2017 when it began to take place each year in Saudi Arabia, as the host nation of the GCC, whose Secretariat is based in Riyadh. The other level is technocratic and is represented by the participation of Kuwaiti delegates in the issue-specific ministerial committees, which are the primary fora for the more humdrum moves towards harmonization and standardization of regulations that make the common market and customs union a GCC reality. On both levels, Kuwait has exercised a prominent role in part because the country has kept itself out of intra-GCC skirmishing which periodically led other members to downgrade or threaten to withhold participation in the political (as opposed to the technocratic) workings of the GCC (Guzansky, 2016, p. 548).

Kuwait's two-pronged approach was fully visible (and tested to the hilt) during the blockade of Qatar by three GCC members—Bahrain, Saudi Arabia, and the UAE, plus Egypt—between June 2017 and January 2021. Emir Sheikh Sabah al-Ahmad embarked on a round of shuttle diplomacy on a bilateral basis, rather than through the GCC, whose own settlement dispute mechanism was not activated, to ensure that the immediate crisis in June 2017 did not escalate further. "Thank God, now, what is important is that we have stopped any military action," the Emir stated in September 2017 during a press conference with US President Donald Trump in Washington, D.C., raising eyebrows with his use of words (White House, 2017). This was a reprise of Emir Sabah's actions in a previous round of crisis between Qatar and the three neighbouring GCC states, in 2013–14, when the Emir positioned himself as a mediator and worked hard to achieve a diplomatic solution in the Riyadh Agreement of November 2014, working in tandem with his foreign minister and other senior officials in the Ministry of Foreign Affairs (Coates Ulrichsen, 2020, p. 59).

In addition, Kuwait was, fortuitously, scheduled to host the annual GCC leaders' summit in December 2017, six months into the blockade of Qatar. The summit provided the first opportunity for political leaders to gather, and Kuwaiti officials pushed hard for the meeting to take place, even resisting an attempt to move the summit away from Kuwait, lest Qatar get disinvited (Kabalan, 2018, p. 26). In the event, the summit was marred by downgraded delegations from Saudi Arabia, Bahrain, and the UAE, and broke up in disarray after less than a day, indicating how deep-rooted the dispute had become. With the prospects of a mediated solution off the table, at least for the time being, Kuwaiti officials switched to ensuring that the GCC survived at the technocratic level even as the political level was at a stalemate. In the critical years of 2017, 2018, and 2019, when political tensions remained high, Kuwait City, together with Muscat in Oman, hosted meetings of many of the GCC's technocratic committees, allowing them to convene in neutral "safe spaces" with the participation of delegates from all six states, including Qatar, whose diplomats were unwilling or unable to travel to Riyadh for meetings at the GCC Secretariat. Meetings in Kuwait during this period included the GCC chiefs of staff, the committees of finance and economy ministers, health, housing affairs, and commerce, and the Gulf Water Conference and Gulf Health Council (Coates Ulrichsen, 2019).

Intra-Gulf Dynamics   97

Ultimately, the GCC rift over Qatar was not resolved until January 2021, four months after Emir Sabah died, aged 91 years, in September 2020, thereby preventing the last surviving "heavy-hitter" from the formation of the bloc from seeing the group come back together and the longest and deepest crisis in its history. On several occasions towards the end of his life, Emir Sabah had expressed his concern that the continuation of the rift within the GCC could threaten the very fabric of Gulf politics as well as the viability of the GCC. In November 2017, the Emir addressed the opening parliamentary session of the National Assembly and warned of the rift that "Any escalation will bring with it an outright call for regional and international intervention, which will destroy the security of the Gulf and its people" (The New Arab, 2017). In January 2018, Emir Sabah reiterated his call for regional harmony in remarks to a meeting of representatives of all six GCC states' assemblies in Kuwait City, a meeting, which, as noted above, could happen in Kuwait due to its credibility as a safe space for all participants. On this occasion, the Emir stated that:

> We are all aware of the conditions around us and unfortunately of their deterioration that represent a serious challenge to us all (…) Collective work is our way ahead in the confrontation and the best way to protect us to deal with the challenges and to preserve the achievements of our people and countries.
>
> (The New Arab, 2018)

Despite Emir Sabah's declining health and subsequent passing, Kuwait's leadership was able to play a role in the final resolution of the GCC rift in 2020–21. In February 2020, Nayef bin Falah al-Hajraf, a former Minister of Education and Minister of Finance in Kuwait, was appointed the Secretary-General of the GCC, succeeding Abdullatif bin Rashid al-Zayani, who had held the post since 2011. This was significant, as al-Zayani, as a Bahrani national (who was appointed Bahrain's Foreign Minister after he left the GCC), struggled to be perceived as impartial during the rift, given that Bahrain was one of the blockading states. The appointment of a Kuwaiti, first al-Hajraf and then, in January 2023, Jassim bin Mohammed al-Budaiwi, a diplomat of 30 years' standing, to head the GCC, was important for the message it sent of the GCC seeking to restore balance after a period of unprecedented internal disharmony. In December 2020 and early January 2021, after Emir Sabah's death, Kuwaiti diplomats also worked closely alongside U.S. counterparts to facilitate the Al-Ula Agreement that settled the rift at the annual GCC leaders' summit held at the Saudi heritage site of the same name on January 5, 2021 (Theros, 2021).

Into the Post-Sabah Age

While the GCC survived the rifts of the 2010s and emerged with its technocratic functions intact, both the GCC and Kuwait in a "post-Sabah" era face numerous challenges. The GCC must reckon with the emergence of a trio of headstrong leaders in Saudi Arabia (Mohammed bin Salman, Crown Prince at the time of writing in 2023), Qatar (Emir Tamim bin Hamad), and the UAE (President Mohammed bin Zayed) whose age means they are likely to dominate the regional landscape for the foreseeable future and into mid-century. While the anger and animosity between Qatar and the three GCC states involved in the blockade have cooled, and Qatar and Saudi Arabia especially have developed close relations since 2021, the possibility remains that other regional issues could become points of tension, including growing and increasingly direct economic competition between Saudi Arabia and the UAE (Gardner, 2021). Going forward, it may be that the GCC exists more visibly in the technocratic arena than in the political as leaders in the six-member states prioritize their own pursuit of national (rather than GCC-wide) interests. If this proves the case, it will present a challenge for Kuwait to maintain balance in a more assertive regional context.

Kuwait post-Sabah has faced its own succession of political difficulties as the new Emir, Sheikh Nawaf al-Ahmad Al Sabah, acceded to power at the age of 84 years and in poor health that necessitated frequent trips and medical stays in Europe. In his absence, influence over policymaking passed to the new Crown Prince, Sheikh Mishal al-Ahmad Al Sabah, the 81-year-old brother both of Emir Nawaf and former Emir Sabah with a career-long background in the security forces and national guard. One of Crown Prince Mishal's first moves, in March 2021, was to announce the formation of a National Security Council under his chairmanship, while in November 2021, a decree transferred some of Emir Nawaf's constitutional powers to Crown Prince Mishal (Associated Press, 2021). In parallel, Kuwait experienced a period of deep political stasis, unusual even by the standards of the sclerotic relationship between the executive and parliamentary branches during Sheikh Sabah's 14 years as Emir, which saw seven elections and more than a dozen governments rise and fall between 2006 and 2020 (Allarakia & Albloshi, 2021).

Although elections to the National Assembly were held in December 2020 and September 2022, the body largely ceased to function on an effective basis as members of the appointed cabinet engaged in a prolonged standoff with elected members of parliament. The cabinet resigned in January and November 2021 and April 2022, ahead of motions of no confidence tabled in the assembly and continued in a caretaker capacity during which time parliamentary business slowed to a trickle (Coates Ulrichsen, 2022). The feeling of political crisis deepened in March 2023 as the Constitutional Court annulled the results of the September 2022 elections to the National Assembly (in which opposition candidates performed strongly) and reinstated the 2020 parliament, which failed to achieve a quorum (Arab News, 2023). While this was not a unique development in Kuwaiti history, having happened in 2012, the decision added to a growing sense that the *status quo* was becoming unsustainable from a governmentality perspective.

Against this backdrop of domestic uncertainty, the post-Al Ula thawing of regional tensions provides some respite to Kuwaiti policymakers, even if, as noted, intra-GCC tensions could yet recur. The "outbreak" of diplomacy across the Gulf in 2022, when the UAE resumed full diplomatic relations with Iran, and in 2023, when Saudi Arabia and Iran agreed to restore ties, moved the centre of gravity onto a landscape favourable to Kuwait's pragmatic approach to foreign affairs. The appointment of a second consecutive Secretary-General of the GCC from Kuwait likewise indicated that Kuwaiti representatives could still play a prominent role in regional leadership despite the political gridlock at home. At some point in the 2020s, the Kuwaiti ruling family will need to identify a pathway to a new generation of leaders, and in the meantime, it may be the case that technocratic engagement offers an alternative strategy in the absence of viable political will, just as it did in the intra-GCC crisis between 2017 and 2019.

Despite the passage of time and the transition in leadership, Kuwait's interests within the GCC and across the Gulf and wider region are largely unchanged. The geographical extent and size of its population mean that Kuwait is fated to remain a small state surrounded by larger and more conventionally powerful neighbours. The rapprochement between Saudi Arabia and Iran offers a bright spot for regional stability, as do the signs that Iraq is at last emerging from more than two decades of conflict that followed the toppling of Saddam Hussein in 2003. Prior to 2003, Iraq was a threat to Kuwait in the hardest possible sense, a "fierce" state with military capability and intent to use it against Kuwaiti sovereignty, while after 2003 the threat posed by Iraq changed to one of the potential overspills of violence and instability resulting from the breakdown of internal security and governing institutions as civil conflict intensified. Closer political, diplomatic, and above all economic and energy ties between Kuwait and Iraq could produce a "peace dividend" in a manner similar to that between France and Germany after the Second World War when they joined in the European Coal and Steel Community, a forerunner of the European Union. The planned connection of Iraq to the GCC's Interconnection Authority by 2025, which will see electricity from the GCC grid flow to Iraq via a substation in Kuwait, is a step towards closer economic integration (MEES, 2023).

Conclusion

Pursuit of survival within the GCC has therefore been a consistent feature of Kuwait's pragmatic regional approach, one that recognizes the limitations in power projection inherent in a small state yet also builds on the specific strengths that Kuwaiti leaders have accumulated over the years. The record for relative impartiality and reluctance to pick sides in regional disputes is one that has given Kuwait good standing on both sides of the Gulf and has enabled Kuwait to play a significant role in developing the GCC. If one result of the gradual disengagement of the United States from the Middle East (should it take root) is an internationalization of the Gulf, with greater participation of states, such as China and India, which maintain productive working relationships with all parties, that also may lead to greater regional balance. The near future may therefore see a move in Kuwait's interests as a consensus has formed among states in the region in support of cooperation over confrontation, especially after the tumultuous post-Arab Spring decade between 2011 and 2020 that produced no clear geopolitical winners. Irrespective of which path forward is taken, the challenges facing Kuwait, and a new cadre of Kuwaiti leaders and officials, will stay broadly similar to the ones that have defined Kuwait's past participation in the GCC.

References

Abdulla, A. (1999). The Gulf Cooperation Council: Nature, origin and process. In M. Hudson (Ed.), *Middle East dilemma: The politics and economics of Arab integration* (pp. 150–170). New York: Columbia University Press.

Abu-Hakima, A. M. (1983). *The modern history of Kuwait 1750–1965*. London: Luzac & Co.

Allarakia, L., & Albloshi, H. (2021, March 11). *The politics of permanent deadlock in Kuwait*. Arab Gulf States Institute in Washington. Retrieved from https://agsiw.org/the-politics-of-permanent-deadlock-in-kuwait/.

al-Awsat, A. (2017, February 23). Emir of Kuwait concludes visit to Oman. Retrieved from https://eng-archive.aawsat.com/theaawsat/news-middle-east/emir-kuwait-concludes-visit-oman.

Al-Ebraheem, H. A. (2016). *Kuwait and the Gulf: Small states and the international system*. London: Routledge.

Al-Marashi, I. (2009). Iraq's Gulf Policy and Regime security from the monarchy to the post-Ba'athist Era. *British Journal of Middle Eastern Studies*, *36*(3), 449–461.

Al-Mazrouei, N. S. (2016). *The UAE and Saudi Arabia: Border Disputes and International Relations in the Gulf*. London: I.B. Tauris.

Al-Nakib, F. (2012). The lost "two-thirds": Kuwait's territorial decline between 1913 and 1922. *Journal of Arabian Studies*, *2*(1), 19–37.

Al-Rashoud, T. (2021). Schools for the Arab homeland: Kuwait's educational mission in Sharjah. In S. Sooud Al Qassemi & T. Reisz (Eds.), *Building Sharjah*. Basel: Birkhauser(pp. 217–248).

Al Sabah, S. (2015). *Abdullah Mubarak al-Sabah: The transformation of Kuwait*. London: I.B. Tauris.

Altiok, H. (2023). Kuwait's mediation in the gulf crisis: Dynamics of Kuwait's foreign policy approaches. In Md. Mizanur Rahman & A. Al-Azm (Eds.), *Social change in the Gulf region: Multidisciplinary perspectives* (pp. 597–618). Singapore: Springer.

Alvandi, R. (2010). Muhammad Reza Pahlavi and the Bahrain question, 1968–1970. *British Journal of Middle Eastern Studies*, *37*(2), 159–177.

Anscombe, F. (1997). *The Ottoman Gulf: The creation of Kuwait, Saudi Arabia, and Qatar*. New York: Columbia University Press.

Arab News. (2023, March 19). Kuwait reinstates old parliament after annulling 2022 vote. Retrieved from https://www.arabnews.com/node/2271376/middle-east.

Assiri, A. R. (1990). *Kuwait's foreign policy: City-state in world politics*. Boulder: Westview Press.

Associated Press. (2021, November 15). Kuwait emir transfers some duties to crown prince. Retrieved from https://apnews.com/article/united-arab-emirates-dubai-kuwait-middle-east-d9ce941287d676e11af1253afd2c74cb.

Baaboud, A. (2005). 'Dynamics and determinants of the GCC States' foreign policy, with special reference to the EU. In G. Nonneman (Ed.), *Analyzing Middle Eastern foreign policies* (pp. 254–282). London: Routledge.

Caldwell, D. (1996). Flashpoints in the Gulf: Abu Musa and the Tunb Islands. *Middle East Policy*, *4*(3), 50–57.

Coates Ulrichsen, K. (2017, August 9). Walking the tightrope: Kuwait, Iran relations in the aftermath of the Abdali affair. *Gulf State analytics*. Retrieved from https://gulfstateanalytics.com/walking-the-tightrope-kuwait-iran-relations-in-the-aftermath-of-the-abdali-affair/.

Coates Ulrichsen, K. (2019, June 4). Working around the Gulf impasse. Chatham House Expert Comment. Retrieved from https://www.chathamhouse.org/2019/06/working-around-gulf-impasse.

Coates Ulrichsen, K. (2020). *Qatar and the gulf crisis*. London: Hurst & Co.

Coates Ulrichsen, K. (2021). Kuwait as a mediator in regional affairs: The gulf crises of 2014 and 2017. *The International Spectator*, *56*(4), 119–133.

Coates Ulrichsen, K. (2022, October 18). Parliamentary elections are unlikely to alter Kuwait's political landscape. *Arab center Washington.* Retrieved from https://arabcenterdc.org/resource/parliamentary-elections-are-unlikely-to-alter-kuwaits-political-landscape/.

Cooper, A., & Momani, B. (2011). Qatar and expanded contours of small state diplomacy. *The International Spectator, 46*(3), 113–128.

Cordesman, A. (1997). *Kuwait: Recovery and security after the Gulf War.* Boulder: Westview Press.

Gardner, D. (2021). Saudi-UAE competition threatens to upend the GCC. *Financial Times,* July 7. Retrieved from https://www.ft.com/content/054f0788-e5f4-4b59-80c6-2e9cfd7b0a5a, July 7.

Gordon, E. (1971). Resolution of the Bahrain dispute. *The American Journal of International Law, 65*(3), 560–568.

Gulf States Newsletter. (2015, July 16). Emir Sabah's Response to Mosque Bombing May Define Leadership. *39*(997).

Guzansky, Y. (2016). Lines drawn in the sand: Territorial disputes and GCC unity. *Middle East Journal, 70*(4), 543–559.

Halliday, F. (2005). *The Middle East in international relations: Power, politics and ideology.* Cambridge: Cambridge University Press.

Heard-Bey, F. (2006). Conflict resolution and regional cooperation: The role of the Gulf Cooperation Council 1970–2002. *Middle Eastern Studies, 42*(2), 199–222.

Herb, M. (2009). Kuwait: The obstacle of parliamentary politics. In J. Teitelbaum (Ed.), *Political liberalization in the Persian Gulf* (pp. 135–155). London: Hurst & Co.

Jones, C., & Stone, J. (1997). Britain and the Arabian Gulf: New perspectives on strategic influence. *International Relations, 13*(4), 1–24.

Jones, J., & Ridout, N. (2015). *A history of modern Oman.* Cambridge: Cambridge University Press.

Kabalan, M. (2018). Kuwait's GCC mediation: Incentives and reasons for failure. In Z. Azzam & I. Harb (Eds.), *The GCC crisis at one year: Stalemate becomes new reality* (pp. 23–30). Washington, DC: Arab Center Washington.

Kechichian, J. (1999). Trends in Saudi national security. *Middle East Journal, 53*(2), 232–253.

Kechichian, J. (2014, February 24). The gulf security pact: Another GCC dilemma. *Al Jazeera.* Retrieved from https://www.aljazeera.com/opinions/2014/2/24/the-gulf-security-pact-another-gcc-dilemma.

Khalaf, S. (1992). Gulf societies and the image of unlimited good. *Dialectical Anthropology, 17*(1), 53–84.

Koch, C. (2012, December 22). GCC confronted by dichotomy. *Gulf News.* Retrieved from https://gulfnews.com/opinion/op-eds/gcc-confronted-by-dichotomy-1.1122050.

Louis, W. R. (2003). The British withdrawal from the Gulf, 1967–71. *Journal of Imperial and Commonwealth History, 31*(1), 83–108.

MEES. (2023, February 10). Kuwait-Iraq power link deal. *Middle East Economic Survey.* Retrieved from https://www.mees.com/2023/2/10/news-in-brief/kuwait-iraq-power-link-deal/d3ab4960-a953-11ed-9a37-bda361e062de.

Miller, R. (2016). *Desert kingdoms to global powers: The rise of the Arab Gulf states.* New Haven: Yale University Press.

Mills, R. (2022). Iranian claims cloud Kuwaiti-Saudi neutral zone deal Arab Gulf States Institute in Washington. Retrieved from https://agsiw.org/iranian-claims-cloud-kuwaiti-saudi-neutral-zone-deal/.

Munro, A. (1996). *An Arabian affair: Politics and diplomacy behind the Gulf War.* London: Brassey's.

Plotkin Boghardt, L. (2006). *Kuwait amid war, peace, and revolution: 1979–1991 and new challenges.* Basingstoke: Palgrave Macmillan.

Smith, S. (2001). The making of a neo-colony? Anglo-Kuwaiti relations in the era of decolonization. *Middle Eastern Studies, 37*(1), 159–172.

Takriti, A. R. (2016). *Monsoon revolution: Republicans, sultans, and empires in Oman, 1965–1978*. Oxford: Oxford University Press.

Tetreault, M. A. (1991). Autonomy, necessity, and the small state: Ruling Kuwait in the twentieth century. *International Organization, 45*(4), 565–591.

The New Arab. (2017, October 25). Kuwait ruler says Qatar crisis could herald GCC breakup. Retrieved from https://www.newarab.com/news/kuwait-ruler-says-qatar-crisis-could-herald-gcc-breakup.

The New Arab. (2018, January 8). Kuwait emir calls for GCC cooperation amid Qatar crisis. Retrieved from https://www.newarab.com/news/kuwait-emir-calls-gcc-cooperation-amid-qatar-crisis.

Theros, P. (2021, January 11). What the Al-Ula summit has (and Has Not) accomplished. Gulf International Forum. Retrieved from https://gulfif.org/what-the-al-ula-gcc-summit-has-and-has-not-accomplished/.

Toth, A. (2005). Tribes and tribulations: Bedouin losses in the Saudi and Iraqi struggles over Kuwait's frontiers, 1921–1943. *British Journal of Middle Eastern Studies, 32*(2), 145–167.

White House. (2017, September 7). *Remarks by President Trump and Emir Sabah al-Ahmed Al-Sabah of Kuwait in joint press conference* [Press release]. Retrieved from https://trumpwhitehouse.archives.gov/briefings-statements/remarks-president-trump-emir-sabah-al-ahmed-al-jaber-al-sabah-kuwait-joint-press-conference/.

Wiegand, K. (2012). Bahrain, Qatar, and the Hawar Islands: Resolution of a gulf territorial dispute. *Middle East Journal, 66*(1), 79–96.

7 Kuwait's Relations with the Global Powers

US, Russia, and China

Giorgio Cafiero

Introduction

Like all Gulf Cooperation Council (GCC) members, the State of Kuwait has existed under the United States' (US) security umbrella for several decades. The US is undeniably Kuwait's most important military ally in the world. For the foreseeable future, it is difficult to imagine another global power supplanting the US as the security guarantor for Kuwait or any other GCC state. Mindful of the American role in Kuwait's 1991 Liberation from the Iraqi occupation, the US has a special place in the hearts of Kuwaitis and continues to safeguard Kuwait's national sovereignty from external threats.

The US and Kuwait entered into a Defense Cooperation Agreement (DCA) and an Acquisition and Cross-Servicing Agreement (ACSA) in 1991 and 2013, respectively. Washington designated Kuwait as a Major Non-NATO Ally (MNNA) in 2004. Relying on Washington for its national defence, Kuwait is home to an American military presence. Roughly 13,500 US forces are based in the Gulf country, mainly at Camp Arifjan and Ali al-Salem Air Base (US Department of State, 2021). No Middle Eastern country hosts more US forces than Kuwait, and worldwide only Germany, Japan, and South Korea do.

Nonetheless, Kuwait's leadership has pragmatically conducted a foreign policy in which its closeness to the US does not prevent the Kuwaitis from developing strong relationships with non-Western powers, including Washington's geopolitical adversaries. This chapter examines Kuwait's foreign policy balance between the US, Russia, and China in a world that is becoming more multipolar with each passing day. The chapter sheds light on Kuwait's approach to international relations against the backdrop of intensifying great power competition that plays out in the Gulf and beyond.

The main argument is that Kuwait's leadership has been successful in maintaining a careful equilibrium that enables the Arab Gulf country to maximize the extent to which it benefits from its relationships with Washington, Moscow, and Beijing. Furthermore, the nature of Kuwait's relationships with Russia and China has created less controversy among US officials compared to, for example, the United Arab Emirates (UAE) and Saudi Arabia's partnerships with Moscow and Beijing. Such dynamics limit the need for Kuwait to worry about problems in Washington stemming from its ties with America's top two geopolitical foes.

DOI: 10.4324/9781003435259-7

104 *Giorgio Cafiero*

When analysing Kuwait's foreign policy strategies, it is difficult to overstate how much the legacy of the 1990–91 crisis informs Kuwaiti perspectives. Iraq, with its far more heavily armed military, invaded and began occupying Kuwait on August 2, 1990. Saddam Hussein's forces smashed the oil-rich Gulf state's sovereignty and territorial integrity. This existential crisis taught the Kuwaitis important lessons that are relevant to their current approach to balancing their relationships with larger powers on the international stage. Ultimately, Kuwait's interest has been in ensuring that (a) no power with the means to invade and occupy Kuwait would choose to do so, and (b) should any such crisis unfold, Kuwait would have sufficient support from powerful actors throughout the region and beyond who would come to the defence of its sovereignty and territorial integrity.

The traumatic experience of the Iraqi invasion and occupation in 1990–91 remains fresh in the minds of Kuwaitis. Within this context, policymakers in Kuwait have attempted to maintain a foreign policy approach comparable to the Turkish doctrine of "zero problems with neighbors" as developed in the 2000s by Ankara's then-chief diplomat Ahmet Davutoglu. Striving to avoid making enemies in its neighbourhood and maintaining positive relations with all countries near Kuwait is a high priority for the country's policymakers because it is critical to the balance that serves the interests of peace and security in Kuwait. In Kuwaiti thinking, this is considered a form of "positive neutrality" (Chay, 2023). Beyond the immediate neighbourhood, Kuwaiti foreign policy decision-makers have long worked to enhance cooperation with as many states worldwide. Their assumption is always that when in trouble or threatened, it is best to have more friends who would come to the country's aid (Freer, 2023).

Understanding Kuwait's alliance with the US and its partnerships with Russia and China requires a historical context, which brings us back to some of the hottest periods of the Cold War. As this chapter explains, Kuwait was the first among the Western-backed Gulf monarchies to genuinely seek mutually respectful, cooperative, and trustful relationships with non-Western powers such as the Union of Soviet Socialist Republics (USSR) and the Peoples' Republic of China (PRC). Today, in 2023, as the Middle East and other parts of the Global South are under greater Russian and Chinese influence, the Kuwaiti leadership, to its credit, has managed to balance its ties to Washington, Moscow, and Beijing in ways that effectively serve the Gulf country's national interests.

Kuwait and Russia: Historical Context

Russia views Kuwait as a Moscow-friendly country, which is easy to understand given the history of bilateral ties dating back to the Cold War era when US–USSR geopolitical and ideological competition played out on the Arabian Peninsula and the Gulf. Although today all GCC states are friendly towards Russia and work with the Kremlin to various degrees, Kuwait was ahead of the curve in terms of fostering a constructive partnership with Moscow. Beginning in the 1960s, Kuwait stood out among the Gulf monarchies for formalizing ties with the Soviet Union relatively early on. Oman (Teslova, 2023) and the UAE (United Press International, 1985) were the second and third Gulf monarchies to officialize their diplomatic ties with

Kuwait's Relations with the Global Powers 105

Moscow, and they did not do so until 1985. Qatar and the Soviet Union formalized relations in 1988 (New York Times, 1988). Saudi Arabia (Katz, 2009) and Bahrain (Toumi, 2016) did not establish formal relations with the USSR until after Iraq's 1990 invasion of Kuwait, which was the year before the Soviet Union's implosion.

According to former American and British diplomats who served in the Gulf States during the 1960s, 1970s, and 1980s, the Kuwaitis had grave concerns about Washington's foreign policy (Ramani, 2023). The expanding US military presence in the Gulf combined with Washington's relationship with the fiercely anti-Communist Shah of Iran, which Kuwaitis feared would shift the balance of power in the Gulf in undesirable ways, were concerns for Kuwaitis—far more than anything that the Soviet Union was doing in the sub-region such as supporting the Marxist regime in South Yemen. To this day, such pro-Moscow sentiments among the royal Al-Sabah family endure (Ramani, 2023).

Despite the USSR backing Baghdad amid the 1961 Kuwaiti crisis, by 1963 the Kuwaitis and Soviets established formal diplomatic relations. In 1964–65, Kuwait and the USSR signed agreements on technical cooperation and cultural cooperation, resulting in the development of some trade links (Melkumyan, 2015). By March 1975, Kuwait and the USSR concluded a military agreement which entailed the Soviets delivering artillery and missile launchers to the Gulf country.

Iraq's Ba'athist government perceived a grave threat from Iran's nascent Islamic Republic, which was emboldened with revolutionary fervour and zeal in 1979–80. Fearful that Ayatollah Ruhollah Khomeini's theocracy in Tehran was seeking to export Iran's Islamic revolution to Shi'a-majority Iraq, Saddam Hussein's military invaded Iran in September 1980, resulting in the Iran–Iraq War (1980–88). The bloody eight-year war created circumstances that were extremely harmful to Kuwaiti interests. The leadership in Kuwait City supported defending Iraqi sovereignty after the war's tide turned with Iran bringing the conflict to Iraqi soil while also urging the international community to take necessary action to resolve the conflict between both Islamic nations of the Gulf.

> Traditionally, interference in another country's affairs has been a red line for Kuwait, notably during Iran–Iraq War when Kuwait shifted stances when Tehran began escalating military operations against Baghdad. Sheikh [Al] Sabah then moved to call for the passing of a UN resolution to use all necessary means to halt the crisis.
>
> (Chay, 2023)

After this conflict erupted, Kuwait saw strengthening its relationship with the USSR as necessary for its own geopolitical interests and national security. The Iran–Iraq War's destabilizing impact on the Gulf and falling oil prices served to strengthen the Kuwaiti–Soviet relationship amid a period in which officials in Kuwait City and their counterparts in Moscow shared many concerns. In 1981, Kuwait's then-Minister of Foreign Affairs Sheikh Sabah Al-Ahmed Al-Jaber Al-Sabah led a Kuwaiti delegation on an official visit to the Soviet Union, where the two countries issued a joint statement addressing the Palestinian question (Melkumyan, 2015).

106 *Giorgio Cafiero*

While the war between two of Kuwait's neighbours was raging, the Kuwaitis grew concerned about the threat of Iranian warplanes, prompting Kuwait to request Stingers from the US in May 1984 (Atkinson, 1984). Washington declined, maintaining that Saudi Arabia, which had received 400 of these antiaircraft missiles from the US earlier that month through President Ronald Reagan's executive emergency authority, needed to accept responsibility for protecting Kuwait from Iran (Atkinson, 1984). Another factor was pressure from lawmakers in Washington who believed that delivering Stingers to Kuwait risked undermining Israel's national security. The *New York Times* reported:

> The concern of members of Congress about the Stingers in connection with Kuwait is that they could fall into the hands of terrorists and then be used against civilian aircraft. There are large numbers of Palestinians in Kuwait, and some members of Congress have charged that security was not good enough in Kuwait to warrant the risk of the loss of the missiles.
>
> (Gwertzman, 1984)

Not even the then-Kuwaiti Foreign Minister's assurances to Washington that his country was not requesting the Stingers "to declare war" against Israel could convince the US to deliver the missiles (Gwertzman, 1984). Kuwait responded to Washington's decline by pursuing deeper military cooperation with Moscow, resulting in the Soviets and Kuwaitis signing a $300 million defence contract, which entailed Soviet weapons and military specialists going to Kuwait. Towards the end of the Iran–Iraq War, Kuwait suffered from the "Tanker's War," which further internationalized the conflict, and Moscow responded by chartering tankers to assist Kuwait with the transportation of its oil.

Despite Kuwaiti–Soviet military cooperation remaining limited during the 1980s and 1990s, with only a few dozen Soviet military specialists in the Gulf country, industrial cooperation at the bilateral level deepened during this period. In 1986, Kuwait City and Moscow signed a protocol for Soviet expertise to help with Kuwaiti oil industrial projects. During the second half of the 1980s, the USSR's diplomatic ties with Kuwait improved as did Moscow's relationships with Bahrain, Oman, Qatar, and the UAE. In late 1987 and early 1988, a special envoy from Moscow visited the UAE and Kuwait. In one government report, a Soviet representative wrote that GCC states are "very friendly" to the USSR and "eager to develop cooperation" (Melkumyan, 2015).

Iraq's 1990 invasion of Kuwait was the Middle East's last major crisis that unfolded during the USSR's existence. That Premier Mikhail Gorbachev's government did not side with the Soviet Union's traditional partner, Iraq, in that conflict spoke volumes about the extent to which Moscow's relationships with Kuwait and the other five GCC states (save Saudi Arabia) had improved during the previous decade. The cooperation with Washington and other Western capitals underscored how the USSR's foreign policy grew less ideologically confrontational towards the West and more geared towards upholding international law. "The Gulf crisis of 1990–91 was a watershed moment for the Soviet strategy in the Gulf region, and

Kuwait's Relations with the Global Powers 107

saw Moscow cooperate with the United States in condemning Iraq and legitimating the use of force against the Iraqi army" (Melkumyan, 2015).

The Soviet Union's implosion and establishment of the Russian Federation in 1991 resulted in Moscow being less active in the Gulf. No longer sharing a land border with Iran, the Russians were somewhat less connected to the body of water. During the 1990s, Moscow did not attempt to compete with Washington for influence in the Gulf. Yet, Russia's leadership continued to view the sub-region as critical to the security of the former Soviet Republics in the Southern Caucasus and Central Asia, where Moscow did intend to remain the dominant external player. Within this context, Russia intended to strengthen its relationships with all GCC states throughout the 1990s. Kuwait City's historic relationship with Moscow, going back to 1963, led to a defence agreement being signed in August 1993. By December of that year, Russian and Kuwaiti military forces took part in joint exercises with Moscow delivering the Kuwaitis an S-300V ITBM system. Although Russia's fiscal crisis caused that agreement to freeze at a later point, Kuwait and the UAE established themselves as the GCC's only members to purchase weapons from the Russian Federation during those years. In the mid-1990s, the Kuwaitis and Russians also signed a Protocol of Consultations between the two countries' foreign affairs ministries, an intergovernmental commission to facilitate greater investment and information cooperation, and an operating plan aimed at bolstering cultural cooperation.

The insurgency in Chechnya during the 1990s was a source of tension between GCC states and Russia. After Vladimir Putin's rise to power in 1999, however, relations between the Gulf monarchies and Russia improved with Kuwait and other GCC members declaring the situation in Chechnya to be an internal Russian issue. Between 2000 and 2002, Kuwait and Russia took steps to deepen bilateral relations with contracts between their parliaments and Moscow hosting a session of the Russian–Kuwaiti Commission for Trade, Economic, Scientific and Technological Cooperation which resulted in investment and taxation agreements and Moscow affirming its interest in expanding ties with Kuwait across a host of domains such as agriculture, infrastructure, irrigation, energy, and civil construction. In addition, during that period, Kuwait's then-Minister of Defence Jaber Al-Sabah visited Russia, securing an agreement to enhance bilateral military cooperation. The minister said, "Kuwait is interested in Russian modern technology and modern weapons including tanks."

The deepening of Kuwaiti–Russian relations during Putin's first ten years in power must be seen in the wider context of Moscow's relationship with the GCC as a six-member bloc improving in the 2000–2010 period, largely due to the warming of Saudi Arabia's relationship with Russia and the Organization of Islamic Cooperation (OIC) granting Russia observer status. By 2008, the GCC and Russia began their preparations for strategic dialogue, which led to the formal establishment of a mechanism for consultations and cooperation between the sub-regional institution and Moscow in late 2011. The Kuwaitis hosted the third ministerial meeting for GCC–Russia strategic dialogue in 2014 (Melkumyan, 2015).

108   *Giorgio Cafiero*

After the Arab Spring uprisings and revolts erupted across the Middle East and North Africa in 2010–11, the conflicts in Syria and Yemen grew increasingly relevant to Kuwait's relationship with Russia. Although the Syrian crisis pitted Kuwait City (a supporter of the rebels) against Moscow (a supporter of Bashar al-Assad's government), Kuwait established itself as a "venue for Russia-Gulf dialogue" on Syria (Ramani, 2021). An important factor was Kuwait's more balanced position on Assad's regime compared to the stance of Saudi Arabia and Qatar.

> Although Kuwait closed its embassy in Syria in 2012, it broke with the majority of its Gulf allies by keeping a Syrian Embassy open in Kuwait City. The Kuwaiti government also refused to officially sanction arms transfers to Syrian rebel forces, though Kuwaiti businessmen still donated funds to Islamist opposition factions in Syria.

Moreover, despite Kuwait's continued refusal to normalize relations with Assad's regime, Kuwait and Russia had some common cause in relation to Syria. For example, in April 2019, the Kuwaiti parliament Speaker Marzouq al-Ghanem praised Moscow for opposing the Trump administration's recognition of the Syrian Golan Heights as Israel's territory (Ramani, 2019).

Regarding the conflict in Yemen, there has been diplomatic outreach from Moscow to Kuwait beginning years ago. Having hosted Yemen peace talks in 2016 while serving a mostly diplomatic and symbolic (as opposed to militaristic) role in the Saudi-led coalition's anti-Houthi campaign, Kuwait's foreign policy vis-à-vis Yemen has received support from the Kremlin. The Russians have seen Kuwait, as well as the Sultanate of Oman, as having the potential to help wind down the conflict(s) in Yemen by supporting efforts to bring the different Yemeni factions towards a political solution (Ramani, 2019).

After Saudi Arabia, the UAE, Bahrain, and Egypt imposed a blockade on Qatar in mid-2017, Kuwait played a critical role in the efforts from within the region to restore the GCC as a cohesive institution and harmony among its six members. Russia, like many other global powers, lent support to such Kuwaiti efforts aimed at resolving the intra-Gulf feud. Two months after the blockading states began sieging Qatar, Russia's top diplomat, Sergei Lavrov, visited Kuwait to demonstrate Moscow's support for Kuwait's attempts to mediate in the GCC crisis (Ramani, 2019). While in Kuwait, Lavrov stressed the importance of unity among the Gulf monarchies, and he announced his country's plans to spearhead Russian-backed efforts aimed at complementing Kuwaiti mediation attempts if the rest of the GCC would agree to it (Ramani, 2019). Nonetheless, Moscow's diplomatic initiative hardly gained much traction, illustrating limits to Russia's ability to arbitrate in the 2017–21 Gulf crisis.

a Kuwaiti–Russian Relations in Light of the Ukraine War

Kuwait responded to Russia's overt invasion of Ukraine on February 24, 2022, based on its own national interests. Kuwait and its fellow GCC states have supported a diplomatic solution to the conflict while wanting to avoid being drawn

Kuwait's Relations with the Global Powers 109

into the war to the point whereby the Gulf countries would come under greater pressure to either side with Ukraine and its NATO backers or Russia. Nonetheless, Kuwait and Qatar have stood out as the GCC states with positions that are most aligned with the West (Ulrichsen, 2022). Not only was there sympathy in Kuwait for Ukraine and its citizens, but also a strong belief that it was necessary for the international community to strongly condemn a larger state invading its smaller neighbour. Modern Kuwaiti history was highly relevant as memories of Iraq's aggression towards Kuwait in 1990–91 were refreshed in Kuwaiti minds after Russia invaded Ukraine in 2022.

On February 24, 2022, the day of the Russian–Ukrainian War's eruption, Kuwait's Ministry of Foreign Affairs issued a statement condemning the "use, threat to use or displaying of force" to settle disputes between UN member states. One day later, Kuwait was the only Arab country out of 80 worldwide to co-sponsor the UN Security Council resolution which rejected the use of force, called for upholding the UN Charter, and reaffirmed Ukraine's sovereign rights (Ulrichsen, 2022). Subsequently, Kuwait has voted with the US and against Russia on numerous UN General Assembly resolutions concerning the Ukraine War. Nonetheless, the conflict in Ukraine has not resulted in any notable damage to the Kuwait–Russia relationship. With the conflict in Ukraine not affecting Kuwait and Russia's economic relationship, and with high-level officials from both countries meeting with each other since February 2022, the relationship remains in place (Freer, 2023).

Kuwait never implemented any of the West's sanctions on Moscow in response to its aggression in Ukraine, just as Kuwait did not do so in response to Russia's 2014 annexation of Crimea (Mostafa, 2022). One sign that Kuwait's relationship with Russia has remained healthy came on March 12, 2023, when the two countries celebrated the 60th anniversary of their establishment of bilateral relations. Kuwait's Foreign Minister Sheikh Salem Abdullah Al-Jaber Al-Sabah and his Russian counterpart exchanged messages, "stressing on the strong relations and bonds of friendship between the two countries and their endeavors towards developing bilateral relations in various fields," and emphasizing "the importance of abiding by principles adherence to international law and international legitimacy, and their keenness to restore security and stability in the region and the Middle East," according to Kuwait state-run media (KUNA, 2023). In the words of Freer:

> [The Kuwaitis] are not completely isolating Russia in the same way [as Western states are doing]. Kuwait recognizes the need not to become potentially politically close to Russia. But it can maintain this economic relationship and maybe [keeping] your friends close and your enemies closer in maintaining cordial ties with the state which has shown aggressive behaviors is certainly one way of handling that state.
>
> (Freer, 2023)

Kuwait and China: Historical Background

Beginning in 1949, China's revolutionary agendas on the international stage prompted Beijing to foster relations with the "radical" and left-leaning Arab

110   *Giorgio Cafiero*

regimes such as Egypt, Iraq, Libya, and South Yemen. Seeing the Middle East very much through revolutionary lenses, Mao Zedong's government gave support to anti-monarchical actors on the Arabian Peninsula such as the People's Democratic Republic of Yemen (PDRY) and the Popular Front for the Liberation of the Occupied Arabian Gulf (PFLOAG), which later changed its name to the Popular Front for the Liberation of Oman and the Arabian Gulf (Wakefield, 2011). Nonetheless, by the late 1970s, the Asian giant grew increasingly dependent on Gulf oil, which led to Beijing softening its stance towards Western-backed Gulf states. China began approaching the monarchies on the Arabian Peninsula far more pragmatically and less ideologically. During those years, China became less opposed to Gulf rulers cracking down on Marxist, Leftist, and Arab nationalist movements (Wakefield, 2011).

One of the reasons why Kuwait has long been important to China is the fact that in 1971 Kuwait became the first Gulf monarchy to establish formal relations with the PRC (Niazi, 2009). The next one to do so was Oman in 1978 (Zambelis, 2015), followed by the UAE (Chang, 2019), Qatar (Xinhua, 2018), and Bahrain (Chaziza, 2020) in the 1980s, and lastly Saudi Arabia (Fulton, 2020) in 1990. That Kuwait was ahead of the curve in terms of recognizing the PRC as China's only legitimate government did much to earn the Kuwaitis goodwill in Beijing. During Kuwait's 1990–91 crisis, that goodwill paid off. By the time of the Iraqi invasion and occupation of Kuwait, China came to the Gulf emirate's defence and Beijing was one of the first capitals to praise the Liberation of Kuwait in 1991. Five months after the US-led coalition ejected Iraqi forces from Kuwait, China's then-Prime Minister Li Peng paid a visit to Kuwait to congratulate the country on its liberation (Niazi, 2009).

a. *Deep Economic Relations Strengthened by the Belt and Road Initiative*

Throughout the 21st century, China and Kuwait have both been serious about strengthening their bilateral ties. Kuwait joining the Asia Cooperation Dialogue (ACD) in 2003 was a major step in the Gulf country's "Look East" drive, which intensified following the 2008 financial crisis that caused investments to shift from North America and Europe toward Asia.

Like the other GCC states, the oil exports of Kuwait have been to the East much more than to the West as the world's centre of economic gravity has shifted towards China and the rest of Asia. China is currently Kuwait's top trading partner in the world (Omar, 2023). In 2022, Sino–Kuwaiti trade reached $31.48 billion, marking a historic high (Omar, 2023). Year-on-year there was an increase in trade by 42.3 per cent with Chinese exports to the Gulf emirate at $4.97 billion and Kuwait's exports to China at $26.51 billion (Omar, 2023).

Kuwait and China established a strategic partnership in 2018, further consolidating the closeness between both nations and increasing mutual political trust between them (Xinhua, 2018). This strategic partnership opened the door to more bilateral cooperation in various domains from energy to trade and development of

Kuwait's Relations with the Global Powers 111

megacities to investment. When the late Kuwaiti Emir Sheikh Sabah Al-Ahmad Al-Jaber Al-Sabah was at the Great Hall of the People in Beijing during July 2018, he met with Chinese President Xi Jinping for talks about the strategic partnership. During that meeting, President Xi hailed the bilateral relationship as one between two nations which have remained "tried and true friends" since the early 1970s (Xinhua, 2018).

In September 2021, China's ambassador to Kuwait Li Minggang spoke about the two countries' relationship on the 50-year anniversary of diplomatic relations being established. In addition to addressing bilateral cooperation between Kuwait and China in dealing with the COVID-19 pandemic, he also stressed that the two countries' relationship has "stood the test of time, involving international changes and fluctuations," reported Kuwait's state-run KUNA (KUNA, 2021). The Chinese ambassador went on to explain that the two countries made much progress in terms of advancing practical cooperation across multiple domains since the signing of their strategic partnership in 2018 and that over 70 projects in the Gulf country benefited from the participation of Chinese firms (KUNA, 2021).

As the first Arab state to partner with China's ambitious Belt and Road Initiative (BRI), Kuwait views this grandiose Chinese initiative as complementing the Gulf country's own Vision 2035 (a.k.a. the "New Kuwait"), which seeks to end Kuwait's dependence on oil and diversify its economy. In practice, Vision 2035 rests on the future of Kuwait's culture, commerce, finance, logistics, and tourism sectors. Kuwait's ambition is to become an established hub in the northern Gulf in all these domains.

One pillar of Vision 2035 is Madinat Al Hareer (Silk City), a plan that began developing in 2014 which seeks to establish Boubyan Island as the location for a megacity with an economic zone complete with a state-of-the-art port. In February 2019, the Kuwaitis and Chinese signed a $82.2 billion deal to develop Silk City, meaning that this massive development project has much potential to elevate the Sino–Kuwaiti relationship to new heights. The expectation is that this megaproject will create 200,000 new jobs and housing for as many as 700,000 people. This new metropolis will include an Olympic stadium, a skyscraper, retail areas, workplaces, an international airport, and entertainment facilities (Castelier, 2019).

So far, the Silk City project has faced some stalling in no small part due to political paralysis since the country's current head of state ascended to the throne in 2020. Nonetheless, there is a general sense of optimism in Kuwait about the Mubarak al-Kabeer port on Boubiyan Island, which has attracted much attention from Chinese investors and businessmen. "According to Kuwaiti sources, both sides have come to terms on port investments, and what is left is a black-and-white ratification of Chinese involvement. If signed, this will boost Kuwait's plans for the port to transform into a major shipping hub" (Chay, 2023).

BRI provides the Chinese with a,

> smart way to gain a foothold in the Gulf and to do that not in a way that forces [GCC] states to choose to either have a relationship with China or a relationship with the US. Kuwait can and does maintain good ties with the

US, maintains a US military presence, and yet still has managed to get these promises of massive Chinese investment which speaks to Kuwait's ability to balance.

(Freer, 2023)

In the space of diplomacy, Kuwait and China see their agendas complementing each other. Sharing similar approaches to navigating the Middle East's complicated and constantly evolving geopolitical environment, Kuwait City and Beijing both strive for a "no enemies" foreign policy in the region. The leaders of both countries have worked to help various actors in the Gulf lower tensions and find common ground.

There is a rich history of Kuwait being a diplomatic bridge between Arab states, recently underscored by the role of Kuwaiti mediation in the lead up to the historic al-Ula summit of January 2021 that brought the 2017–21 Gulf crisis to an end as well as the rift between several GCC members and Lebanon in 2021–22. Like Russia, China very much saw a resolution of the feud between Qatar on one side and several of its Arab neighbours on the other as serving Beijing's interests.

The Chinese-brokered diplomatic agreement between Saudi Arabia and Iran reached on March 10, 2023, highlighted Beijing's growing influence in the Gulf as a mediator. Given Kuwait's own interests in seeing GCC states and Iran manage their tensions diplomatically without letting conflicts of interest and threat perceptions lead to another war in the region, the official response from Kuwaiti officials to the diplomatic deal brokered in Beijing in March 2023 was no surprise. Additionally, China's calls for resolving the Israeli-Palestinian conflict based on international law with the establishment of a Palestinian state aligns with Kuwait's firm stance on the question of Palestine. Kuwaiti efforts to resolve conflicts and lower temperatures in the Middle East will naturally lead to further alignment between the Gulf country and Beijing, creating new synergies based on shared interests in greater stability and opportunities for more prosperity in the region.

b. Xinjiang and Taiwan

The Kuwaiti media's coverage of China also speaks to the strength of bilateral ties. For example, the Kuwaiti media space is accepting of Beijing's official narratives about the plight of Uighurs and other Muslim groups in China's Xinjiang province (Ramani, 2023). Although some Kuwaiti lawmakers have criticized their country for being highly accommodating of China vis-à-vis the Uighur issue (Ramani, 2023), there is no pushback or criticism from either the media or the royal Al-Sabah family.

Despite Kuwait's history of supporting various pan-Islamic causes from Palestine to Myanmar and Bosnia, the situation in Xinjiang is unlikely to be one where Kuwait positions itself as a defender of oppressed Muslims. Instead, buying into Beijing's official narrative of a "securitization campaign" or "pacification drive" will enable Kuwait to avoid antagonizing China, a country of too much economic importance to any GCC state to risk upsetting.

Beijing is appreciative of Kuwait's stance not only on Xinjiang, but also on the Taiwan issue. As a close US ally, Kuwait did not join some other Arab states such as Egypt, Syria, and the UAE in voicing opposition to then-US House Speaker Nancy Pelosi's August 2022 visit to Taiwan (Salacanin, 2022). However, during that moment of intense friction between Washington and Beijing, the Kuwaitis made it clear that they remain fully committed to the one-China principle (Salacanin, 2022). In the aftermath of Pelosi's visit to Taipei, Kuwait's Deputy Minister of Foreign Affairs, Majdi Ahmed al-Dhafiri, took advantage of the opportunity to affirm the stance of his country towards the Taiwan issue when meeting with China's ambassador to Kuwait, Zhang Jianwei. Al-Dhafiri "stressed the need for all sides to respect the basic norms governing international relations to maintain world peace and stability," according to the Chinese state-run media outlet *Xinhua* (Xinhua, 2022).

Throughout the foreseeable future, it would be difficult to imagine Kuwait and China's relationship not improving and deepening. The extent to which China can be a major investor in Kuwait's Vision 2035 and the Gulf country's significance to BRI make these two nations extremely important to each other. With Kuwait's oil exports set to continue going to China, this bilateral relationship shows all the signs of being able to endure for many years if not decades. In light of the China-brokered Saudi–Iranian diplomatic accord on March 10, 2023 (Hafezi, 2023), the Kuwaitis are set to see Beijing's rising influence in the Middle East's affairs as all the more reason to invest in a stronger relationship with the Asian giant.

Among Kuwaiti elites, intellectuals, lawmakers, and businessmen, there has long been an understanding that their country must look eastward towards China given all the ways in which Kuwait can benefit from deeper ties with Beijing. Having faced no significant problems with Washington over its relationship with China, Kuwait is set to continue embracing Beijing as an extremely important economic, trade, business, investment, and diplomatic partner. By working to bring Sino–Kuwaiti relations to new heights, Kuwait is building on its legacy of being the first monarchy on the Arabian Peninsula to establish diplomatic relations with the People's Republic of China.

Looking ahead, it will be important to monitor Kuwait's relationship with the Shanghai Cooperation Organization (SCO). The SCO is a Chinese- and Russian-led Eurasian political, economic, and security organization, which was formed in 2001 as a product of the Shanghai Five. This international institution consists of its two main leaders—China and Russia—plus four Central Asian republics Kazakhstan, Kyrgyzstan, Tajikistan, and Uzbekistan—along with India, Iran, and Pakistan. Kuwait now joins Bahrain, Egypt, Qatar, Turkey, Saudi Arabia, and the UAE in having Dialogue Partner status at the SCO (Essaid, 2023).

Within the context of the international geopolitical landscape growing increasingly multipolar, Kuwait and other Middle Eastern nations see the SCO as an important organization as they look East more than West in terms of their economic, trade, and energy relations. Although the SCO is not comparable to NATO in the sense that it is not a military alliance, the organization provides its full-fledged members and Dialogue Partners a forum for addressing security challenges from

114 *Giorgio Cafiero*

the situation in post-US Afghanistan to terrorism and ethnic separatism throughout Eurasia.

After obtaining Dialogue Partner status at the SCO's Council of Foreign Ministers meeting in Panaji, India, in May 2023, the Kuwaiti ambassador to India, Jassim al-Najem, explained that this marks the first step in the Gulf country's path towards full membership (Essaid, 2023): "This move is in line with Kuwait's key foreign policy objectives, because trade, economic cooperation, global supply chain and food and energy security are among the areas that Kuwait attaches great importance to." The Kuwaiti diplomat stressed how his country is pursuing integration into the SCO in no small part due to Kuwait's interests contributing to the institution's efforts to counter terrorism and enhance security in Eurasia (Essaid, 2023).

Naturally, as East–West bifurcation accelerates with tensions rising between Washington, on one side, and Russia and China, on the other, the onus will continue to be on Kuwaiti policymakers to ensure that their integration into the SCO—itself an institution that aims to challenge US hegemony—balances itself with the Gulf country's decades-old alliance with the US.

Conclusion

Kuwait's history of conducting a mostly non-aligned foreign policy will continue to influence its relationships with global powers in this increasingly multipolar world. As the first GCC state to establish diplomatic relations with the USSR and Communist China, Kuwait is not geopolitically concerned about power becoming increasingly diffused on the international stage in a new global environment that is less US-centric (Coates Ulrichsen, 2023). Based on a pragmatic and non-ideological approach to foreign affairs, as well as a willingness to work with diverse parties, Kuwait is set to maintain its careful balance between Washington, Moscow, and Beijing.

In general, GCC states' growing economic relationships with China are not at the heart of Washington's concerns. Officials in the US have essentially accepted that China's astonishing economic ascendancy and thirst for Gulf hydrocarbons in the 21st century have created a geo-economic landscape in which GCC members have an eastward, not westward, orientation. It is in the domains of defence and security that Washington is most worried about—its allies and partners in the Gulf moving closer to Russia and China.

Policymakers in the US were alarmed by a report published by *CNN* in December 2021 about Saudi Arabia's indigenous ballistic missile production efforts receiving Chinese support (Cohen, 2021). Additionally, Chinese drone deliveries to Riyadh have also unsettled officials in Washington who fear that the defence and security dimensions of Sino–Gulf Arab relations can further develop in the years ahead.

Similarly, both the Trump and Biden administrations have attempted to put pressure on the UAE to avoid deepening military cooperation with Beijing. In November 2021, the *Wall Street Journal* reported that US intelligence agencies suspected that the Chinese were building a secret military facility at Khalifa port, located 50 miles north of Abu Dhabi (Lubold, 2021). The following month, another *Wall Street Journal* article claimed that the Emiratis, while under pressure from Washington, shut down that Chinese facility (Strobel, 2021).

Nonetheless, in the case of Kuwait, its dominant ties with China are based on commercial, investment, business, and trade relations, which means its partnership with Beijing is less likely to raise concerns in Washington compared to Saudi Arabia or the UAE's relationships with China. Nonetheless, there are scenarios whereby Kuwait may find it too challenging to avoid picking sides in great power politics. In terms of Kuwaiti–Russian relations, the prolongation of the Ukraine War increases the risks of Moscow using nuclear weapons as a last resort, especially if Russia's control of Crimea appears to be in jeopardy. Under such extreme circumstances, Kuwait would probably find itself shifting into greater alignment with the West against Putin's government. Additionally, if tensions between the US and China over Taiwan escalate into a military confrontation, Kuwait and its fellow GCC states would face a serious dilemma, especially if Washington used its leverage to try to pressure the Gulf monarchies into halting their oil sales to China.

Kuwait's interests are in seeing to it that such catastrophic scenarios do not unfold. Therefore, Kuwait will likely be eager to support actions taken by fellow GCC states which aim to cool friction between the US and Russia or the US and China. Saudi Arabia has already voiced its willingness to attempt such diplomacy, underscored by the Kingdom's Finance Minister Mohammed al-Jadaan's remarks at the World Economic Forum in Davos, Switzerland, in January 2023. When al-Jadaan was asked what issues worried him the most, he raised the need for "collaboration, cooperation, avoiding more geopolitical tensions, and calling for calm and political solutions to geopolitical solutions" while highlighting Riyadh's ability to facilitate fruitful dialogue between the world's major powers as the Ukraine War rages on (Turak, 2023). "We made our position very clear on these issues—whether it is in the general assembly in the United Nations or other forums," said the minister. In response to a question about the Kingdom's ability to facilitate dialogue between Washington and Beijing, al-Jadaan replied, "We have a very strategic relationship with the US, and we have a close relationship with China, and we think we can bridge the gap."

As a state that prioritizes stability and balance in the Gulf and greater Middle East, Kuwait will probably continue to navigate the challenges of this new international environment defined by accelerated East–West bifurcation by working closely with its Arab neighbours in the GCC's multilateral regional framework. Doing so will enable the Arabian emirate to benefit from greater collective depth if pressures on Kuwait intensify amid a period of greater polarization between Russia and China on one side and the US and its NATO allies on the other. Ultimately, Kuwaiti policymakers will remain focused on finding ways to benefit from the country's relationships with Washington, Moscow, and Beijing to the maximum extent possible while seeking to resist being drawn into siding with one of these powers against another.

116 *Giorgio Cafiero*

References

Atkinson, R., & Hiatt, F. (1984, May 31). Kuwait asks U. S. To Sell it stinger antiplane missiles. *The Washington Post*. https://www.washingtonpost.com/archive/politics/1984/05/31/kuwait-asks-us-to-sell-it-stinger-antiplane-missiles/65b0f62c-2109-4be2-86ce-5e0eb7af1ab3/

Bismarck, H. V. (2009). He Kuwait crisis of 1961 and its consequences for Great Britain's Persian Gulf policy. *British Scholar*. https://doi.org/10.3366/brs.2009.0105

Castelier, S. (2019, June 3). *Can Kuwait's Silk City project overcome Islamist opposition in parliament?* Al Monitor. https://www.al-monitor.com/originals/2019/06/kuwait-silk-city-bump-unanticipated-obstacles.html#ixzz7wSySmaL3

Chang, I. W. J. (2019, August 14). *The UAE: An oasis for trade and friendly ties with Taiwan*. Global Taiwan Institute. https://globaltaiwan.org/2019/08/the-uae-an-oasis-for-trade-and-friendly-ties-with-taiwan/

Chaziza, M. (2020). China-Bahrain relations in the age of the belt and road initiative. *Strategic Assessment, 23*(4).

Cohen, Z. (2021, December 23). *CNN Exclusive: US intel and satellite images show Saudi Arabia is now building its own ballistic missiles with help of China*. CNN. https://www.cnn.com/2021/12/23/politics/saudi-ballistic-missiles-china/index.html

Essaid, S. (2023, May 8). In boost to China, UAE and Kuwait become 'dialogue partners' in Shanghai Cooperation Organization. Al Monitor. https://www.al-monitor.com/originals/2023/05/boost-china-uae-and-kuwait-become-dialogue-partners-shanghai-cooperation#ixzz81KpYWWK0

Fulton, J. (2020, August 25). *Strangers to strategic partners: Thirty years of Sino-Saudi relations*. Atlantic Council. https://www.atlanticcouncil.org/wp-content/uploads/2020/08/Sino-Saudi-Relations_WEB.pdf

Gwertzman, B. (1984, June 20). U.S. tells Kuwait it can't have missiles. *The New York Times*. https://www.nytimes.com/1984/06/20/world/us-tells-kuwait-it-can-t-have-missiles.html

Hafezi, P., Abdallah, N., & Yaakoubi, A. (2023, March 10). *Iran and Saudi Arabia agree to resume ties in talks brokered by China*. Reuters. https://www.reuters.com/world/middle-east/iran-saudi-arabia-agree-resume-ties-re-open-embassies-iranian-state-media-2023-03-10/

Katz, M. N. (2009, October 1). *Saudi-Russian relations: 1979–2009*. Middle East Institute. Retrieved March 25, 2023, from https://www.mei.edu/publications/saudi-russian-relations-1979-2009

Lubold, G., & Strobel, W. (2021, November 19). Secret Chinese port project in Persian Gulf rattles U.S. relations with U.A.E. *The Wall Street Journal*. https://www.wsj.com/articles/us-china-uae-military-11637274224

Melkumyan, E. (2015, December 4). *A political history of relations between Russia and the gulf states*. Doha Institute. https://www.dohainstitute.org/en/lists/ACRPS-PDFDocumentLibrary/A_Political_History_of_Relations_between_Russia_and_the_Gulf_States_Elena_Melkumyan.pdf

Mostafa, A., & Naar, I. (2022, June 1). GCC members stand united on Russia-Ukraine crisis, Saudi foreign minister says. *The National*. https://www.thenationalnews.com/gulf-news/saudi-arabia/2022/06/01/russias-sergey-lavrov-meets-gcc-foreign-ministers-in-riyadh/

Niazi, K. (2009, September 1). *Kuwait looks towards the east: Relations with China*. https://www.mei.edu/publications/kuwait-looks-towards-east-relations-china

_____. (1988, August 2). Qatar opens ties to Moscow at time of strains with U.S. *New York Times*. https://www.nytimes.com/1988/08/02/world/qatar-opens-ties-to-moscow-at-time-of-strains-with-us.html?mcubz=0

Omar, F. (2023, March 9). China-Kuwait trade ties flourish. *Kuwait Times*. https://www.kuwaittimes.com/china-kuwait-trade-ties-flourish/

Ramani, S. (2019, May 7). *Russia, Kuwait discuss common ground in regional conflicts*. Al Monitor. https://www.al-monitor.com/originals/2019/05/russia-kuwait-gulf-syria.html

Ramani, S. (2019, May 7). *Russia, Kuwait discuss common ground in regional conflicts*. Al Monitor. https://www.al-monitor.com/originals/2019/05/russia-kuwait-gulf-syria.html

Ramani, S. (2021, March 25). *Russia's expanding cooperation with gulf Arab countries on Syria*. The Arab Gulf States Institute in Washington. https://agsiw.org/russias-expanding-cooperation-with-gulf-arab-countries-on-syria/

Salacanin, S. (2022, August 17). *Why Arab states are standing by China over the US on Taiwan*. The New Arab. https://www.newarab.com/analysis/why-arab-states-are-standing-china-over-us-taiwan

_____. (2021, July 22). U.S. security cooperation with Kuwait. U.S. Department of State. https://www.state.gov/u-s-security-cooperation-with-kuwait-2/#:~:text=Approximately%2013%2C500%20U.S.%20forces%20are,Ambush%20Protected%20vehicles%20in%20Kuwait.

Strobel, W. (2021, December 9). U. A. E. Shut down China facility under U.S. pressure, emirates says. *The Wall Street Journal*. https://www.wsj.com/articles/u-a-e-confirms-it-halted-work-on-secret-chinese-port-project-after-pressure-from-u-s-11639070894

Teltsch, K. (1961, July 8). Soviet veto bars British U. N. Plan to Shiel Kuwait; security council defeats U.A.R.'s rival proposal for troop withdrawal 4 days' debate ended Russians support Iraqis' claim to Sheikdom -- Arab talks may settle issue plan for Kuwait vetoed by soviet. *The New York Times*. https://www.nytimes.com/1961/07/08/archives/soviet-veto-bars-british-un-plan-to-shield-kuwait-security-council.html

Teslova, E. (2023, March 23). Putin, Sultan of Oman hold 1st phone call since establishment of diplomatic relations. *Anadolu Agency*. https://www.aa.com.tr/en/world/putin-sultan-of-oman-hold-1st-phone-call-since-establishment-of-diplomatic-relations/2854080

Toumi, H. (2016, September 5). King Hamad to hold talks with Putin in Russia. *Gulf News*. https://gulfnews.com/world/gulf/bahrain/king-hamad-to-hold-talks-with-putin-in-russia-1.1891027

Turak, N. (2023, January 16). *Saudi Arabia can 'bridge the gap' between the U.S. And China, finance minister says*. CNBC. https://www.cnbc.com/2023/01/16/saudi-arabia-can-bridge-the-gap-between-the-us-and-china-finance-minister-says-.html

Ulrichsen, K. C. (2022, March 22). *The GCC and the Russia-Ukraine crisis*. Arab Center Washington DC. https://arabcenterdc.org/resource/the-gcc-and-the-russia-ukraine-crisis/

_____. (1985, November 15). United Arab Emirates establishes ties to Moscow. United Press International, Inc. https://www.upi.com/Archives/1985/11/15/United-Arab-Emirates-establishes-ties-to-Moscow/6370500878800/

Wakefield, B., & Levenstein, S. (2011). *China and the Persian Gulf*. Woodrow Wilson International Center for Scholars. https://www.wilsoncenter.org/sites/default/files/media/documents/publication/ASIA%20Program_China%20and%20the%20PG.pdf

_____. (2018, July 5). *China, Qatar celebrate 30 years of diplomatic relations*. Xinhua. http://www.xinhuanet.com/english/2018-07/05/c_137303729.htm

_____. (2018, July 10). China Focus: China, Kuwait agree to establish strategic partnership. Xinhua. http://www.xinhuanet.com/english/2018-07/10/c_137312795.htm

_____. (2021, September 23). *Kuwait, China willing to cement strategic partnership*. KUNA. https://www.kuna.net.kw/ArticleDetails.aspx?id=2999526&language=en

_____. (2022, August 9). *Kuwait firmly supports one-China principle*. Xinhua. https://english.news.cn/20220809/b32f1d351e3245af831bf3b402afb38a/c.html

_____. (n.d.). *Kuwait, Russia celebrates diplomatic ties' 60th anniversary*. KUNA. Retrieved March 12, 2023, from https://www.kuna.net.kw/ArticleDetails.aspx?id=3084247&Language=en#

Zambelis, C. (2015, November 16). *China and the quiet kingdom: An assessment of China-Oman relations*. The Jamestown Foundation. https://jamestown.org/program/china-and-the-quiet-kingdom-an-assessment-of-china-oman-relations/#.VmAIpnarSUk

Interviews

Interview with Dr. Clemens Chay (2023, March 30).
Interview with Dr. Courtney Freer (2023, March 13).
Interview with Dr. Kristian Coates Ulrichsen (2023, March 23).
Interview with Dr. Samuel Ramani (2023, March 20).

8 Kuwait and the Palestinian Cause

Mutual Search for National Pride

Meshari Hamad Alruwaih

Introduction

Support for the Palestinian cause in the Arab world has been declining since the counter-revolutions that ended the waves of protests that have come to be known as the "Arab Spring." Although this shift is harder to substantiate among Arab populations, it can be easily observed in discourse and policies among Arab political regimes and elites. Moreover, Gulf states have assumed a leading role in this move away from the political, moral, and emotional "burdens" that are usually associated with the Palestinian cause. It seems that, finally, the Arab Gulf states have decided on their position on the continuum between pan-Arab-Islamic issues on one side and sovereignty and national interest on the other, decisively choosing the latter, while actively and boldly constricting the former.

Today, Kuwait remains an exception. At the official level, it has demonstrated what could be described as a reluctance to join the move away from the Palestinian cause and pan-Arab-Islamic issues in general. At the level of the public, Kuwaitis are among the fiercest supporters of the Palestinian cause, despite waning support in many other parts of the Arab world. What makes this Kuwaiti position more puzzling is the fact that it was Kuwait that witnessed the steepest decline in support for the Palestinian cause after the Iraqi invasion and during the 1990s. This chapter explores the reasons behind Kuwait's continued support for the Palestinian cause, despite the decline in other Gulf Cooperation Council (GCC) states.

Until recently, the foreign policy of the GCC was usually characterized by an assumption of sameness. Mainstream international relations theory, although witnessing a decline of its own, continues to support this assumption, emphasizing a structural-material understanding of threats and forcing the logic of survival on states. This logic is especially applicable to small states, which have limited options, namely bandwagoning or finding a balance through alliances with foreign powers, leaving little room for these states to support moral causes.

Although recent research has conceded greater agency and freedom of action to small states, states like Qatar and the United Arab Emirates (UAE) (Ennis, 2018) are the subjects of most of the available empirical studies, with only a few exceptions considering Kuwait (Mansour, 2020). This focus is understandable given that Kuwait has long been moving towards the passive side of the passive–active continuum, at least compared to these other states.

DOI: 10.4324/9781003435259-8

120   *Meshari Hamad Alruwaih*

This state of research makes support for moral causes by small states at best either absent or instrumental. Writing on Arab nationalism and the foreign policy of Kuwait in the 1960s and 1970s, Wafa Alsayed called on researchers studying Arabism to move beyond instrumental views of the behaviour of Arab states (Alsayed, 2022), specifically criticizing Michael Barnett's work, which subsumes cultural and normative concerns in Arab politics into security competition between Arab states (Alsayed, 2022, 200). Instead, Wafa offers a combined historical–sociological and constructivist approach to argue that Kuwait's Arabist foreign policy in the 1960s and 1970s largely stemmed from its distinctive history.

Foreign policy analysis can offer a more diversified toolkit to escape assumptions of sameness, as it focusses on the making of foreign policy rather than on the outcomes of foreign policy. In his article "Roles, Identity, and Security: Foreign Policy Contestation in Monarchical Kuwait," Sean Yom uses role theory, a foreign policy analysis tool borrowed from social theory, to explain the Kuwaiti government's failure to impose and ratify the Internal Security Pact (Yom, 2019), which is an innovative project designed to enhance cross-border repression of domestic opposition and thus bolster collective security among GCC states. These states faced what Yom described as an existential threat to the six Gulf monarchies during the Arab Spring. Although clearly vulnerable, the prospect of the Sabah family imposing this mechanism of greater repression was incompatible with the regime's historical role of tolerating domestic pluralism and protecting Kuwait from foreign pressures. According to Sean Yom, this role conception of a tolerant protector flowed from historical understanding and collective memory, and is cognitively tied to a national self-conception of "Kuwaitiness" (Yom, 2019, p. 2).

These contributions clearly go beyond the instrumentalism and survival logic contained in structural–material ontological views of the region. Of equal importance, they challenge the associated sameness assumption and emphasize the distinctiveness of the Kuwaiti case. The question remains, however, distinctive from what? Wafa gives an implicit answer, while Sean Yom, because of the nature of his research, gives an explicit answer: other GCC states. However, again, because of the scope of their research, they do not develop the theoretical implications of this answer.

Between sameness and distinctiveness, this chapter takes a relational approach emphasizing the ideational and emotional interplay between Gulf states as an important dimension to understanding their sometimes divergent positions on regional issues, including the range, degree, and intensity of support for the Palestinian cause.

In this context, the chapter argues that Kuwait's support for the Palestinian cause has always been an expression of self-conception, but one that is viewed in relation to other Arab Gulf states. This relational dimension of Kuwait's self-conception versus other Arab Gulf states takes different forms: Democratic, pluralist, open, active, progressive, and modern. This expression was not taken in isolation but was always based on the assumption that "other" Arab Gulf states are non-democratic, tribal, closed, and traditional. From the 1930s until the Iraqi invasion of Kuwait, and especially during the 1950s and 1960s, supporting Arab causes, particularly the Palestinian cause, was a "requirement" for being progressive and an opportunity to showcase Kuwaitis' ideational and material success compared to their peers in other Gulf states. In other words, Kuwaitis took *pride* in supporting the Palestinian cause, a very important self-conscious emotion.

In this chapter, the literature on self-conscious emotions plays an important part in developing the theoretical framework guiding the navigation of the ideational and emotional ground so that Kuwait's support for the Palestinian cause can be better understood. As the theoretically aware reader may have guessed by now, the use of the phrase "self-conception" points to the purpose of role theory in this chapter. In this context, I build on Sean Yom's application of role theory to Kuwait's foreign policy, but with differences, as will be shown later. I also build on Wafa Alsayed's historical–sociological treatment of Kuwait's Arabist foreign policy, although I give more weight to the Palestinian influence.

From a theory perspective, I will attempt to integrate role theory and self-conscious emotions, namely pride and shame, arguing that doing so sheds light on the emotional dimensions of the application of a few ideas associated with the use of role theory in the field of foreign policy, including self-defined national conceptions, self-representations, and role enactment (Thies, 2010). This self-conscious emotional dimension is essentially relational, which, in turn, serves to capture the relational context of performing roles in different social settings, including regional and international settings. The integration of role theory and self-conscious emotions, it will be argued, can contribute to different fields of literature, including social-emotional rewards and sanctions on moral actions in international politics, support for moral causes within competitive status-seeking by small states, and, in general, the emotional turn in both international relations theory and foreign policy analysis. The first part of this chapter develops the link between role theory and self-conscious emotions, while the second part applies it to the Kuwaiti case with an eye on the emotional and ideational milieu that links Kuwaitis to the Palestinian cause through phases of regional transformation.

This chapter uses role theory and the literature on self-conscious emotions to trace the status of the Palestinian cause among the Kuwaiti public. It argues that role enactment involves emotional investment, demonstrating in turn that assuming roles in international politics and maintaining the social status associated with these roles necessarily involves self-conscious emotions, namely pride and shame.

Further, the chapter argues that from early on, the Palestinian cause has been present in the development of 20th century Kuwait's national self-representation and national conceptions, allowing Kuwait to successfully enact the regional role of a "progressive Gulf state." In addition, the chapter traces Kuwait's role-enacting and status-seeking behaviour as a small state, through different phases of regional transformation, highlighting the changing structure of the regional role as a result of economic globalization and arguing that Kuwaitis continue to find pride in supporting the Palestinian cause, turning shame and anger from failure to exploit economic globalization into virtuous anger.

Role Theory and Self-conscious Emotions: Emotional Investments in Role Enacting

The theoretical framework developed in this chapter argues that role enactment in any social setting involves an emotional dimension. Different definitions of role theory, whether in its original sociological meaning or within foreign policy analysis, agree on the cognitive content of social roles in general; this is, at least implicitly, in line with Holsti's emphasis on "role conception" over role expectations, implying an emphasis on cognitive dimensions (Holsti, 1970, p. 243).

More explicitly, Sarbin and Allen agree that locating oneself in the role system is a cognitive process (Sarbin & Allen, 1968, 507). Walker, who has written extensively on role theory and foreign policy analysis, defined symbolic interactionist and cognitive approaches to role theory as those referring to roles as "repertoires of behavior inferred from others' expectations and one's own conceptions, selected at least partly in response to cues and demands" (Walker, 1992, p. 23).

Recent studies in psychology and neuroscience, however, have suggested that cognition and emotions are not separate; on the contrary, emotions are involved in the sensory processes where information about the external world is translated into an internal code or representation (Duncan & Barrett, 2007, p. 1185). Within foreign policy analysis and international relations theory, researchers seem to agree and have been pushing for an emotional turn for some time (Stein, 2012, p. 133). It is at this intersection of role theory and the study of emotions, namely self-conscious emotions, that the theoretical framework in this chapter is advanced.

On role theory, it is useful to go back to basics, that is, to Holsti's work, where he made the earliest attempt to borrow role theory from sociology and apply it to the field of foreign policy analysis. Although Holsti's introduction of role theory to the field has benefited from subsequent development and refinement by others (Walker, 1992, 2004), his empirical effort in identifying 17 roles in international politics based on studying 72 states remains exceptional. Conveniently for the purpose of this chapter, Kuwait was one of the 72 states.

Writing in the middle of the Cold War, Holsti criticized limitations on the study of roles in international politics resulting from balance of power theory and polarity models, where only three roles can be envisioned, namely an aggressor state or group of states, a defending state or group of states, and "balancer" (Holsti, 1970, p. 234). This treatment of roles, Holsti argued, ignores the great variety of roles that small states in particular play in the system and in their respective regions; these states were primarily analysed as objects of rivalry between the great powers.

Thus, Holsti included more than a few small states in his empirical study, although Kuwait always stood out as one of the most active, and not just among small states. Evidently, after introducing different findings, he kept going back to the Kuwaiti case, highlighting it as an "exception." For example, on the ratio of national role conceptions per source, Kuwait scores higher than expected and was mentioned by Holsti as "one of a few surprises" (Holsti, 1970, p. 281). Also, according to his findings, Kuwaiti policymakers held five national role conceptions. Qualitatively, the types of national self-conceptions held by Kuwait (mediator, integrator, developer, independent, faithful ally) place it among the most active states in the system.

On the theoretical level, Holsti derived four concepts to help analyse foreign policy through role theory: (1) role performance, which encompasses the attitudes, decisions, and actions governments take; (2) their self-defined national role conceptions; (3) the role prescriptions emanating, under varying circumstances, from the external environment; and (4) a position within which action always takes place, that is, a system of role prescriptions (Holsti, 1970, p. 240).

Although clearly acknowledging the intersubjective and structural dimensions of role performance, throughout Holsti's framework, self-conceptions seem to always to take precedence. While important to preserve agency and agential cognitive and emotional capacities, relational dimensions that actualize these cognitive and emotional capacities are underdeveloped.

In his *Oxford Review of Role Theory and Foreign Policy*, Cameron Thies suggested making more use of the concepts and language of role theory as developed in the sociological literature, specifically, role enactment, role expectations, role demands, role location, and audience (Thies, 2010). He suggests treating role enactment as a dependent variable to be explained, with role expectations, demands, location, and audience effects as independent variables. While overlapping and underspecified, these concepts can indeed be useful as descriptive background for bringing in self-conscious emotions, which play the explanatory role in this chapter. In addition, due to the redundancy of the above concepts, at least as introduced by Thies, this chapter only makes use of role enactment, role expectations, and the audience effect.

Sarbin and Allen (1968, pp. 491–497) identified three key dimensions of role enactment: the number of roles, the effort expended upon a particular role, and the time spent in one role in comparison to other possible roles. Role expectations are norms, beliefs, and preferences concerning the performance of any individual in a social position relative to individuals occupying other positions (Sarbin & Allen, 1968: 497; Holsti 1970: 244). The audience or observers of role enactment play an important role according to Sarbin and Allen, who mention several functions of the audience, including establishing a consensual reality for the role and engagement in social reinforcement through the positive and negative sanctions associated with role enactment (Sarbin & Allen, 1968: 534).

Those who are familiar with self-conscious emotions should have spotted a few familiar terms, such as expectations, social enforcement, positive and negative sanctions, and of course, audience or observers. To demonstrate this familiarity, the following quote by Jennifer Beer is instructive:

> In order to experience a self-conscious emotion, one must have an awareness of self (self-perception), an awareness that others are judging that self (person inference), and an awareness that there are a set of rules or social norms that determine whether the actions of the self are "right" or "wrong" (social norms).
>
> (Beer, 2007: 53)

This quote seems to include components emphasized by role theorists as influencing role enactment: Self-perception (self-conception), judgment by others (audience), and rules and social norms (role expectations). Moreover, positive and negative sanctions provided by the audience of role enactment are essential to understand the role of self-conscious emotions, especially negative emotions like embarrassment, shame, and guilt that arise from social misdeeds. These emotions are sufficiently unpleasant that, once they have been given a taste, people are highly motivated to regulate their behaviour to avoid experiencing them (Beer, 2007: 53). In other words, questions like "what happens when an actor fails to meet role expectations?" or "what happens to an actor when the normative and ideational context of the role changes and the role loses the social status associated with it?" can better be investigated by bringing self-conscious emotions on board.

The realization that components emphasized by role theorists can accommodate an emotional dimension suggests a fruitful integration between role theory and literature on self-conscious emotions that could contribute to our understanding of motivations and incentives influencing behaviour and foreign policy of states beyond forcing material-structural determinants, especially on small states. Compared to basic emotions (fear, happiness, etc.), self-conscious emotions (pride, shame, guilt, and embarrassment) have not received enough attention even in their home field: Psychology. Recent interest within the fields of cognitive and neuroscience, however, has advanced exploration of the role played by these emotions in decision-making processes and, to a lesser degree, social relations.

Self-conscious emotions are divided into positive (pride) and negative (shame, guilt, and embarrassment) emotions. In this chapter, we are concerned with pride and shame. In the literature, pride is usually conceptualized in terms of two distinct facets: One reflecting authentic feelings surrounding achievements and mastery, and the other reflecting hubristic feelings of arrogance, grandiosity, and superiority (Tracy & Robins, 2007, p. 266). Although an important distinction at the individual level, it is less so at the group level, especially in national groups, where both facets are interwoven in a narrative of national pride, reflecting "national greatness." Shame is the opposite of pride but can also be divided along the same lines, as shame of one's behaviour and shame of oneself. Moreover, the mechanism that produces these two different experiences is the same: (1) the actor has succeeded/ failed to live up to some cultural standard for behaviour, (2) others are aware of this success/failure, and (3) the actor is aware of others' knowledge in this regard (Fessler, 2004). These mechanisms producing self-conscious emotions can be used to enhance our understanding of role enactment and how it is related to role expectations and audience, although not without qualification.

First, going back to Sabrin and Allen's dimensions of role enactment, specifically the time and effort an actor invests in performing a role, one cannot rule out the emotional relations an actor develops with the role, a kind of emotional investment, to use Ernesto Laclau's term. Actors, especially in international politics, take *pride* in the roles they choose to perform on the international stage. Roles, in this regard, are social status, reflecting others' acknowledgement of success and the achievements of the collective national self. Where national narratives of greatness meet international recognition, or in self-conscious emotional terms, where actors are aware of others' knowledge of their success, the positive experience of

Kuwait and the Palestinian Cause 125

national pride is elicited. In other words, role enactment is both an ideational and an emotional undertaking.

Second, and subsequently, the interaction between self-defined national role conceptions and role expectations or prescriptions emanating from the external environment necessarily involve emotions; this is especially true when the level of ideational and emotional investment in the role is high. Any discrepancy between ideational and emotional investment can trigger an identity and emotional crisis on the part of the actor enacting the role. One possible path towards this state is when the norms and beliefs that constitute role expectations are allowed to be a part of defining national self-conceptions, which is to an extent true in the case of Kuwait, as will be argued.

In this context, it is important to point to the beneficial distinction made in the literature on self-conscious emotions and the psychological literature; that is, the distinction between self-awareness and self-representation. Although both point to a sense of self, the former is usually described as the "I" self and the latter as the "Me" self: The mental representations that constitute one's identity (Tracy & Robins, 2007, p. 5). In the usage of role theory in foreign policy analysis, national conceptions usually capture the "I" sense of self, before allowing this sense of self to interact with the external ideational environment. In contrast, the "Me" sense of self comprises relational, social, and collective self-representations, reflecting how we see ourselves vis-à-vis close others. Bringing the national "Me" in between the "I" of national self-conceptions and role expectations from the external environment can contribute to a richer analysis, including capturing the emotional interplay between role enacting and the international audience.

Third, the audience effect on role enactment is differentiated and multidimensional, resulting from the fact that the audience or observers of role enactment are themselves ranked in a social hierarchy. If role enactment is in itself a status-seeking effort, especially by small states, then recognition of social status through successful role enactment can only be "awarded" by those of higher rank in the international social hierarchy.

Daniel Fessler refers to prestige hierarchies, arguing that these hierarchies have come to replace dominance hierarchies (Fessler, 2007, p. 176). In the latter, a superordinate social position is obtained through the use or threat of force, while in the former, selected individuals are elevated to superordinate positions by observers; in short, a dominant position is *taken* from others, but a prestigious position is *given* by others.

Moreover, Fessler argued that prestige hierarchies are not competitive, focussing on shame; he claimed that although shame can be elicited by subordination or defeat, the prototypical eliciting situation is not a competitive one, but rather a situation in which the actor has failed to conform to some cultural standard. Rather than addressing issues of hierarchical ranking, shame often revolves around failing to meet a threshold for social acceptability (Fessler, 2007, p. 178).

Although we can see the value of Fessler's arguments in enhancing our understanding of the relationship between audience and role expectations on one hand, and role enactment on the other, we do not need to go as far as denying the competitive nature of prestige hierarchies, particularly in international politics where competition is an essential dimension of interactions between states. In fact, I argue that prestige and status as intangible rewards in international politics are usually subject to competition, and this competition can take place through role enactment. In this competition, success or "winning" is awarded by those of higher rank in the international social hierarchy: the creators of role expectations and prescriptions. In addition to peers and competitors, these constitute the most important segment of the audience of role enactment.

For Michael Barnett and Raymond Duvall, this capacity to produce role expectations for others is called "structural power" (Barnett & Duvall, 2005, p. 52). It concerns the co-constitutive, internal relations of structural positions that define what kind of social beings actors are. It produces the very social capacities or subject positions in direct relation to one another, and the associated interests that underlie and dispose action. Barnett and Raymond go further, assigning the capacity of "productive power" to some actors. While structural and productive powers overlap, the authors explain that structural power is the capacity to produce and reproduce internally related positions of super- and subordination, or that actors occupy, and productive power is the constitution of all social subjects with various social powers through systems of knowledge and discursive practices (Barnett & Duvall, 2005, p. 55).

Although important, we do not need to go as far as suggesting that all social subjects are constituted through systems of knowledge and discursive practices, and instead argue that agents have essential emotional and idealist capacities, risking a post-structuralist view of subjectivity as pointed out by the authors themselves (Barnett & Duvall, 2005, p. 56). As previously mentioned, preserving the emotional and ideational agential capacities is important to the story I want to tell about Kuwait's support for the Palestinian cause. It is a story with a number of actors, interacting mainly through role enacting, in a multidimensional setting where the emotional dimension plays an important part. The fact that agents practice resistance and reluctance and go through crises means that it must be assumed that there are strong emotional and ideational-agential capacities that should not be overlooked.

Bringing in notions of structural and productive power in the context of prestige hierarchies should broaden the theoretical space to relate role enactment to the concept of audience. In this context, there are three sides to the interaction between role enactment and the audience: Two sides competing for higher rank in the prestigious international hierarchy through role enactment, and an observer enjoying a level of structural and productive power awarding status and prestige to the actors who succeed in meeting role expectations, set, or at least valued by these observers.

To sum up, role enactment on the international stage is a type of ideational and emotional investment as well as a status-seeking behaviour, where actors seek recognition from other actors for their national narratives of greatness, uniqueness, or exceptionalism and, in turn, maintain a positive image of the national self and preserve their sense of national *pride*, which is a self-conscious emotion. For this emotion to be elicited and maintained, however, the actor must succeed in meeting

Kuwait and the Palestinian Cause 127

norms and beliefs associated with the role (role expectations) and be aware of others' knowledge and approval, of this success (audience). That said, failure for different reasons, including peers outperforming an actor in a particular role enactment or the ceasing of a role because of ideational structural change in the regional and international environment, can produce an identity crisis along with negative self-conscious emotions, namely shame, especially when investment in the role is high. This chapter argues that Kuwait has gone through emotional and ideational ups and downs in this race towards regional and even international status and, more importantly, that support for the Palestinian cause has always been present in times of both pride and shame.

Kuwait and the Palestinian Cause: From National Conceptions to Regional Roles

"The people of this republic are one of the freest peoples in the world."
E. Reclus (1884)

Although clearly a subjective observation, this short sentence summarizes an important element of Kuwaitis' national self-conception, of course settling for "in the Gulf and Arab Peninsula" instead of "in the World." Almost all accounts of the history of Kuwait reflect a narrative of exceptionalism, whether they confirm or deny this narrative. Mary Ann Tetreault included (2000, p. 11) exceptionalism as one of the founding myths of the Kuwaiti narrative; Sean Yom used exceptionalism in building his explanation based on role theory of Kuwait's strategic behaviour, particularly in the difficult times of the Arab Spring (Yom, 2019). In addition, Wafa Alsayad (2022) employed exceptionalism as the foundation to challenge instrumental views of Kuwait's Arabist foreign policy in the 1960s and 1970s.

More importantly, this narrative is "out there" as part of Kuwaitis' self-defined national conception. Kuwaitis pride themselves not just on the peaceful consensual establishment of Kuwait but also on subsequent political reforms, including the 1921 Shura Council, which is seen as an unprecedented system of consultation between the ruler and Kuwait's leading citizens. This consultation was "the first formal attempt at democratic rule in Kuwait, and for that matter, in the Persian Gulf and Arab Peninsula" (Tetreault, 2000, p. 59). The narrative of exceptionalism has tied Kuwaiti self-conception and self-representation since then.

Exceptionalism is necessarily relational, as it implies uniqueness compared to others, especially "close others" and in this case, the "close others" are societies of the Gulf and Arab Peninsula. To give more context, this exceptionalism was to be read as follows: Societies of the Gulf and Arab Peninsula are traditional, closed, and tribal *except* Kuwait." In other words, the "I" of Kuwait in the early 20th century was entangled from the start with the "Me" as explained above, meaning that Kuwaitis developed their national self-conceptions relationally; they saw themselves vis-à-vis close others, that is, other societies in the Gulf and Arab Peninsula.

More detailed accounts explain that this sense of "Kuwaitiness" developed on the border of the town of Kuwait, dividing Kuwaiti (*hadhar*) or city-residents and (*Badu*)

128　*Meshari Hamad Alruwaih*

tribal populations surrounding the town. Although suffering the greatest burden of building and protecting physical borders (*Alsoor*), the tribal population was still seen as outsiders, especially socially and culturally (Tetreault, 2000, p. 65).

It is in this context that we should understand, for example, the *Ikhwan man ata'a Allah* (Brethren of those who obey God) threat to Kuwait in the early decades of the 20th century. Although the religious character of this movement is well known, it is also important to imagine how this threat might have presented itself to Kuwaitis at the time. The Ikhwan movement, which might have been an exception to religious movements and groups, was known for its brutality and backwardness, further confirming Kuwait's self-representation versus its close surroundings, including the tribes who again suffered the burden of fighting the Ikhwan movement. However, in the Kuwaiti *hadhar*'s imagination, they were all alike and different from the population of the town of Kuwait.

Subsequent political reforms and modernization have further contributed to positive national self-conceptions versus their close surroundings, but important elements of self-representation and role allocations were still missing. Earlier, the Ottomans failed to penetrate the Kuwaiti "collective cognition" as a valued audience, while the British were not yet heavily involved, at least culturally, to play that role in Kuwaitis' construction of their mental image. Elements of self-representation and role allocations would have to wait until the start of the actual institutional and educational modernization of the Kuwaiti state, which started around the late 1930s and the 1940s, coinciding with the arrival of the early waves of Palestinians.

Following the discovery of oil reserves and the commencement of commercial exploitation in 1938, Kuwait underwent a period of rapid development and transformation. It soon became a magnet for Palestinian immigrants (Zelkovitz, 2014, p. 86). The first wave of Palestinian refugees to arrive in Kuwait comprised no more than a few hundred persons, the majority of whom belonged to the Palestinian intelligentsia, who were considered to be one of the most qualified and capable workforces in the Arab world. By virtue of their pedagogical achievements, this group was regarded highly by an impressed local elite (Zelkovitz, 2014, p. 87).

Not only the local elite but also wider segments of the Kuwaiti population were highly and rightly impressed by early waves of Palestinian immigrants coming to Kuwait. Their work in education gave the immigrants wider opportunities to interact with the local society, where they could demonstrate their capacities and, more importantly, tell their story. Soon, Palestinians and the Palestinian cause became a cultural and emotional magnet for Kuwaitis, who were offered a moral cause where they could support an Arab population, namely, the Palestinians who were cultured, civil, and capable. Moreover, one could argue that it was the Palestinian cause that attracted Kuwaitis more than the skills and wide knowledge of the Palestinian intelligentsia.

Although both Palestinian character and skills were present in Kuwaitis' development of their self-representations, it was the moral cause that represented itself as a gate to a new moral and cultural space where Kuwaitis could further express their perceived exceptionalism; an "Arab space," yet one that was not traditional, tribal, or backward. This space was more modern, civil, intellectual, and vibrant.

Progressive Kuwait in the Eyes of Arab Nationalism

It was a space where Kuwaitis' self-conceptions could be realized. This time, however, the elements of self-representation, and later, role enactment, were present. There were "close others" in other Gulf and Peninsular societies that formed the audience, while the standard of assessment was support for the Palestinian cause and Arab causes in general by a modern progressive society. In other words, this time, Kuwaitis had someone to look at and say that "societies of the Gulf and Arab Peninsula are traditional, closed, and tribal *except* Kuwait."

Kuwaitis understood that their gate to this new space was, at least partly, support for the Palestinian cause, and thus they invested heavily; emotionally, ideationally, and politically in this cause. This was not an instrumental state policy, but rather an attraction to a moral cause that seemed to energize self-defined national conceptions and the assertion of national positive representations in a wider space. In other words, it was support for the Palestinian cause that brought Kuwait to Arab nationalism and the pursuit of an Arabist foreign policy, and not the other way around.

During the 1940s and 1950s, Kuwaitis literally stepped into this space through educational missions and scholarships to Arab states, including Egypt and Lebanon. This attraction to other Arab states and societies did not detract from Kuwaitis' attraction to the Palestinians and the Palestinian cause, since these states, especially Egypt, valued the Palestinian cause and made support an essential norm by which to assess other states. Thus, if anything, the Egyptian bid for regional leadership contributed further to Kuwaitis' investment in the Palestinian cause.

It was not until the 1960s and 1970s that Kuwait endorsed regional roles and enacted them in its foreign policy. As mentioned, Holsti suggested a number of roles associated with Kuwait's foreign policy, namely regional mediator/integrator, developer, independent, and faithful ally. The abstract nature of these roles is clear and understood given the aims of Holsti's study. When considered alongside regional dynamics at the time Holsti wrote his work, it becomes clear that these roles point to Kuwait's heavy involvement and active role in regional politics under the umbrella of Arab nationalism, with its concerns, aspirations, and competitions.

Regional mediation and integration were defined by Arab nationalism rather than, for example, Islamic nationalism and, at heart, supported the Palestinian and Arab struggle against Israeli occupation. Moreover, the role of "developer" cannot be understood outside the same context of Arab nationalism and support for Arab states, especially those sharing borders with Israel. Interestingly, where Holsti's findings concerned convergence between role and behaviour, he singles out "faithful ally" (to Western powers) as a case of divergence between Kuwait's role and behaviour, suggesting that Kuwait prioritized its commitment to Arab nationalism and the Palestinian cause over its alliance with Western powers.

In addition to these important findings, and after putting them in context, I propose a "progressive Gulf state" as the main role that guided Kuwait's foreign policy during the 1960s and 1970s. This proposal, of course, needs some explanation.

130 *Meshari Hamad Alruwaih*

First, it could be argued that the "progressive Gulf state" is a national self-conception or, at best, a self-representation, not a regional role. However, going back to the ideational structure of the region in the context of the Cold War and the dominance of left-leaning Arab nationalism, one can find sufficient ideological, normative, and discursive evidence that such structures included two opposite roles, one positive (progressive), and the other negative (traditional or backward). Leading Arabist states like Egypt may not have enjoyed the productive power of these roles, but nevertheless enjoyed sufficient structural power to reproduce these progressive and traditional/backward, internally related positions or roles at the regional level, frequently placing Gulf states in what was viewed as an inferior position or role (traditional/backward).

Second, the use of the term "progressive" did not have to carry the entire leftist burden; it also meant at the regional level, a state or society that was rapidly modernizing socially and economically in addition to supporting Arab causes, at the heart of which was the Palestinian cause. This meaning was particularly true when assessing the progressiveness of Gulf states that were not *expected* to endorse a fully fledged progressive agenda.

Together, one can envision the expectations of the role of the progressive Gulf state as follows: support for Arab nationalism, championing the Palestinian cause and other Arab causes, and demonstrating rapid social and economic modernization. Kuwait seemed to satisfy these expectations nicely and, most importantly, not in absolute terms but in relative and relational terms compared to other Gulf states and societies that were less active in supporting Arab nationalism and the Palestinian cause, and, for the most part, were falling behind Kuwait in social and economic modernization. In other words, Kuwait was progressive, but only in relation to other Gulf states and societies, hence the role: "progressive Gulf state."

The emotional, social, and even political rewards for Kuwaitis resulting from satisfying this role and the associated expectations were substantial. National *pride* was at its highest during the 1960s and 1970s, and so was the social and political status of Kuwait, at least at the regional level. The investment in the Palestinian cause appeared to pay high rewards, which Kuwaitis seemed to enjoy.

Doubts and Crisis: Shattered National Conceptions

After the 1970s, several changes shook not only Kuwaitis' sense of national pride but also the role structure of the region. During the 1980s, an economic slowdown and political deadlocks on one hand, and the rise of other Gulf states on the other, affected Kuwaitis' sense of exceptionalism among Gulf states. At the regional level, increasing conflict between Palestinian factions and around the Palestinian cause, in addition to the changing role and behaviour of Egypt towards Arab nationalism, contributed to a hesitant Kuwaiti regional policy, as did the dominance of less inspiring or "likeable" Arab nationalist discourse by other Arab states, mainly Syria, Iraq, and Libya.

It was not until the Iraqi invasion in 1990 that Kuwait would suffer an ideational and material crisis, which would shatter not only its capacity for role enactment but also its self-representations and self-defined national conceptions. Kuwait was occupied for seven months by another Arab state, mainly in the name of Arab nationalism; an occupation cheered by Arab populations, including Palestinians and, worse still, by Palestinians living in Kuwait. Of course, there is a good deal of generalization in this description, yet public opinion in a good number of Arab countries was not firmly set against the occupation.

The occupation and its aftermath represented a threat not only to Kuwait's survival goals but also to its identity and social goals. After the Iraqi invasion, it could be argued that Kuwait went through a sort of identity crisis, having invested heavily in Arab nationalism and the Palestinian cause. According to Stefano Guzzini (2012, p. 56), a leading constructivist scholar in international relations, for such a crisis to occur, there must be a mismatch between the significance of a certain event and the subject positions or the roles that are embedded in foreign policy imagery. He elaborates further:

> Hence, for a crisis to occur, interpretations given to the event must be such as to make role conceptions no longer self-evident; in other words, these conceptions need to justify themselves. An identity should come naturally; the moment it needs consciously to justify its assumptions, we can say that a crisis has occurred. Such a definition is weaker than one that would add that such justification should turn out to be impossible.

Given the magnitude of the event, one would choose the stronger definition where the justification for self-conceptions and identity assumptions turned out to be impossible in the case of Kuwait. In other words, the justification for Kuwait's self-representation and regional role as a "progressive Gulf state" was no longer possible since the expectations of this role were closely related to Arab nationalism and the Palestinian cause. Consequently, Kuwaitis were no longer emotionally and ideationally capable of embedding these expectations in their self-representations.

Such a crisis of identity and social goals should result in withdrawal behaviour, which could be interpreted as mediated by basic emotions, such as fear, or self-conscious emotions, such as shame (Tracy & Robins, 2007, p. 15). Although withdrawal was reflected in Kuwait's foreign policy after the invasion, there was no evidence of a sense of national shame at the time; this came later and for different reasons, as is argued later in this chapter.

Kuwaitis and the Palestinian Cause: Between Limited Islamism and Shame of Globalization

Luckily, at least for Kuwaitis, the ideational and role structure of the region witnessed a broad transformation, the victim of which was Arab nationalism. By the mid-1990s, two forces were competing for structural and productive power to constitute roles and role expectations in the region: Islamism and globalization. Moreover, these two forces had great influence on the status of and approaches to the Palestinian cause and, of equal importance, redistributed status among Gulf states. Initially, it seemed that Kuwait, again, was positioned for a head start in the race towards regional status compared to other Gulf states.

The way these two forces represented themselves and how the conflict between them played out, proved more challenging for Kuwait with its hesitant foreign policy, messy politics, and complex political economy compared to other Gulf states that had more assertive foreign policies and centralized development plans. Nevertheless, these regional changes allowed Kuwaitis to rediscover their moral attraction and emotional bond to the Palestinian cause. Islamists in Kuwait were highly organized and playing a more prominent part in Kuwaiti politics and society since the late 1970s. Likewise, by the mid-1990s, it was clear that the Palestinian cause was taking an Islamist direction. In other words, praising Arab nationalism, which was almost non-existent by that time, was no longer a requirement for supporting the Palestinian cause. On the ground, military confrontations between Israel and Hezbollah, and then Hamas, both non-state Islamist organizations, recharged Kuwaitis' support for the Palestinian cause while freeing them from Arabist and even the Palestinian Liberation Organization (PLO) support. In Kuwait, both Sunni Islamists, namely the Kuwaiti branch of the Muslim Brotherhood, and Shia Islamists built on these confrontations and used them to make political gains, locally, in Kuwaiti politics.

Although there was wide support for both Hamas and Hezbollah among Arab and Muslim populations, including within the Gulf states, it was Kuwait's more open form of politics that allowed this support to be more visible regionally compared to support in other Gulf states. That said, Islamism had its limits, both as a source of national self-conception on the Kuwaiti side, and as a source for role expectations at the regional level. On the Kuwaiti side, although Kuwaitis could be described as fairly religious, with active Islamist movements, these elements were never sufficiently dominant to constitute a self-defined national conception. Islamism was a latecomer to Kuwaiti politics, which had long been dominated by secular-leaning Arab nationalism.

At the regional level, and unlike Arab nationalism at its height, Islamism comprised mainly transnational movements and organizations that did not hold structural or productive power to constitute an ideational structure with social roles that regional actors could occupy in an Islamist-defined social and political hierarchy. This capacity has always been associated with states, and regional states were reluctant, even resistant, to such an ideational change at the regional level. No leading states supported Islamism, at least not as openly as was the case with Arab nationalism. These limitations became more apparent during the Arab Spring and its aftermath, when Islamism clearly became a burden. In short, Islamism might not have solved Kuwait's identity crisis or helped it regain its sense of national pride at the regional level; nevertheless, it did open an alternative path for Kuwaitis to re-establish their support for the Palestinian cause.

It was not just national pride and status-seeking that Kuwaitis were after. They also wished to escape shame, and here again, the Palestinian cause came to the rescue. Understanding the influence of the Palestinian cause, however, calls for consideration of the other force that came out victorious in the race to constitute regional roles and role expectations; that is, globalization.

Kuwait and the Palestinian Cause 133

Again, at a superficial level, Kuwait seemed to be better positioned to invest in globalization than other Gulf states. After all, globalization was supposed to be a process that diffused liberal norms. As a semi-democratic open society compared to other Gulf societies, Kuwait should have had the most to gain; however, this was not how globalization made its way into the region. Instead, it was mainly an economic process, linking national economies with the global economy, changing the public spaces of these societies into procedural and technological infrastructure; that is, into global economic hubs. Globalization in the region was, and continues to be, about spaces not people. How else can one explain the fact that countries such as the UAE and Qatar have more conservative societies yet more open public space, while Kuwait, with a more open society, enjoys less open public space?

Globalization in the region thus needed a strong centralized authority to, using Freidman's old and worn term, "flatten" the public space and make it more hospitable for economic globalization; that is, where Kuwait, with its messy politics and complex political economy, could not compete with other Gulf states, which enjoyed more assertive, centralized, and ambitious regimes that seemed to embrace these forces, especially in the UAE, then Qatar, and lately Saudi Arabia. If anything, these "close others," who always served as a platform where Kuwaitis could justify their progressiveness, modernization, and exceptionalism, are now outperforming Kuwait in almost every respect, standard, and expectation associated with economic globalization and economic development in general.

This type of globalization prefers a strong state rather than a strong society. It was this combination of a strong state and economic globalization that made its presence strongly felt after the Arab Spring and its counter-revolution against democratically elected Islamists, especially in Egypt. This counter-revolution was led by two Gulf states: Saudi Arabia and the UAE. It could be argued that it was not a counter-revolution against democratic reforms; rather, it was against transnational and pan-ideologies competing with the model of a strong state and economic globalization. Furthermore, it could be argued that the Palestinian cause has always been a point of attraction to transnational movements and pan-ideologies in the region, whether Arabist or Islamist, an emotional and cultural "magnet" that attracts followers and mobilizes support across national borders. Only a strong state can coerce its society away from this attraction and safeguard the public space from such "radical" ideas.

The Kuwaiti regime was supportive of the counter-revolutions but lacked the assertiveness and resolve of the regimes in Saudi Arabia and the UAE, to the point that Kuwait could be described as a "free rider," enjoying the benefits of the counter-revolution while not really contributing much to it. Likewise, Kuwaitis are divided and hesitant, with an eye on the rising prestige and status of other Gulf states, which never miss an opportunity to take pride in almost everything; from diplomatic attention by superpowers to the opening of new malls and resorts. Kuwaitis compare these states with their own pluralist and democratic legacy that continues to produce political and economic failure. Politically impaired and economically falling behind Gulf societies, Kuwaitis are aware of their place in the newly configured hierarchy and they feel *ashamed* of it.

134   *Meshari Hamad Alruwaih*

The top level in this hierarchy is reserved for those who can enact the role of a "successful globalized economic hub." Role expectations here are procedural rather than normative and include the administrative and procedural know-how to manage economic networks, supply chains, and state-of-the-art infrastructure in a space where global financial, legal, and technological firms and their human capital come together in a globalized economic hub. These hybrid human, digital, and procedural hubs are assessed according to economic competitiveness, business-friendly environments, and investment destinations by global economic organizations that rank states according to how closely they enact the role of a "successful globalized economic hub." The audience this time comprises global, mainly Western, political and economic actors who hold structural and productive power, allowing them to constitute the ideational structure of globalization. In short, Gulf states are competing in this hierarchy where status and prestige are awarded to those who succeed in satisfying the expectations of the role of a "successful globalized economic hub." In this hierarchy, according to most rankings, Kuwait comes in a distant sixth.

Following Kuwaiti discussions, whether in *Diwaniyas* (workplaces) or on social media, it is not hard to sense a collective feeling of bitterness. When interacting with other Gulf citizens, Kuwaitis feel that they always need to prepare an answer for frequently repeated questions: "What is wrong?" and "What is happening in Kuwait?" Whatever answer they give, it seems that it is always underlined by a sense of shame. Just like pride was relational, that is, in relation to the lack of progressiveness of other Gulf States, so is shame relational to the success of other Gulf states.

To be more accurate, it might be better to describe collective Kuwaiti feelings regarding their economic and developmental failure compared to other Gulf states as one of resisting shame, a more complex state of defensive psychological mechanism that might be even more appropriate for describing collective feelings of national groups in general. National groups do not succumb easily to feelings of shame, not for long anyway, as the opposite self-conscious emotion of pride is built into nationalism itself (Mearsheimer, 2011, p. 8). Therefore, national groups demonstrate a higher capacity than individuals to resist feelings of shame. Nevertheless, defensive mechanisms might be shared by groups too, including for example, distancing oneself from shame-provoking events (Lickel, Schmader, & Spanovic, 2007, p. 360); another is to "turn the tables" defensively, externalizing blame and anger onto a convenient scapegoat (Tangney, Stuewig, & Mashek, 2007, p. 27). I believe these defensive mechanisms shed light on the way Kuwaitis deal with the newly distributed status and prestige among Gulf states and societies and the resulting sense of shame. However, these mechanisms do not have to be seen as negative, self-serving, or instrumental, as described in the literature on self-conscious emotions.

That said, it is evident that Kuwaitis seek to escape events, discussions, or news that spotlight the economic and developmental gap between Gulf states and Kuwait. Kuwaitis may discuss this gap among themselves all the time, but when interacting with others on a regional or international level, they prefer to escape any status-distributing event, emphasizing the successful enacting of roles of Gulf states associated with economic development and international status. Moreover, it is also evident that the people of Kuwait feel more comfortable with events, discussions, and news emphasizing the role of public opinion and social forces in supporting transnational Arabists, and to a lesser extent Islamic causes. This is a "turning the tables" as described in the literature on self-conscious emotions, yet it is not directed towards other Gulf states and societies, at least not explicitly, since one can hardly blame those states and societies for their success.

Instead, I argue that Kuwaitis are turning this shame and resultant anger into what can be described as virtuous anger, an alternative mechanism that seeks moral and social acceptability (Tangney, Stuewig, & Mashek, 2007, p. 21). Thus, virtuous anger becomes, when expressed, a moral behaviour that should result in a positive self-conception and self-representation. Shweder, Much, Mahapatra, and Park (1997) offered a framework identifying three "ethics" that inform our standards for moral behaviour: Autonomy, community, and divinity. The ethic of autonomy focuses on individual rights, justice, and especially the prohibition of harming others physically, psychologically, or spiritually. The ethic of community focuses on duty, loyalty, and shared social conventions, standards, and rules that support community and hierarchy. The ethic of divinity encompasses interrelated concepts of divinity and physical purity.

While clearly some elements of these "ethics" go beyond the purposes of this discussion, it is also clear that others point to what can be described as an ideational toolkit that allows Kuwaitis to form a national self-representation that is resistant to the newly constituted regional role structure and is more in line with Kuwait's national self-representation. This national self-representation goes as follows: The people of Kuwait, given their legacy of a semi-democratic system, are among the few remaining populations in the Arab world, and maybe the only remaining in the Gulf, who can still express virtuous anger against injustice and harm directed at other groups and individuals in the region. The Kuwaiti people are still capable of showing loyalty and duty to the transnational communities and identities in the region. In other words, Kuwaitis represent themselves as capable of demonstrating the "ethics" of autonomy and community on a regional level, which can only be sustained through the country's exceptionally strong society and semi-democratic politics.

Despite everything, and perhaps not for long, support for the Palestinian cause remains the standard by which moral behaviour and ethical standards are measured in this region, and Kuwaitis again find themselves emotionally and morally entangled with the Palestinian cause. Kuwaitis' virtuous anger needs the Palestinian cause in order to function socially and emotionally at the regional level, producing a degree of national pride and helping Kuwaitis "turn the tables" on endless rankings that keep reminding Kuwaitis of their failures, eliciting feelings of national shame.

Instrumental or not, virtuous anger is needed in this region. How long Kuwaitis can enact this anger is hard to tell, especially without a role structure supporting this anger or an audience showing much interest.

Conclusion

This chapter was an attempt to provide an account of Kuwaitis' relationship with the Palestinian cause through regional transformation. It was also an account of a small state seeking status and recognition at the regional and international levels. Despite the relatively limited academic interest, compared to the study of more active Gulf states like Qatar and the UAE, the Kuwaiti case continues to offer richer accounts, especially for theoretical purposes. The strong involvement of the Kuwaiti public in regional issues throughout different phases of regional transformation, and their continuing search for national pride and the desire to repair their national self-representation, can serve as a case study to broaden approaches to status-seeking by small states. The case of Kuwait is unlike others, where national conceptions and national self-representations seem to be artificially imposed in a top-down fashion. Such broader approaches will have to make use of both ideational and emotional dimensions in analysing behaviour. As shown in this chapter, roles are tightly related to status, and status floats in an ideational and emotional milieu where pride and shame are always present, at least in the eyes of observers, or in the eyes of the status-seeking actors when observing the observers.

The chapter offered a step forward in bringing theoretical tools, namely, role theory and literature on self-conscious emotions, to study status-seeking behaviour by small states. Moreover, the particularity of the Kuwaiti case sheds light on an important research question that deserves investigation: Does support for moral causes enhance or impair status-seeking, especially by small states, and particularly when the moral cause is losing popularity, thus increasing political cost?

This question, in turn, points to another contribution that is hopefully offered by this chapter. That is, the position and moral status of the Palestinian cause in regional transformation, where role expectations do not favour moral transnational issues. Will the Palestinian cause be a victim of these transformations? Will it sustain its moral status? What constitutes national pride in the current regional order? In other words, can a state or society claim national pride without taking a supportive position on the Palestinian cause? Is it still shameful to abandon the Palestinian cause? How will virtuous anger interact with the model of a strong state and economic globalization? Hopefully, this chapter will serve as a step towards rethinking these questions.

References

Alsayed, W. (2022). Beyond instrumentalism: Arab nationalism and the foreign policy of Kuwait in the 1960s and the 1970s. *Middle East Journal, 76*(2), 199–221.

Barnett, M. (1993). Institutions, roles, and disorder: The case of the Arab states system. *International Studies Quarterly, 37*(3), 271–296.

Barnett, M. Sovereignty, nationalism, and regional order in the Arab states system. *International Organization, 49*(3), 479–510.

Barnett, M., & Duvall, R. (2005). Power in international politics. *International Organization, 59*(1), 39–75.

Beer, J. (2007). Neural systems for self-conscious emotions and their underlying appraisals. In J. Tracy, R. Robins, & J. P. Tangney (Eds.), *The self-conscious emotions, theory and research* (pp. 53–67). New York and London: The Guilford Press.

Duncan, S., & Barrett, L. F. (2007). Affect is a form of cognition: A neurobiological analysis. *Cognition and Emotion, 21*(6), 1184–1211.

Ennis, C. A. (2018). Reading entrepreneurial power in Small Gulf states: Qatar and the UAE. *International Journal, 73*(4), 573–595.

Fessler, D. M. T. (2004). Shame in Two Cultures: Implications for Evolutionary Approaches. *Journal of Cognition and Culture, 4*(2), 207–262. "https://psycnet.apa.org/doi/10.1163/1568537041725097 "https://doi.org/10.1163/1568537041725097

Fessler, D. (2007). From appeasement to conformity: Evolutionary and cultural perspectives on shame, competition, and cooperation. In J. Tracy, R. Robins, & J. Tangney (Eds.), *The self-conscious emotions, theory and research* (pp. 174–193). New York and London: The Guilford Press.

Guzzini, S. (2012). *The return of geopolitics in Europe? Social mechanisms and foreign policy identity crisis.* Cambridge: Cambridge University Press.

Holsti, K. J. (1970). National role conceptions in the study of foreign policy. *International Studies Quarterly, 14*(3), 233–309.

Lickel, B., Schmader, T., & Spanovic, M. (2007). Group conscious emotions: The implications of others' wrongdoing for identity and relationships. In J. Tracy, R. Robins, & J. P. Tangney (Eds.), *The self-conscious emotions, theory and research* (pp. 351–371). New York and London: The Guilford Press.

Mansour, I. (2020). The BRI is what states make of it: Evaluating Kuwait's engagement with China's belt and road initiative. *Middle East Journal, 74*(4), 538–558.

Mearsheimer, J. (2011). Kissing cousins: Nationalism and realism. Prepared for the Yale Workshop on International Relations.

Sarbin, T. R., & Allen Vernon, L. (1968). Role theory. In G. Lindzey & E. Aronson (Eds.), *Handbook of social psychology*, 2nd ed. Reading: Addison: Wesley Publishing Company.

Stein, J. G. (2008). Foreign policy decision making: Rational, psychological, and neurological models. In S. Smith, A. Hadfield, & T. Dunne (Eds.), *Foreign policy: Theories, actors, and cases* (pp. 488–567). Oxford: Oxford University Press.

Tangney, J. P., Stuewig, J., & Mashek, D. J. (2007). What's moral about the self-conscious emotion? In J. Tracy, R. Robins, & J. P. Tangney (Eds.), *The self-conscious emotions, theory and research* (pp. 21–38). New York and London: The Guilford Press.

Tetreault, M. A. (2000). *Stories of democracy: Politics and society in contemporary Kuwait.* New York: Columbia University Press.

Thies, C. (2010). Role theory and foreign policy. *Oxford research encyclopedias.* https://doi.org/10.1093/acrefore/9780190228637.013.334

Tracy, J., & Robins, R. W. (2007). The self in the self-conscious emotions: A cognitive appraisal approach. In J. Tracy, R. Robins, & J. P. Tangney (Eds.), *The self-conscious emotions, theory and research* (pp. 3–21). New York and London: The Guilford Press.

Walker, S. G. (1992). Symbolic interactionalism and international politics: Role theory's contributions to international organization. In M. Cottam, C. Shih, & Paeger (Eds.), *Contending dramas: A cognitive approach to international organizations.* New York.

Walker, S. G. (2004). Role identities and operational codes of political leaders. In M. G. Hermann, Elsevier, & Amsterdam (Eds.), *Advances of political psychology.*

Yom, S. (2019). Roles, identity, and security: Foreign policy contestation in monarchical Kuwait. *European Journal of International Relations, 26*(2), 569–593.

Zelkovitz, I. (2014). A paradise lost? The rise and fall of the Palestinian Community in Kuwait. *Middle Eastern Studies, 50*(1), 86–99.

9 Role of Urbanization in Changing Social Norms to Laws

Impact on Status of Kuwaiti Women

Muyassar H. Suleiman

Introduction

Kuwait has undergone a rapid process of urbanization since the discovery of oil in the 1930s. This chapter defines urbanization as one aspect of the development process which was adopted by the state of Kuwait since the 1930s. The city's urban planning phase began in 1951 with the first master plan by the British firm Minoprio, Spencely, and McFarlane (Mahgoub, 2008). Their main objectives were to create a foundation for improvements which they considered necessary for the development of the State of Kuwait in accordance with the highest standards of "modern town planning" (Minoprio, Spencely, and McFarlane, 1951). The issues of primary importance were developing infrastructure, a modern road system, and public buildings. In the late 1950s and early 1960s, Kuwait implemented the first master plan by the Ministry of Public Works under the supervision of the Kuwait Development Board, which was established in 1950 and headed by the Emir of Kuwait (Mahgoub, 2008).

Two major factors have contributed to urbanization in Gulf societies: First, oil revenues and second, the outcomes of globalization (Moghadam, 2010). Urbanization seemed more pronounced in the transition from rural to urban areas and the consequent change in social norms. This rural–urban transition of community members has changed the idea of association and belonging. A change in lifestyle requires changing the type of relationships that bind people. Prior to moving to the city, the natural link between individuals was most likely shaped by tribal affiliation. After moving to the city, this relationship shifted to different interests, and the need for public benefit became the dominant paradigm. Consequently, the idea of an imagined community among the people of the city emerged. Urbanization requires a certain pattern of life, services, and concepts and this in turn helped to change many social norms and traditions by the state. In this period of urbanization, state institutions worked to regulate daily life through laws and legislation. Thus, the urbanization process in Gulf cities was not only focused on changing the physical infrastructure but also on changing many of the customs and social norms that existed before urbanization.

This chapter covers three pillars for urbanization (as a development process) in the state of Kuwait, including building state institutions, advancement in education, and legal structure. These three pillars reveal gender in urbanization. In essence,

DOI: 10.4324/9781003435259-9

the urbanization process in the Middle East's developing countries gives women access to state education, while conversely undermining women's status in society through institutions, laws, and regulations, which consider women as second-class citizens before the law—this is evident in the Nationality Law. Moreover, it describes how authority has been transferred from social norms in society to laws and regulations by state institutions. Based on this transformation, gender-based discrimination became legal in the state of Kuwait. This chapter presents the role of urbanization in the state of Kuwait in changing social norms and bringing new social dynamics to society.

In addition, the chapter details the domestic context in which the status of women in Kuwait started to change. This is important because it will help create a context for understanding Kuwait at a critical time in its contemporary political, social, and economic formation. Additionally, emphasis is placed on how the status of women in Kuwaiti society changed under the urbanization process because of the modern state adopting urbanization as a strategy to achieve development. Thus, urbanization represents the framework that the modern state works under. Moreover, this chapter outlines the reasons behind the current contradictions in the State of Kuwait between the National Constitution, the Nationality Law, and its impact on National Development in Kuwait. This will be covered by explaining the negative impact of urbanization on the status of Kuwaiti women in Kuwaiti society, and explaining the current contradiction between the National Constitution and the Nationality Law in terms of gender equality. Finally, the chapter discusses the changing of the development concept globally, and new concepts that have become linked to development.

What Is Urbanization?

Urbanization, as one aspect of the development process, is governed by the fact that the state has a role in changing and providing services to its citizens. The process of development has led to demographic changes and a shift in people settling in a certain place (Al-Ganem, 1997). By leading people to settle, the state has an essential role towards its citizens, such as protection and providing equal rights and opportunities to them, as well as a public platform for opinion. The state's behaviour becomes more specific and determined because the process of urbanization aims to change and transform the lifestyle and "way of life" of the society. Thus, the state works to provide a level of welfare (Al-Ganem, 1997). This results in interfering in and regulating people's lives through institutions and laws. The process of urbanization of the state of Kuwait succeeded in transforming the traditional Kuwait city, which was simple with public houses, unpaved and old roads into an urban city capable of providing services and a welfare lifestyle to its citizens (Mahgoub, 2008). However, it did not work to empower Kuwaiti female citizens in the same way that it empowered male citizens. Moreover, the state institutions, under the process of urbanization, worked to restrict Kuwaiti women through laws; gender and the status of women in society became highlighted and discussed deeply (Ghabra, 2017).

Urbanization in the Gulf is a process that had an impact on the rural population by having transformed the idea of tribes from a rural traditional lifestyle into an urban pattern and setting. Typically, this happens through cultural changes that involve a change in values, attitudes, and behaviour of immigrants towards compatibility and adaptation to local urban patterns. In the context of physical geography, urbanization is defined as a general trend towards urban cities or centres (Moore, 1980). On the other hand, urbanization is also defined as the transition from rural to urban life. This transition happens because of migration which requires individuals or groups to adopt a certain social system of values and culture prevailing in the city. This transition may result in a deterioration of the material and moral values which in turn may result in a return to the village (Ghaith, 1989, p. 499).

Al-Naqeeb (1987) posited that between the 1950s and 1960s there was a change in the position of the traditional social forces (tribal families in the Gulf region), which coincided with the rise of the ruling families to power and their control over the oil revenues. The impact of oil on social construction in the Gulf led to the destruction of the traditional economic sectors and economic activities such as fishing, pearl diving, and trade, which changed the composition of the population in the Gulf. Accordingly, two main eras in the Gulf society appeared, before oil and after oil. This change in social construction as a result of the urbanization policies adopted by the State, which sought to codify laws and customs and gender, was used as a standard in enactment for many laws and legal practices.

Additionally, Al-Naqeeb (1987, p. 136) offered a description of the urban society, which he said was characterized by a division of labour based on "industry." This urban society sought a level of perfectionism that was greater than necessary. While social problems increased along with behavioural and moral deviations, the standard of living and appearance of society improved by dressing up its clothing, food, and housing.

Urbanization has significant effects not only on the habits and patterns of behaviour of groups, but also on patterns of thinking and values. The imagined community is linked to urban mobility mechanisms, as urbanization creates an interactive environment that takes different forms. The urban population is not homogenous; there is a clear contrast between the city's urban population in knowledge and cultures. For example, in cities that have grown rapidly, the level of cultural and cognitive change is lower than it is in the cities that have grown gradually. This change is supposed to be a direct result of the migration of the population from the countryside to the city. In the case of rapid urban growth, rural people maintain their values and habits in the city rather than adapting to the demands of urban life (Moghadam, 2013). This phenomenon is similar to the experience in Gulf cities; as cities have grown and developed rapidly, the population has moved from a rural to urban environment. However, the strength of the community tribe has prevailed in the city, while also maintaining its customs and traditions.

In addition, the integration of society and its incorporation of new values were not quite clear in an emerging urban city. This is contrary to the idea of urbanization, from which the state is expecting a certain contribution from its citizens. Society is supposed to have a distinct role in the development of knowledge and

Urbanization in Changing Social Norms to Laws 141

culture and cannot achieve a distinct urban life in the absence of civic awareness. Additionally, it requires the integration of people to be aware that they have the potential and capabilities to contribute positively to social development in the city. Thus, urbanization refers to the requirements of civic life based on awareness, mutual interest, and the continuous interaction between citizens and the institutions (Ghaith, 1989; Moghadam, 2013).

Pillars for Urbanization Subjected by Gendered Code in Kuwait

The most rapid growth in urbanization in the Gulf region occurred in the oil-exporting GCC countries. The urbanization in Gulf cities was influenced by the oil revenues, especially in the period between 1960 and 1980 (Moghadam, 2010). Accordingly, oil revenues encouraged Gulf urbanization, reflecting different levels of development in the region. Urbanization has brought about a better life in most of the region, but some countries continue to face difficulties with the provision of services. In Gulf cities, urbanization can be most clearly seen in the buildings, state institutions, and high-level living services (Tawadrous, 2014).

Cities in the Gulf have been recognized in different ways. Cities should consider the demographic, geopolitical, and social dimensions of such population settlements. Moreover, the most important one is the need for the legal structure to help in organizing the urbanization process (Konuk, Turan, & Ardali, 2016). Moghadam (2010) pointed out that urbanization in Gulf cities brings many deep changes to the populations as well as to the cities. For example, in its history, the idea of a young unmarried woman (under 20 years) was completely unaccepted in the Muslim world, for the concept of patriarchal honour is built around the idea of virginity, which reduces a woman's role to its sexual dimension: Reproduction within an early marriage. Moreover, the concept of unmarried women is linked with social corruption (*Fitna*). In the contemporary period after the oil boom revolution, these things have largely become socially acceptable because the economic transformation has led to social transformation as well.

However, Moghadam believes that urbanization has created social problems. For example, in Gulf countries, because of gender differences in education, employment, and income, women are especially exposed to poverty during periods of economic difficulty or in the event of divorce, abandonment, or widowhood. Rapid urbanization and population growth have transformed the size and structure of the labour force. In most countries, the population has shifted from engagement in primarily rural and agriculture production systems to involvement in various types of urban industrial and service-oriented economic activities (Al-Naqeeb, 1987). This level of potential instability happened because of the cultural norm of the male breadwinner and female homemaker ideal. At the same time, urbanization created opportunities for the citizens to work as a collective group and encouraged the emergence of many non-governmental organizations (civil society organizations) which have an influential role in many of the social dynamics that happen in the region currently. The social dynamics include changes in norms, customs, and traditions. Moreover, urbanization in some Gulf cities created an awareness of

142   *Muyassar H. Suleiman*

internal issues related to citizens such as women's rights and social mobility. This is largely due to the idea that urbanization has brought social advances and social inequalities, both of which have helped to generate women's groups. From this change, dynamic women's movements and campaigns emerged for the repeal of discriminatory laws, specifically the Sharia-based family laws, which place women in the position of a minor, dependent, or subordinate in the family. Furthermore, the region has seen the emergence of women's movements and organizations calling for reform of family law, equal nationality rights, laws against domestic violence, and increased economic and political representation (Tawadrous, 2014).

Advancement in Education

Social changes are associated with the rise of mass education in Kuwait. Thus, the advancement of education is one of the important factors and markers of urbanism because of the development it ensures. In general, educational institutions in the Middle East have undergone major growth since the mid-20th century. In the Gulf countries, education has served a central role in the development of modern states and citizenship. At the same time, the emergence of international organizations and human rights conventions focussed on human development (human capital), mainly on education. As a result of this, education became a basic right, as well as a key institution of development, and the provision of education has become essential to state legitimacy. Gulf education rates are much higher than those in the other countries of the region. For instance, Morocco, Yemen, and Egypt currently have the lowest women literacy rates in Middle East and North Africa (MENA) region, at 56, 59, and 66 per cent, respectively, while just 10 per cent of women are illiterate in the UAE and Qatar (Moghadam, 2010).

Most of the Gulf countries started the process of development years before earning independence; the state's policies were directed towards the promotion and training of an indigenous, local, and professional labour force and towards an integrated economy. The expansion of formal education and the establishment of higher education institutes were a reaction to the requirements for human capital, affected largely by the lack of sufficient and broad literate infrastructure. Thus, Gulf cities needed to expand access to education to every societal group in the country. Accordingly, educational attainment became the main feature of educational policies in Gulf countries. Free public education is subsidized by the state; as a provision of social welfare services, it can be seen as an integrated part of the state policy to ensure its legitimacy. Thus, the social transformation in certain aspects in the Gulf countries was influenced primarily by education. This is reflected in the transformation in both the political and economic dimensions under the development process in Gulf countries (Tawadrous, 2014).

Urbanization process which led to the formation of state institutions, encourages educating women. It brought new concepts related to social change in Gulf society. Women's gross enrolment rates have improved since the 1970s. In developing countries, women tend to specialize in the humanities and social sciences, and this led to a mismatch between education and labour market demands. This

Urbanization in Changing Social Norms to Laws   143

is related to society's perspective towards women, that they should study specific majors considered suitable for them and enable them to work in places free of men (Moghadam, 2010). Moreover, there were personal and social returns to women of higher education and unintended consequences for political activism and cultural change. State's policy works to create the "New Muslim Woman," through the school curriculum while education provided a platform for women's increased gender and political awareness. For example, the feminization of higher education accompanied the growth of women's rights because education provides urban women with the capacity to raise awareness and engage in collective action (Al-Mughni, 2001).

Creation of Legal Structure and Its Impact on the Status of Kuwaiti Women in Society

Urbanization changed the social power of society while it also brought to the forefront many of the social dynamics and the new situation of women in Kuwait. Social dynamics were represented mainly in the emergence of women's movement and associations in Kuwait after 1961 (Al-Mughni, 2001, p. 68). Women from merchant classes who were well educated at that time and had a different sort of social power in Kuwaiti society played a significant role in opening women's associations. These associations worked to raise awareness of society towards many issues related to women (Moghadam, 2010). Most of these issues emerged with urbanization that was accompanied by state institutions, laws, and legislation (Moghadam, 2010). Thus, the emergence of the urban city had positive and negative effects on the lives of Kuwaiti women. On the one hand, urbanization contributed to raising the level of education for women and helped to create awareness about the importance of civil and women's work, and the emergence of women's associations that demanded the political rights of Kuwaiti women. On the other hand, urbanization has created new concepts about the role of women and restricted women in the house or certain places only for work, whereas before Kuwaiti women had full freedom to go to all places without restriction and even take the responsibility of their family (Al-Mughni, 2011; Moghadam, 2010).

In Kuwait, as in other Gulf countries, urbanization influenced state formation and worked towards building institutions and draughting laws (Mahgoub, 2008). Urbanization has a negative impact on people's freedom and specifically on women's freedom (Moghadam, 2010). The government, "the main actor" controls society through laws and regulations which limit people's freedom in exchange for some services (Moghadam, 2010). This is happening by interfering in individuals' issues to regulate society, and a few numbers of people are in power and influence the types of legislation and laws that are legislated (Ghabra, 2017). Based on this, the state, under the process of urbanization, worked on codifications for space; this resulted in gender-segregated spaces (Sonbol, 2012). The State of Kuwait's practices resulted in spaces as a gendered subject. Thus, gender becomes an organizing principle of social life thoroughly saturated with power relations (Al-Mughni, 2001, p. 64).

144   *Muyassar H. Suleiman*

As mentioned earlier, Kuwaiti contemporary history can be divided into two distinct periods. Before the discovery of oil, the State of Kuwait was a trading place for nomadic tribes and sea traders; the inhabitants depended on the Gulf for their livelihood through fishing, pearling and travel (Mahgoub, 2008). Kuwaiti women have played an active role in Kuwaiti society as well as in the family. For example, Kuwaiti women have successfully managed the economic and social affairs of the family in the absence of men for many months in the journey of diving and travelling in search of livelihood (Tétreault & Al-Mughni, 1995). Thus, before urbanization, women were responsible for the house. This was socially acceptable within the society and even considered as part of norms and customs at that time (Sonbol, 2012). On the other hand, after the urbanization process, women were treated as second-class citizens before the laws and based on this, many of the legislations and laws started to differentiate between male and female citizens in rights and duties. The most important one was the Nationality Law in 1959 and other laws that followed such as the Personal Status Law 1984 and the Penal Code Law 1960. State institutions started to discriminate between male and female citizens in rights and duties based on their sex or "Biological Differences." The legislators believe that this discrimination is legal because rights and duties were distributed between citizens based on their biological differences and not based on their citizenship (Tétreault & Al-Mughni, 1995).

For instance, Kuwait's Housing Law No. 47 of 1993 is a marker of rights and duties for citizens and stipulates that the Kuwaiti male citizen married to a non-Kuwaiti citizen has the right to take housing by giving him a loan from the government bank and land to build a house while Kuwaiti female citizen married to a non-Kuwaiti citizen does not have the same right. This is despite the fact that the Kuwaiti Constitution (1962) in Article 29 states that "people are equal in human dignity and are equal before the law in public rights and duties, without discrimination on grounds of race, origin, language or religion."

However, the Constitutional Court explained this discrimination between male and female citizens as legal, arguing that housing care is provided by the head of the family, who is the man. The explanation given to justify this discrimination is that the Kuwaiti family can be defined only by the Kuwaiti father, regardless of his wife's nationality, and not the other way around. Thus, the Constitutional Court declared that the man is the sole guardian of the family. Another problem emerges in that the law has not given any exception for the abandonment of women or the divorced women who are the guardians of the family. Thus, we can see a discrepancy in the law that emerged after the period of urbanization and how legal perspectives affect women. Before urbanization, women were responsible for the family and independent for long periods of time (Sonbol, 2012). Whereas after urbanization, women's status became constructed and controlled by the state. Such an example given is to show how the status of women in Kuwait before and after urbanization has been affected (Alkaldi, 2018).

Nationality Law in Kuwait 1959

(Kuwait: Ministerial Decree No. 15 of 1959 promulgating the Nationality Law", 2014)

a. Article 2

Any person born in, or outside, Kuwait whose father is a Kuwaiti national shall be a Kuwaiti national himself.

b. Article 3

The Minister of the Interior may, by decree, grant the Kuwaiti nationality to a person born in Kuwait from a Kuwaiti mother if the father was unknown, or his father was not legally proven.

c. Article 5

Kuwaiti women's children are treated as Kuwaitis when she divorced, or her husband died or captured.

Kuwait Nationality Law in Article 2 is a clear example of how state institutions in Kuwait undermine Kuwaiti female citizens and discriminate against them in other laws. Article 2 discriminates against Kuwaiti female citizens married to non-Kuwaiti citizens by denying the children of such marriages the Kuwaiti nationality based on blood ties. The example of such discrimination is given to prove that the nationality law in Kuwait affects the status of female citizens and all other laws. The pervasive bias against women is observed at three levels of the state: In political institutions, in gender-related discourses and policies, and in legal status. Accordingly, the concept of citizenship that exists in Kuwait remains ambiguous; importantly, it is rooted in the belief that women are allowed to be members of society, but not rightful citizens in the state. Kuwaiti Nationality Law regulates women's lives based on their imposed role in society rather than on their citizenship (Al-Mughni, 2001, p. 126). This has negative implications for the family of the Kuwaiti females' citizens (including the husband of a Kuwaiti female and her children). For example, this prevents family stability and unification because the Nationality Law is the main determinant of rights and duties. More specifically, the National Constitution of Kuwait (of 1962) considers all Kuwaiti citizens as having equal rights and opportunity while the Nationality Law discriminates on the basis of gender itself in Article 3, and further distinguishes among births by married women and those who give birth out of wedlock. The pervasiveness of such discrimination against Kuwaiti female citizens can be observed in the outcome of sustainable development policies. The irregularity in the concept of female citizen hinders the development process as a result of female citizens who are unable to enjoy their full rights and duties. This shows how state institutions consider only the Kuwaiti father as the core of the family and based on this all other rights for children come only from the Kuwaiti father not Kuwaiti mother. From this, there follow four negative consequences which will be explored in the following sections.

Negative Impact of Urbanization on the Status of Kuwaiti Women

In the 1960s, 1970s, and 1980s, the urbanization process had not yet resulted in more restrictions on women in terms of social norms, as women still had a large

146 *Muyassar H. Suleiman*

space in Kuwaiti society. For example, there were no written laws concerning the education, work, and travel of women. However, after the liberation of Kuwait in 1991, the conservative school emerged and was influenced by Salafist tendencies (Ghabra, 2017, p. 118). People who ascribe to Salafist thought have narrowed the public sphere for women. For example, Abdullah al-Mutawa, president of the Social Reform Association, has stressed the importance of implementing Sharia law in a fast and direct manner in Kuwait, especially on matters related to (Al-Hodood) the Quran such as cutting off the hand of the thief, whipping the adulterer, and preventing mixing between the sexes in public spaces. This did not correlate with Kuwaiti law; the legislation was defined by flexibility in the interpretation of Islamic law, such as punishing the thief without cutting off their hand (Ghabra, 2017, p. 119).

In addition, at that time a group of parliamentarians in the National Assembly was focused on women's issues in society including marriage, the veil, and gender segregation in workplaces, schools, and universities. After that, the National Assembly members proposed a law to separate education at Kuwait University, which since its establishment in the mid-1960s was a university for joint education of both sexes. This policy of gender segregation in higher education and in public spaces has paved the way for many social and personal distortions in Kuwaiti society (Ghabra, 2017, pp. 154–155).

The Islamist and the government positions towards women resulted in strict regulations and control of women's sexuality during the period of urbanization, which Islamic Jurists regarded as a threat to civilized society. However, they believed that the requirements of modernization are incompatible with traditional Muslim structures (e.g., women should stay at home, and women should work only in the home) and the ensuing contradictions present in nearly all Muslim countries. In Kuwait, urbanization had a disorientating effect on modern life and male–female relations as it looks at the male–female unit as a basic element of the structure of the Muslim world (Mernissi, 1987).

The parliament in Kuwait is supposed to reflect a minimum of democracy, freedom, and rights for the Kuwaiti citizens. Thus, the parliament in Kuwait is the legislative authority, which means that it is the only authority responsible for legislating laws in the state (Herb, 2016). The persuasion of the members of the Council is reflected in the type of laws they legislated in the state and even on the laws that they amended in the state (Ghabra, 2017). For instance, in the 1990s after the Iraqi occupation for Kuwait, the Islamic fundamentalist (Asolya / Salafe) faction in the parliament had seen government legislation as non-Islamic according to their own perceptions of Islam and wanted to change it (Ghabra, 2017). Additionally, the Islamic fundamentalists were in power and neglected the development and corruption issues, focussing instead on women's issues and raised the awareness towards many new ideas related to women in Kuwaiti society. In the same period, the Islamist movement developed harsh interpretations of the relationship between women and men in Kuwaiti society. Consequently, all the interpretations and attention were from a sexual perspective towards women which reduced women's perspective as a human (Al -Mughni, 2001, p. 45).

Urbanization in Changing Social Norms to Laws 147

Accordingly, the Islamic movement in Kuwait focused on women's hijab, clothes, and the places where women were allowed and not allowed to go. Thus, their focus was never on women's production, development, and contribution in society, but on controlling women and restricting them. This was because their perception of women's emancipation was that it will lead to moral issues and social corruption (*fitna*) in Kuwaiti society. In addition, the Islamist movement opposed all women's political rights until 2005 when Kuwaiti women gained the right to vote (women's right to vote in Kuwait in 2005 was very late compared to neighbouring Gulf countries and compared to the period in which Kuwait began urbanization). These issues related to gender dominated the efforts of the Islamic Movement in Kuwait. Therefore, all other issues related to development, modernization, and corruptions were absent. Ghabra (2017) questions how the society will be able to move forward while one half of it is preoccupied with controlling the other half, or even the decision-makers who are preoccupied with how to confront women in society for religion, moral, or other reasons.

Changes to women's political, economic, and social status during the urbanization period in Kuwait have been gradual and limited. These changes were focused on education and women's movements only (Al-Mughni, 2001). Thus, the entire policy of the state of Kuwait has been designed to perpetuate patriarchal relationships and to maintain the traditional role of women—homemaking and reproduction—without enhancing their role outside the home. Furthermore, the barriers or "mechanisms of social control" and restrictions increased for women. The transition from social authority, customs, and traditions to state authority resulted in increasingly codified and written norms. Kuwaiti society, like other patriarchal Arab and Islamic societies in the region during the period of state formation and institution building, produced laws that were detrimental to the status of women and codified discrimination between male and female citizens in law.

The drafting of the Nationality Laws in Kuwait was influenced by other laws such as Family Law and Personal Status Law (*Al-Issa, 2013*). Historically, the Nationality Laws of the Arab and Gulf countries as well were influenced by French-Napoleonic Law, which was built based on the Patriarchate. For example, in the Christian religion, women lose their eligibility, money, and names when they marry, and they always follow men while that is not the case in the Islamic religion. The Patriarchate influenced the status of women in the Nationality Law at the time, but patriarchalism, the culture of power and the domination of men over women, also existed in Arab and Gulf culture and helped in preventing any change for the Nationality Law in favour of women citizens. As a result, the Nationality Law in Kuwait does not treat women as full citizens (Al-Mughni, 2001, p. 155).

Thus, all the policies of the Kuwaiti state are built upon the premise that women are weaker than men and in need of protection. Under this argument, women are placed under the guardianship of men father/husband/brother/uncle/son; for the state, it is inconceivable that they could exist without the protection of men and be capable of standing on their own. Women are defined as family members whose rights and obligations are circumscribed by their roles as mothers, wives, and daughters (Al-Mughni, 2001, p. 64). Therefore, women are framed as mothers,

148 *Muyassar H. Suleiman*

sisters, caregivers, wives, but are not referred to as citizens with equal, constitutionally sanctioned rights. Based on this, women are not treated as rightful citizens (Al-Mughni, 2001, p. 50; Alhewail, 2017, December). When women are subjugated to in-laws, they are subjugated in the home as well, and by this, women are exposed to different types of violence (Alhewail, 2017, November). Moreover, laws in the state of Kuwait are made by men and societies shaped by a patriarchal history, with men drafting the laws which discriminate against female citizens (Allanana, 2013) Accordingly, gender equality can only be achieved by correcting the imbalances in the laws (Chaudhary, 2018).

Contradiction between Constitution and Nationality Law in Terms of Gender Equality

Kuwait witnessed the building of state institutions and the legal structure in the 1940s (Mahgoub, 2008). In the 1950s, there was a need to define the Kuwaiti citizen. The Kuwaiti Nationality Law was established in 1959. The legislature defined the Kuwaiti citizen under certain conditions. The legislature established the conditions, deciding that a person could be a Kuwaiti only if the father is Kuwaiti. The reason behind this condition remains unclear until today; however, there are two explanations for this legislation. The first one is that when the legislature chose the Kuwaiti father only to be the means to gain the Kuwaiti nationality through the blood tie, they were mixing between the descent and nationality tie. The second explanation is that there was a preference for the male citizen to give him the right to grant his nationality to his children while ignoring the same right to a female citizen and to her children. In 1959, there were no sustainable developments and no internal trends in the state of Kuwait or even globally on the importance of equality between males and females in legislation. There was no universal awareness of the concepts of discrimination against women and based on gender. Therefore, many of the laws that were adopted after the law of nationality in that period did not consider the female citizen as a citizen. Consequently, the legal and institutional violence that women were subjected to was due to insufficient awareness. After that, the concept of gender began to appear, as well as many conventions at the state and the international conferences that began by talking about the social, legal, and political situation of women in light of the modern state and the new legal systems.

The National Constitution was adopted in 1962 and it prevents any discrimination based on sex. However, the Nationality Law in Kuwait legitimates discrimination based on gender. The chapter argues that there exists an inconsistency between Articles 7 and 8 of the state of Kuwait Constitution that states,

> Article 7: Justice, freedom, and equality are the pillars of society; and cooperation and compassion are the firm link binding all citizens. Article 8: The State shall preserve the pillars of society and shall guarantee security, tranquility and equal opportunity to all citizens.

And, Article 2 of the Nationality Law, which states, "Any person born in, or outside, Kuwait whose father is a Kuwaiti national shall be a Kuwaiti national himself." The Constitution considers Kuwaiti citizens as having equal rights and opportunities, while Nationality Law in Article 2 discriminates against Kuwaiti female citizens married to non-Kuwaiti men by denying the children of such marriages the Kuwaiti nationality based on blood ties. Examples of such discrimination are given to prove that the nationality law in Kuwait is discrepant with the Constitution and affects the status of female citizens and all other laws.

The legal pyramid indicates that the national constitution is the supreme authority in the state. Therefore, any law that existed before the national constitution should not be in contradiction with the national constitution. That is why there is an explanatory memorandum for any law. All laws must be consistent with the principles of the National Constitution, not the opposite. The Nationality Law is considered one of the sovereign acts established by the Law on the Organization of the Judiciary, Decree No. 23 of 1990, and Article 2: The Courts shall not look into the sovereign acts. "The Nationality Law is one of the sovereign laws in the State (Decree-Law No. 23 of 1990—dated 10/3/1990 Law on the organization of the judiciary). The Prince is the one who grants citizenship and withdraws it, this means he signs the Emiri Decree because some articles in the nationality law state it may grant the nationality not should or is required" (Almassri, 2017).

The idea of adoption of national legislation in accordance with international assessments in the State of Kuwait is not strange to legislators. The State of Kuwait has responded to external changes with regard to several things and has changed several domestic legislations to comply with external pressures. As for women's affairs, especially Kuwaiti female citizens, no related articles have been changed in the Nationality Law. Moreover, the legislature responded to external pressures that discussed the granting of citizenship to a foreign wife and the principle of the unification of the nationality of the family and the issue of dual nationality. The Nationality Law stipulates that the wife of a citizen shall be granted citizenship under certain conditions and this legislation shall be applied to facilitate family matters and the principle of preserving the family, motherhood, and childhood provided for in the Kuwaiti Constitution. Article 9 of the Constitution says, "The family is the corner-stone of society, it is founded on religion, morality, and patriotism. Law shall preserve the integrity of the family, strengthen its ties, and protect under its support motherhood and childhood" (1962 Constitution of the State of Kuwait). In contrast, the Kuwaiti legislature ignored the same right of Kuwaiti citizenship in women having the right to grant nationality to her children and her husband under the same principle, which is to protect the family unity.

Most of the conventions designed to prevent discrimination against women aimed at directing states to amend their domestic legislation that discriminates against women in order to harmonize their laws with international standards. In 1953, the United Nations Economic and Social Council (ECOSOC), under the direction of the Commission on the Status of Women, issued an agreement to the States Members of the United Nations concerning the nationality of married persons. Article 1 of the Convention states:

150 *Muyassar H. Suleiman*

Each Contracting State shall not discriminate on the basis of The Convention on the Rights of the Child, adopted by the General Assembly of the United Nations and submitted for signature, ratification and accession by its resolution 34/180 of 18 December 1979, and by reference to the provisions of this Convention, the first paragraph of article 9 States are required to grant women equal rights with men to acquire, change and retain their nationality, and to ensure in particular that neither marriage nor change of nationality by a spouse during marriage can automatically change the nationality of a woman, make her stateless, Her husband and the nationality of the children. Indeed, the second paragraph of this article gave women equal rights with men with regard to the nationality of their children, stating that States Parties shall grant women equal rights with men to acquire, retain or change their nationality. In particular that the marriage shall not result in a foreigner or change the nationality of the husband during marriage, the nationality of the wife shall automatically change, become stateless, or the husband's nationality shall be imposed upon her. (Convention on the Nationality of Married Women New York, 20 February 1957)

Furthermore, "States Parties shall accord to women equal rights with men with respect to the nationality of their children" (United Nations Treaty Collection). The Kuwaiti legislature has responded to these global changes that advocate the importance of uniting the nationality of the family. The law of nationality has been amended only for the wife of a Kuwaiti citizen, who has the right to apply and take Kuwaiti nationality in order to preserve the principle of family unity, while at the same the right for the husband of Kuwait citizen was ignored. The Kuwaiti Nationality Law in both Articles 3 and 5 states that

Article 3: The Minister of the Interior may, by decree, grant the Kuwaiti nationality to a person born in Kuwait from a Kuwaiti mother if the father was unknown, or his father was not legally proven; Article 5: Kuwaiti women's children are treated as Kuwaitis when she divorced, or her husband died or captured.

Moreover, in Article 8,

Kuwaiti nationality may be granted by Decree upon the recommendation of the Minister of the Interior to a foreign woman who marries a Kuwaiti national provided that she declares her wish to acquire Kuwaiti nationality and that the marriage shall have lasted for at least 15 years from the date of her declaration.

New Concepts Linked to Development

The concept of development is a dynamic and variable concept. Development in the twentieth century was meant to increase the average per capita income before

Urbanization in Changing Social Norms to Laws   151

it became focused on education and health (Amin, 1983). At the beginning of the 21st century, development became a means for human development and recently the international community discourse in development is related to sustainable development (Soares Jr. and Quintella, 2008). These sequential changes were a response to the external changes in the international community in the 20th century, which was represented by the emergence of international organizations and civil society organizations that brought new concepts and linked them to the development necessitating a change to many particular existing policies. This included gender equality and the rights of special needs, child rights, and women's rights. These concepts have played an important role in preventing violence and oppression against vulnerable groups in society. Thus, international attention to these issues raises awareness on the importance of protecting vulnerable groups in society. Gender equality is one of these new concepts linked to development and it became essential to discuss gender equality as a part of the development process in many aspects (Aoláin, Cahn, Haynes, & Valji, 2018).

The 20th century witnessed an emphasis on defending issues such as justice and freedom and linked them to equality between male and female citizens in the political system. The 1960s marked a new turning point in the social and cultural life of the world. This was due to the emergence of new social theories such as the second wave of feminism, the expansion of human rights trends, the emergence of civil society organizations, and the governments of the welfare state and the economic prosperity that led to the development of many concepts in society in the 1980s (Moghadam, 2010). There have been many political movements that call for raising awareness of gender-based discrimination. Gender-based discrimination was the result of abnormal factors such as education, socialization, and the environment that established misconceptions about the roles of each sex in society. Biological difference was also linked to the distribution of the political rights and duties in the modern state (Al-Mughni, 2001). This discourse was in a world full of transformation. Therefore, it was necessary to reconsider the fixed social roles established by society and later on by the modern state in their laws for both female and male citizens.

The concept of gender has many dimensions and angles. A gender perspective aims to create a gender balance, justice, and development; in fact, it is discrimination based on sex (discrimination based on biological differences). It focusses on achieving justice that considers the difference between men and women and considers the differences between the needs of each sex (Aldabag & Ramadan, 2013). The characteristics of gender are classified into what is attributed to nature and what is acquired. Nature imposes male and female, and they are completely different from each other in terms of natural biological characteristics and differences. On the other hand, the concept of gender imposes traditions or social customs by the local culture of a society. The prevailing stereotypes in this society give males or females social roles (AlSeda & Abbas, 2015). Thus, the qualities acquired from the environment and social group confirm the masculinity or femininity of each sex. Therefore, sex is the biological difference (sexual identification) while gender is the image given by the society or the "social identity." Local culture plays a

152 Muyassar H. Suleiman

major role in cultivating specific values and principles that are specific to a particular society. This local culture establishes certain concepts, characteristics, and special roles for both sexes. This social identity is reflected in the form of daily transactions, policies, rights, duties, and the social role that each gender must follow. For instance, all the policies of the State of Kuwait are built upon the perspective that women are weaker than men and they are always in need of protection (Al-Mughni, 2001, p. 64).

The evolution of the concept of development globally and gender-based discrimination coincides with the internal women's groups movement of Kuwaiti society (Tetreault and Al-Mughni, 1995). In Kuwait, women have played a major role in demanding the elimination of all forms of legal and institutional discrimination based on gender. Urbanization brings social advances and social inequalities, both of which have helped to generate women's groups and movements. From this population growth, dynamic women's movements and campaigns for the repeal of discriminatory laws have emerged, as discussed in the previous chapter.

In one respect, urbanization was accompanied by greater access to education while it was also accompanied by inequalities in social, political, and cultural realms (Tetreault & Al-Mughni, 1995). Especially among young people, this generated demands for greater participation and rights. This happened because of cultural norms of the male breadwinner and female homemaker ideal. A lack of government programmes to involve low-income women in the labour force, and Muslim family laws that discriminate against women with regard to inheritance encourage female dependence on male "guardian" in the family. In Kuwait, the role of education under urbanization meant the opening of schooling and gave public spaces to women. Moreover, it has affected the traditional family and prescribed gender roles, replacing the patrilocally extended family with the nuclear family, creating many more opportunities for women, and affecting attitudes towards sexuality (Moghadam, 2013). In Kuwait, the emergence of women's movements and organizations calling for family law reform, equal nationality rights, and increased economic and political representation came about over the last several decades. These laws are seen as old and useless by much of the female population and the activist generation.

The urbanization process encourages education that contributes to women's capacity to mobilize around grievances and goals. At the same time, the global women's rights agenda by the United Nations conferences of the 1990s and 1994, the International Conference on Population and Development, created favourable opportunity structures that allowed increasing women's organizations in the Middle East (Moghadam, 2010). Among these are the non-governmental organizations that advocate for women's equality and rights, and participate in campaigns for family law reform, equal nationality rights, electoral quotas, and the introduction of anti-sexual harassment laws, and the prevention of all forms of violence against women (Moghadam, 2010). Women's rights activists rely on a parallel strategy of maintaining a strong civil society presence. In addition, civil society serves as an arena for women's activism through which they can increase their access to decision-making positions.

Urbanization in Changing Social Norms to Laws 153

The relationship between women's education, employment, and civic engagement is clear. Women's education not only correlates with employment and involvement in professional and civic associations, but it is also a powerful predictor of women's rights activism. Educated women have spearheaded the movements, organizations, and campaigns mentioned above—most of whom are also urban professionals in an array of fields, including the arts, media, the university sector, and business. Indeed, urbanization is a key aspect of social change and economic development in cities (Abu-Lughod, 1983). It plays a central role in social movements as well as in globalization processes. For instance, in Kuwait in 1963, two women's societies were established: The Cultural and Social Society (CSS) and the Arab Women's Development Society (AWDS) and, until today, they remain the only official organizations to speak on behalf of Kuwaiti women. Moreover, these organizations represented the history of the women's movement in Kuwait and evolved as a result of a male society eager to modernize itself without being ready to make a serious change in the gender relations in this period (Al-Mughni, 2001: 67). Thus, the period of establishment of these associations represented the spread of education in Kuwait and the presence of women from the merchant class who changed the discourse around women.

Additionally, these groups are working to rehabilitate them and change the stereotype of the status of women who were urged to be a wife and housewife. On the other hand, the pre-period of urbanization women's social status was customary, and their authority was limited to a certain tribe (Tetreault & Al-Mughni, 1995). There were no laws related to women's affairs such as work and study. After urbanization that brought the institution and the legal structure, the authority transferred from society to states and customaries became laws and legislation by the states. All of this was built on the assumption that women are weak, emotional, and irrational, and based on this, the state classifies female citizens as second-class citizens. More specifically the state's perspective of female citizens never comes from the concept of citizenship, but it comes from their social role and their social identity based on their nature and by "default" they have limited abilities compared to their male counterparts. Therefore, female citizens are considered based on their biological difference that they are less than men are, and thus, they should not be equal to the male citizen in citizenship rights.

Conclusion

The process of urbanization was driven by the global changes that happened in building the modern state in Kuwait which was started before Kuwait's independence in 1951. The concepts of development globally in the international community affected the level of development in Kuwait as well as the formation of state building. Urbanization had an impact on changing the social and cultural norms in the state of Kuwait. Economic change and the discovery of oil have also been one of the main factors that led to the social transformation in norms and values. Kuwaiti urbanization represents the framework that shapes state formation in building institutions, the legal structure, and the educational

154 *Muyassar H. Suleiman*

institutions. Education has been the most positive aspect in terms of changing the status of women. Society's awareness and the level of education have stimulated the establishment of civil society and social organizations in Kuwait and raised awareness of the political, social, and economic rights of women. The building of state institutions and the legal structure has adversely affected women's status through codification of women's affairs in laws that reduce the space of freedom that existed before, as well as transferring authority from society to the state because, under urbanization, a legal structure was established to regulate society's affairs.

In the State of Kuwait, the process of urbanization has not changed the culture of society from being conservative to more open, but it has put more restrictions on gender agency. As a result, in the State of Kuwait, the urban city (laws and legislation) does not reflect the social urbanization because development was not reflected in the political status of female citizens. The city in Kuwait refers to a Kuwaiti female citizen as a member of the social system (wife, sister, daughter… etc.) rather than a member of the political institution. In Kuwaiti society, after urbanization and especially after the Kuwait liberation in 1991, women's position in society became more restricted and controlled by the state. The government has contributed to gender inequality through legislation and laws that discriminate against Kuwaiti female citizens, such as the Nationality Law, Family Law, Penal Code Law, and Personal Status Law.

The State is responsible because it has the capacity to implement policies through the State's institutions, legislation, and laws. The Kuwaiti Constitution prevents any discrimination based on sex without mentioning gender, which means that gender found in law acts as a base of legal discrimination against female citizens. In both Article 7 and 8 of the Kuwaiti Constitution, it states that:

> Article 7: Justice, freedom, and equality are the pillars of society; and cooperation and compassion are the firm link binding all citizens. Article 8: The State shall preserve the pillars of society and shall guarantee security, tranquility, and equal opportunity to all citizens.

This state, institution, and the parliament, or "Legislature," in Kuwait believe that laws in Kuwait towards women are legal and do not discriminate against them because based on biological differences, rights and duties are determined between male and female citizens.

Footnote

Foucault's analysis of the effects of power on bodies refers to the notion of "biopower," which means state regulation of the population. Under urbanization, the process in which the body becomes a "political field" is inscribed and constituted by power relations. The state gives a symbolic code to certain spaces and these spaces become gendered, some places for men and other places for women. Thus, the transition in the identity in a modern regime of power was focused on sex,

Urbanization in Changing Social Norms to Laws **155**

gender, and proliferation to subjectify discourses on sexuality. This is done through legislation and laws established by states' institutions (Deveaux, 1994).

Arabic References

Al-Ganem, K. (1997). *Qatari society from diving to urbanization: A study of socio-economic composition and social classes and building strength*, 2nd ed. Doha: Dar Al-Sharq.

Alkaldi, K. (2018, January 15). No housing sponsorship for Kuwaiti women. Alaraby.

Almassri, M. (2017, January 22). Al-Enezi: Issues of nationality are not subject of sovereignty and administrative decisions are subject to the control of the administrative judiciary- cancellation and compensation. Kuwait News Agency. Retrieved from https://www .alanba .com .kw /ar /kuwait -news /incidents -issues /715937 /22 -01 -2017-العنزي مسائل-الجنسية-تخضع-لأعمال-السيادة-والقرارات-الصادرة-بشأنها-إدارية-تخضع-لرقابة-القضاء-الإداري-الإلغاء-وتعويضا.

Alnaba (2016). A Kuwaiti woman married to a non-Kuwaiti: The only mother that can not see her children grow up. *Newspaper News*.

Alseda, H., & Abbas, A. (2015). Women and memory forum. Feminist and historical studies. Decree No. 23 of 1990 on the law of the organization of the judiciary. Eastern Law Network. Retrieved from https://site.eastlaws.com/GeneralSearch/Home/ArticlesTDetails?MasterID=119378&MasterID=119378.

Ghaith, A. (1989). Urban sociology, Dar Al - Maarefah, Cairo. Ghabra, S. (2017). *Kuwait study in the mechanisms of the state, power and society*, 2nd ed. Johar Town: Afaq Publishing.

Ghabra, S. (2017). *Kuwait study in the mechanisms of the state, power and society*, 2nd ed. Beirut, Lebanon: Afaq Publishing.

English references

(1962). Kuwaiti constitution. Retrieved from http://www.wipo.int/edocs/lexdocs/laws/en/kw/kw004en.pdf.

Al-Mughni, H. (2001). *Women in Kuwait: The politics of gender*, 2nd ed. London: Saqi Books.

Al-Naqeeb, K. (1987). *The society and the state in the Gulf and the Arabian Peninsula*. London: Routledge.

Abu-Lughod, J. (1983, May–June). Urbanization and social change in the Arab world. *Ekistics*, 50(300), 223–231.

Aldabag, M., & Ramadan, A. (2013). Gender: Towards rooting the concept in the Arab world and using it to formulate effective policies. *Arabic Journal Sociology*, 23–24, 118. Retrieved from http://0-search.mandumah.com.mylibrary.qu.edu.qa/Record/489725.

Aoláin, F. N., Cahn, N. R., Haynes, D. F., & Valji, N. (2018). *The Oxford handbook of gender and conflict*. New York: Oxford University Press.

Konuk, N., Turan, N. G., & Ardali, Y. (2016). The importance of urbanization in education. *ISRES*, 5, 232–236. Retrieved from http://dergipark.gov.tr/download/article-file/334823.

Kuwait: Amiri Decree No. 17 of 1959 issuing the Aliens Residence Law. Gulf migration. Retrieved from http://gulfmigration.org/amiri-decree-no-17-of-1959-issuing-the-aliens-residence-law-3/.

Kuwait: Ministerial Decree No. 15 of 1959 promulgating the Nationality Law. Retrieved from https://www.ilo.org/dyn/natlex/docs/ELECTRONIC/83364/91990/F734821664/KWT83364.pdf.

Mahgoub, Y. (2008). *Kuwait: Learning from a globalized city: The evolving Arab city - Tradition, modernity and urban development*. New York: Routledge.

156 *Muyassar H. Suleiman*

Mernissi, F. (1987). *Beyond the veil: Male-female dynamics in modern Muslim society.* Bloomington: Indiana University Press.

Minoprio, S., & Macfarlane, P. W. (1951, November). Plan for the town of Kuwait. Report to his highness Sheikh Abdullah Al-Salim Al-Sabah, The Emir of Kuwait.

Moghadam, V. (2010). Urbanization and women's citizenship in the Middle East. *Brown Journal of World Affairs, 17*(1), 19–34. Retrieved from http://www.jstor.org/stable/24590755.

Moghadam, V. M. (2013). *Modernizing women: Gender and social change in the Middle East.* Boulder: Lynne Rienner.

Soares, J., & Quintella, H. R. (2008, April/June). Development: An analysis of concepts, measurement and indicators. Brazilian administration review. Retrieved from http://www.anpad.org.br/bar.

Sonbol,A. (1996).*Women, the Family and Divorce Laws in Islamic History. With a foreword by Elizabeth Warnock Fernea.* Syracuse: Syracuse University Press.

Sonbol, A. (2012). *Gulf women.* London: Bloomsbury Academic.

Tawadrous, N. (2014). Education and development in the Arab region. Master's degree studies in international and comparative education at Stockholm University. Retrieved from https://www.edu.su.se/polopoly_fs/1.404842.1538747723!/menu/standard/file/Master%20thesis-%20Nermeen.pdf.

Tétreault, M. A., & Al-Mughni, H. (1995). Gender, citizenship and nationalism in Kuwait. *British Journal of Middle Eastern Studies, 22*(1–2), 64–80. https://doi.org/10.1080/13530199508705612.

Conferences and lectures

Alhewail, F. (2017, November). *The reality of Kuwaiti citizenship married to non-citizens.*

Alhewail, F. (2017, December 11). Lecture on Kuwaiti Nationality Code, a rule of law v. a rule of man. *Annual Gulf Studies International Interdisciplinary Conference: Gulf Culture, Identity, and Society.* Doha, Qatar: Qatar University.

Gulf Forum: The reality of Gulf women married to non-citizens - 11/14/2017- State of Kuwait, 2017, December 6. Youtube.

10 Political Economy of Kuwait through the Prism of Its Hydrocarbon Sector

Nikolay A. Kozhanov

Introduction

Russia's invasion of Ukraine had a controversial impact on the energy security of the Gulf region. In terms of its external dimension, the Ukraine war moved the focus of the international community from security of demand towards security of supply by making the Western countries see the Gulf oil producers as potential replacements for Russia at the European energy market and beyond. In other words, the Ukrainian war presented the Gulf with a rare opportunity to enrich. High oil prices, boosted by the Russian aggression against Ukraine, not only replenished oil producers' coffers emptied by COVID-19 but also positively affected their macroeconomic growth indicators. Yet, each coin has two sides. On the one hand, the unwillingness of the Gulf producers to cooperate with oil consumers in order to slow down or even reverse the growth of oil prices makes the consumers seek alternative ways to change the situation in their favour. The range of potential responses is wide and it varies from the search for alternative suppliers outside of the Gulf to the adoption of legislation negatively affecting the activities of the OPEC+. Moreover, despite the fact that the Gulf countries' economies have a higher level of tolerance towards the negative outcomes of the war (such as rising fuel prices, high inflation rates, and growing cost of inputs) than the other countries of the Middle East, even the least vulnerable economies started to feel the negative pressure of rising fuel prices and energy costs. The high oil incomes also slow down the growth of the non-oil sectors of the Gulf economies and make them less interested in the implementation of diversification programmes. In the long term, this impact will only be growing, potentially making the Gulf players reconsider their market strategies.

The overall situation is aggravated by the fact that the last eight years preceding the war in Ukraine were in general a difficult period for the oil-producing monarchies of the Persian Gulf and they have not yet completely recovered from experienced troubles. These problems, in turn, were caused by those changes in world politics and economics that made the future of the global oil market unpredictable and full of various challenges. The roots of these transformations that began in the late 2000s and hit the regional markets by the mid-2010s are connected to two factors: The impact of the US shale revolution on the global hydrocarbon market and the beginning of the global energy transition to non-carbon fuels.

DOI: 10.4324/9781003435259-10

The Shale Oil Strom and Kuwait Interests

The US shale revolution is a term marking the beginning of the active use of the combination of hydraulic fracturing, horizontal mining, and seismic technologies that allowed the United States to substantially increase the production of oil and gas in the late 2000s and 2010s, subsequently turning the country into one of the world's largest producers and exporters of hydrocarbons. In the 2000s, new ways of tight oil and gas extraction were massively introduced in the US, which allowed the American hydrocarbon producers to significantly increase their domestic output within a relatively brief time. This not only changed the situation at the global oil market by turning the US into one of the largest hydrocarbon producers, but set an example for some other countries and created a shale oil industry whose life cycles and principles of functioning substantially differed from those of the conventional oil sector, threatening the global oil market with oversupply and often creating challenges for traditional producers such as the GCC countries (Yergin, 2020).

Thanks to the shale revolution (de facto, new technological revolution), the US not only became the largest producer and exporter of hydrocarbons, but also stimulated the emergence of new market players in other countries. Driven by these factors, the growth rates in global oil supply have been steadily surpassing growth in oil demand since 2011, causing the markets' oversupply in the 2010s. Due to the specifics of shale oil production, neither the 2014–2016 price war waged by Saudi Arabia in an attempt to bankrupt its global rivals, nor OPEC+'s subsequent efforts to regulate the market through the reduction of oil output could remove or eliminate this oversupply. Unsurprisingly, by the beginning of the COVID-19 pandemic in 2020, the global oil market was already oversupplied and even without factoring in the coronavirus, the volume of market supply was set to surpass demand by 2 million barrels per day, making the fall in oil prices inevitable. The market oversupply swung the oil market in favour of buyers and significantly weakened the position of sellers. This change stripped the importance of hydrocarbons as a "unique" resource, giving its consumers the right to choose between suppliers offering the cheapest price. Suddenly, the GCC countries found themselves scrambling to ensure their own sustainable access to markets in order to guarantee the adequate development of their own economies, particularly the oil, gas, and petrochemical sectors. In other words, the energy security focus of the GCC countries shifted from protecting the interests of oil consumers to protecting the interests of oil producers.

Under these circumstances, it is not a coincidence that the new round of Kuwait's economic troubles began almost simultaneously with the rise of US shale oil production. The country has never fully recovered from the 2014–2016 fall in oil prices, which was caused, for the first time in history, by the rise in shale oil output (see Table 10.1). After 2014, its GDP growth rates significantly dropped, sometimes even recording negative values, and the oil incomes of the key players never returned to previous levels (see Table 10.1, Figures 10.1 and 10.2) (Table 10.1).

Table 10.1 Real GDP Growth of GCC Member Countries 2012–2022 (%)

	2012	2013	2014	2015	2016	2017	2018	2019	2020	2021	2022[1]
Saudi Arabia	5.4	2.7	3.7	4.1	1.7	-0.7	2.4	0.3	-4.1	3.2	7.7
UAE	4.5	5.1	4.3	5.1	3.1	0.5	1.7	1.3	-6.1	2.3	4.2
Qatar	4.7	4.4	4	3.7	2.1	1.6	1.5	0.1	-2.7	1.5	3.4
Oman	9.1	5.1	1.4	4.7	4.9	0.3	1.8	0.5	-2.8	2	5.6
Kuwait	6.6	1.2	0.5	0.6	2.9	-4.7	1.2	0.7	-8.9	1.3	8.2
Bahrain	3.7	5.4	4.4	2.9	3.5	3.8	2	1.8	-4.9	2.2	3.3

Source: IMF

The increased competition of Kuwait with other market players was also a result of the shale revolution that changed the hydrocarbon trade patterns. The US has ceased to be an important market, instead becoming another exporter and diverting a significant portion of global hydrocarbon exports to Asia, thus, increasing competition in the main consumer market for Kuwait and other GCC oil and gas producers. At the same time, the high sensitivity of shale oil production to oil prices subsequently shortened the duration of global oil price cycles and changed their amplitude. Given the ability of shale oil producers to quickly increase output if encouraged by positive market dynamics, oil prices were unable to rise too high and/or for too long, forcing GCC countries, including Kuwait, to say goodbye to the era of ultra-high incomes until 2021. (Figure 10.1).

Under the influence of these factors, in the late 2010s, Kuwait supported the decision of OPEC to somewhat move away from the strategy of maximizing its market share (by offering moderate oil prices and squeezing out competitors with higher production costs) towards the idea of maximal monetization of natural resources to generate funds necessary to develop its own economy in order to meet the needs of the ongoing energy transition. Price damping is, in general, a risky endeavour as it launches price wars whose outcomes also depend on the ability of other players to change their output and decrease the cost of production. The 2014–2016 price war that Saudi Arabia was waging against shale oil producers by increasing its oil production showed that this strategy was only strengthening the Saudi rivals by getting them motivated to further cut production costs and adjust their output levels. Meanwhile, extremely moderate market gains were not justifying financial losses from low prices (Fattouh, Poudineh, & Sen 2016, pp. 223–240). Apart from that, the new approach implied, among other things, keeping the cost of a barrel of oil at the highest possible level by regulating (cutting) production volumes while increasing the production spare capacity in order to be able to both

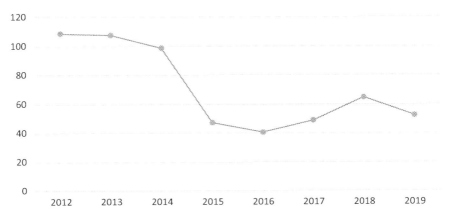

Figure 10.1 Oil Export Revenues of Kuwait in 2012–2019 (billion USD). (*Source:* Middle East Economic Survey)

regulate the market and maximize the volume of exports once oil prices are stabilized at the acceptable level.

By 2020, the shale revolution significantly weakened Kuwait and other GCC oil producers' positions in the oil market, shortened oil price cycles, and created a threat of long-term oversupply of hydrocarbons. Yet, this was only one part of the challenge faced by Kuwait and its oil-producing neighbours. The energy transition that was also partially boosted by the shale revolt sharply raised the question of possible stagnation and decline in global oil demand in the long term, putting the future prosperity of conventional oil producers, including Kuwait, under question (Yergin, 2020).

Kuwait and Energy Transition Challenge

As the analysis of the existing academic and research literature shows, not all researchers and policymakers understand the complexity of the nature of the fourth energy transition and the problems it poses for consumers and producers of traditional energy resources. The situation is often simplified by a definition of the energy transition as a grand replacement of hydrocarbon resources in the energy sector with renewable energy sources (S&P Global, February 24, 2020). Such a definition overemphasizes the environmental factor of the energy transition and can create a false feeling that the replacement of hydrocarbons with renewable energy sources is the main goal of the energy transition. Thus, some experts argue that the "energy transition is [about] reducing our ecological footprints—we should stop wasting materials (food, water, etc.) and quit polluting the environment" (METGroup, July 29, 2021).

The definition of the energy transition given by the International Renewable Energy Agency (IRENA) somewhat improves the situation by saying that the energy transition is "a pathway toward transformation of the global energy sector from fossil-based to zero-carbon by the second half of this century. At its heart is the need to reduce energy-related CO2 emissions to limit climate change" (IRENA, 2020). In other words, the use of renewable energy sources is only a part of the energy transition, which is a complex combination of the processes of the global transformation of energy systems, including the processes of decarbonization, energy efficiency improvement, digitalization, and reforming regulatory systems of energy trade (including through decentralization). However, this definition is also not complete.

In considering the fourth energy transition only as a response to the challenges posed by climate change, researchers miss the most important thing: this response not only affects all elements of the global energy system (production, transportation, and consumption), but also implies a global restructuring of society and the world economy based on the principle of sustainable development. This principle is a distinctive feature that distinguishes the current energy transition from all previous transformations of the energy market, such as the transition from the use of coal to the use of oil, during which the imperative was to increase energy efficiency and accelerate economic growth. The impact of the fourth energy transition on

162   *Nikolay A. Kozhanov*

the development of the world economy and society may be even more profound than previous transitions. According to Mills (2020, p. 116), the current energy transition "is not simply the introduction of new technologies, but also involves the changes in markets, institutions and regulations that allow or are induced by technological changes."

The global scale of the upcoming changes inevitably affects the interests of hydrocarbon-producing resources. According to researchers (Mills, 2020, p. 116), in the medium- and long-term, adaptation to a new energy order will require Gulf Cooperation Council (GCC) oil and gas producers to:

- Restructure their economies and revise their social contracts to withstand a decline in demand and prices for oil and gas resources.
- Ensure the survival of their oil and gas industries.
- Rebuild their energy systems for a lower-carbon future.
- Cope with the growth of competition in traditional Asian markets.

For Kuwait, the issue of adapting to new conjunctures is perhaps more acute than for most of its neighbours in the Gulf. This is, firstly, due to the peculiarity of the structure of its economy and the existing social contract, the existence of which directly depends on petrodollar receipts. The country possesses approximately 6 per cent of the world's known oil reserves. The oil and gas sector is responsible for more than half of Kuwait's GDP while oil export revenues form more than 92 per cent of the export revenues and a lion's share of budget incomes (Kim, 2023, p. 208). At the same time, Kuwait was and still is a state with a specific form of social contract that is typical for rentier states. It implies that the ruling elite of a country buys the loyalty of its citizens and imposes certain restrictions on political freedoms in exchange for the guarantees of a comfortable life. The high level of living standards is ensured, amongst all, through the provision and distribution of direct and indirect subsidies. This rather expensive social contract between the Kuwaiti society and state is funded by high oil revenues and is dependent on their sustainability. Under these circumstances, the market instability of the 2010s determined by the fallout of the US shale revolution clearly showed the danger of such reliance, while the ongoing energy transition put the country's prosperity under the big question.

Oil Kingdom

According to many researchers, Kuwait represents an extreme example of a rentier state (Commins, 2012, p. 149; Embassy of Switzerland in Kuwait, 2022, p. 1; Herb, 2014, p. 192). Indeed, during the 20th and early 21st centuries, oil was and remains the main pillar of state building and economic development of the country. And, to a certain extent, the early gains from oil dependency were not so negative. The first commercial oil well was drilled in 1938 and the first export consignment was sent abroad in 1946. Yet, it was not until the 1950s when Kuwait started receiving substantial incomes from the oil trade (Commins, 2012). This was

Kuwait's Hydrocarbon Economy: Main Trends 163

largely determined by two factors: The 1951 renegotiation of Kuwait's profit share with Kuwait Oil Company (established in 1934 by Anglo-Persian Oil Company and American Gulf Oil Corporation) and the 1953 attempt by the Iranian government to nationalize its own oil industry. In the first case, the Kuwaiti authorities were able to increase their share in oil export incomes to 50 per cent. Meanwhile, the nationalization movement in Iran made Iran's traditional consumers look for alternative sources of supplies, naturally drawing their attention to the Arab part of the Gulf. Both of these factors substantially increased the incomes of the state and helped its leadership to speed up the state building processes (Commins, 2012, p. 148). These events also coincided with the rise of a new ruler, Sheikh Abdullah Al Salim, who, in 1950, inherited the Kuwaiti throne from his predecessor, Sheikh Ahmad. According to Commins, "Sheikh Abdullah presided over the formation of Kuwait's rentier bargain, the exchange of generous public services funded by oil wealth for citizens' loyalty to the ruler. His administration provided free education and medical care to ordinary Kuwaitis. The sheikhdom became the Gulf's leader in specialized medicine with the construction of several hospitals. Furthermore, the government expanded the range of jobs available only to Kuwaitis as the number of expatriate workers grew in medicine and education. The political effect was profound and lasting. For instance, during the years of Arab nationalist ferment that caused so much concern in Saudi Arabia and Bahrain, Kuwait saw limited activism, primarily among expatriate Arab workers from Iraq and Egypt. Only during the height of the Suez Crisis did Kuwaitis join with Egyptian, Lebanese, and Palestinian workers in demonstrations to denounce the British and criticize the ruling clan for its pro-British posture" (2012, p. 149).

Oil resources allowed Kuwait to quickly launch modernization processes. The country was one of the first in the region to achieve independence from British control. It took part in the creation of OPEC and, for the most part, successfully maneuvered in the turbulent climate of the Middle East of the 20th century. Up until today, Kuwait remains one of the leading oil exporting countries in the region and the world. By 2023, oil production in the country was at the level of 2.70 million barrels per day, of which 1.92 million barrels per day were exported, 762,000 barrels per day were consumed by the petrochemical sector of Kuwait, and 22,000 barrels per day were used as fuel for local power plants. The main volume of Kuwaiti oil supplies falls on Asia. As of 2022, the largest consumers of Kuwaiti oil were China (665,000 barrels per day), South Korea (447,000 barrels per day), India (250,000 barrels per day), Japan (214,000 barrels per day), and Vietnam (175,000 barrels of oil per day) (Al-Maleki, December 23, 2022).

As part of the ongoing process of economic diversification, Kuwait is making a serious bet on the development of its petrochemical production. By 2024, the country's leadership plans to bring the country's refining capacity to the level of 1.416 million barrels per day: The results should bring 30 billion US dollars invested in the construction of the Al-Zour petrochemical complex, as well as the modernization of two existing refineries—"Mina al-Ahmadi" and "Mina Abdullah." Most of the products of the Kuwaiti refineries are intended for export. By 2023, its volumes were 695,000 barrels per day (Al-Maleki, December 23, 2022). At the same time,

164 *Nikolay A. Kozhanov*

so far oil remains the main source of the country's budget revenues and a way to maintain the aforementioned social contract.

Wasted Money?

Unfortunately, by the beginning of the 21st century (if not before), the initial successes in state-building secured by the rentier state model had been compensated by the triumph of factors constraining this development. One of the main problems has become the ever-increasing cost of the social contract, which significantly reduces the amount of money that the government can direct to the development and restructuring of the economy. Thus, in 2021–2022, 88 per cent of Kuwait's budget expenditures (US$62.7 billion out of US$71.1 billion) accounted for current expenses. Of these, US$41.6 billion were spent on paying salaries to employees of the public sector, where the majority of the Kuwaitis (up to 80 per cent) are employed, and another US$12.6 billion were spent on paying various subsidies. At the same time, the share of citizens in Kuwait is only one-third of the 4.45 million people living in the country (Al-Maleki, January 27, 2023).

However, the absorption by the social contract of funds that could be directed to the development of the economy is only one of the consequences of the existing sociopolitical system. The negative impact of the rentier state model is also evident in other issues of the country's economic development (Shehabi, 2021, p. 5). Among other things, these include:

- Excessive dependence of the country's socioeconomic system on the sustainability of petrodollar revenues.
- Underdevelopment of the tax system.
- Lack of interest among citizens of the country to work in the private sector with unreasonably high salaries in the public sector, where priority is given to hiring Kuwaitis.
- Opacity and corruption in the economic environment.
- Oligopolistic nature of the Kuwaiti economy.[2]
- Use of reserve funds to cover the budget deficit and finance social programmes instead of investing these funds in the development of the country's economy (Shehabi, 2019).

Kuwait's economic problems directly affect the business environment, according to the *2023 Index of Economic Freedom*, published by the Heritage Foundation. In 2023,

> Kuwait's economic freedom score is 56.7, making its economy the 108th freest in the 2023 Index. Its score is 1.6 points lower than last year. Kuwait is ranked 9th out of 14 countries in the Middle East/North Africa region, and its overall score is below the world and regional averages. Institutional weaknesses continue to constrain overall economic freedom. The judicial system lacks the capacity to defend property rights effectively. Despite some

progress, corruption continues to undermine prospects for long-term economic development. There have been efforts to enhance the efficiency of the business regulatory framework, but overall progress has been mixed.

(Kim, 2023, p. 208)

The right of the population to social benefits and protection is enshrined in the Constitution of the country and practically elevated to the status of a "sacred cow" that cannot be touched. Meanwhile, it is assumed that the state should play the role of defender of this inviolability. In other words, the revision of the social contract may even be associated with a challenge to the legitimacy of the ruling elite. At the same time, the existing system of distribution of oil benefits is inefficient and leads to their excessive consumption, as well as the creation of a negative model of economic behaviour of citizens who prefer to remain unemployed if they cannot get a place in the public sector (Saad, 2021, p. 9). Free social support programmes create an excessive demand for them, which, in turn, increases financial pressure on the budget and the only main source of income is oil exports (Saad, 2021, p. 9). The country's tax system remains undeveloped (1.8 per cent of the country's GDP) (Kim, 2023, p. 208). Under these circumstances, a natural question arises regarding the sustainability of the entire financing system of Kuwait's social contract: since 2014, the country's oil revenues have significantly decreased and are highly volatile (Saad, 2021, p. 9). At the same time, due to the strict limits on external borrowing, the country must cover the resulting deficit from financial reserves that initially it was planned to use for economic development. Moreover, since 2014, the country's budget has been in deficit (see Figure 10.2) (Figure 10.2).

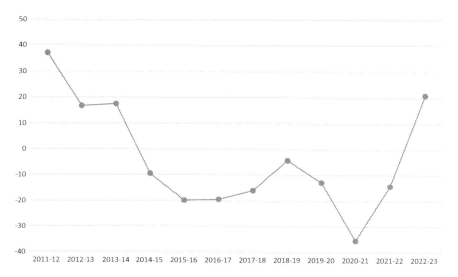

Figure 10.2 Dynamics of Kuwait's Budget Deficit in 2011–2023 (billion USD)
Source: Middle East Economic Survey

166 *Nikolay A. Kozhanov*

Reforms, such as the introduction of VAT and the development of the taxation system, the reduction and restructuring of the subsidy system, the promotion of the development of the private sector of the economy, and active economic diversification could solve the problems in many ways (Agha, 2021, p. 2). However, this is not happening. Moreover, even the political life of Kuwait does not contribute to the removal of existing constraints on economic development. Rather, on the contrary, it is such a limiter in itself.

Political Deadlock

On the one hand, the almost incessant political crisis in the relations between the Majlis (National Assembly) and the executive power in recent years does not allow the government to fully build and implement long-term development plans for the country (Blanchard, 2023, p. 5). The latter are largely declared, but rarely or with delays are executed in practice. Moreover, from the end of 2018 to the end of 2022, four people were replaced as oil minister, which also does not contribute to building a long-term vision (Al-Maleki, January 27, 2023).

On the other hand, populism has become one of the important levers of influence in the domestic political struggle in Kuwait. Neither the executive power nor the opposition is ready to embark on full-fledged transformations that may infringe on the interests of citizens. As a result, the Kuwaiti parliament has been postponing the implementation of VAT for many years. Moreover, instead of dismantling a rather cumbersome system of state support, the same parliament seeks only to strengthen the existing social contract. According to Olver-Ellis,

> one of the most important functions of the National Assembly has been to represent and protect the socio-economic rights of Kuwaiti citizens. Elected members, who are described as "service MPs," have often put pressure on the government to increase the socio-economic privileges available to their constituents. In November 2016, for example, with a populist backlash against the government's reform agenda, the opposition returned to the National Assembly after a four-year absence and won 24 of the 50 seats. Opposition MPs promoted themselves as guardians of their constituents, opposing the government's austerity measures that included the cutting of subsidies and public sector employment.
>
> (2020, p. 14)

Under the current circumstances, such a role of the Majlis creates more problems than it serves for the benefit of the interests of the country. Thus, in January 2023, the Kuwaiti government was forced to resign, having not found a common language with the parliament, which demanded to direct the excess revenues received from oil to additional payments to the population. Back in late 2022, the Financial Committee of Majlis decided that the government should pay citizens' debts related to consumer and personal loans (Al-Maleki, January 27, 2023). The

Kuwait's Hydrocarbon Economy: Main Trends   167

committee also wanted to raise pensions. The issue of personal debts is very serious for Kuwait: According to the country's Central Bank, over one-third of the Kuwaitis owe US$48 billion in loans; out of these, US$5.5 billion were consumer loans while the other US$42.5 billion were housing loans (Al-Maleki, January 27, 2023). The payment of these debts by the state would definitely help to strengthen the legitimacy of the political regime, but undermine its capacities to develop the economy in the long run.

According to the researchers, the uniqueness of the political structure of Kuwait, which, unlike other GCC countries, has a parliament endowed with decision-making power, has become its own curse (Saad, 2021). The Majlis, which can reject government laws, cross-examine cabinet ministers, and challenge the will of appointed government ministers, also makes it difficult to make decisions on necessary budget adjustments, reforms, and meaningful diversification plans. The long political crisis has demotivated the executive branch to carry out the necessary reforms, including plans to diversify the Kuwaiti economy. Meanwhile, recent events are increasingly demanding radical steps from Kuwait (Saad, 2021).

COVID-19 and Putin's War in Ukraine as a Last Warning?

The COVID-19 pandemic that hit the region in 2020 only amplified the impact of the negative impact of existing trends (both external and domestic) on Kuwait's economy. Firstly, the global oil glut has forced the GCC countries to wage a severe price war in the hydrocarbon market. Moreover, in spring 2020, oil producers had to fight not so much for the expansion of their market presence, but rather to protect their position while being pressured by a devastating fall in demand. As one commentator observed, this turned the market competition into a bloody knife fight where anything goes (Henderson 2020). At the same time, the excessive crude reserves accumulated by some traditional consumers during the period of low prices in the spring of 2020 also tempted them to temporarily become exporters when prices started to recover. This made life for traditional oil producers even harder; for instance, in July 2020, the Chinese oil traders suddenly announced their intention to resell about 1 million barrels of oil from their reserves to Asian consumers at a price lower than those set by Saudi Arabia, the UAE, or Kuwait (as the GCC member countries included transportation costs which were higher than those of Chinese traders whose stocks were already located in the region) (Bloomberg, 2020).

Kuwait's macroeconomic indicators have deteriorated significantly amid lower revenues caused by the fall in oil prices and the all-out war for market shares (see Table 10.1, Figures 10.1 and 10.2). The resulting fall in oil incomes, accompanied by the need to support non-oil sectors hit by the global lockdown, has triggered significant budget deficits, putting Kuwait at risk of running out of foreign exchange reserves (Ingram, May 15, 2020). Given the dominant role of government institutions in financing GCC economic development, any reduction in oil revenues inevitably slowed down the implementation of key development programmes. Together with the downturn in economic activity, this led to Kuwait's negative GDP growth rates with impacts on social indicators (See Table 10.1).

168 *Nikolay A. Kozhanov*

Under these circumstances, the beginning of Putin's invasion of Ukraine and the hike in oil prices caused by oil market instability were, to a certain extent, a blessing in disguise for both Kuwait and its GCC neighbours. It slowed down the process of energy transition, extending the age of hydrocarbons and demonstrating the need for greater international investment in the upstream sector. Profits from increased oil prices allowed Kuwait and GCC members to mitigate the financial losses of previous years and improve their macroeconomic indicators, directly resulting in the strengthening of their domestic economies. This allowed Kuwait to speak again on the need to speed up the implementation of mega projects that were to boost its presence in the international oil market and help diversify its economy (Al-Maleki, May 12, 2023).

The Russia–Ukraine war also shifted the focus of the international community from the security of oil and gas demand to the security of supply by prompting Western countries to prioritize GCC hydrocarbon producers as a potential replacement for Russia in the European energy market and beyond. This, in turn, created additional levers of influence for the GCC when building a dialogue with their Western partners. Despite the objective factors that prevented GCC countries from acting as a full-fledged and immediate replacement for Russia in the EU's oil and gas market, their presence in Europe notably grew and was not limited exclusively to hydrocarbon supplies. Gulf countries were also able to increase their presence in the petrochemical industry of Europe; and that is where Kuwait was able to use the momentum. Since the end of 2022, Kuwait has begun commissioning its newest Al-Zour oil refinery, which successfully coincided with the European embargo on Russian oil products and the increased interest of the EU and the United States in the Middle East as a source of alternative supplies. The Kuwaiti authorities have officially confirmed that they benefit from extremely high demand in the United States and Europe amidst the economic confrontation between Russia and the West. The new plant is aimed specifically at the production of medium distillates, mainly diesel fuel and jet fuel, which will allow Kuwait to successfully find its place in the European market. It is estimated that by the beginning of 2023, the export of Kuwaiti petroleum products to Europe reached a record level of 219,000 barrels per day (from 56,000 barrels before the war) (Al-Maleki December 9, 2022; Ingram, March 10, 2023a). Back in 2021, Kuwait exported only 8,000 barrels per day of gas oil and diesel fuel to Europe. This figure has increased to an average of 22,000 barrels per day in 2022. At the beginning of 2023, the largest component of Kuwait's petrochemical exports to Europe is jet fuel, the volumes of which usually exceed 100,000 barrels per day. Of these, more than 70 per cent of the volume falls on kerosene for jet engines. It is believed that because of the transformation of the supply chains of petroleum products, Kuwait has become the largest supplier of jet fuel to Europe by 2022. (Al-Maleki, December 9, 2022).

At the same time, the existing gains of Kuwait and other GCC countries are, to an extent, counterbalanced by the market challenges created by the conflict. Firstly, Moscow is more and more successful in redirecting its export flows to Asia, the traditional consumer market of Kuwait's oil exports. This, in turn, increases the

Kuwait's Hydrocarbon Economy: Main Trends 169

intensity of competition. In 2022, cheap, albeit toxic, Urals oil was traded at a historically high discount rate and attracted the attention of Indian and Chinese consumers, limiting options for Kuwait and other Gulf producers to strengthen their presence there.

Secondly, the determination of Gulf producers to maintain high oil prices in spite of growing dissatisfaction among oil consumers and, first of all, the US, can create new challenges for GCC producers (Cahil, 2022; Smith & El Wardany, 2022). The American failures to persuade the Arab monarchies of the Gulf to limit their price ambitions make the US not only search for alternative (and not always producer-friendly) ways to bring the barrel prices down but also try to encourage other consumers to act against the interests of the GCC hydrocarbon producers (Hunnicutt & Renshaw, 2021). In addition, these US efforts are gradually acquiring the flavour of a market war.

Thirdly, the impact of the Ukraine crisis on the domestic energy and economic security of Kuwait is not as positive as in the case of its oil and gas exports. The country feels the negative pressure of rising fuel prices, inflation, and increasing energy costs. High oil incomes also slow down the growth of non-oil sectors by rendering them less of a priority in the framework of diversification programmes.

Finally, the transition to a new model of energy consumption globally, which entails a decrease in hydrocarbon demand in the long run, might be delayed outside of Europe by the current economic conditions, but not cancelled (Brendon, 2022). Moreover, the negative impact of the oil market instability on the global economy together with some other factors might even create additional incentives to speed up the energy transition in the long run, thus leaving Kuwait and the GCC with even more limited time to adjust to the new realities (Kanawa, 2023; Mendiluce, 2022). Meanwhile, in order to successfully integrate into the new "post-oil" economic system while ensuring the extended demand for hydrocarbon resources, traditional oil producers of the Gulf need to start implementing ambitious and complex economic programmes, including measures aimed at the decarbonization of oil, gas, and petrochemical production, the diversification of their economies, the development of sustainable energy sources, and reconstruction of their own energy systems. All of these require substantial funds generated by oil incomes. Yet, as it will be shown later, the current situation cannot guarantee their steady flow.

Currently, the energy market is experiencing an unprecedented and intense struggle between political and systemic economic factors, whose interaction determines oil prices. The eventual outcome of this ongoing struggle is still not yet clear. Political factors presented by the war in Ukraine, instability in Libya (whose 1.2 mln barrel production capacity were the hostage of protracted political turmoil and amounting maintenance issues leading to occasional and sometimes abrupt cut in the country's oil production and exports), the uncertainty of the future of Iran's nuclear programme, unclear prospects for Iran–Saudi relations and broader instability in the Middle East, are pushing prices up. Meanwhile, fundamental economic factors in the market are pulling them down. Among these economic factors are the unpredictability of demand in China, the global restructuring of oil flows due to the EU's decision to limit dependence on Russia's hydrocarbons, and the expected slowdown in global economic growth caused by high oil and gas prices as well as the initial disruptions in supply chains of oil and oil products from Russia to Europe. In comparatively more peaceful times in international relations, the influence of market fundamentals on hydrocarbon trade is always stronger than political factors. This influence, as a rule of thumb, is of a long-term nature.

The set of solutions for the problems created by geopolitical factors affecting the supply side are relatively easy to apply. Given the availability of alternatives, the market can restructure the chains of supply to replace "problematic" sources. Once this is achieved, the political factor loses its sharp destabilizing influence on the market that drives price volatility. This, for instance, was the case in 2019, when US sanctions were placed on Venezuela. Venezuela's heavy and sour oil that could not reach the global market due to sanctions was swiftly replaced by its Russian equivalents. The economic factors, on the contrary, are mostly connected to the demand side. They can be caused by deep and complex structural changes in the global economy. Their impact on the oil market is not always direct and solutions—as in the case of the current energy transition process—are not always obvious. All of these reasons make the impact of the economic fundamentals on the market situation deeper and long-lasting. However, the world is currently going through abnormal times. Political factors no longer have a short-term impact on the market that can be easily compensated by the redirection of oil flows: the Kremlin's aggression in Ukraine and the accompanying games with "oil weapons" between Russia and the West will affect oil prices for a long time, bringing acute unpredictability to the hydrocarbon market. Russia's size and importance as an oil and gas producer play one of the key roles in this: For the first time in recent history, the sanction war is waged against one of the largest hydrocarbon and petrochemical producers whose absence from the market cannot be easily compensated by other actors.

It appears unlikely that the end of the pandemic crisis and Putin's war in Ukraine will lead to a return to the pre-COVID-19 situation, when the problem of Gulf energy security was solely related to the stability of consumers' access to regional hydrocarbons. In the long run, the world is more likely to see relatively low oil prices, frequent market fluctuations, limited potential for growth in oil demand, and intense competition. And yet, neither the COVID-19 pandemic nor energy transition nor current market instability should be considered an exceptional evil for Kuwait and other producers of hydrocarbons from among the Gulf countries. The trials that fell to their lot allowed them to develop a certain behaviour strategy that should help them prepare for the energy transition. GCC countries are forced to adapt to new conditions, implementing adjustment strategies for the development of their oil sectors. Given the current instability of the market and future challenges of the energy transition, they are betting on a long-term strategy aimed at ensuring the competitiveness and profitability of hydrocarbons in the global market. The key elements of this strategy include:

- Constant work to maintain low production costs.
- Creation of spare production capacity.

- Interaction with key partners in Asia by "binding" them to GCC oil through long-term contracts and stimulating their demand for oil from the GCC through investments in the Asian petrochemical sector.
- Active "greening" of the oil production process.
- Investments in the development of alternative energy sources (both to decrease the CO_2 footprint of hydrocarbon production by switching the domestic oil and gas sector to the use of green energy sources and to diversify their energy exports in the future).
- Investments in the oil production and refining sectors of other countries (including competitors).
- Preservation of OPEC as an effective lever of influence in the oil market.

In other words, the road map already exists, being suggested by such players as Saudi Arabia, the UAE, and Qatar. Yet, it is unclear whether Kuwait will be able to use it given the current model of its economic development.

Conclusion

Most probably, the implementation of the above-mentioned road map will be a challenge for Kuwait. Already the first two points—maintaining low production costs and creating additional production capacities—can be difficult to implement. In the second half of the 2010s, it was assumed that the country would be able to increase its oil production capacity to 4 million barrels per day by 2020. However, this did not happen. Moreover, the timing of reaching this indicator is constantly shifting. Now it is believed to be achieved by 2035 (Al-Maleki, May 12, 2023). Kuwait's problem is a banal lack of funds for development. On the one hand, they are constantly absorbed by current expenses. On the other hand, the conditions for the presence of foreign companies in the oil and gas sector are unprofitable and unattractive (for the sake of populist reasons, the country is trying to maximize its sovereignty over the process of producing and exporting hydrocarbons by offering unprofitable contracts to foreigners). As a result, Kuwait practically does not develop its own gas fields, and oil fields have been showing a steady decline in production since 2017, when oil production reached its peak of 3.15 million barrels per day (Ingram, March 10, 2023b). The country is facing a very acute issue of implementing costly EOR programmes: Their implementation is impossible without additional financial injections, which are difficult to attract.

As of the spring of 2023, Kuwait officially planned to invest $15 billion annually in increasing oil production over the next five years. However, as argued by Ingram,

> these are large sums, but are dwarfed by the figures from nearby states. In Abu Dhabi, Adnoc announced an 18 per cent increase in its planned capex in November and intends to invest $150bn over 2023–27 ($30bn annually)— double the KPC [Kuwait Petroleum Company—NK] figure. Saudi Aramco

meanwhile guided for $40–50bn for 2022 capex, although supply chain issues mean that spending likely came in below this figure.

(March 10, 2023b)

This, in turn, can explain why Saudi Arabia and the UAE expect to accomplish their production expansion plans by 2027, much earlier than Kuwait. The situation with the oil production cost, which is constantly growing, is also alarming. It allows Kuwaiti oil to remain competitive on the world market, but makes it look worse against the background of other oil production leaders in the Persian Gulf. According to Al-Maleki, "KPC's average per-barrel production costs have soared by 90% over the past decade from KD1.35 ($4.87) in 2012 to KD3.31 ($8.52) last year, a 75 per cent increase in dollar terms" (July 22, 2022).

The problem with free financial resources for the implementation of economic development programmes is likely to limit Kuwait's ability to invest in solving the problem of falling production costs and stimulating demand for its oil abroad. All this is complemented by highly controversial management decisions, such as the preservation of a very cumbersome management structure for the development of the country's oil sector, as well as the preservation of the use of fuel oil in the production of electricity within the country (Al-Maleki, November 11, 2022).

The global financial and energy crisis, which is gaining momentum and has led to a rise in energy prices, has an ambiguous impact on Kuwait's economic strategy. On the one hand, like most Arab countries of the Persian Gulf, Kuwait is in a winning position, since the revenue part of its budget is 90 per cent generated by profits from the sale of oil and gas. Thus, the excess profit extracted in 2022–2023 increases financial stability in the country and provides opportunities for investment in long-term development. On the other hand, high dependence on hydrocarbons in the context of the global crisis can torpedo Kuwait's accelerated transition to a sustainable economy. The once-priority plans for the diversification of the national economy, which were conceptually reflected in the national strategic plan "New Vision of Kuwait until 2035," have been greatly slowed down.

Of course, some efforts made by the Kuwaiti authorities in the course of economic diversification should not be underestimated. In particular, in 2022–2026, it is planned to create a so-called "northern economic zone" in Kuwait, including the Silk City project, as well as an investment of US$6.5 billion for the construction of the modern port of Mubarak al-Kabir. The revenues from the sale of oil and gas extracted against the background of the commodity super cycle will be partially directed to the creation of this new modern infrastructure.

In the context of the de facto political crisis, we should expect further stalling of steps to implement a new economic course on diversification, calculated until 2035. This will lead to delays in the implementation of promising projects for the modernization of social, physical, and transport infrastructure.

Accordingly, the horizon of planning and implementation of targeted investment projects in Kuwait for a sufficiently long term will depend on the dynamics of oil prices on world markets. If the current trend continues, the country's authorities will be able to delay the introduction of unpopular austerity measures and cuts in social programmes, and even distribute part of the excess profits for the implementation of the development plan until 2035. For this purpose, in the next few years, Kuwait will be able to actively use the funds of the sovereign investment fund, which as of June 2022 reached the volume of US$740 billion.

Thus, it seems that the issue of reducing dependence on the oil and gas industry in the national economy is key to solving the problem of its diversification. This process is lengthy and requires the adoption of a set of thoughtful measures. It includes various tax and management measures to stimulate the transition of oil companies to more sustainable solutions in the non-oil sector, but with careful balancing to preserve their profitability. In the conditions of the current commodity super cycle and high oil prices, the implementation of such initiatives is not possible. The transition to green technologies in the oil sector is also fraught with difficulties today in the absence of quick profits. However, Kuwait actively supports and implements the idea of redirecting part of the excess profits extracted from the sale of hydrocarbons to green technologies, especially in terms of creating technologies for desalination of seawater, expansion of solar energy, investments in green transport infrastructure, and smart cities (electric vehicles, smart city lighting, etc.). At the same time, the Kuwaiti authorities are conducting an active information campaign on sustainable development, involving civil society, youth, academic institutions, and business in these efforts.

The traditional model of economic management formed in Kuwait, in which the well-being of citizens depends entirely on oil revenues, as well as on knowledge, technology, and human resources attracted from abroad, resists this new paradigm and does not allow taking full advantage of the chance for cardinal diversification of the economy, as well as the transition to sustainable development. The transformation process seems to be lengthy and requires important decisions in the field of management, tax, and investment regulation and legislation.

Notes

1 IMF assessments.
2 According to existing estimates, seven family-owned companies contribute to more than 60% of the country's GDP and employ 80% (Embassy of Switzerland in Kuwait, 2022).

References

Agha, Z. (2021). Kuwait's best strategic options to utilize its petroleum resources and energy performance. *Journal of Petroleum and Environmental Biotechnology, 9,* 428.
Al-Maleki, Y. (2022, November 11). Kuwait reshuffles oil & gas sector leadership. *The Middle East Economic Survey*. Retrieved from https://www.mees.com/2022/11/11/geopolitical-risk/kuwait-reshuffles-oil-gas-sector-leadership/38e4bc40-61c3-11ed-809e-1d99694d9744.
Al-Maleki, Y. (2022, December 9). Kuwait looks to capitalize on Europe oil products sales. *The Middle East Economic Survey*. Retrieved from https://www.mees.com/2022/12/9/refining-petrochemicals/kuwait-looks-to-capitalize-on-europe-oil-products-sales-opportunity/a7e324c0-77be-11ed-bbf5-155b55ec1530#:~:text=Kuwait

174 Nikolay A. Kozhanov

%20Looks%20To%20Capitalize%20On%20Europe%20Oil%20Products%20Sales%20Opportunity&text=Having%20invested%20%2430bn%20in,begin%20profiting%20from%20its%20investments.

Al-Maleki, Y. (2022, December 23). Kuwait oil exports set for radical shift in 2023. *The Middle East Economic Survey*. Retrieved from https://www.mees.com/2022/12/23/refining-petrochemicals/kuwait-oil-exports-set-for-radical-shift-in-2023/b52b65a0-82c7-11ed-a640-e18d98edd97b.

Al-Maleki, Y. (2023, 27 January). Kuwaiti government resigns. Again. *The Middle East Economic Survey*. Retrieved from https://www.mees.com/2023/1/27/geopolitical-risk/kuwaiti-government-resigns-again/da8825c0-9e46-11ed-86c4-9dba9ba12d42.

Al-Maleki, Y. (2023, 12 May). Kuwait targets 2030 for delivery Of $19bn in megaproject. *The Middle East Economic Survey*. Retrieved from https://www.mees.com/2023/5/12/oil-gas/kuwait-targets-2030-for-delivery-of-19bn-in-megaprojects/585a3d10-f0ca-11ed-b8bf-391487feb99b.

Blanchard, C. (2023). *Kuwait: Issues for the 118th congress*. Washington DC: CRC.

Bloomberg. (2020, July, 20). OPEC has new competitor as China ships oil from swelling storage. Bloomberg. Retrieved July 24, 2020, from https://www.livemint.com/market/commodities/opec-has-new-competitor-as-china-ships-oil-from-swelling-storage-11595210555611.html.

Brendon, K. (2022, December 20). The cost-of-living crisis: Accelerating or delaying a green transition? SEI. Retrieved from https://www.sei.org/perspectives/rising-cost-living/.

Cahil, B. (2022, October 6). OPEC+ deepens producer-consumer rift. CSIS. Retrieved from https://www.csis.org/analysis/opec-deepens-producer-consumer-rift.

Commins, D. (2012). *The gulf states. A modern history*. London: I.B.Tauris.

Embassy of Switzerland in Kuwait (2022). Economic Report, 2022. Kuwait.

Fattouh, B., Poudineh, R., & Sen, A. (2016). The dynamics of the revenue maximization—Market share trade-off: Saudi Arabia's oil policy in the 2014–15 price fall. *Oxford Review of Economic Policy*, 32(2), 223–240.

Henderson, S. (2020, March 10). Russia and Saudis in a knife fight over oil — But we may be the victims. The Hill. Retrieved July 24, 2020, from https://thehill.com/opinion/energy-environment/486761-russia-and-saudis-in-a-knifefight-over-oil-but-we-may-be-the-victims.

Herb, M. (2014). *The wages of oil*. London: Cornell University Press.

Hunnicutt, T., & Renshaw, J. (2021, November 18). U.S. asks Japan, China, others to consider tapping oil reserves. Reuters. Retrieved from https://www.reuters.com/business/energy/exclusive-us-asks-big-countries-coordinate-releases-oil-reserves-sources-2021-11-17/.

Ingram, J. (2020, May 15). Kuwait risks exhausting financial reserves. *The Middle East Economic Survey*. Retrieved from https://www.mees.com/2020/5/15/news-in-brief/kuwait-risks-exhausting-financial-reserves/be312a90-96bf-11ea-9894-7d512e4a1b26.

Ingram, J. (2023a, March 10). Al Zour ramp up. *The Middle East Economic Survey*. Retrieved from https://www.mees.com/2023/3/10/refining-petrochemicals/al-zour-ramp-up/c0c349c0-bf45-11ed-a251-49e15bc5b47c.

Ingram, J. (2023b, March 10). Kuwait Targets 3.1mn b/d End-2023 Capacity. *The Middle East Economic Survey*. Retrieved from https://www.mees.com/2023/3/10/oil-gas/kuwait-targets-31mn-bd-end-2023-capacity/830a8090-bf41-11ed-91e3-495eaf15f9a3.

IRENA. (2020). Energy transition, IRENA. Retrieved from https://www.irena.org/energytransition#:~:text=The%20energy%20transition%20is%20a,emissions%20to%20limit%20climate%20change.

Kanawa, K. (2023, March 14). Renewable energy transition speeds up during Ukraine war, led by China. Nikkei Asia. Retrieved from https://asia.nikkei.com/Business/Energy/Renewable-energy-transition-speeds-up-during-Ukraine-war-led-by-China.

Kim, A. (2023). *2023 index of economic freedom*. Washington, DC: heritage Foundation.

Mendiluce, M. (2022, November 7). No more excuses to delay the shift to clean energy. EURACTIV.com. Retrieved from https://www.euractiv.com/section/energy/opinion/no-more-excuses-to-delay-the-shift-to-clean-energy/.

METGroup. (2021, July 29). Energy transition: Definition and solution,". Retrieved from https://group.met.com/en/media/energy-insight/energy-transition.

Mills, R. (2020). A fine balance: The geopolitics of the global energy transition in the Middle East. In M. Hafner & S. Tagliapietra (Eds.), *The geopolitics of the global energy transition* (pp. 115–150). Singapore: Springer.

Olver-Ellis, S. (2020). *Building the New Kuwait: Vision 2035 and the challenge of diversification*. London: LSE Middle East Centre.

Saad, W. (2021). *Kuwait common Country Analysis (CCA)*. Kuwait: UN.

Shehabi, M. (2019). *Diversification in Gulf hydrocarbon economies and interactions with energy subsidy reform*. Oxford: Oxford Institute for Energy Studies.

Shehabi, M. (2021). *Quantifying long-term impacts of COVID-19 and oil price shocks in a Gulf oil economy*. Oxford: Oxford Institute for Energy Studies.

Smith, G., & El Wardany, S. (2022, March 31). OPEC+ refuses to heed consumers' call for more oil. Al Jazeera. Retrieved from https://www.aljazeera.com/economy/2022/3/31/opec-refuses-to-heed-consumers-call-for-more-oil.

S&P Global. (2020, February 24). *What is energy transition?* Retrieved from https://www.spglobal.com/en/research-insights/articles/what-is-energy-transition#:~:text=Energy%20transition%20refers%20to%20the,well%20as%20lithium%2Dion%20batteries.

Yergin, D. (2020). *The new map: Energy, climate and the clash of nations*. New-York: Penguin Press.

11 Citizenship, Identity, and Human Rights in Kuwait

Ghanim AlNajjar

Introduction

Identity politics plays a major role in shaping societies. Although it tends to be projected as a stable phenomenon, and it may indeed present itself as such, however, it changes over time. Within the Gulf Cooperation Council (GCC) countries, it could be seen through a major division between citizens and non-citizens. It creates several layers of identities, both within the expat communities, as well as the citizens of each country. It is exacerbated by the fact that most GCC countries are predominantly composed of non-citizens. Several studies have focused on the composition of the expat communities, while less emphasis has been given to the identity politics of citizens of each country. Kuwait in this regard stands alone in its political dynamics of the citizenry because it extends itself into political participation. Kuwait opted to have a constitution and a parliamentary system with an electoral system as early as 1962 (Alnajjar, 2004, p. 26). Although the political process in Kuwait is marred with crises, especially in the last 15 years, it remains dynamic and has the potential of transforming a traditional society into a more participatory form of governance. The Constitution of Kuwait, despite political crises, remains influential in protecting the basic rights for both citizens and non-citizens alike. In many rulings of the Constitutional Court, rights were protected against the government's actions (Selvik & Alnajjar, politics of crisis, 2015, p. 27).

Citizenship as a Cornerstone of Kuwaiti Nationality: Structuring the Political System

A key aspect of political science, attributed to its nature of methodological inquiry, is understanding political and power dynamics within a country, including the domestic political considerations, international diplomacy, and relations with other nations and states. A power structure in a country (a formal organization of political power) is typically structured so that there is an individual or ruling elite that has decision-making authority. Power is often dependent on the elite class, as well as the positioning of those structures within other relationships, including the roles of identity, citizenship, and human rights in the country. The political culture in Kuwait is complex and multifaceted. It is a reflection of the country's dynamic history, which has seen it experience different shapes of governance under

DOI: 10.4324/9781003435259-11

Citizenship, Identity, and Human Rights   177

different protection arrangements until becoming a fully independent state in 1961. Internally, Kuwait, as a political entity for centuries, was rarely interfered with by foreign powers, which left local politics developing by its local power structures. The culture includes a range of influences from customs, economy, geography, interaction between different groupings, and reactions with surrounding countries and communities. As with any society, this unique blend of politics shapes relationships between government and citizens—and reveals much about how governments interact with their people (Smith, 1999, p. 18).

Kuwait, as it is known today, is a hereditary rule, with a ruling family (Al-Sabah). However, the existence of the country approximately four centuries ago was instituted through the consensus of migrant tribes (Utub), originated from the heart of Arabia. Such a consensus created what could be called "Joint Governance," whereby the ruler governs the country while other influential segments of society provide him with the financial support. This resulted in a model of less absolute governance by the ruler (Alnajjar, 2004 p. 26). However, things have changed over time, in favour of more power in the hands of the ruling family. This political discourse came as a result of the accumulation of oil wealth, managed by the ruling family. Although the concept of Joint Governance faded away and weakened, it remained shaping power politics and political alliances between the ruling family and other influential segments of society.

The Development Plan of the early 1950s, undertaken as a result of the sudden increase of oil income, pushed many people from the region and far beyond coming to Kuwait for work. It was not until 1959, that a comprehensive law about citizenship was issued, defining what it means to be a citizen in contrast with non-citizens (Alragam, 2017, p. 2; Alnakib, 2014, p. 1). Over the years, such a law was subject to numerous amendments in all directions. The debate over the law and its components has been a major feature of politics for more than six decades. Major disagreements were apparent over citizenship and took place within the constitution committee, which drafted the Constitution of 1962. The Constitutional Committee minutes revealed major differences in the rights of citizens, in particular revoking citizenship (Constitutional Committee minutes, 1962). The Law of Citizenship created two major types of citizenships, "Original," and "Naturalized," with five articles explaining the reason behind naturalization (Citizenship Law of 1959 no.24).

Within this political culture, Kuwaiti citizens enjoyed many of the rights and responsibilities associated with citizenship. The Constitution of 1962 defines Kuwait as a democratic state, guaranteeing its people the fundamental rights to practice freedom of religion and speech, enjoy personal privacy, and social justice. This includes disallowing discrimination based on race, gender, or status. It also guarantees free access to public services, including healthcare, education and employment opportunities. However, the reality does not go that far, as several laws were issued contrary to the constitutional principles, by restricting freedom of public space (Kuwait Constitution, 1965).

The ideas of citizenship, identity, and human rights can be understood in a manner that is completely unlike to one another, depending on the period in question, both politically and historically. It is essential to begin by identifying the three

178   *Ghanim AlNajjar*

concepts that are discussed in the chapter (citizenship, identity, and human rights), as well as the inextricable relationship that each of these concepts must unavoidably have with the others, in order to guarantee that there is no confusion.

Citizenship, Identity, and Human Rights

Citizenship is a legal status that is recognized by a certain state and confers on the individual who holds a particular set of rights and responsibilities within that state. Citizenship is the legal status of an individual as a member of a particular nation-state or other political entity. Citizenship, by default, grants citizens specific rights and obligations under the jurisdiction of the state, such as the ability to vote, the right to possess property, and the right to gain state protection.

A person's sense of identity is their perception of who they are (Austead, 2014, p. 40). It is made up of an individual's social connections, roles, and responsibilities, in addition to the perceptions, beliefs, and attitudes that give them their own distinct identity. An individual's identity may be shaped by a variety of factors, including their culture, religion, language, and gender. Identity is a multifaceted notion that encompasses both an individual's sense of who they are and how others in the society in which they live see them. It has a strong connection to the social and cultural expectations that people in a specific culture have of one another.

In essence, human rights are rights that are regarded as universal, unalienable, and inherent to all individuals regardless of their identification, citizenship, or any other criteria (Joppke, 2007, p. 12). These rights are thought to be a part of a person's own essence. The relationship between citizenship, identity, and human rights can be seen in the way that an individual's identity, along with the rights and obligations associated with it, is determined by the state in which an individual holds citizenship. This demonstrates the connection between citizenship, identity, and human rights. The identity that an individual is accorded by the state is directly related to the rights and responsibilities, that are bestowed upon that individual by the state. For instance, citizens are granted particular rights as an independent entity, and not in accordance with the identification markers of their race, gender, and other categories.

On the other hand, the rights that an individual possesses owing to their identity, citizenship, and several other criteria can have an effect on who they are. This underlines the tight connection that exists between citizenship, identity, and human rights, as well as the interconnected nature of these three concepts. Recognizing this relationship is key to understanding how individuals perceive and interact, with their environment, and how the rights and obligations associated with their identity and citizenship affect their life.

Suffice it to mention the dynamics of international law, in that it plays an important role in protecting these rights and responsibilities, by creating a set of standards that all countries must adhere to. The development of the international human rights regime since 2006 was made more relevant in addressing specific issues by transforming the Human Rights Commission into the Human Rights Council, with an innovative mechanism of the Universal Periodic Review (UPR). The UPR, which is in its 4th cycle, obliges all members of the United Nations to present national reports on conditions of local human rights practices and provide recommendations on how to fix human rights shortcomings (UPR, Human Rights Council Website). Through International Human Rights Law (IHRL), citizens of different countries are provided with basic rights and freedoms that protect them from abuse and injustice. IHRL also ensures that people in different countries have access to the same opportunities, regardless of their backgrounds. Furthermore, international law provides a framework for resolving disputes between countries, as well as for developing collaborative solutions to global challenges. By promoting the rights and responsibilities of its citizens through international law, a country can create a more equitable, just, and secure society. International treaties, particularly within the framework of the IHRL, present a reference point and model practice for countries to follow in achieving human rights protection. In this regard, Kuwait has been a party to most human rights treaties since 1994. Yet, despite the presence of international treaties on human rights, many countries still fail to meet their obligations to their citizens. To ensure that international law is respected and followed, countries must be held accountable for their actions. Unfortunately, there is no such accountability mechanism that handles countries. International law is a powerful instrument for pursuing justice in an increasingly interconnected world. By defining the rights and responsibilities of citizens, international laws foster security, stability, and peace. From the big questions related to national identity to more specific matters such as individual civil liberties, international laws help create a just and secure world. However, we must be cognizant that while legal frameworks are essential, they cannot be seen in isolation. In order to understand their impact on issues of citizenship, identity, and human rights, we should look at the social, political, and cultural contexts in which these laws operate and are interpreted. Only by looking beyond the scope of mere legal instrumentation can we contemplate how respective societies shape fundamental ideas about identity, belongingness, and human rights. This should be looked at within the broader picture of social, political, and cultural contexts in which the laws are interpreted. In light of the failure of the international community in providing a safe haven to protect vulnerable communities, there is a need for more concerted efforts to provide a minimum standard of protection.

Exploring the Impact of Identity Politics in Kuwait

Identity politics is a major factor in understanding Kuwait's complex political culture. Citizenship is the most powerful instrument that political systems employ to create an individual's rights, obligations, and advantages in a given society. As a result, discussions over national identity have become the focal point of public discourse, and intense ideological power struggles have broken out between various conceptions of citizenship and nationhood (Elkatiri, 2011, p. 7).

Kuwait Citizenship Law was issued in 1959, in preparation for independence that took place two years later in June 1961. Granting citizenship was done in a simple and straightforward manner (Alnajjar, 2004, p. 26). Several committees were created, composed of knowledgeable personalities of who is who in Kuwait, and they made the decision of who is a citizen and who is not. The process continued for a few years and it was closed for a short period. In the following years, the process of naturalization started by the government with no criteria. With the introduction of the electoral process and parliamentary politics in 1962, citizenship took on a more political function. It even affected the relationship within factions of the ruling family. A constant story that appears time over time again in Kuwait's history is that a ruling family member, who wanted to strengthen his position in parliament, was able to grant citizenship to many of his tribal lineage (Alkhatib, 2007, p. 29). This particular talk has always been present in any public debate on citizenship. Another controversial issue is dual citizenship, which is illegal under Kuwaiti law but continued to be a major issue in the political discourse. Many blame the government for being lenient in allowing hundreds of thousands to have dual citizenship. The heated debate continues until today. The right of naturalized citizens and their descendants to have political rights is becoming an issue of contention. In 1994, the National Assembly passed unanimously an amendment to the 1959 law that made all Kuwaitis born to a naturalized citizen be recognized as an original citizen by birth. Until 1994, the government wrongly interpreted the law whereby a child born to a naturalized citizen should be registered as his/her father's status. In 1994, the law was explained clearly that they are to be considered original citizens. For some reason, a campaign started by some individuals in 2023 calling for revoking the 1994 law (Aljarida Newspaper, May 2023). Another example was a major amendment of the citizenship law in the 1971 parliament. The 1971 amendment paved the way for granting citizenship by allowing the Minister of Interior to grant citizenship, in meeting the minimum requirements such as being born in Kuwait and finishing secondary school locally. Although the change was passed by parliament with the government's presence, it was later revoked. In 1976, the government dissolved parliament and suspended the constitution, and the law was changed to a more restrictive practice, claiming that the practice was taken advantage of and negatively affected national security.

Blaming the government, or some members of the ruling family, for inflating the number of citizens through continuous naturalization over the years, to strengthen its power through the electoral process, became part of public culture. It is known as "chaotic naturalization." The controversies are regularly confused with dual citizens or those who obtained their nationality by forgery. The citizenship law does not allow dual citizenship, yet it seems that it is widespread, as the government never replied to official parliamentary questions.

Revoking citizenship is another contentious issue. It is normally practised either because of obtaining citizenship by forgery or because of discovering a dual citizen who did not declare his status. In two periods, however, revoking citizenship for political reasons became more visible. The first was during the 1980s under the shadow of the Iraq–Iran war. However, most of those whose citizenship was revoked had their citizenship reinstated again in the 1990s (Alnajjar, 2000). It happened a second time during a major protest movement after 2012, targeting some activists. Although some revoked citizenships were returned later through political

Citizenship, Identity, and Human Rights 181

negotiations, some are still waiting. Revoking citizenship is an absolute right of the government, with no legal review to remedy it. As it has been the case, the solution comes within a politically negotiated framework. While granting citizenship is recognized as a sovereign right, on the other hand, revoking citizenship is looked upon as an administrative action for courts to look into cases. Due to such an understanding, several court rulings ruled against the Ministry of Interior, with the latest ruling taking place in May 24, 2023. Later in 2023, a judicial body issued a statement to unify courts' treatment by preventing them from looking into cases of citizenship.

In addition, one of the dimensions of citizenship is the shape and structure of the official institution dealing with citizenship. Although there has been an organ of some sort, the Higher Citizenship Committee, and/or the Citizenship Department, there is an ongoing campaign running from the beginning of 2023 that calls for establishing an official structure that handles all citizenship affairs. The campaign claims that establishing such an organ will solve all citizenship issues, focusing on forgery (obtaining citizenship through illegal means) and exposing those who are dual citizens, among other issues. The understanding of power politics in creating such a body is very difficult, since it might change the dynamics of citizenship affairs (Aljarida and Alqabas dailies May 17, 2023).

Another contentious issue relating to citizenship is the *bidoon* population of Kuwait. The *bidoon-bidūn-*, which is short for *bidūn jinsiyya* (without nationality), are stateless people (Alnajjar, 1998, p. 34). For various reasons, the *bidūn* population has been deprived of citizenship based on the 1959 law. Over the years, the phenomenon rose, reaching up to 250,000 stateless people before August 1990, with illicit government encouragement. Until August 1990, approximately 80 per cent of the army, and possibly a similar number of the police force, were *bidūn*. Unlike the stateless population in most other parts of the world, who have always been always mistreated, here it is different (Alnajjar, 1998, p. 34). Until 1986, *bidūn* were treated almost like citizens. They enjoyed most of the rights as citizens without obtaining citizenship. However, from 1986 onwards, things changed, with denying them all rights. It seems that such a change was related to the Iran–Iraq war. To add insult to injury, two years after the cessation of hostilities in August 1988, another war started. This time the field of operation was Kuwait itself, with Iraq invading Kuwait and occupying it in August 1990. Aside from all the ramifications of the invasion itself, as far as the *bidūn* were concerned, it exacerbated the situation for the *bidūn*. When Iraq invaded Kuwait, thousands of *bidūn* were held in Iraqi prisons, taken from Kuwaiti military bases. They were imprisoned in places such as Mosul, Tikrit, and Ramadi. They were released after Kuwait's liberation in February 1991, through the International Committee of the Red Cross. This time, however, they returned to a less welcome environment, which continues until today. The author visited them while in prison in Iraq several times until he was taken prisoner later in February 1991 (Alnajjar, 2021).

The *bidūn issue* presents a major dilemma from legal, political, and human rights aspects. There does not seem to be any serious intention to solve the problem. The government's argument is that the *bidūn* hide their true nationality,

182   Ghanim AlNajjar

claiming that they are stateless. Submitting their real nationality will restrict them from all the major privileges they enjoyed before 1986. So far, the policy has not been successful according to statistics provided by the government. Although the government acknowledged in 2012 that around 34,000 of the *bidūn* (in total they are approximately around 100,000) were registered in the 1965 census of Kuwait, which is one condition for naturalization, no action has been taken in this regard (Alnajjar, 2021).

The *bidūn* issue, being directly related to identity and citizenship, has become increasingly politicized due to the presence of a system of exclusion in operation. Over the years, a complex network of regulations and restrictive rules has been introduced, targeting the *bidūn*. This has gradually made them a fully marginalized segment of the population, resulting in a high degree of social exclusion. It has created a layer within society with an identity of its own. This is especially true for individuals from different backgrounds who lack the proper documents and paperwork needed to pass muster with the relevant authorities. The reality is that these individuals find themselves facing barriers not just in obtaining Kuwaiti citizenship, but also in accessing basic rights such as employment, education, and healthcare, amongst others. In addition to this, the government has imposed a series of restrictions on their economic and social rights, such as the denial of access to public services, education, health, etc. This can foster a culture of exclusion and prejudice, which may further alienate them as a minority. Finally, it can also question the government's commitment to human rights and international law (Alnajjar, 2021). It is worth mentioning that the *bidūn* issue in Kuwait, as compared to the GCC, is highly present in the public domain, whether in the media, activism, or most importantly within parliament, where there is a special commission on *bidūn*. Also, many proposals and initiatives have been presented in parliament to address the plight of the *bidūn*, but they were largely obstructed by the government.

The argument above clearly relates to political culture and citizenship in Kuwait. It highlights the discrimination that the *bidūn* people have faced for many years. It shows how the Kuwaiti government has enacted policies that resulted in marginalizing and isolating the *bidūn* people. On the other hand, the continued political controversy over the *bidūn* affects public attitude not only towards the *bidūn*, but towards citizenship as a whole.

These overarching thematic clusters, citizenship, identity, and human rights, have the potential to become sites of struggle and power. On the one hand, the struggle to determine citizenship, identity, and human rights conduct will largely determine the future political character, including how governance and political leadership occur, which will feed into the precarious nature of Kuwaiti politics.

One controversial aspect of the citizenship debate is, who is responsible for issuing decisions on citizenship, and whether there is room for due process, either in granting, or in revoking a citizenship. The government's view is that decisions concerning citizenship should be the sole business of the government, as a sovereign right of the state. This was clearly reflected in the Administrative Court Law, which prohibits accepting cases related to citizenship. This means that if a person's citizenship is revoked, the relevant court—in this case the administrative court—is

Citizenship, Identity, and Human Rights 183

prevented from looking into this case. There is a reasonable degree of consensus on the absolute right of the state in granting citizenship being regarded as a sovereign issue. However, there is no consensus on revoking citizenship, since it is considered an administrative matter, which should be allowed for the courts to look into.

Citizenship has been a key factor in the development and transformation of Kuwait because it provides the basis for political participation, protection of human rights, and social justice. In addition, it is a significant contributor to the nation's sense of identity and cohesion, since it fosters a collective sense of belonging and solidarity among its nationals. The concept of citizenship became more relevant with the introduction of the election of the Constituent Assembly in 1962, which drafted the Constitution in November 1962, making citizenship the basis of protected identity. In a similar vein, citizenship has had a considerable influence on the organizational structure of the political system in Kuwait. It has opened up opportunities for residents to take part in the political process, and as a result, it has been an essential contributor to the growth of civil service in Kuwait (Longva, 2006, p. 16).

Politics of Fear: Immigration, Identity, and Its Consequences in Kuwait

Since the early 1950s, with the sudden increase of oil wealth and the huge undertaking of the first Development Plan, an influx of expats from different countries rushed to Kuwait. As a result, two main groups appeared in Kuwait's population: Citizens and non-citizens. Citizens felt overwhelmed by the newcomers. This has led to a growing sense of identity politics, which manifested itself in a variety of forms, such as fear, exclusion, or the promotion of some aspects of Kuwaiti identity. Some of these elements were reflected in the citizenship law of 1959. In other words, the cultural fabric of Kuwait was strengthened by the influx of expats from different backgrounds, yet how this citizenry interacts has revealed a concerning trend in identity politics (Longva, 2006, p. 16; Stoke, 2017, p. 93). As interactions between citizens and expats grew, Kuwaitis felt pressured with the concern of exclusion and marginalization. This was due to concerns about the security of jobs and housing which manifested itself in policies favouring citizens and further strengthening local identity politics. Identity politics can have lasting implications, as it affects relationships between natives and expats, potentially leading to further divisions within the population.

Moreover, an increase in the number of expats has also led to an increase in xenophobia. The political atmosphere in the 2000s—which has witnessed an increase in populist rhetoric and sentiments—pushed the agenda towards job security in the public sector, which employs over 90 per cent of citizens. Over the course of the past several years, there has been a call on government to restrict public jobs to citizens, which has become increasingly common in Kuwait's elections. Politicians have frequently employed this rhetoric in an effort to boost their popularity and garner support for the policies that they advocate. This rhetoric has been used in recent years as a method of capitalizing on the public's fear and gaining greater

184 *Ghanim AlNajjar*

support from voters. This has been exacerbated by repeated working visa scandals related to forged visas. In some cases, the culprits were citizens, officials, and non-citizens, in what is being publicly nicknamed "Residency Traders." This anxiety is a result of the public's perception that the number of expats entering the country is far more in number than what the country needs. Some politicians have effectively stoked unreasonable anxieties among both residents and newcomers by appealing to such worries in order to further their own popularity (Selvik & Alnajjar, 2015). The immediate consequence of this was more restrictive policies.

In addition, anxieties of "the other" are generally at the root of all policies favouring citizens, whether in employment, healthcare, education, and other public policy issues. Some politicians frequently portray expats as a danger to the country's culture, economy, and national security. This discourse is frequently coupled with a desire for more restrictive visa regulations and the promotion of policies that give priority to citizens. As such, identity politics has become an increasingly important factor in Kuwait's political system, as it is used to shape the way citizens are represented and their access to resources. The concept of citizenship can be understood from three varying perspectives. At its highest level, citizenship is an international legal term. At its lowest level, citizenship is a personal identity. In between is the sociopolitical understanding of the citizen as a fundamental institution of modern society that relates to social, political, and institutional structures and definitions of rights. It is always the case that modern society has its ancient antecedents; and the form of governance of Kuwait is no exception.

The mixture of social groupings shaped what Kuwait is today (Longva, 2006, p. 171; Alnakib, 2014, p. 20). The pattern of tribes and tribal confederation has great significance to the constitution of power structure within the new nation-state. As an intermediate step, an understanding of citizenship as a sociopolitical institution is essential. Citizens mobilize themselves in the political process in different social affiliations; citizenship becomes an identity that acts as a catalyst of individual self-awareness and group-orientation that creates unity, while at the same time creates otherness. It is through such self-orientation, as one that is part of a cohesive population sharing interests, experiences, and identity recognition, that one can one experience and share with the national collectivity. The collective society then becomes a central aspect of the new identity. Being a "citizen" of Kuwait constitutes a privileged social category: Those who fit into this category may experience the greatest mobilization into citizenship, involving an identity that is formed through everyday experience and participation within such an organizational structure.

The Kuwaiti citizenry, because of its own dynamics, created several layers of identities, in the form of social groupings. Social groupings are normal structures in any society; however, they are easily observable in Kuwait, since there have been ongoing political elections (17 parliamentary elections since 1963). Elections in Kuwait are common. Not only are there parliamentary elections, but also elections in all aspects of life, from schools, universities, cooperative societies, municipal councils, civil society organizations, trade unions, sporting clubs, and many more organized structures. This means that the culture of elections is well based in

Citizenship, Identity, and Human Rights 185

the society. Over the years, elections have gradually become a reflection of identity politics, reflecting social, ethnic, sectarian, tribal, and other social group's affiliations. As a modern state, Kuwait has tried to be a melting pot, creating a national identity. For all social groupings, the ongoing identity politics and its dynamics have helped in creating new group identities to contest elections. Instead of diminishing socially based solidarity mechanisms, it seems that elections have played a major role in creating identity politics for some groups that they have never thought of. While the state strives to establish a general affiliation to unified state values rather than smaller grouping to win elections, the situation seems to be going back to a more traditional solidarity. While the state was moving, it seems, in the direction of "detribalization," elections have pushed back towards "retribalization." The difficulty in changing the tribal sociopolitical nature of society to a more national identity stems itself from the fact that the ruling family structure itself is tribal in nature (Alnajjar, 2000, p. 43).

There is no clear-cut definition of affiliation of social groupings. Yet, many will argue, vaguely, that Kuwaiti citizens are divided into three major groups: *hadhar* (sunna), *bedouin* (not to be confused with the Bidoon), and Shi'a. As vague and interconnected as it may seem, these three major groupings reflect the identity politics. Many candidates run for elections based on these groupings. Those social divisions could map out a picture, however, a very misleading and confusing one. For example, what is supposed to be a large group, the *bedouin*, with tribal affiliations, is divided into sub-groupings that do not make it a valid definition (Longva, 2006, p. 177; Nosova, 2016). In addition, many of the *hadhar* group have tribal affiliations yet they might be excluded from the group. As for the Shi'a, it is not clear whether they are considered *hadhar* or not. Most of the *bedouin*-affiliated candidates are said to be geographically located in the so-called remote areas. Although the concept of the tribal definition of identity politics is a vague and confusing one, it remains paramount in affecting the thinking of any political understanding of local Kuwaiti politics. The definition also ignores the appearance of new groups, while amounting to new tribes. One of the major measurable indicators for political/social affiliations among identity politics is the primary elections of the tribes in the country. It is a process that started in 1971—some say 1967—to filter and minimize the number of candidates running for general elections from the same tribe. In earlier studies, the author attended some of those tribal primary elections until it was banned by law in 2004 (Alsaidi, 2021, p. 36). The banning of tribal primary elections came as a surprise because such elections started with the support of the government when most tribal candidates were fully in line with the government in parliament.

Although all primary elections were tribal, there were, however, two primaries held in 1981 and 1985, on a sectarian basis by Sunni groups against Shia, conducted under the shadow of the Iraq–Iran war. However, such sectarian primaries took place in one constituency only, and ceased to exist. The Iraq–Iran War lasted for eight years from 1980 until 1988, during which sectarianism was at its highest.

On the other hand, tribal primary elections were important in strengthening tribal identity and affiliations, as opposed to a more general nationalist identity.

186 *Ghanim AlNajjar*

However, the dynamic of primary elections affected the internal cohesion of each tribe by strengthening the identity of each sub-clan against other sub-clans within each tribe. At the end of the day, it is all about numbers. On another front, tribal primaries affected the internal power structure of the tribe (Alsaidi, 2021, p. 54). The traditional tribal sheikh, after the introduction of primaries, had no entitlement to represent the tribe in the electoral process. Under this mechanism, tribal sheikh, if a tribal sheikh intends to run for elections, he will have to win his seat through primary elections. Over the years, a number of popular candidates refused to participate in their tribal primaries and won in the general elections, disregarding their tribe's candidate. Although tribal primaries were banned by law and constitute a criminal offence, the government did not show a determination in implementing the law until the recent 2022 elections, when organizers of primary elections were sentenced. It is also important to note that although women were granted full political rights since 2005, they do not participate in primary elections. It remains to be seen if the government will continue its active approach against primary elections. One of the major influences on elections is the shape, boundaries, and components of electoral constituencies. Since elections started in 1962, constituencies have been changed at least five times, both in boundaries and in the number of seats.

One of the most profound policies enhancing citizenship identity, as well as elections, was the housing policy. The government, being a welfare state, launched its housing policy in the late 1950s. By the 1960s, large parts of residential areas were designated as model areas, specifically for citizens. Housing became a major factor in creating citizenship identity, where citizens reside in certain areas. It also affected the electoral constituencies.

Human Rights

The Kuwaiti Constitution guarantees human rights. There is a full chapter of the constitution that deals with human rights. Looking at that chapter, it is noticeable that it resembles the articles of the Universal Declaration for Human Rights. However, those articles are not necessarily implemented in full. One reason for such discrepancy is that most of the human rights articles are referred to in laws. As a result, several laws were issued, such as the Publication Law or Law of Gatherings (most articles were revoked later by the Constitutional Court) and Public Benefits Societies, but they did not comply with the basic principles of human rights. In 1965, during the first parliamentary session, eight members of parliament resigned in protest against some laws restricting freedoms. It is clear that the excessive laws that permit the government to violate human rights happen during times of Constitution suspension and parliament dissolution. During Kuwait's history, parliament was dissolved and the Constitution was suspended twice: The first time between 1976 and 1981, and the second time from 1986 until 1992. One positive point from a human rights perspective is that change is possible in the direction of complying with human rights principles. Many laws were abolished after October 1992, such as the draconian State Security Law in 1994. Even after Kuwait was liberated in February 1991, martial law was declared and lasted only four months,

Citizenship, Identity, and Human Rights   187

and was lifted in June 1991. In addition, all death sentences ruled during the martial law period were commuted.

The case of the death of Muhamed Almaimooni (2011) at the hands of police is a case in point. While it was a personal crime in nature, not a politically motivated one, it shook society. The Minister of Interior, replying to parliamentary questioning, denied any responsibility of his staff. However, when some MPs in the public parliamentary session presented official medical reports of torture, the Minister assured the parliament that he would resign. In addition, the police officers were also tried and, eventually, sentenced.

Another functioning tool in protecting human rights is the courts, whether they are lower courts or the Constitutional Court. Three examples of different court rulings may explain the potential of the courts in protecting human rights. The first case concerns a case about the law of passports, which regulates issuing passports. Article 15 of the law prevented women from obtaining passports without the consent of the husband. In 2008, a married Kuwaiti woman's application for a passport was denied. The Ministry of Interior refused to hand in the woman's passport because she needed the consent of her husband. Unable to obtain his consent, she complained to the Administrative Court, challenging the Minister of Interior. She claimed that the Law of Passports, are unconstitutional, because it is against the principles of Article 29 of the Constitution, which emphasized equality (Law of Passports). The case took off from the Administrative Court to the Constitutional Court, which ruled that Article 15 is unconstitutional, allowing women as well as men to obtain passports without any conditions based on gender. Although the Constitutional Court's ruling was clear, some Ministry of Interior staff continued the old practice based on their traditional leaning. With pressure from some MPs, the Minister of Interior was poised to make a public statement calling on all passport staff to issue passports to women in compliance with the Constitutional Court ruling. Another example was about discrimination against female students' admission to Kuwait University. For many years, the university administration, in order to lower the percentage of female students within the university population—female students are between 65 per cent and 70 per cent of the student population—implemented a discriminatory policy by implementing a quota on the number of female students in three colleges, namely medicine, engineering, and dentistry. So, admission to these three colleges was not based on merit, but on the gender of the applicant, contrary to Article 29 of the Constitution. When a young female student applied to the college of dentistry, her application was refused based on her gender. Although she was offered to apply to another college, the student, with the support of her father, went to the Administrative Court against the Minister of Education and the university administration, challenging the legality of such a policy. In the court, the government defended the discriminatory policy, but the court ruled in favour of the student, ordering the university to admit her immediately. The court went even further by ordering the university to abolish its discriminatory policy. The university complied and implemented the ruling, and after that the whole policy was abolished (Court CASE, 2014). On a different note, in 2016, the parliament amended the law of the Constitutional Court, allowing,

188 *Ghanim AlNajjar*

for the first time, individuals to access the Constitutional Court directly. It was a historical decision. It allows individuals to seek justice in their personal capacity through the Constitutional Court.

The above-mentioned amendment in the law of the Constitutional Court brings us to the third example. In 2022, a man was arrested, charged with emulating the other sex, according to an article in the Penal Code. The man went to the Constitutional Court, claiming that his arrest violated his constitutional rights. The court ruled that the Penal Code article, which was added by an earlier parliament, making emulating the other sex an offence, punishable by fine or imprisonment, was unconstitutional because it did not define what it meant by "emulating the other sex" and as a result, the article was abolished. In many other cases, several changes took place by the late Amir, who returned the law that allows for death penalty for those who insult God, the prophet, and others. Although the parliament and government supported that law, the Amir returned it using his constitutional prerogatives, which allows him to return legislation, and if the parliament insists on it, they can vote on it in a year by a two-thirds majority. The same could be applied to the Law on DNA or the law on the rights of the child and several others. This shows that there are several tools and legal structures that allow individuals to complain against violations of their rights. Although those tools are functioning, they are not sufficient.

Conclusion

Following the independence of Kuwait in 1961, identity politics was intertwined with citizenship. The law of citizenship issued in 1959 became the focal point of political discourse, as well as that of identity politics. Citizenship gained momentum after the country chose parliamentary system as a form of governance. With elections becoming the tool for political participation, citizenship became the cornerstone of the political structure. Electoral politics was directly related to citizenship. With the society growing in number and diversity, several layers of identities were gathering pace. While granting citizenship remains until today a matter causing a sense of resentment and claims of meddling with the integrity of citizenry, electoral politics became more of sub-groups' identities. As such, tribal primary elections became a constant feature of any elections until it was banned in 2004. However, the government was lenient on such practices, and hence, it was blamed for encouraging them. However, the government changed course during 2022 elections and began clamping on several primaries, by arresting organizers of the primaries, trying them and have them jailed.

Things have changed in the elections of 2022, when several disguised primary elections were clamped on number of the organizers were arrested, indicted, and jailed. While the goal of the state is to have national identity over other identities through implementing a policy of detribalization, the process of primary elections is a manifestation that the country is moving towards retribalization. However, tribal primary elections cut through the traditional tribal structure by enhancing the sub-identities of sub-clans. In addition, it challenges the traditional power structure of the sheikhdom of the tribe. The existence of a constitution, with its wide provisions protecting human rights, laid the foundation of a reasonable legal infrastructure, which could be a basis for potential safeguarding of human rights.

In general, Kuwait's political system offers many tools for continued change; ranging from challenging the government in court, to the separation of the office of crown prince from the prime minister (2003), to granting women political rights (2005), to changing electoral constituencies (1981, 2006, 2012), to the election of the head of state in parliament (during the succession crisis December 2006), and to the protection of women's rights. Thus, change is the constant phenomenon within the system, despite the constant political crises that appear to be a permanent feature of Kuwaiti politics. The pace of change is likely to determine the degree of stability of the political system in the country. Despite such important changes that affect the decision-making process, the remaining issue that has never changed is the balance of power.

References

Alnajjar, G. (2000). Challenges facing Kuwaiti democracy. *Middle East Journal. 54*(2), 242–258.
Al-Nakib, F. M. (2014). Revisiting visitiand BADŪ in Kuwait: Citizenship, housing, and the construction of a dichotomy. *International Journal of Middle East Studies, 46*(1), 5–30.
Al-Ragam, A. (2017). Negotiating the politics of exclusion: Georges Candilis, housing and the Kuwaiti welfare state. *International Journal of Urban and Regional Research, 41*(2), 235–250.
Beaugrand, C. (2017). Borders and spatial imaginaries in the Kuwaiti identity. *Geopolitics, 23*(3), 544–564.
El-Katiri, L., Fattouh, B., & Segal, P. (2011). *Anatomy of an oil-based welfare state: Rent distribution in Kuwait* (pp.165–187). Routledge.
Ghabra, S. N. (1997). Kuwait and the dynamics of socio-economic change. *Middle East Journal, 51*, 358–372.
Herb, M. C. (2009). A nation of bureaucrats: Political participation and economic diversification in Kuwait and The United Arab Emirates. *International Journal of Middle East Studies, 41*(3), 375–395.
Joppke, C. (2007). Transformation of citizenship: Status, rights, identity. *Citizenship Studies, 11*(1), 37–48.
Longva, A. N. (2006). Nationalism in pre-modern guise: The discourse on hadhar and BADU in Kuwait. *International Journal of Middle East Studies, 38*(2), 171–187.
Nosova, A. (2016). *The merchant elite and parliamentary politics in Kuwait: The dynamics of business political participation in a rentier state* [PhD Thesis]. London School of Economics and Political Science.
Smith, S. C. (1999). Kuwait, 1950–1965: Britain, the al-Sabah, and Oil., British Academy postdoctoral fellowship monographs.
Stokke, K. (2017). Politics of citizenship: Towards an analytical framework. *Norsk Geografisk Tidsskrift - Norwegian Journal of Geography, 71*(4), 193–207.
Kuwait . Kuwait Government Press, 1965.
Kuwait Constitution Committee Minutes 1962. National Assembly Website.
LAW, O. F. Citizenship, 15/1959, Alkuwait Alyawm.
alkanderi and others (2021). *Social transformations in the Arab gulf countries, identity, tribe, and development (ARABIC)*. Arab Center for Research and Policy Studies.
Alnajjar, G. (2004). *Introduction to Kuwaiti political development*. Qurtas Publishing Press.

190 *Ghanim AlNajjar*

Alnajjar, G., & Selvik, K. (2015). Kuwait, Politics of Crisis, in a book (ed.) *Oil States in the New Middle East*. Taylor & Francis.

Universal periodic review. Human Rights Council [Website].

Alkhatib, A. (Memoire) (2007). *From Emirate to state (Arabic)*. The Arab Cultural Center.

Aljarida Newspaper 16 May 2023.

During the National Assembly of 1971, on July 10th 1972, a new article was added to Law 15/1959 (citizenship law) by amendment number 41/1972 allowing for obtaining citizenship specifically targeting the Bidoon. However, just after the national assembly was dissolved in 1976, the government cancelled the article by law number 100/1980 on December 20th 1980, citing harm caused by implementing the change of 1972.

DEBATE Alriai, Alqabas, and Aljarida dailies 17,18,19, May 2023.

Alnajjar, G. (1998). The Bidoon, the root causes and its future. *Alzaman, Kuwait*, 32–53.

Alnajjar, G. (2021). The Bidoon, between 10 facts and one illusion, Platform Website.

Alsaidi, H. (2021). *Primary elections for Kuwaiti national assembly, 1967–2020* [MA Thesis]. Department Of Political Science, Kuwait University.

For details on the death of Muhamed Almaimoni see Aljarida newspaper 30 November 2011.

Court Case, 2009.

Court Case, 18 June 2014.

AUESTAD, L. (2014). *Nationalism and the body politics*. Karnak.

Blackburn, R. (Eds.). (1993). *Rights of citizenship*, London: Mansell Publishing Ltd.

Herb, M. (2014). *The wages of oil, parliaments and economic development in Kuwait and UAE*. Cornell University Press.

Beaugrand, C. (2018). *Seatless in the gulf, migration, nationality, and society in Kuwait*. I.B.Tauris.

Joyce, M. (1998). *Kuwait:1945–1996, an Anglo American perspective*. Frank Cass.

12 Kuwait's Publication Law

A Civil Act to Protect Freedom of Expression

Tahani Alterkait

Introduction

The amendments to Law 03/2006 on Press and Publications, belatedly passed in August 2020, brought an end to a decades-long period of futility in Kuwait, which had severely impacted on its cultural scene and standing. These amendments could not see light without the diligent efforts and active civil movement of devoted activists, who argued that freedoms in Kuwait should be protected through open, democratic channels.

When examining the political system of Kuwait, many would consider that democracy has been, as a bare minimum, stumbling. Amending the laws, which contradict the spirit of the Kuwaiti Constitution, became an objective for many activists: Who want to bring an end to the continual political instability the country has experienced ever since its liberation from Iraq in 1991. Kuwait's vibrant civil society renders it an ideal case study through which we can reflect on the sociopolitical dynamics of this small state and its active citizenry. This chapter sheds light on the civil initiative and campaign *Sout al-Kuwait* to amend Law 03/2006: An anti-censorship, pro-democracy civic movement, which ultimately succeeded. An overview of the most critical articles of Law 03/2006 on Press and Publications and where the Constitution of Kuwait stands of freedom of expression is addressed in this chapter. In addition to the historical background of the law amendments since it was adopted in the 1950s (Al-Jerri, 2018).

Despite the Constitution of Kuwait guaranteeing personal freedoms and encouraging academics and writers to conduct free and independent research, local records in 2018 revealed a huge drop in writers, publishers, and book collectors being allowed to write, publish, sell, and buy local and international books from the Kuwaiti market. This became apparent when Mohammad al-Jabri, the Minister of Information, responded to a parliamentary request by revealing:

> There have been 4370 books banned by the Ministry [of Information] on the grounds that these books contain texts that might influence youth against their religious beliefs, or might affect national security in terms of censoring local and international books before selling them in Kuwait.
>
> (Al-Jerri, 2018)

DOI: 10.4324/9781003435259-12

192   *Tahani Alterkait*

Public opinion, civil society, and non-governmental organizations reacted with vehemence, demanding that the Ministry of Information and its Censorship Department abide by Article 36 of the Kuwaiti Constitution: "Freedom of opinion and of scientific research shall be guaranteed. Every person shall have the right to express and propagate his opinion verbally, in writing or otherwise, in accordance with the conditions and procedures specified by the law" (The Constitution of Kuwait, 1962). The response from the government was procedural: Claiming that the Ministry's role is executive, not legislative. It pointed critics towards Law 3/2006 on Press and Publications: Originally issued on January 26, 1961, and amended several times since, most recently in 2018 (Al-Jeri, 2018).

The chapter takes Law 03/2006 on Press and Publications as its case study by both examining the roots and origins of book censorship in Kuwait and scrutinizing recent amendments. These enable the Censorship Department of the Ministry of Information to oversee and ban books prior to their publication. The Law enforces criminal charges against any publication deemed as stirring up sectarianism, tribalism and/or racism. Moreover, content restrictions are applied in case a publication includes any written violation of the person of the emir, Islam, and any other sensitive issues deemed unethical and/or morally unacceptable. Thus, how far does the amended law still protect the rights of Kuwaiti citizens; and to what extent does the country's mixed political system still provide for democracy and freedom?

The Constitution of Kuwait: Freedom of Press and Publication

The Law of Publication was ratified on June 16, 1956, yet has featured many serious shortcomings in spite of numerous amendments. Guaranteeing freedom of expression is the basis of the democratic system, which Kuwait identifies as its system of government in Article 6 of its Constitution, ratified in 1962: "The System of Government in Kuwait shall be democratic, under which sovereignty resides in the people, the source of all powers. Sovereignty shall be exercised in the manner specified in this Constitution" (The Constitution of Kuwait, 1962). Furthermore, the Constitution explicitly guarantees the freedoms set out in Article 36: "Freedom of opinion and of scientific research shall be guaranteed. Every person shall have the right to express and propagate his opinion verbally, in writing or otherwise, in accordance with the conditions and procedures specified by law" (Ibid.). Thus, Kuwait's supreme law pledges freedom of expression and scientific research as a fundamental human right. Moreover, the Constitution's section on Public Rights and Duties is very specific on freedom of press and publication in Article 37: "Freedom of the press, printing and publishing shall be guaranteed in accordance with the conditions and manner specified by law" (Ibid). Yet some articles of Law 03/2006 remained controversial and plainly contradicted the civil spirit of the Constitution.

Law 03/2006 on Press and Publications

Law 03/2006 on Press and Publications has continually ignited debate, dividing public and civil society. Book banning and censorship have always represented hugely emotive totems: Dividing those who wish to protect personal freedoms and constitutional rights, from opponents who believe that banning books is necessary to protect national and Islamic identity. Curbing freedoms is therefore justified as part of the government's responsibility to protect society and religion. No formal translation of Law 03/2006 exists. This chapter attempts to translate its major articles, in order to explain the most recent amendment that took place in 2018. The Law is broad and manifold in explaining all relevant matters regarding the press, publications, and printing: all of which applies to newspapers, printing houses, magazines, and workers in this field. The focus of this chapter is dedicated to the import, circulation, and publication of books in Kuwait. For example, Article 7 enacts:

> It shall be permitted to enter, circulate, or sell the prints that are imported from abroad after obtaining permission from the competent Ministry and after checking their contents regarding the prohibited contents in accordance with the Articles stipulated under Section Three of this Law. Without prejudice to any severer penalty stipulated by another law, the local distributor shall be considered responsible in case of violating any one of the provisions of this Law, and he shall be penalized according to its provisions.
>
> (Information, 2008)

As we can see, Article 7 stresses that all prints need to be scrutinized and approved by the Ministry of Information before being made available for sale and circulation in Kuwait. In other words, book censorship is required prior to publication, circulation, and sale (Ibid.). Therefore, what are the "prohibited contents" which Article 7 refers to: Which are mandatory for the Ministry of Information Committee to check before approving publication?

Under "Matters Prohibited from Publishing in Print or Newspaper and Penalties" can be found Section Three of Law 03/2006. This defines "prohibited contents," and effectively entitles the Ministry of Information to penalize any violation. Article 19 states:

> It shall be prohibited to meddle in matters related to God, the Holy Quran, Prophets, the Noble Companions of Prophet Muhammad, Wives of the Prophet, peace be upon him, or persons who are part of the Prophet's family, peace be upon them, by meddling, defamation, slander, or mocking in any forms of expression that are stipulated under Article (29) of the Law No (31) for the year 1970 on Amendment of Some of the Provisions of the Penalty Law No (16) for the year 1960.

Article 20 of Law 03/2016 goes further in listing the prohibited contents, but this time it is more secular unlike the sacredness and religious spirit of Article 19.

In this context, Article 20 underscores that, "No challenge may be made to the person of the country's emir of the State of Kuwait by criticism, and no statement shall be attributed to him except by a special written permission from the Emiri Diwan." Further, Article 21 details that:

194   *Tahani Alterkait*

It shall be prohibited to publish anything that would:

1. Disdain or contempt the Constitution of the State.
2. Disdain or insult jurists or members of the public prosecution or to state something that is considered as a disparagement of the integrity and impartiality of the judicial system or to publish something which the courts or the investigating parties decide to maintain in secret.
3. Insulting the public morals or instigating to violate the public order or to violate the laws or to commit crimes, even if the crime did not occur.
4. News regarding official secret communications and publishing of agreements and treaties which the government of Kuwait concludes, before publishing them in the Official Gazette, except by a special permission from the concerned Ministry.
5. Influencing the value of the national currency or what would lead to worries about the economic status of the country or publishing news about the bankruptcy of businessmen or the commercial companies or banks or the money exchangers, except by a special permission from the competent court.
6. Revealing what goes on in any meeting or what is written in the papers or documents or decrees, or any papers or prints which the Constitution or any law decided that they are to be kept in secret or not to publish them, even if the published topic was true, and the publishing was limited to the official statements that are issued in that regard.
7. Infringement on the dignity of the persons or their lives or religious beliefs, and instigating hatred or disdain of any of society's strata or to publish information about their financial statuses or to reveal a secret which would harm their reputation or wealth or their trade names.
8. Encroachment into the private life of an employee or a person who is charged in a public service, or attributing statements or acts not true to him which would cause harm or insult to his person.
9. Causing harm to the relationships between Kuwait and other Arab or friendly countries if that is done through the press campaigns.
10. If the specialized newspaper went beyond the purpose of the license which is granted to it.

Article 26 sets out the penalties for any of the above.

> For each violation of the provisions of the First Section's Articles of this Law, the violator shall be penalized with a fine not less than five hundred Dinar and not exceeding one thousand Dinar. If the print contained something which contradicts the national interest or if it served a foreign authority or state or if it infringes on the social or political system of Kuwait, the penalty shall be a fine not less than three thousand Dinar and not more than ten thousand Dinar; even though without prejudice to any severer penalty that is stipulated under another law. Judgment shall be made for confiscating the print in all cases.

As for Article 28, it is more specified to any attempt to overthrow the political system. It states:

> If an instigation was published to overthrow the ruling regime in the country and this instigation included an enticement to change this system by force or through illegal means, or by urging to use force to change the social and economic system that exists in the country, or to adopt creeds which aim at destroying the basic statutes of Kuwait through illegal means, the chief editor and the article writer shall be penalized by the penalty which is stipulated under Article (29) and paragraph (1) of the law No (31) for the year 1970 on Amendment of Some of the Provisions of the Penal Law No (16) for the year 1960.

Historical Background

Understanding the rationale behind the various attempts and initiatives of civil campaigns to amend Law 03/2006 entails a historical and legal survey of the Law's content; perhaps above all, why it was adopted even before Kuwait's independence in 1961. In *Forbidden to Publish: A History of Censorship in Kuwait*, Hamza Olayan emphasizes the importance of what had happened in December 1954, when Dawood Musaad Al-Saleh, the Chief Editor of *The Weekly News*, received an order from the government ceasing the issuance of all newspapers until the enactment of a new law to organize all matters related to press and publications in Kuwait. His abiding with this order did not stop him from expressing his point of view, published in the final issue of his newspaper: "A country which ceases a publication until it promulgates a law does not deserve to have journalism" (Olayan, 2013, p. 39).

When the Department of Publications was established, it was required by the High Executive Committee (the equivalent of the Council of Ministers in modern Kuwait) to censor all newspapers. All were obliged to send copies of their issues to the Department[1] before printing and distribution. This, effective from June 1, 1955, marked the beginning of the censorship trajectory in Kuwait. It was followed by ratification of Law of Press and Publications on June 16, 1956, by H.H. Sheikh Abdullah al-Salim Al-Sabah, emir of the State of Kuwait (1950–1965).

The new law organized the relationship between the government and owners of printing houses and newspapers, as well as protecting the rights of all workers in the field. It consisted of 35 articles: Five of which focused on what was forbidden, while a further seven related to punishment and penalties.

Between 1961 and 1970, Hussein Khalaf al-Sheikh Khazaal, author of a five-volume Political History of Kuwait, encountered several difficulties with censorship. He took great care over meticulously documenting the nation's history despite a scarcity of resources, and realized many could be upset but maintained his objectivity and integrity throughout. The fourth volume, published in 1965, faced many challenges from conservatives; but the final volume was banned from entering Kuwait. "The final say was from the ignorant bunch who know nothing about the history of their country without building the book banning on apparent

196 *Tahani Alterkait*

reason or clear argument." Remarkably, Khazaal did not single out any individual for blame (Olayan, 2013).

From 1975 onwards, the issue of book banning, and censorship would provide main headlines in daily newspapers and other media: Mostly during the Annual Book Fair, which took place each November. The Kuwait Book Fair is ranked the third most important in the Arab world, after its counterparts in Cairo and Beirut. The National Council on Culture Arts and Letters receives books from publishers worldwide; and presents all books to the Ministry of Information's Censorship Committee, which decides on their eligibility for distribution or otherwise. On November 19, 1997, the Committee banned 176 books. The Minister of Information, Sheikh Saud al-Nasser Al-Sabah, requested a list of the banned books: which he reconsidered before allowing their release. Conservative MPs considered the minister's decision as transgressing the law, arguing that the books in question impinged on God, Islamic ethics, and values. Mohammad Abdullah al-Olaim, Waleed Musaad al-Tabtabae, and Fahad Saleh al-Khena interrogated the minister in January 1998. Ten MPs sought to withdraw confidence in the minister; but the government resigned the day before this would have taken place.

The issue of censorship, in other words, would bring down the entire government. Yet it would take a further two decades before a popular tumult around thousands of banned books made international headlines and finally resulted in long overdue reform.

Protests and Change: 2018–2020

Books by local and international writers were banned, including Buthaina Al Eissa, Saud Alsanousi, and Elif Shafak. This served to ignite the whole question of censorship and greatly divide public opinion. Al Eissa's novel, *Kharayet Altayah* (*Maps of Loss*) was published in Lebanon and Saudi Arabia, yet could not be distributed in Kuwait.

> The novel is about a boy who gets lost during the hajj pilgrimage, and an organ trafficking gang kidnaps him. It tells how this gang was pursued and how the parents dealt with this situation. The censorship department accused my novel of provoking regime overthrow and not respecting public morals. Simply, it's a Taleban-esque policy.
>
> (Kuwait Times, 2018)

In 2015, Alsanousi's novel, *Mama Hessa's Mice*, was banned on the grounds that it was advocating sectarianism and fanaticism. The writer appealed the decision and won. The Court ruled, "the mere mention [of sectarianism in the mouths of characters] in no way correlates to the author adopting or promoting these views" (Fattahova, 2018). Shafak's *Forty Rules of Love* can be bought in English in Kuwait, but not in Arabic. Such decisions reflect the arbitrary nature of the bans. The censorship department at the Ministry of Information found individual words like "breast" or "thigh" offensive. Similarly, one publisher's edition of Orwell's *1984* was banned, while that by a different publisher was allowed.

Kuwait's Publication Law   197

Around 80 activists gathered in Irada Square opposite the National Assembly to protest against the banning of books by the Ministry of Information. This was the second gathering by the activists after they held a similar protest in front of the Information Ministry (Ibid.).

The Censorship Committee

With various award-winning books also banned, the Committee had begun to act as though it knew the value of literature better than the judging panels of international literary prizes. Anti-censorship activists, scholars, and non-governmental organizations view the Censorship Department as unqualified: especially given around 5,000 books had been banned in just five years. The Committee does not discuss the reviewed book, but merely a report about it: With one-page memos highlighting supposedly offensive words, phrases, and pictures: All items taken completely out of context. They refuse even to provide a reason, instead highlighting the offending pages, as though the problem with them were self-evident.

Defending this, Muhammad al-Awash, assistant undersecretary at the Ministry of Information stated:

In Kuwait, over the past five years only 4,300 books were banned out of 208,000 books—which means only 2 percent are banned and 98 percent are approved ... Some books are being banned in the US, Europe, Beirut and other countries, too.

Over the preceding 11 months, censors had approved 3,600 books, while 700 were banned. Yet al-Awash insisted that '"since its inception, Kuwait has always been known for its sponsorship of literature and culture".

On Twitter, the hashtag "Forbidden in Kuwait" (mamnou' fi al-kuwait) posted screenshots of the Censorship Committee's reports. It was glaringly obvious from these that zero consideration or thought lay behind the bans. It even showed that the Committee and its members lacked even the most basic reading skills—and were thus unable to differentiate between sacrilege and historical context or artistic license. Consequently, a novel containing a character who believes in magic, or a book that uses the words "angels," "Adam," "Eve," "Satan," or even Nahj al-Balagha (a book of letters and sermons by Ali ibn Abi Talib, cousin and son-in-law to the Prophet—peace be upon him) are all banned under the claim that they transgress on the sacred (AlAmmar, 2018).

Many books have been banned for allegedly promoting a sectarian ideology. This is despite the reality that certain topics in the Arab world cannot be properly explored without using sectarian characters or referring to sectarian tensions. However, despite vocal opposition to the bans from various democratic, liberal, and progressive organizations, multiple opinion pieces by prominent literary figures and critics in daily newspapers, and a small but passionate protest outside the Ministry of Information, there was a rather disturbing streak of public apathy or even inability to grasp the basic point. Contrasting with the Twitter storm were

198 *Tahani Alterkait*

responses such as, "well, I hated that book, so it should be banned"; or "that book was silly and unnecessary, so I agree with banning it" (Ibid.).

> This is emblematic of the problem that, on a larger scale, we face with the Ministry. It is this bizarre notion that one man's individual taste and preferences ought to be applied to the masses. It is a rudimentary misunderstanding of pluralism that should be the hallmark of any democracy, a pluralism that is tolerant of different views and varied opinions. If you think a book is trash, do not read it. It is as simple as that.

A lot of questions have been asked in the wake of this abuse of power—questions about the random nature of the bans, about what precisely the justifications are for them, who exactly is the one wielding the pen and what makes him qualified to do so, just how far this will go. However, one thing no one has asked was: What are they afraid of that they ban all these titles?

We do not ask because we know very well what they fear. The ability to read, and read critically, is a kind of magic. It is what Proust called "that fruitful miracle of communication in the midst of solitude." When you read, you find you are not alone. When you read, you commune with the past. When you read, you have a conversation with the writer. You are free to fall in love with them, to critique them, to detest them. You are free to think, to criticize, to question—attributes the Ministry of Information does not want citizens to have (Flood, 2020).

One could argue that these bans are an assault on the rights to freedom of thought and expression that the Kuwaiti Constitution grants to all its citizens. Kuwait prides itself on being a democracy, but it should be remembered that democracy does not begin and end with a ballot box. It extends as a mode of thought and a way of life that prizes plurality and tolerance. In the words of Potter Stewart, former associate justice of the United States Supreme Court, "Censorship reflects society's lack of confidence in itself." I would go further in saying that censorship is fear and ignorance. It is a tool of oppression. It is offensive because it quite simply assumes the human mind cannot function properly and must be contained. Censorship constitutes the drawing of a line in the sand, and sand is an impermanent medium. It is quite easy for someone to come along, erase that line and draw a new one. A decade ago, mentioning Allah or the Prophet—peace be upon him—in certain contexts was seen as crossing the line. Today, comparing a woman to an angel in poetic verse is where the line is. Where will it be tomorrow?" (AlAmmar, 2018).

Kuwaitis like to think of their country as an enclave of intellectual freedom in the conservative Persian Gulf, a haven that once welcomed exiled Arab writers. However, that self-image is becoming harder to sustain. Responding to the demands of a growing conservative bloc in parliament, the government is increasingly banning books. In August, the government acknowledged that it had banned 4,390 books since 2014, hundreds of them this year, including many works of literature that had once been considered untouchable, setting off street demonstrations and online protests. Sometimes the 12-member censors committee (six Arabic readers, six English readers) that rules on books for the Ministry of Information gives a reason: The anthology *Why We Write* was banned because its editor, Meredith Maran, had falsely accused her father of molestation.

In other cases, the justification is obscure, such as with *The Art of Reading* by Damon Young. Maya Angelou is honoured with a postage stamp in America, but her memoir, *I Know Why the Caged Bird Sings*, is forbidden in Kuwait.

Prizewinners are not immune—in fact, they seem to be frequent victims. *One Hundred Years of Solitude* by the Nobel Prize winner Gabriel Garcia Marquez is banned because of a scene in which a wife sees her husband naked, as is *Children of Gebelawi* by the Egyptian author Naguib Mahfouz, the first Arabic-language writer to win the Nobel in literature. If all that seems rather Orwellian, George Orwell's *1984* is also banned, in at least one Arabic translation, though it is allowed in another (Yousef, 2020).

Kuwaiti readers have struck back with a mix of brio and scornful mirth. Some posted photographs on Twitter and Facebook of piles of banned books they have in their home libraries. Authors suggested that online delivery services from abroad could evade the ban, which applies mostly to bookstores and local publishers. "Now books are becoming like drugs," said Hind Francis, an activist with a Kuwait anti-censorship group called Meem3. "You have to have your banned-book dealer." Activists and writers gathered to protest the book ban three times in September, most recently on Saturday, the last day of the international Banned Books Week. Kuwait is one of the few Gulf countries that allow public protests, although they are strictly controlled. The protests have been lightly attended, but any outdoor crowd has to brave temperatures that still reach 100 degrees.

"It's a challenge, but we tell them we'll keep it to only an hour," said Fatima Matar, a law professor, and a founder of the protest effort. With the country's book fair—the third largest in the Arab world, after Cairo and Beirut—scheduled in November, officials have pushed back. "There is no book banning in Kuwait," read a recent statement by the Ministry of Information. "There is a book censorship committee that reviews all books. It is a particularly sensitive issue because Kuwait's late emir, Sheikh Sabah al-Ahmad al-Sabah (2006–2020), has pushed to make his country a regional cultural hub. While theatre, dance and music are under royal patronage and exempt from censorship, books are not. "That cultural hub just cannot happen when you have a book massacre like this, all these books being banned," said Bothyana Al-Essa, a Kuwaiti author (Saeed, 2020). Bans have for the first time extended to many international books and reference books already on Kuwaiti shelves, at least in part because of parliamentary pressure, critics say. "This year they've gone into the ridiculous," said Shamayal AlSharikh "Children's stories and books by Kuwaiti authors. Even works produced by the government's own publishing house in the Public Council for Culture, Arts and Literature have been banned, such as a scientific study of hymens," according to Ms. Francis. Kuwait's history of literary freedom is, activists say, the reason book banning is so distressing to the intelligentsia. "Kuwait has had a significant amount of progress when it comes to civil liberties," Al Sharikh said. "We are the trendsetters in the Gulf region and have been for many decades. The Kuwaiti Parliament is the most independent in the Gulf, but that has also become the problem, bibliophiles complain." In effect, "democracy has become the enemy of democracy," Fatma AlMatar said. "They believe we should all think alike."

Because Kuwait's parliament has the authority to call a vote of confidence on individual ministers, and has forced resignations, the ministers tread carefully, especially on explosive social issues. Authors and their supporters say the Ministry of Information has responded to parliamentary pressure by giving the censors sweeping powers to ban books, even though the Kuwaiti Constitution guarantees intellectual freedom. Arwa Alwagayan, a Kuwaiti author, said her book *Be Well* was banned because of a passage that said the Islamic State was attracting teenagers "in the mosques." The censors demanded she change that to "in some mosques," and she refused. For some local authors, having their books banned has created a sales opportunity. After Mohamed Ghazi's book *Blue* was banned over a passage on page 56, Ghazi, an Iraqi who writes in English and lives in Kuwait, used Twitter to invite readers to buy it to find out why. His sales more than doubled, he said. Such defiance is rife. Many banned books are still on sale in bookstores in Kuwait; recently, at the country's largest, the Jarir Bookstore in Shamiya, there were books on display by Márquez and Orwell, along with one not-very-risqué copy of Hans Christian Anderson's bikini-clad mermaid. However, other outlets, mindful of heavy fines, are removing offending titles. "It's happening gradually, but slowly and surely books are disappearing," Fatma AlMatar said. New books by Kuwaiti authors are especially vulnerable, because if banned they cannot be printed and distributed. Matar's book of poetry was banned from sale when she refused to delete an offending line, she said.

'We don't want to get to that stage where we go to our bookshops and only find cookbooks and books about Sharia law', she said.

Underground banned-book dealers are already doing a brisk business serving literary scofflaws. According to one young author, who said he supplements his income that way, many use Instagram's disappearing photo feature to display their wares, take orders and stay a step ahead of the law. At a bookstore in Kuwait City, the proprietor showed off a secret cupboard full of contraband books behind the cash register and a basement storeroom with even more. "It's a cliché that book banning helps book sales," she said. "As a bookseller, I can tell you I would much rather have the books out on display."

The bookseller did have a banned copy of *Zorba the Greek* on display, discretely, since it could result in a minimum fine of about $1,650 if Ministry of Information inspectors saw it. She said she was not too worried. "You can always spot them when they come in," she said. "You can tell they're not readers" (Nordland, 2018). The information ministry has banned 4,390 books over the past five years, Minister of Information and Minister of State for Youth Affairs Mohammad Al-Jabri has confirmed. Responding to an inquiry by MP Khaled Al-Shatti, Jabri said that the ministry's grievances committee—formed according to ministerial resolution number 13/2017—had investigated complaints against two books and agreed to reconsider banning them. He added that the banned list was 70 pages long, including religious, cultural and historical books (Al-Khonaini, 2011).

Kuwait's Publication Law   201

Notably, Shatti had inquired about the long list of banned books, noting that he had 16 cartons full of the banned books' titles. He said after reviewing some of the banned books, he emerged with a feeling that we are living a "real freedom of thought dilemma," warning that censorship is killing ideas and creativity. "It is as if we are living in the medieval ages," he added, noting that some of the justifications for bans were feeble. (Kuwait Times, 2018).

Amendments to Law 03/2006, August 2020

"Kuwait's National Assembly yesterday voted to change the 2006 publications law on media and publications that required all books to have prior approval, resulting in the ban of more than 4,500 books," as parliamentary observer, Abdulla Khonaini, wrote on Twitter on August 15, 2020.

This meant that books would no longer be subject to a required prior censorship, although they could still be challenged in court on a case-by-case basis. This change has been the result of the work of many authors and activists including—as Kuwaiti novelist Layla AlAmmar commented on Twitter—Khonaini; novelist and bookseller Bothaina Al-Essa; and Hind Francis. AlAmmar said:

> What the law means is that banning will no longer be the default position, whereby, like in the case of *Mama Hessa's Mice*, the author has to go to court, at great personal expense, to get it unbanned. Instead, the person who wants it banned would have to go to court for a ruling.[2]

According to the Kuwait News Agency, importers will be required to provide a list of authors and titles to the Ministry of Information, but without submitting the books to a committee and waiting on approval. Thus, "the importer alone bears the sole legal responsibility for the ideas and opinions expressed in this publication, according to the amended article."

Khonaini added that "there is still a long way to go, in moving toward the free exchange of books, and that, what happened today is a very small step in a much longer journey."

There are still questions about the thousands of books that have been banned—some seemingly on a whim—in the 14 years that law has been in force. As AlAmmar asked on Twitter, "question though, what happens with more than 4500 books that are already banned? Do they remain so or automatically lifted?"

According to the news reports, "forty-nine lawmakers were reportedly in attendance; forty approved the change and nine voted against" (ARABLIT, 2020).

"After banning almost 5,000 books in the last seven years, Kuwait's government has relaxed its book censorship laws in a move that has been welcomed by writers and free speech activists."

Kuwaiti state media reported that the country's parliament had voted 40 to 9 in favour of lifting the Ministry of Information's control over books imported into the country. Previously, the ministry had blacklisted more than 4,000 books since

202 *Tahani Alterkait*

2014, with titles including Victor Hugo's *The Hunchback of Notre Dame* and *One Hundred Years of Solitude* by Gabriel García Márquez falling foul of its censorship committee. All books published in the country had to receive prior approval from a 12-member committee that met twice a month before they could be released, with offences ranging from insulting Islam to "inciting unrest" and committing "immoral" acts.

The new rules mean importers and publishers will only have to provide the Ministry of Information with book titles and author names, with the importer alone bearing responsibility for the book's contents. According to the *National*, only an official complaint from the public will spark legal action against a book, with a ban only to be implemented by the courts, rather than the Ministry of Information. The International Publishers Association said the ruling put "an end to the mandate of the Kuwaiti book censorship committee."

AlAmmar said that, in the nearly 15 years that the committee was in place, almost 5,000 books were banned in a "largely arbitrary fashion" and that the law had 'throttled an already fledgling publishing industry and market where piracy is rampant."

Campaigners have both welcomed the news and shared reservations. "The Ministry of Information is no longer the judge when it comes to books and I believe this is a most important achievement," Essa told *Gulf News*. "We will continue to work towards achieving greater freedoms."

However, Khonaini said:

> The freedom of expression is already restricted in Kuwait on multiple levels. This law does not fix it. The amendment shifts the power of censorship away from the executive branch to the judicial branch. We still need to work on the prohibition section in the law, which needs a stronger political lobby and mature political and societal awareness.

AlAmmar pointed to the case of International Prize for Arabic fiction winner, Saud al-Sanousi, who went to court to get a ban on his book annulled. "It remains unclear what the fate of the banned books is: Does the ban automatically lift? Must they pass through some other authorising committee or bureaucratic procedure before their sale is allowed? None of this has been addressed," she said (Flood, 2020).

The news has also been welcomed by two of the region's biggest literary awards. The Sheikh Zayed Book Award's secretary general, Dr Ali bin Tamim, tells the *National* that the new amendments will strengthen the region's literary and academic fields.

> Commitment to creativity is better than being committed to censorship guidelines that, if biased, surely derail cultural efforts and scholarly work. The Kuwaiti parliament's decision to waive censorship on written work is commendable because it supports the literary and cultural momentum, imposing a creative and scientific responsibility on the author and publisher.
>
> (Ibid.)

Fleur Montanaro, administrator of the International Prize for Arabic Fiction, says the changes will be good for Kuwait's already strong literary scene, citing the international success of 2013 Ipaf award winner Saud Alsanousi (*The Bamboo Stalk*) as an example of its fertile landscape.

> The Kuwaiti literary scene is a lively one, with active book clubs and many talented writers, including Alsanousi. Hopefully, this means writers in Kuwait will feel greater freedom and be able to look forward to their books being enjoyed in their home country, which has a history of openness.
>
> (Saeed, 2020)

Conclusion

What's next? On August 19, 2020, Kuwait's National Assembly had voted 40 out of 9 in favour of lifting the Ministry of Information's control over books imported into Kuwait. According to Kuwait News Agency,

> Importer will now be required to provide a notice to the ministry indicating their name along with the publication's title and name of the author. The importer alone bears the sole legal responsibility for the ideas and opinions expressed in this publication according to the amended article. Another article was amended to a penalty issued for those who violate public morals or incite the violation of laws and crimes, even if the crime incited does not occur another article prohibits publishing ideas that stir up sectarian or tribal division or that are deemed racist or demeaning of groups of people or are an incitement to an act of violence for this purpose.
>
> (Kuna, 2020)

The diligent efforts of *Sout Al Kuwait* activists and authors did not go with the wind. However, they still believe there is a great chance for more amendments. In his words, Abdullah al-Khonaini commented on passing the bill, "there is still a long way to go, in moving toward the free exchange of books, and that what happened today is a very small step in a much longer way" (ARABLIT, 2020).

One could argue that the campaign to amend law 03/2006 is twofold:

The amendments could not see light, if it was not for the determination and perseverance of a well-organized civil group "*Sout Al Kuwait*" and group of dedicated novelists and writers who the censorship in their own country shattered their aspirations to make Kuwait again the literary cradle of arts and literature not only in the Gulf region, but also in the Arab World.

Abolishing censorship on press and publications is a public civilized act. Therefore, all the rallies and protests that took place between 2018 and 2020 embodied the voices of 24 non-governmental organizations, civil groups, and

204 Tahani Alterkait

activists to protect personal freedoms and other constitutional rights and defend them against any violations.

Civil campaigns reinforce that the civil movement in Kuwait is a fundamental partner and contributor in nation building based on democratic values. Kuwaitis consider that the ratification of the Kuwaiti Constitution in 1962 is their social contract between the ruler and ruled.

Historically, the first three international book fairs convened in Kuwait were not submitted to any form of prior censorship. Yet, it did not violate or distort societal values or traditions.

Moreover, it is illogical and useless in the age of information technology and mass media revolution to keep the same old tools of censorship. Therefore, developing the mechanisms of censorship is more feasible. For example, the Ministry of Information should classify publications based on the age group and grant parents and guardians the freedom of choice.

Censorship is a system which excludes, prevents, and confiscates the rights of others and the continuation of books banning contradicts the principles of freedom which is guaranteed in the Constitution of Kuwait. A campaign like *Sout Al Kuwait* need to be acknowledged and encouraged to continue their civil initiatives as the outdated laws need to be amended and reconsidered.

Notes

1 First established in Kuwait on 13 December 1954.
2 Twitter, August 20, 2020 @Layla_AlAmmar.

References

4390 Books Banned in Five Years (2018, March 16). *Kuwait Times.* Retrieved from https://www.kuwaittimes.com/4390-books-banned-in-five-years/.

Abdullah Al-Khonaini, Dalal Al-Shayji and Deema Al-Ghunaim (2011). Peace treaty with books, Sout Al Kuwait. http://soutalkuwait.com/booklets/censorshipbook-web.pdf

Agency, K. N. (2020). *Kuwaiti Parliament amends media and publications law.* Kuwait News Agency. Retrieved from https://www.kuna.net.kw/ArticleDetails.aspx?id =2916517&language=en.

AlAmmar, L. (n.d.). Book Banning in Kuwait: Whatever Next? Al-fanar Media. Retrieved from https://www.al-fanarmedia.org/2018/09/book-banning-in-kuwait-whatever-next/.

Alshammari, A. (n.d.). https://arablit.org/. Retrieved June 6, 2023, from https://arablit.org /2018/09/10/literary-massacre-in-kuwait-the-state-of-book-banning/.

Fattahova, N. (2018, September 15). Activists stage protest against book Banning. *Kuwait Times.* Retrieved from https://www.kuwaittimes.com/activists-stage-protest-against -book-banning/.

Flood, A. (2020, August 25). Kuwait relaxes book censorship laws after banning thousands of titles. *The Guardian.* Retrieved from https://www.theguardian.com/books/2020/aug /25/kuwait-relaxes-book-censorship-laws-after-banning-thousands-of-titles.

Information, M. O. (2008). *Press and publication law.* Kuwait: Kuwait Government Press.

Kuwait Parliament Votes to Abolish Censorship Committee for Books. (n.d.). *Arablit & Arablit quarterly.* Retrieved from https://arablit.org/2020/08/20/kuwaiti-parliament -votes-to-abolish-censorship-committee-for-books/.

Kuwait's Publication Law 205

Kuwait Parliament Votes to Abolish Censorship Committee for Books. (2020, 8 20). *Arablit & Arablit quarterly*. Retrieved from https://arablit.org/2020/08/20/kuwaiti-parliament-votes-to-abolish-censorship-committee-for-books/.

Maha Naji Ghannam, A. G.-S. (2014). *The civil state and the civilized deadlock: The case of Kuwait*. Beirut: Difaf Publishing.

Nordland, R. (2018, October 1). *The New York Times*. Retrieved May 16, 2023, from From Orwell to 'Little Mermaid,' Kuwait Steps Up Book Banning.

Olayan, H. (2013). *Not for publication: History of censorship in Kuwait*. Kuwait: That AlSalasil.

Saeed, S. (2020, August 24). Kuwait writers welcome change to book censorship laws. *The National News*. Retrieved from https://www.thenationalnews.com/arts-culture/books/kuwaiti-writers-welcome-change-to-book-censorship-laws-1.1067837.

Tetreault, M. A. (2000). *Stories of democracy in Kuwait: Politics and society in contemporary Kuwait*. New York: Coloumbia University Press.

Yousef, M. A. (2020). *Controlling the narrative: Censorship laws in the gulf*. The Arab Gulf Sattes Institute in Washington. Retrieved from https://agsiw.org/: https://agsiw.org/controlling-the-narrative-press-and-publication-laws-in-the-gulf/.

13 Culture, Politics, and Citizenship in Kuwait

Courtney Freer

Introduction

Kuwait, like other oil-wealthy Gulf states, has since the discovery of oil and since independence in 1961 put in place measures to regulate the number of national citizens. Because citizenship in rentier states carries with it substantial material benefits, this practice has been common throughout resource-rich states. These policies, however, have had legal, social, and political consequences that will be assessed in this chapter.

In terms of legal categories, aside from citizens and expatriates, the category of *bidūn jinsiyya* (without nationality) has emerged across the Gulf states to describe communities, which lack any documentation of their nationality and therefore cannot be naturalized as full citizens of any state. This has contributed to the social and political marginalization of such populations, despite government efforts to address the issues of this population.

Because citizenship laws have been based on dates when families settled in Kuwait and had documentation to prove their presence there, members of the more sedentary merchant elite class who historically lived and worked in Kuwait City received citizenship first, leading some members of that population to consider themselves "original" Kuwaiti citizens. Heritage projects in Kuwait reflect the importance of the state's past as a port city, and social and political differences have emerged between those citizens earlier settled, *hadhar* (literally "civilised," but meaning those settled in Kuwait City from an earlier period) and *badu* (tribal populations who became sedentarized later). In what follows, I trace Kuwait's citizenship policies and the social and political effects they have had within the state.

A History of Kuwaiti Citizenship Policies

Following the discovery of vast hydrocarbon resources in the 1940s and 1950s, state authorities throughout the Arabian Peninsula went about creating generous social welfare systems for their citizens. Because citizenship suddenly became a source of material benefit in these new rentier economies, often involving the provision of free education, healthcare, and housing, in addition to state employment, all of these states put in place stringent limitations on citizenship. Kuwait started defining citizens shortly after its vast oil reserves began to be traded on global

DOI: 10.4324/9781003435259-13

markets after World War II. In 1948, the first requirements for Kuwaiti citizenship were codified: Residents had to prove they had had ancestors in Kuwait since 1899, and Arab or Muslim children born in Kuwait and living there for up to ten years could also apply for citizenship (al-Nakib, 2014, p. 12). Others could be naturalized on the condition that they had lived in Kuwait ten years, were employed, and spoke Arabic or "by special order for valuable services" (Longva, 2000, p. 185). In 1950, 11 years prior to independence from Britain, Kuwaiti Amir Shaykh Abdullah al-Salim launched efforts at modernizing and centralizing the state. As al-Nakib explains, "[t]he institution of Kuwaiti citizenship was key to this state-building project, and to maintaining the stability of the new state" (al-Nakib, 2014, p. 11). Efforts at building up a unified and distinctly Kuwaiti national citizenry therefore emerged, and this involved an overhaul of state-provided social welfare, as well as a reformulation of citizenship policies.

Another reason that citizenship became redefined in Kuwait was that, as early as 1957, as the oil industry grew through an influx of foreign workers, more than 45 per cent of the population consisted of non-Kuwaitis, and so a 1959 nationality law removed the option to gain citizenship through birth or long-term residence (al-Nakib, 2014, p. 12). Al-Nakib explains:

> The law defined Kuwaitis "originally" (*asāsan*) as those persons whose families were "settled in Kuwait" (*al-mutawaṭṭinūn fī al-kuwayt)* by 1920. The only option for people who did not meet these requirements to be naturalised as Kuwaiti was by decree from the minister of the interior.
>
> (al-Nakib, 2014, p. 12)

Notably, the date of 1920 had been chosen since it marked the Battle of Jahra, which effectively solidified Kuwaiti independence, albeit with British assistance, from Saudi Arabia, which was an important step in subsuming formerly disparate tribal identities under a national Kuwaiti identity. Longva specifies that Kuwait City, rather than Kuwait as a whole, was central to the Battle of Jahra, as the construction of a wall around the town centre had helped to withstand attack (Longva, 2000, p. 186). In her words, the battle,

> created a special bond between the town dwellers who had taken part in it and invested them with legitimacy of membership in the Kuwaiti community. This event, it is often said in Kuwait, saw the birth of an explicit Kuwaiti 'national' awareness by creating a nucleus of citizenry encompassing those who had taken part in the events and their descendants.
>
> (Longva, 2000, p. 186)

This date has continued to be important in demarcating varying segments of the Kuwaiti citizenry based on when they became sedentarized in Kuwait City.

Kuwait became independent in 1961. Shortly before that, however, the government had attempted to register all citizens using the 1959 legislation and by requiring them to present proof of their status to committees throughout the country

208   *Courtney Freer*

(al-Nakib, 2014, p. 13). This process, notably, favoured people whose families had been settled for generations, mainly in Kuwait's urban centre, and therefore disadvantaged people whose families had remained nomadic for a longer period. An additional amendment in 1960 limited naturalization to non-Gulf citizens to 50 per year (Longva, 2000, p. 185). Al-Nakib explains:

> The townspeople could furnish adequate documentation—land deed, birth and death certificates, travel documents—as proof of settlement in Kuwait by 1920. The tribes that grazed and camped beyond the *sūr*, however, were not permanently settled and did not possess such documentary evidence. About one-third of the Kuwaiti population (not counting recently arriving foreigners with nationality papers from other countries) was recognized as qualifying for "original" citizenship and classified as Kuwaitis *bi-l-ta'sīs*, meaning "by establishment" or funding. These were predominantly town-dwellers and some villagers. Another third, consisting mainly of members of Bedouin tribes who had not permanently settled in Kuwait Town before oil [....] occupied a more ambiguous category. These were individuals or families who did not meet the legal requirements for citizenship *bi-l-ta'sīs* but were naturalized as citizens by ministerial decree.
>
> (al-Nakib, 2014, p. 12)

From the start, then, various tiers of citizenship were delineated depending on the time that one's family became *settled* in Kuwait, privileging those whose families had lived in the town and relied on trade, rather than living in the desert, relying largely on animal husbandry, and therefore not settled in one place. Further, the fact that the state itself was named after Kuwait's primary port city has led many conflate urban dwelling, not outlying tribes, with citizenship itself (Calderwood, 2011). The requirement that people demonstrate proof of their family's having settled also created a group of people who were unable to present any proof of settlement in Kuwait or in another country, known collectively as the *bidūn jinsiyya* (without nationality), hereafter referenced as the *bidūn*. They tended to be included in tallies of Kuwaiti citizens as a different class of citizen for decades (Plotkin-Boghardt, 2006, p. 137).

In the 1980s, as the Middle East faced the turmoil of the Lebanese civil war, Iran–Iraq war, and fallout of the Iranian Revolution, efforts were made to nationalize, or Kuwaitise, the workforce, which had long been dominated by expatriates. This plan was meant to insulate Kuwait from nefarious or harmful external influences that could destabilize the state. As a result, changes were made to the 1959 Nationality Law. In 1981, an amendment required naturalized Kuwaitis to be Muslims (Longva, 2000, p. 185). Two additional changes were made in 1982. The first involved an amendment to Article 4 to require that Arab expatriates hoping to be naturalized live in Kuwait for 15 years, rather than 8 years (Eldemerdash, 2015, p. 86). The second change, made in 1987, involved an amendment to Article 8, which "imposed a 'continued marriage' requirement of 15 years for spouses of Kuwaiti citizens seeking naturalisation, where previously there had been no residency requirement for wives" (Eldemerdash, 2015, p. 86). Another amendment to Article 3 meant that children of Kuwaiti mothers and *bidūn* men could not inherit Kuwaiti citizenship (Eldemerdash, 2015, p. 86).

These strict citizenship policies have led scholars like Longva to equate Kuwait with an ethnocracy: "government by an ethnic group [....] In Kuwait and the rest of the Gulf, the defining feature is not race, language or religion but citizenship conceived in terms of shared descent – so it's a '"civic' ethnocracy'" (Longva, 2013, p. 119). In some ways, then, citizenship is linked to a specific lineage, rather than to a race, religion, or language, all of which are relatively homogeneous in Kuwait. Demonstrating the importance of maintaining this lineage, institutional encouragement exists for nationals marrying nationals, whereby nationals receive KD2,000 each (6,600 USD) upon marrying Kuwaitis— as well as free housing or a generous housing loan for a Kuwaiti couple (Alsharekh & Freer, 2021, p. 86). Further, in 2015, the Kuwaiti parliament passed a law, set to come into action in November 2016 that required DNA testing for all residents and visitors to make a comprehensive list of criminals and terrorists. Those failing to comply would face a fine of KD10,000 ($30,000) and up to one year in prison (Arabian Business, 2016). Many Kuwaitis feared that the law, although meant to be used for security, could be used as a means of revoking citizenship for political reasons (Arabian Business, 2016). Ultimately, the Constitutional Court ruled against the legislation in 2017 on the grounds that it violates constitutional provisions for personal liberty (Coghlan, 2017). Despite the overturning of the law, bloodlines still matter— particularly when it comes to determining who is and is not a Kuwaiti national.

Kuwait's *Bidūn* Population

Because all Gulf states have put in place similarly restrictive citizenship policies due to the handsome disbursements granted to citizens, populations of those falling within two potential citizenships have emerged across the Arabian Peninsula. In the Kuwaiti case, these restrictions date back to the 1959 Citizenship Law, although the group of *bidūns* did not become legally distinguished from other Kuwaiti citizens until the 1980s. The Kuwaiti authorities initially extended education and healthcare rights to the *bidūn* population. Rather than regulating their status legally, the state instead "offered the *Bidūn* the social privileges of citizenship—education, healthcare, housing—through military and police service, thus ensuring that it had a constant source of recruits for its army and police forces" (Eldemerdash, 2015, p. 85).

In 1986, when Kuwait was in the midst of regional strife and facing a spate of violent attacks at home, rules were altered regarding the *bidūn*. They were collectively reclassified as "illegal residents," since it was suspected that many had in fact come to Kuwait from surrounding countries to gain access to the handsome benefits of Kuwaiti citizenship, destroying their original citizenship documents in the process (Beaugrand, 2018, p. 3).

As of 1989, the population of *bidūn*, according to officials, numbered 250,000 (Plotkin Boghardt, 2006, pp. 136–137). Plotkin Boghardt (2006, p. 137) links the change in dubbing *bidūns* as citizens to late 1988 after efforts began to nationalize the workforce. In her words,

210 *Courtney Freer*

> The concern remained [...] that the loyalty of *bidūns* might shift if a more lucrative offer, potentially from Iraq, were to emerge. This concern was linked to Kuwait's belief that most *bidūns* were of Iraqi origin, and would have been particularly pronounced after the Iran–Iraq ceasefire and the presumable end to Iraq's special war-related partnership with Kuwait. The suspicion over the issue would prove well-grounded in some cases in the context of the Iraqi invasion.
>
> (Plotkin Boghardt, 2006, p. 137)

On the eve of the Iraqi invasion in 1990, *bidūns* comprised about three-fourths of Kuwait's total army (Plotkin Boghardt, 20061, p. 48). This proportion changed markedly after the invasion due to concerns about their loyalty to the Kuwaiti state.

In 2000, parliament passed legislation delineating those *bidūns* whose families had arrived in Kuwait before 1965 from those who had arrived after that date (Albloshi, 2019). Legislation states that those who arrived before 1965, which was thought at the time to number 34,000 people, could be naturalized, but there has been considerable confusion about that process, and it has therefore not been straightforward (Albloshi, 2019). Adding to the confusion, "[t]he same law requires the government to naturalize 2,000 *bidūns* every year, but the government has not reached that target. The government agreed to naturalize up to 4,000 people in 2019, but again it has the ultimate discretion over how many it will naturalize" (Albloshi, 2019).

Reliable statistics are difficult to find, but authorities appear to estimate Kuwait's *bidūn* population today to number just over 100,000 people (Albloshi, 2019). This figure reflects a decrease in the *bidūn* population after the Iraqi invasion and occupation of Kuwait in 1990–1991 when the population was thought to number 220,000 (Albloshi, 2019). As Albloshi explains:

> Many *bidūns* left Kuwait at that time to go back to their countries of origin, although a significant number of them stayed in the country during the occupation, with some taken as prisoners or war or killed by Iraqi forces. Their numbers have declined for other reasons as well. The authorities say that more than 8,000 *bidūns* declared their original nationalities and became foreign residents in Kuwait between 2011 and 2016. Others were naturalized.
>
> (Albloshi, 2019)

In 2010, seeking to address the issue, the Kuwaiti government established the Central System for the Remedy of the Situation of Illegal Residents led by former MP Saleh al-Fadhalah, who announced that the system, along with Kuwaiti ministries, had gathered some 5 million documents dating back to the 1960s to allow it to trace the "original" nationality of some 87,000 people (Albloshi, 2019). Some *bidūn* activists have criticized the body, claiming that their living conditions have worsened since its establishment, citing the rise in suicide among members of the *bidūn* population (detailed below) as evidence (US Department of State, 2021). Kuwait's *bidūn* population today can be divided broadly into three categories:

Culture, Politics, and Citizenship in Kuwait   211

those whose ancestors failed to apply for nationality or lacked the necessary documents at Kuwaiti independence; those recruited from abroad (like Iraq, Syria, and Jordan) to work in the Kuwaiti army or police during the 1960s; and children of Kuwaiti mothers and stateless or foreign fathers.

(Diwakar, 2021)

MPs and more specifically speakers of parliament have put forward plans to resolve the issue of the *bidun* more decisively than legislation has to this point, outlined below, but no plan has yet been put into action. Indeed, since 2011, as traced by Beaugrand, Kuwait's *bidūns* have become increasingly visible and vocal about their situation (Beaugrand, 2018). Perhaps in response, in 2016, reports emerged that the Kuwaiti government had entered into negotiations with the Comoros Islands to grant citizenship to Kuwait and the United Arab Emirates' *bidūn* population in exchange for economic assistance (Mansour-Ille, 2016). Kuwait's foreign minister at the time denied these negotiations or the existence of an agreement as of 2014 to grant Comorian citizenship to Kuwait's *bidūns* (Toumi, 2016). The plan reportedly would have granted the *bidūn* what is known as economic citizenship of the Comoros Islands, which would have given them the ability to reside in Kuwait through self-sponsorship, as well as secure access to free education and healthcare, in addition to access to jobs in Kuwait (Toumi, 2016). In return, Kuwait would build schools and open a branch of the Zakat House (Toumi, 2016). A report produced by the Comoran Parliament in 2017 found the scheme resulted in "suspected embezzlement of public funds," as a substantial amount of the revenue went missing (Lewis & Ahmed, 2018). Ultimately, the plan was never implemented. Thus, far, then, so long-term solution has been found for the *bidūn* population, yet this is by no means the only social distinction in Kuwait.

Kuwait's *Badu-Hadhar* Division

Although the majority of the Kuwaiti citizen population (who comprise some 30 per cent of the total population of the state) is Sunni and Arab, which has led many to consider the state homogeneous, there exists a deep political and social division between long-time urbanized citizens (*hadhar*) and more recently naturalized tribal figures (*badū*, or bedouin). While a *hadhar* is defined as a Kuwaiti "whose forefathers lived in Kuwait before the launch of the oil era (1946) and worked as traders, sailors, fishermen, and pearl divers," (Longva, 2006, p. 172) *Badū* are often described as "immigrants, mostly from Saudi Arabia, who used to live on animal pastoralism" and moved to Kuwait between 1960 and 1980 (Longva, 2006, p. 172).

As noted above, citizenship laws have emphasized differences between citizens based on when their families arrived in Kuwait. Over time, this separation became concretized through housing policies that have leant social and geographic separation to groups that were already socially distinct. As al-Nakib has noted, state housing policies between the 1950s and 1980s physically segregated the *hadhar* and *badū* (al-Nakib, 2014, pp. 14–15). Members of the *badū* population tended to be moved to "self-contained" communities outside the centre of

212   *Courtney Freer*

Kuwait City, thereby making it unnecessary for them to mix with the *hadhar* population, who mainly lived in the city centre (al-Nakib, 2014, p. 21). In peripheral areas, which were developed later than the city itself, the *badū* received state services of lower quality and smaller housing plots than did city dwellers, with access to healthcare and education not guaranteed until the end of the 1980s (al-Nakib, 2014, p. 21).

Despite this history of relative underdevelopment, many Kuwaitis consider *badū* communities today to be more reliant on the state, and on the ruling family, for their survival than urban communities. Indeed, tribal Kuwaitis are often believed to be over-represented in public employment, particularly in the military. They also, traditionally, have been considered politically quiescent and loyal to the state; indeed, it is perhaps for this reason that, "[b]etween 1963 and 1975, the electoral power of the *badu* more than doubled," (Longva, 2006, p. 187).

Further, the state encouraged the movement and settling of the Bedouin population because they needed laborers and preferred to employ Kuwaiti nationals (Ghabra, 1997, p. 364). Political ideology was part of the consideration of the state's naturalisation policies. As Ghabra recounts:

> Policymakers also believed that the traditional bedouins would be more loyal to the emirate than the more radical and urban-oriented Lebanese, Palestinians, and Syrians. They also hoped that government-provided services and employment opportunities made available to the bedouins would lead to electoral support at the polls and, in part, counter the rising opposition from the urban commercial establishment. In order to change the electoral balance of power to the disadvantage of the urban commercial elite, the Kuwaiti government gave, in the 1960s and 1970s, a percentage of newly naturalized bedouins the right to vote.
>
> (Ghabra, 1997, p. 364)

This urbanization initiative, an effort at "integrating tribes into the fabric of Kuwaiti society," fuelled tensions between the formerly Bedouin populations and those who had long lived in Kuwait City (Ghabra, 1997, p. 365). Still, Bedouins became important in the army, police, and other security forces through this process (Ghabra, 1997, p. 365). Ghabra recounts how the tribal population in Kuwait City and the suburbs grew rapidly due to higher birth rates, becoming 65 per cent of the total population; nonetheless, the *hadhar* have remained dominant politically and economically, largely through their control of Kuwait's private sector (Ghabra, 1997, pp. 365–366). However, the numbers made tribes difficult to marginalize completely.

Ghabra calls the process of "desertization" as the course of action by which members of the tribal population in the city "transfer the desert's customs, traditions, beliefs, dress codes, and mentality into the city." This process was accelerated when the leadership role of the commercial class and the major urban families

Culture, Politics, and Citizenship in Kuwait   213

was weakened in the 1980s" (Ghabra, 1997, p. 367). Due to their differences, which are illustrated in much writing about Kuwait,

> urbanites looked down at the bedouins, making them feel politically and socially marginalized, and pushing them to cling more tenaciously to each other and to their tribal values and relations. Furthermore, as migrants continued to settle next to their fellow tribesmen, the areas they inhabited became overpopulated. Over time they also began to suffer from inadequate services.
>
> (Ghabra, 1997, p. 367)

What had initially been a distinction in terms of lifestyle, specifically a means of making one's livelihood, then, became a geographic, social, and political divide. In Tetreault's (2000, p. 46) words, "as carefully selected cohorts of *badu* were awarded full Kuwaiti citizenship with its plenitude of social rights, to boost support for the regime, indiscriminate prejudice against tribal Kuwaitis by *hadhar* Kuwaitis intensified."

Even today, some segments of the urbanized Kuwaiti elite consider the tribal population to be somehow less committed to the very concept of a democratic nation-state, only taking citizenship in the state and maintaining loyalty to the government to secure material benefits, since these families arrived after the discovery of oil (Longva, 2006, p. 173). Reflecting on this attitude, according to Longva, "a critical attitude toward the government is an important feature in the definition of hadhar identity. In contrast, *badu* are said to revere governmental authority, with their attitudes towards the ruling family described by several hadhar as 'obsequious hand kissing.' Badu, they say, are brought in "to serve the government's purposes" Longva, 2006, p. 173). While these perceptions were present in the late 1980s when Longva conducted fieldwork, the interests of the merchant population have grown increasingly linked to the government, as tribal populations are associated more and more with the political opposition in the 2000s and 2010s.

The arrangement of parliamentary elections, particularly voting districts has taken into consideration the political split between the *hadhar* and *badū*, especially as these populations tend to live in self-contained and separate areas of Kuwait. In recent years, tribal constituencies have demonstrated a growing self-awareness of their clout as powerful voting blocs, becoming essentially, as one Kuwaiti scholar put it, "political parties you're born into" (Interview, 2018). Nathan Brown argues that as Kuwait's largest tribes have become increasingly aware of their ability to influence political outcomes, they have managed to use their clout to block government initiatives to protect their own interests (Brown, 2009). As he explains:

> [t]he tribes themselves have grown far more sophisticated and demanding with regard to their political agendas [....] Tribal primaries have allowed tribal members to use their votes in a more united manner [....] And no longer can tribal deputies be bought cheaply – they represent sizeable constituencies now and do not follow the government blindly.
>
> (Brown, 2009)

214 *Courtney Freer*

Al-Nakib likewise describes a shift in tactics over time, as "[t]he fact that the tribal deputies now represented such sizeable populations made it difficult for the government to buy them out, as MPs began listening to their constituencies instead" (al-Nakib, 2014, p. 24). For their part, the *hadhar* seem to consider this shift in tribal tactics as evidence of a so-called tribal mentality, which they describe as the rent-seeking desire to use parliament to gain more services and goods for tribal constituencies, at the expense of others and to the detriment of the political system; they fear that such a mentality can seep into other aspects of politics, essentially reducing parliament to a distributive institution rather than a space for genuine political debate (Interview, 2017). Survey data from the Arab Barometer confirm, however, that there is nothing qualitatively different in how Kuwaitis from tribal and urban backgrounds see democracy (Freer & Leber, 2021, p. 14). Nonetheless, such perceptions remain.

Longva goes so far as to argue that one of the reasons for political differences between these two segments of the population has to do with varying conceptions of citizenship, which affect how each group sees the political leadership. In her words:

> The tribes in Kuwait understand nationality and citizenship in the sense of *taba'iyya*, which can be translated as the "following" of or "allegiance" to a leader, in this case Kuwait's ruling family. The root verb of *taba'iyya* means, among other things, "to walk behind someone, to be subordinate to, to be under someone's command." The concept is clearly built on an idea of hierarchy and vertical allegiance. Urban Kuwaitis, on the other hand, understand citizenship as *jinsiyya*, from the root verb *jns*, meaning "to make alike, to assimilate, to naturalize." [....] There is here an idea of similarity and horizontal community; whether one can assume, by extension, an idea of equality is a matter of interpretation—a claim that can also be made about the term *citizenship*. What is clear is that / *jinsiyya*, unlike *taba'iyya*, does not posit a priori an idea of hierarchy or supreme authority. In this sense, it is much closer to the Western concept of citizenship.
>
> (Longva, 2006, pp. 192–193)

Longva further makes the claim that *jinsiyya*, particularly for urban Kuwaitis, is linked to the city itself, rather than to Kuwait writ large (Longva, 2006, p. 193). As she explains:

> being Kuwaiti in the sense of *jinsiyya* implies an indissoluble bond between the citizen and the state of Kuwait; it is a condition that requires the existence of a national community, a national territory, and a state. Being Kuwaiti in the sense of *taba'iyya*, on the other hand, means that one's allegiance goes to a leader whom one follows and not to a territorialized sovereign state [....] a change of the ruling family would make a critical difference to the citizens by *taba'iyya* because it would entail a change in the very object of their loyalty.
>
> (Longva, 2006, p. 193)

Culture, Politics, and Citizenship in Kuwait 215

For Longva, then, dissimilarities between *badu* and *hadhar* are linked to fundamentally different conceptions of and relationships with state authority. For the *badu*, she argues, personal ties matter more than a sense of belonging to a territorial nation-state, and so the emir figures prominently among these individuals. In my view, this appears to be an over-generalization about a large population in the state, yet differing conceptions about state power (considering the emir as first among equals rather than viewing Kuwait itself as an entity worthy of loyalty) may help explain political stances generally taken by these communities.

Social and Cultural Developments

The variety of communities within Kuwait's national population has meant that a variety of social and cultural contributions have been made. Indeed, members of the *bidūn* population have become more visible as contributors to popular culture in Kuwait in recent years. A number of novels have been released, particularly since 2011, by members of Kuwait's *bidūn* population. In March 2019, there was an attempt to host a Bidūn Cultural Week; it was ultimately broadcast online (Alshammari, 2019). Nonetheless, visibility matters: "the presence and prevalence of *bidūn* literature and the rise of *bidūn* literary voices serve as a form of 'soft power for instigating change in the long term; it is an affirmation of existence, saying I am here, listen to me' as Mohammed Al Attabi describes it" (Alshammari, 2019).

In recent years, there has also been a relatively high incidence of suicide among members of Kuwait's *bidūn* population, bringing further attention to that population and the social and economic marginalization its members face. There were three high-profile incidents in November 2019 (Kholaif, 2020), followed by the death of a 32-year-old *bidūn* man in prison in December 2020 (Kholaif, 2020). In the case of the suicide of Zayid al-Asami who died in November 2019, his father shared alleged screenshots of a WhatsApp exchange showing that his son felt "deeply humiliated." Bader Mirsal al-Fadhli, who also died in November 2019, had posted a video on Twitter detailing his frustrations with his circumstances before taking his life. In May 2019, another incident took place when a medical student attempted suicide (Kholaif, 2020). In July 2019, a 21-year-old *bidūn* man committed suicide after failing to obtain a job because he lacked an identification card (Kholaif, 2020). These deaths led some to use hashtags on social media like #BidoonLivesMatter and #ICan'tBreath, drawing on slogans of the American Black Lives Matter movement (Baksh, 2021).

Still, such incidents have continued to take place. In December 2020, a 27-year-old *bidūn* man set himself on fire, leading MPs to submit a draft law demanding rights for the *bidūn* community (Baksh, 2021). In June 2021, a 12-year-old *bidūn* child was hit by a car while working as a street vendor (Amwaj Media, 2021). Days later, a 60-year-old *bidūn* man self-immolated, and in February 2021, 12-year-old Ali Khaled hanged himself (Diwakar, 2021). These incidents have received considerable media attention and have placed pressure on the government to amend the situation. In March 2022, a group of *bidūns* launched a hunger

216   *Courtney Freer*

strike to garner attention for the group; it was suspended 18 days after it began, with calls for a conference to address issues of the *bidūn* population (Amwaj Media, 2022).

When it comes to the social and cultural division between *hadhar* and *badu*, as al-Nakib has noted, the two communities have developed largely separately from one another due to the fact that they live in geographically distinct areas. Geographic separation has harboured social distinction.

Further, Alanoud Alsharekh and I have written elsewhere about the effect this has had on heritage projects in particular. Kuwait's tribal past has often been reimagined through cultural projects like Souq Mubarakiyya and Sadu House, while its past as a flourishing trade centre has also been commemorated through events like the Pearling Festival (Alsharekh & Freer, 2021). In the 1980s, then, Kuwaiti heritage preservation became increasingly important with the creation of *Qaryat Yawm al-Bahhar* (The Seaman's Day Village) on the coast across from parliament as

> a recreational space in which traditional courtyard houses and coffee shops, and reenactments of pre-oil maritime scenes such as shipbuilding and the return from pearling were "displayed and performed in great detail." Like the *souq*, the historic life of the city's seafront became musealized in a confined and controlled space in which Kuwaitis were invited "to experience their past in actualit."
>
> (al-Nakib, 2013, p. 24)

Souq Mubarakiyya, Kuwait City's largest souq, was restored following the Iraqi invasion and today is not only a social gathering place for both Kuwaitis and non-nationals, but also sells a variety of food and clothing items, including some traditional items related to desert life.

Sulayman Khalaf tracks Kuwaiti efforts to preserve national heritage through a yearly government-sponsored celebration commemorating pearl-diving, rather than the state's tribal past: "Kuwaiti sea pearling heritage (*turath al-ghuos*) has become appropriated by the state as a kind of state folklorism" (Khalaf, 2008, p. 63). Khalaf goes on to describe pearling as "an invented tradition," which he says has been used to forge national unity, as well as to portray the emir "as both the guardian of heritage and tradition and a state moderniser, whose wise vision helped in the rapid development and creation of a caring welfare society" (Khalaf, 2008, p. 68). A major part of Kuwaiti heritage, then, appears linked more to its seafaring past than to desert culture. In his analysis of the use of the traditional dhow boat in particular in Kuwaiti heritage projects, Gilbert points out that the boat "represents a past when Arab wealth came from more glamorous endeavours than selling oil," noting that Kuwait's mercantile prowess was intimately tied to the use of the dhow which connected it across the Indian Ocean; it is therefore also a symbol of Kuwait's mobility and demonstrates how connected it was with the rest of the world even in its early days, rather than the inward-facing desert motif often presumed to dominate the Arabian Peninsula (Gilbert, 2011: 64).

Political Implications

Because the various citizen and *bidūn* communities in Kuwait have tended to live in different geographic areas and have developed distinct social communities, it is unsurprising that their political stances have also developed distinctly. We see this most clearly through electoral data, though the issue has also come to the fore in recent parliamentary sessions as an issue in need of a permanent resolution.

Elections

Members of the *bidūn* population do not have Kuwaiti citizenship, and as a result they are unable to vote and therefore will not be considered in this section on elections. Nonetheless, a major social and political cleavage exists between Kuwait's *badu* and hadhar populations. As Andrew Leber and I have shown, members of Kuwait's large tribes tend to be over-represented within the districts in which they are the majority (IV and V) yet are under-represented within the Kuwaiti political system more broadly. As we note, with the exception of a few of the smallest tribes (<2,500 voting citizens each), 75 percent or more of each tribe's voting members were residents of electoral Districts IV (127,000 voters) or V (135,500 voters). Due to imbalances in the number of votes per district, a vote from either of these districts is "worth" less than half of a vote from District I (the smallest district, with a little over sixty thousand voters) (Freer & Leber, 2021, p. 10).

Despite the imbalance across districts in general, there has not been, as some urban Kuwaitis claim, a "tribalisation" of politics in the sense of total tribal domination. As we have found when examining elections held between 1992 and 2022, tribes have tended to hold between 21 and 26 of 50 elected seats (with the exception of 29 in 2020), amounting to some 42–50 per cent of the total elected parliament (Freer & Leber, 2021, p. 18). While this may represent a general increase over time as a general trend, it does not reflect the faster population growth reported in trial districts (Freer & Leber, 2021, p. 18).

While the proportion of tribal MPs has largely remained consistent since 1992, what has certainly changed, however, is the political profile of tribal MPs. While the first generation MPs were widely known as "service MPs," focused solely on securing material disbursements for members of their tribe, recently, opposition figures such as Musallam al-Barrak, Bader al-Dahoum, and Obaid al-Wassmi demonstrate (a) the willingness of tribal figures to become outspoken members of the broad-based political opposition and (b) the ability of such candidates to garner political support from people beyond members of their own tribes. Indeed, al-Barrak and al-Wassmi are the largest vote-getters in Kuwaiti history (Al-Mulla, 2021).

If members of the *bidūn* population were naturalized, this would have significant implications for parliamentary elections, especially depending on where they tend to be concentrated geographically.

218   *Courtney Freer*

Potential Solutions for the Status of Kuwait's *Bidūn* Population

The last two speakers of parliament have put forward plans to address the issue of Kuwait's *bidūn* population. Further, in May 2019, the emir promised a solution to the issue. In November 2019, Marzouq al-Ghanim, who is considered a member of Kuwait's entrenched merchant elite, unveiled his plan to address the *bidūn* population (Kuwait Times, 2019). The law suggested that some members of the *bidūn* population receive "premium" residency of 15 years with the renewal, as long as they provided evidence of their original nationality; those who refused to detail their original nationality would be punished (Kuwait Times, 2019). Notably, premium residency would include free medical service and education, as well as access to ration cards, driving licenses, and jobs in the public and private sectors (Kuwait Times, 2019). Members of the *bidūn* population who had been in Kuwait for decades could have claimed Kuwaiti citizenship, but the government's central body for *bidūn would* first prepare a list of the names of members of the population who would qualify for Kuwaiti nationality, and then Emiri decrees would grant this nationality (Kuwait Times, 2019). *Bidūn* not qualifying for this would be granted one year to reveal their original nationality and would be allowed to apply for Kuwaiti citizenship.

Notably, al-Ghanim announced the bill at a public gathering two days after two *bidūn* men, Bader Mirsal al-Fadhli and Zayid al-Asami, committed suicide. Al-Asami's father claimed that his son was depressed due to discrimination he has faced and produced WhatsApp messages to support that notion (Al-Mulla, 2020). As noted above, there has been a rise in suicides among male members of the *bidūn* population in recent years, leading many Kuwaitis to demand a sustainable resolution of the issue.

When al-Ghanim's plan was put to a vote in October 2020, only two out of five MPs appeared to the relevant parliamentary committee (Interior and Defense), meaning that the issue did not go to a vote (Al-Mulla, 2020). It had previously been backed by six MPs, but lacked sufficient support to be passed (Al-Mulla, 2020). One issue cited was that the law seemed to presume that all *bidūn* have another passport, which is not necessarily the case (Al-Mulla, 2020). Many in the *bidūn* community called the law "discriminatory" because it, in the words of the MENA Statelessness Network, "demonises a whole social group by painting them as a national security threat and by accusing them of hiding this supposed original nationalities [sic] without bearing the burden of proof" (Al-Mulla, 2020). I personally was in Kuwait around the time the bill was announced and saw a small protest against the legislation.

In November 2022, veteran politician and current speaker of parliament Ahmed al-Saadoun introduced another bill seeking to address the *bidūn* issue and nationality more broadly. His draft bill is related to three groups of Kuwaiti residents: those who have applied for nationality through the Higher Nationality Commission of Cabinet, those who have applied at the Martyrs' Office at the Amiri Diwan, and those *bidūn* whose family members were included in the 1965 census (Izzak,

2022). The legislation would require the ministry of interior to assemble a list of all applicants who fall into the three categories, so they can be given renewable civil identity cards for a set period until their claims are settled (Izzak, 2022). The legislation also grants every Kuwaiti citizen the right to bring an objection to any name on the list with documentation (Izzak, 2022). Critically, Saadoun's bill set a timeframe for resolution of the issue: For the first two groups within a year of the publication of the list and for the *bidūn* within a period to be determined by cabinet (Izzak, 2022). With the dissolution of parliament in January 2023 and later election of a new parliament in June 2023, it seems unlikely that al-Saadoun's proposal will produce actual policy results. Al-Saadoun has been elected as speaker of parliament once again, and so he may present the bill for consideration in the new parliament.

Conclusion

As has been demonstrated above, Kuwaiti citizenship is not a straightforwardly homogeneous categorization; rather, it considers historical events, family histories, and political and social dynamics. These dynamics do appear to be changing, despite Kuwait's continued status as one of the world's wealthiest rentier states. Debates about citizenship issues, particularly the status of the *bidūn*, take place openly on social media and in parliament, and are likely to continue to be an area of debate between Kuwaiti citizens of varying backgrounds and the Kuwaiti state.

These debates, aside from having social and political consequences as noted above, also have regional corollaries, as other Gulf states also face the challenge of settling their bidūn populations. With none of the GCC states having found long-term solutions to managing these populations, it is uncertain how resolution will ultimately be found.

In the Kuwaiti case specifically, the stratification between hadhar and badu remains distinctive, particularly due to the consequences it has on parliamentary elections, which are the freest in the Gulf region. This division is also likely to continue to color national politics and heritage discourse, yet is by no means the only meaningful political cleavage in the Kuwaiti state, which also houses a variety of ideologically motivated political blocs.

References

Albloshi, H. (2019, November 8). Stateless in Kuwait. *The Arab Gulf States Institute in Washington*.

Al-Mulla, Y. (2021, May 23). Kuwait: Landslide victory for Al Wasmi in parliamentary by-election. *Gulf News*.

Al-Nakib, F. (2013). Kuwait's modern spectacle: Oil wealth and the making of a new capital city, 1950–90. *Comparative Studies of South Asia, Africa and the Middle East, 33*(1). 7–25.

220 *Courtney Freer*

Al-Nakib, F. (2014). Revisiting 'Ḥaḍar' and 'Badū' in Kuwait: Citizenship, housing, and the construction of a dichotomy. *International Journal of Middle East Studies, 46*(1).

Alshammari, A. (2019, December 2). The Rise of Bidun Literature: Representation and Advocacy in Kuwait. *The Arab Gulf States Institute in Washington.*

Alsharekh, A., & Freer, C. (2011). *Tribalism and political power in the gulf: State-building and national identity in Kuwait, Qatar and the UAE.* London: Bloomsbury.

Assembly speaker unveils bill to resolve problems of Bedoons. *Kuwait Times,* November 4, 2019.

Baksh, S. (2021, January 13). Kuwait's stateless man who set himself alight. *BBC News.*

Beaugrand, C. (2018). *Stateless in the gulf: Migration, nationality and society in Kuwait.* London: IB Tauris.

Brown, J. (2009, February 2). Kuwaiti tribes turn parliament to own advantage. *Financial Times.*

Calderwood, J. (2011, February 22). Fifty years on from Kuwait's birth, arguments still rage over who is Kuwaiti. *The National.*

Coghlan, A. (2017, October 9). Kuwait's plan for mandatory DNA database have been cancelled. *New Scientist.*

Death of 'Bidoon' child reignites citizenship debate in Kuwait, Amwaj Media (8 June 2021).

Diwakar, A. (2021, August 11). Aliens in their own land: Kuwait's stateless Bidoons persist on the margins. *TRT World.*

Eldemerdash, N. (2015). Being and belonging in Kuwait: Expatriates, stateless peoples and the politics of citizenship. *Anthropology of the Middle East, 10*(2).

Freer, C., & Leber, A. (2021). Defining the 'tribal advantage' in Kuwaiti politics. *Middle East Law and Governance.*

Ghabra, S. (1997). Kuwait and the dynamics of socio-economic change. *The Middle East Journal, 51*(3).

Gilbert, E. (2011). The dhow as cultural icon: Heritage and regional identity in the western Indian Ocean. *International Journal of Heritage Studies, 17*(1).

Izzak, B. (2022, November 13). Speaker proposes bill to resolve nationality issues. *Kuwait Times.*

Khalaf, S. (2008). The nationalisation of culture: Kuwait's invention of a pearl-diving heritage. In A. Alsharekh & R. Springborg (Eds.), *Popular culture and political identity in the Arab Gulf states.* London: Saqi in association with SOAS.

Kholaif, D. (2020, December 11). Kuwait's stateless Bidoon population angered by another death. *Global Voices.*

Kuwait to look into constitutional challenges to DNA law, *Arabian Business,* October 18, 2016.

Kuwait's Bidoon remain marginalized after six decades of statelessness. *Amwaj,* May 6, 2022.

Lewis, D., & Amir Ahmed, A. (2018, March 23). Exclusive: Comoros passport scheme was unlawful, abused by mafia' networks – report. *Reuters.*

Longva, A. N. (2000). Citizenship in the Gulf states: Conceptualization and practice. In A. Nils, B. U. Davis, & M. Hassassinian (Eds.), *Citizenship and the state in the Middle East: Approaches and application* (pp. 179–200). Syracuse: Syracuse University Press.

Longva, A. N. (2006). Nationalism in pre-modern guide: The discourse on Hadhar and bedu in Kuwait. *International Journal of Middle East Studies, 38*(2).

Longva, A. N. (2013). Neither autocracy nor democracy but ethnocracy: citizens, expatriates and the socio-political system in Kuwait. In P. Dresch and J. Piscatori (Eds.), *Monarchies and nations: Globalisation and identity in the Arab states of the gulf* (pp. 114–135). London: IB Tauris.

Mansour-Ille, D. (2016). *Cash for citizenship: Rich Arab countries may pay poor islands to take 'stateless' Bidoons.* ODI.

Plotkin-Boghardt, L. (2006). *Kuwait amid war, peace and revolution: 1979–1991 and new challenges.* London: Palgrave Macmillan.

Culture, Politics, and Citizenship in Kuwait 221

Tetreault, M. A. (2000). *Stories of democracy: Politics and society in contemporary*. Kuwait, New York: Columbia University Press.

Toumi, H. (2016, June 20). Kuwait denies Comoros citizenship agreement. *Gulf News*.

US Department of State. (2021). *Country reports on human rights practices*. Kuwait: US Department of State.

Author's interview with Alanoud Alsharekh, London, 13 June 2018.

Author's interviews, Kuwait City, November 2017.

Index

Abdulla, Abdulkhaleq 92
Acquisition and Cross-Servicing Agreement (ACSA) 103
activism 56, 163; anti-censorship 199–200; *bidun* 210; legal 191; Orange Movement 56–57; *Sout al-Kuwait* 191, 203; women's 142–143
al-Adsani, Khalid Sulaiman 16
al-Adwadhi, Hesham 49
al-Alowaish, Ahmad 59
al-Ammar, Layla 201–202
al-Awash, Muhammad, on book banning 197
Alazimi, Istiqlal 71
Alboshi, Hamad H. 5; on *biduns* 210
al-Dahoum, Bader 63
al-Duwaisan, Khaled 60
Alebrahim, Abdulrahman 4–5
al-Eissa, Buthaina 199; *Kharayet Altayah* (*Maps of Loss*) 196
al-Fadhalah, Saleh 210
Alghanim, Marzuq 26, 31
Alhumaidi, Ya'qub 29
al-Jaber, Ahmad 55
al-Jabir, Ahmed 13, 14
al-Jabri, Mohammad 200–201; on censorship 191
al-Jadaan, Mohammed 115
al-Khaled, Sheikh Sabah 63
al-Khalifa, Isa bin Salman 93
al-Khatib, Ahmad 20, 29, 56
al-Khonaini, Abdullah 63–64
Almaimooni, Muhamed 187
Almuhammad, Nasir 37–38
al-Munais, Mohammed 18
al-Najem, Jassim 114
Alnajjar, Ghanim 6, 26; on *diwaniyya* 47
al-Nakib, Farah 50, 211–212, 214; on citizenship 207–208; *Kuwait Transformed* 52

al-Naqeeb, K. 140
Alnawaf, Ahmad 26, 31–32
al-Qatami, Jasim 22, 28, 56
al-Rumaihi, A. H. 55
al-Rushaid, A. 9
Alruwaih, Meshari Hamad 5
al-Saadoun, Ahmed 218
al-Sabah, Jabir bin Mubarak 12, 107
al-Sabah, Mi'shal Alahmad 26
al-Sabah, Mohammed 10
al-Sabah, Mubarak 10–12, 35
al-Sabah, Sa'ad Al'abdallah 29
al-Sabah, Salim bin Mubarak 12
al-Sabah, Sheikh Nasser al-Mohammad 7
al-Sabah, Sheikh Sabah al-Ahmad 88, 90–91, 95–97
al-Sabah, Sheikh Saud al-Nasser 196
al-Sabah family 27, 28; power sharing with merchants 9–10
al-Sabeeh, Nasser 56
al-Saleh, Dawood Musaad 195
al-Salem, Sheikh Abdullah 55–56, 163
Alsalim, Abdallah 27
al-Salim, Sheikh Abdullah 19, 21
al-Sanousi, Saud 202
Alsanousi, Saud, *Mama Hessa's Mice* 196
al-Saqir, Abdullah Mamad 16
Alsayed, Wafa 120, 127
al-Shamlan, Ali 8, 11, 51
Alsharekh, Alanoud 62
al-Sharikh, Shamayal 199–200
al-Shatti, Khaled 200–201
al-Siddiq, Khalid 52
al-Sufiyya farm 9–10
al-Terkait, Tahani 6
al-Utub clan 8
Alwagayan, Arwa, *Be Well* 200
Alzaid, Humud 29
Alzaid, Sarah 73

224 *Index*

Al-Zour petrochemical complex 163–164, 168
amendment of the Constitution 40
American Journal of Men's Health 63
Angelou, Maya, *I Know Why the Caged Bird Sings* 199
appointment 30–31; ministers 29; Prime Minister 30, 31
Arab League 1, 58, 74–75
Arab nationalism 55–56
Arab Spring 7, 108, 119; counter-revolution 133–134
Arab Summit 77
Arab Women's Development Society (AWDS) 153
Arendt, Hannah, "space of appearance" 54
Assiri, Abul-Reda 71, 79
authoritarianism 11–13, 22, 55
autonomy 135
Ayatollah Khomeini 36

badu 206; –*hadhar* division 211–215
Bahrain 48, 91
Bani Khalid tribe 8
Barnett, Michael 120, 126
Bas ya Bahar 52
Battle of Jahra 10, 207
Bedouin 36, 50, 185; urbanization 212–214; *see also badu*
Beer, Jennifer, on self-conscious emotion 123–124
Belt and Road Initiative (BRI) 111–112
Benantar, Abdennour 83
Berridge, G. R. 58–59
bidun jinsiyya (without nationality) 6, 181–182, 206, 208–211, 219; incidence of suicide 215, 218; Nationality Law *see* citizenship; premium residency 218
Bishara, Abdulla 2, 94
book banning and censorship 192, 193, 195–196; al-Awash on 197; Potter on 198; prizewinners 199; for promoting sectarian ideology 197–198; protest 199–200, 203; underground banned-book dealers 200
Bounashi café 52
Bourdieu, Pierre 46
bribes 33, 38
Brown, Nathan 213
bureaucracy, diplomatic 58–59

cabinet 33; attending parliamentary sessions 32; Foreign Secretary 58
cafés 52

Cafiero, Giorgio 5
Camp David Peace Agreement 1, 77
capital: cultural 44, 46, 50; social 46; transmission 46, 50, 51
caravans 51
censorship 6, 192, 203–204; al-Jabri on 191; newspaper 195; Potter on 198; prohibited contents 193–194; *see also* book banning and censorship
Central System for the Remedy of the Situation of Illegal Residents 210–211
chaotic naturalization 180–181
Chay, Clemens 5
checks matter 37–38
China 103; Belt and Road Initiative (BRI) 111–112; –Kuwait relations 109–114; strategic partnership with Kuwait 110–111; Taiwan issue 113; Uighur issue 112
citizenship 19–20, 115, 176–180; al-Nakib on 207–208; *badu* 211–215; based on lineage 209; *bidun jinsiyya* (without nationality) 181–182, 209–211, 214–215, 217–219; chaotic naturalization 180–181; dual 180; economic 211; *hadhar* 211–215; and identity 178; identity politics 183–185, 188; immigration 183–186; nationality and 148; naturalization 180, 207–208, 210; requirements 207–208; revoking 180–181; *taba'iyya* 214
civil society 6
climate change 161–162
clubs 56
coalitions 33, 37, 39
coffee 49–50
community 135
Comoros Islands 211
Conference of 'Uqair 89
Congress of Vienna 58
Constituent Assembly 19–20
Constitutional Committee 29, 177
Constitutional Convention, election 27–28
Constitutional Court 26, 187–188
Constitution of Kuwait (1962) 3, 17–21, 23–24, 28, 72, 177; amendment 40; Article 6 192; Article 29 187; Article 36 192; Article 38 38; Article 56 30; Article 80 30; Article 97 32; Article 101 30; Article 107 26; Article 116 32; Explanatory Note 29–30; position on gender discrimination 148–150
consultation 27
corruption 37; bribes 33, 38
council/s 55; of elders 10–11

court/s: grassroots 52, 53; role in protecting
human rights 187
Covid-19 pandemic 62–64, 158, 170–171;
impact on Kuwait's economy 167
Cox, Percy 73
crisis, parliamentary 40–41
critical thinking 198
Crown Prince 36, 37
Crystal, J. 21
Cultural and Social Society (CSS) 153
cultural capital 44, 50; *diwaniyya* 46
customs tax 15

dakhala (protection) 10
date palm farm/s 11
Davutoglu, Ahmet 104
decision-making 23, 152; authoritarian 12–
13; "majority decision" 15; merchants
55; Shura Council 12–13
Defense Cooperation Agreement
(DCA) 103
democracy 21, 29, 177, 191, 198–200, 214;
freedom of expression 192–193
desertization 212–213
development 128, 164, 171; human 151;
sustainable 151, 161–162; urbanization
138–141; *see also* urbanization
Dhofar War 94
the dignity of the nation (*Karamet Watan*)
38–39
dinar diplomacy 71, 73–75, 84–85
diplomacy/diplomatic relations 84, 89,
98–99, 113; China–Kuwait 109–114;
dinar 71, 73–75, 84–85; face-time 62;
Foreign Secretary 58; grassroots 44;
public 57–62; public policy messaging
62; regional 91; Russia–Kuwait
107–109; shuttle 96; Track I 58–59;
traditional 57–58; US–Kuwait 105–106;
USSR–Kuwait 104–107
discrimination, gender-based 144,
148–150, 187
dishdasha 49
disputes, within the ruling family 35
dissolution of the *Majlis* 26, 27, 31, 33,
38–40
districts 34, 37, 213, 217
divinity 135
diwan 48–50
diwaniyya 3, 5, 13, 22, 44–45, 52–54,
64; administration 47–48; Al-Saqr
55; councils 55; Covid-19 and 62–64;
cultural capital 50; face-time 62;

Ghanim on 47; *majlis* 48; Monday 23,
56; Norton on 47; public diplomacy
57–62; seating 49; social movements
and 49; space of appearance 54;
Tétreault on 46–47; transmission
of cultural capital 46, 50, 51; tribal
customs 49–50
Diwaniyyat al-'Ithnayn 28
Drerejian, Edward 59
dual citizenship 180
Duvall, Raymond 126

economic citizenship 211
Education Council 15, 16
Egypt 1, 28, 74–75; financial assistance
77–78, 83–84
Eickelman, D. F. 8
election/s 3, 21, 23, 38–40; Constituent
Assembly 19–20; Constitutional
Convention 27–28; Covid-19 and
63–64; government intervention 33, 34;
identity politics 184–185; individualism
35; Legislative Council 17–19, 27;
rigging 21, 28; tribal 185–186
electoral districts 28–29
elite/s 10–12, 15–16, 162, 165, 213;
intelligentsia 19; power 176
emotions 122; *see also* self-conscious
emotions
energy 169; market 169–170; renewable
161; security 157, 170–171; transition
161–162, 168, 169, 172
equality, gender 151, 187
estate tax 12
ethics 135
ethnocracy 4
Europe, oil and gas market 168–169
exceptionalism 127
executive power 23, 29; Crown Prince
36, 37

face-time 62; Covid-19 and 63–64
fakhth 8
family 44, 49; lineage 209; men's role in
144; tree 46; women's role in 144
farij 52
Fee, Charles 61
Fessler, Daniel 125
Fletcher, Robert 51–52
foreign aid 2–3, 69, 90; at critical junctures
81–82, 85; to Egypt 83; as foreign
policy tool 70–71, 85; humanitarian
assistance 79, 81; imperatives 71; to

226 *Index*

Iraq 82–83; Kuwait Fund for Arab Economic Development (KFAED) 75, 76; patterns 74; sources 73–74; support for Arab countries 76–78; support for the Palestinians 79; to Syria 83–84
foreign policy 69, 84, 90; analysis 120; coercion through force 70; domestic factors 72; neutrality 2–3, 71; "no enemies" 112; one-China 113; positive neutrality 104; regional diplomacy 91; survival 72–73, 81–82, 88–89; *see also* role theory; self-conscious emotions
Foreign Secretary 58
fourth energy transition 161–162
Francis, Hind 199
freedom: of expression 191–192, 198; urbanization and 143–144
Freer, Courtney 6, 109
frontier states 77

Garcia Marquez, Gabriel, *One Hundred Years of Solitude* 199
gender 5; discrimination 144, 148–150, 187; equality 151, 154, 187; stereotypes 151–153
Ghabra, S. 212–213
Ghazi, Mohamed, *Blue* 200
gifts 9–10
globalization 133–134, 138
Gnehm, Edward 59
governance: authoritarian 11–13; based on consultation 27; council of elders 10–11; joint 27, 49, 56, 177; Municipal Council 15; *Shura* 8–9, 12–14; social contract 9
grassroots diplomacy 44
Gulf Cooperation Council (GCC) 2, 3, 88, 115; formation of 91–93; impact of the fourth energy transition on 162; Kuwait's pursuit of interests 93–97; leaders' summit 96; long-term hydrocarbon strategy 170–171; post-Sabah era 97–99; presence in Europe's petrochemical industry 168–169; –Russia strategic dialogue 107–108; security 1–2; shale revolution impact on 158, 160, 161; technocratic committees 96
Guzzini, Stefano 131

Habermas, Jurgen 56
hadhar 36, 50, 185, 206; –badu division 211–215
Hakima, Abu 51

Hawar Islands 91
heritage projects 206, 216
Hezbollah 78
Higher Citizenship Committee 181
Himdh battle 12
Holsti, K. J. 122–123
housing policy 186
Howell, Nathaniel 59
humanitarian aid 79, 81
human rights 142, 178, 186–188; courts role in protecting 187; treaties 179
Human Rights Council, Universal Periodic Review (UPR) 178–179
Hussein, Saddam 90
hydrocarbon market 169–171; *see also* energy; oil; shale revolution

identity 51; *bidun jinsiyya* (without nationality) 181–182; and citizenship 178; Kuwaiti 184–186; national 179, 188–189; otherness 184; politics 176, 179–185, 188; social 151–152; *see also* *bidun jinsiyya* (without nationality)
Ikhwan movement 128
immigrants/immigration: identity politics 185; Palestinian 128–129; "Residency Traders" 184; xenophobia 183–184
impeachment 37; prime minister 36, 37
Index of Economic Freedom 164–165
individualism 32–33, 35
inequality, gender 154
intelligentsia 19, 199
International Human Rights Law (IHRL) 179
international law 178–179
International Monetary Fund 70
International Prize for Arabic Fiction 203
international relations 5, 70; realist 89
International Renewable Energy Agency, on the energy transition 161
interpellation 94
Iran 89; -Iraq War 1–2, 105–106, 185; nationalization movement 163
Iranian Revolution 1, 36, 82
Iraq 27, 89; financial assistance 81–83; invasion of Kuwait 22–23, 105, 106–107, 131; –Kuwait relations 73
Irhal Nastahiq al-Afdal ("Leave We Deserve Better") 37, 38
Islamic Heritage Society 84
Islamic Republic of Iran 1
Islamic State 81, 95
Islamism 132–133, 135
Israel 1, 77, 106

Jabir, Sabah bin 8–9
jihad 11–12
jinsiyya 214–215
joint governance 27, 49, 56, 177

Karamet Watan (the dignity of the nation)
38–39
Karasik, Theodore 71
Khalaf, Sulayman 216
Khazaal, Hussein Khalaf al-Sheikh
195–196
Khonaini, Abdulla 201, 202
Knox, Stuart 52
Koch, Christian 93
Kozhanov, Nikolay 6
Kutlat al-Aghlabiyya (Majority Bloc)
33, 38
Kutlat al-'Amal al-Sha'bi (Popular Bloc)
32–33
Kutlat al-'Amal al-Watani (National
Bloc) 33
Kuwait 1; Arab nationalism 55–56; Arab
Spring 7; Battle of Jahra 10, 207; *bidun*
issue 181–183, 209–211; Censorship
Committee 197–201; –China relations
109–114; citizenship 19–20, 148,
178–180; clubs 56; Covid-19 pandemic
62–64, 167; Development Plan 177,
183; dinar diplomacy 71, 73–75, 84–85;
districts 34, 37; economic freedom
score 164–165; exceptionalism 127;
executive power 23; First Legislative
Councils 17–19; foreign aid 2–3; formal
diplomatic relations with the Soviet
Union 104–107; heritage projects 206,
216; Higher Citizenship Committee
181; *Himdh* battle 12; identity politics
179–183; immigration 183–186;
intelligentsia 19; Iraq invasion of
2, 22–23, 73, 104, 106–107, 131;
–Iraq relations 73; Islamic movement
146–147; Law 03/2006 on Press and
Publications 191; Madinat Al Hareer
(Silk City) 111; Ministry of Information
192, 193, 196, 203; modernization
163; National Council on Culture Arts
and Letters 196; Nationality Law 145,
147–150; national self-conception 127;
neutrality 3; Official Development
Assistance to Gross National Income
(ODA/GNI) 74; oil and gas sector
71, 162, 167–172; parliament 3, 146;
personal debt 167; political system
3–4; position on the Taiwan issue 113;

position on Ukraine war 109; post-
Sabah era 98–99; pursuit of interests
within the GCC 93–97; residential
areas 53; revoking citizenship 180–181;
–Russia relations 107–109, 115; –Saudi
Arabia relations 89–90; Shura Council
13–15; strategic partnership with China
110–111; subsidy system 162, 164,
166; support for the Palestinian cause
119–121, 129–130; urbanism 51–54;
urbanization 139–141; –US relations
103, 105–106; Vision 2035 111; women
4; *see also* political system
Kuwait Book Fair 196
Kuwait Fund for Arab Economic
Development (KFAED) 58, 69, 75–78,
84, 90–91
Kuwait University, female student quota 187

Lavrov, Sergei 108
Law 03/2006 on Press and Publications
192; amendments 201–203; Article
7 193; Article 19 193; Article 20
193–194; Article 26 194; Article 28
195; historical background 195–196;
prohibited contents 193–194; *see also*
book banning and censorship
Lebanon, financial aid 78
Leber, Andrew 217
Lefebvre, Henri 51
legitimacy 54
Libya 92
lineage 180; citizenship and 209
local culture 151–152
Lodge, Matthew 59–60
Longva, A. N. 50, 209, 213, 214

Madinat Al Hareer (Silk City) 111
Mahfouz, Naguib, *Children of*
Gebelawi 199
majlis 44, 48; Robinson on 48
Majlis movement 29, 55
Majority Bloc (*Kutlat al-Aghlabiyya*) 33, 38
"majority decision" 15
maritime trade 52
market, energy 169–170
Marshall Plan 70–71
Matar, Fatima 199
Meem3 199
members of parliament (MPs):
individualism 35; tribal 217
merchants 9–10, 13, 23, 53, 55; National
Bloc 16–17; *Qibla* 17; resistance against
Mubarak 11–12

228 *Index*

Millennium Development Goals
  (MDGs) 75
Mills, R. 162
ministers 30–31; appointment 29; vote of
  confidence 200
Moghadam, V. M. 141
Monday *Diwaniyya* movement 23, 56
Mumford, Lewis 44
Municipal Council 15
Muslim Brotherhood 3, 84

Nabiha 5 37
National 202–203
National Assembly (*Majlis*) 164, 167;
  appointment of members 22; cabinet 33;
  dissolution 26, 27, 33, 38–40; elections
  21–22; members 30; Olver-Ellis on 166
National Bloc (*Kutlat al-'Amal al-Watani*)
  16–18, 33
national identity 179
nationalism, Arab 55–56, 75, 120, 129–133
national pride 130, 132, 135–136
naturalization 180, 207–208, 210; chaotic
  180–181
network/s: *diwaniyya* 46, 47; social 44
Neumann, I. B. 58
neutrality 2, 3; positive 104
newspapers, censorship 195
non-governmental organizations (NGOs)
  56, 152
Norton, Augustus Richard 64; on
  diwaniyya 47
Nosova, A. 22

Ober, Tristan 71
Official Development Assistance to
  Gross National Income (ODA/GNI),
  Kuwait 74
oil 71, 113, 157, 207; Al-Zour
  petrochemical complex 163–164,
  168; exports to China 110; impact
  on traditional economic sectors 140;
  Kuwait's production expansion plans
  171–172; shale revolution 158, 160,
  161; urbanization and 141–142; *see also*
  energy
Olayan, Hamza, *Forbidden to Publish: A
  History of Censorship in Kuwait* 195
Olver-Ellis, S. 166
one-China principle 113
OPEC 157; price damping 160, 161
Orange Movement 56–57

Organisation for Economic Co-Operation
  and Development (OECD),
  Development Assistance Committee
  (DAC) 70, 74
Organization of Islamic Cooperation 107
Orwell, George, 1984 199
otherness 184

Palestine/Palestinian cause 2, 5, 119;
  financial support 79; Kuwait's support
  for 119–121, 129–130; *see also* role
  theory
Palestinian Liberation Organization (PLO)
  79, 91
pan-Arab movement 75
parliament/ary 3, 29–30, 72, 146;
  attendance of the cabinet 32; blocs
  32–33; coalitions 33; crisis 40–41;
  dissolution 31; *see also* cabinet; *Majlis*
passports 187
pearl diving 216
Pelosi, Nancy 113
Peoples' Republic of China (PRC) *see*
  China
petition 55; Shura Council 13–14
Plotkin Boghardt, Lori 209–210
policy/policymaking 93–99; anti-
  discrimination 154; citizenship 206–209;
  educational 142–143; foreign aid 82–83;
  housing 186; immigration 183–186;
  neutrality 2; regional 130–131
political movements 35–39
political parties 20
political system 72; appointment of
  ministers 29, 30; bribes 33; cabinet 33;
  citizenship 176–178; Constitutional
  Committee 29; Constitutional
  Convention 28–29; crisis 31, 35, 40,
  41, 176; dissolution of the *Majlis* 33;
  electoral districts 28–29; historical
  background 27–28; *Kutlat al-Aghlabiyya*
  (Majority Bloc) 38; *Majlis* 30;
  parliament 29–30; parties 32; populism
  164; presidential system 29; Prime
  Minister 30, 31; ruling family 28
Popular Bloc (*Kutlat al-'Amal al-Sha'bi*)
  32–33
Popular Front for the Liberation of
  Oman and the Arabian Gulf (PFLOAG)
  92, 110
populism 164
positive neutrality 104

power 54, 89, 176–177; executive 23; politics 181; productive 126, 132, 134; ruling family 177; structural 126, 132, 134
premium residency 218
presidential system 29
prestige hierarchies 125–126
price damping 160, 161
pride 124, 126–127, 134; national 132–133
Prime Minister, appointment 30, 31
productive power 126, 132, 134
protection (*dakhala*) 10
protest 38, 83–84; Arab Spring 7, 108; book banning 196–197, 199–200, 204; *see also* activism; social movement/s
Protocol of Consultations 107
public diplomacy 57–62
public sphere 56

Qadiyyat al-Chaykat 37–38
Qaryat Yawm al-Bahhar (The Seaman's Day Village) 216
Qasim, Abdulkarim 27, 73, 90
Qatar 91, 93; blockade 108
Qibla 17

Rabi, Uzi 49
Raqib 50 63–64
Razak, Tatang Budie 61
reform 13, 24, 31, 55, 128, 142, 166; constitutional 22; Education Council 15–16; National Bloc 16–17
regional diplomacy 91
religious scholars, resistance against Mubarak 11–12
renewable energy 161
rentier state model 162–164
revoking citizenship 180–181
Reza Pahlavi, Mohammed 1
rigged elections 21, 28
Riyadh Agreement 96
Robinson, Valerie, on *diwan* 48
role theory 120–121; role enactment 123–127, 131; role expectations 123–125, 134; self-conscious emotions and 122–127
ruling family 28, 30, 34, 58, 180; disputes 35; power 177
Russia 103; –GCC strategic dialogue 107–108; invasion of Ukraine 157; –Kuwait relations 107–109, 115; *see also* Ukraine war

Salafists 84
Saudi Arabia 89, 115; –Kuwait relations 89–90; price damping 160, 161
sectarianism 185–186, 196
security 89; energy 157, 170–171; Gulf states 1–2
segregation, *badu–hadhar* 211–212
self-awareness 125
self-conscious emotions 121; Beer on 123–124; pride 124, 126–127, 134; role theory and 122–127; shame 124, 134–135
self-representation 125; Kuwaiti 128–129, 131
Shafak, Elif, *Forty Rules of Love* 196
shale revolution 158, 160, 161
shame 124, 134–135
sheikhdom: gifts 9–10; power sharing with merchants 9–10; *Shura* 8–9; *see also* governance
Sheikh Zayed Book Award 202
Shi'a 1, 3, 36, 185
Shura 8–9, 49
Shura Council 8, 13–15, 23, 27, 127
shuttle diplomacy 96
Silliman, Doug 61, 62
social capital 46
social contract 9, 17, 23, 44, 162, 164; financing 165, 166
social groups 185
social identity 151–152
socialization, cafés 52
social media 57, 199; "Forbidden in Kuwait" hashtag 197–198
social movement/s 35–36, 38–39; *diwaniyya* and 49; *Irhal Nastahiq al-Afdal* ("Leave We Deserve Better") 37, 38; *Karamet Watan* (the dignity of the nation) 38–39; *Nabiha 5* 37; *Qadiyyat al-Chaykat* 37–38
solidarity 185
Souq Mubarakiyya 216
sources of foreign aid 73–74
Sout al-Kuwait 191, 203
Soviet Union 1, 70; formal diplomatic relations with Kuwait 104–107
space 51; of appearance 54; gendered 143–144
stereotype, gender 151–153
Stewart, Potter, on censorship 198
structural power 126, 132–133
suicide, in the *bidun* community 215–216, 218

230 *Index*

Suleiman, Muyassar H. 5
Sunni Arabs 36, 185
sustainable development 151, 161–162
Syria 28, 108; financial assistance 83–84;
  humanitarian assistance 81

taba'iyya, Longva on 214
tax 11, 165; customs 15; estate 12; value
  added 166
Tétreault, Mary Ann 57, 89, 127, 213;
  on *diwaniyya* 46–47; *Stories of*
  Democracy 49
Thies, Cameron, *Oxford Review of Role*
  Theory and Foreign Policy 123
Track I diplomacy 58–59
trade 144; caravans 51; hydrocarbon 170;
  maritime 52
traditional diplomacy 57–58
treaties, human rights 179
tribe/tribal: affiliation 138; Bani Khalid
  8; elections 185–186; lineage 180,
  209; mentality 214; MPs 217–218;
  politics 217; sheikh 186; *see also*
  badu; Bedouin; *bidun jinsiyya* (without
  nationality)
Twitter 200, 201

Uighurs 112
Ukraine war 108–109, 157, 168–171
Ulrichsen, Kristian Coates 5
UN Economic and Social Council
  (ECOSOC) 149–150
United Arab Emirates (UAE) 91–92
United Arab Republic (UAR) 28
United States 169; 100-*diwaniyyas*
  campaign 62; –Kuwait relations 103,
  105–106; Marshall Plan 70–71; shale
  revolution 158, 160, 161
Universal Declaration of Human
  Rights 186

UN Office for the Coordination of
  Humanitarian Affairs (UNOCHA),
  Financial Track Service 69
UN Relief and Works Agency
  (UNRWA) 79
urbanism 51, 52
urbanization 138–141, 152–154, 212–214;
  advancement in education 142–143;
  impact on patterns of thinking and
  values 140–141; impact on people's
  freedom 143–144; impact on status of
  women 143–144; negative impact on
  the status of Kuwaiti women 145–148;
  social problems caused by 141–142

Venezuela 170
Vision 2035 111
voting 17, 19–20; districts 34, 37, 213, 217;
  women 4; *see also* election/s

The Weekly News 195
women 4, 64; activism 142–143; diplomats
  61; educational achievement 142–143,
  152; female student quota 187; negative
  impacts of urbanization on 145–148;
  passports 187; role in Kuwaiti society
  144; stereotypes 153; unmarried 141;
  see also gender
World Bank 70
World War I 11

xenophobia 183–184
Xi, Jinping 111

Yaghi, Mohammed 5
Yemen 108; humanitarian assistance 81
Yom, Sean, "Roles, Identity, and Security:
  Foreign Policy Contestation in
  Monarchical Kuwait" 120
Young, Damon, *The Art of Reading* 199